ECONOMICS OF CRIME
Deterrence and the Rational Offender

CONTRIBUTIONS
TO
ECONOMIC ANALYSIS

227

Honorary Editor:
J. TINBERGEN†

Editors:
D. W. JORGENSON
J. -J. LAFFONT
T. PERSSON
H. K. VAN DIJK

NORTH-HOLLAND
AMSTERDAM • LAUSANNE • NEW YORK • OXFORD • SHANNON • TOKYO

ECONOMICS OF CRIME
Deterrence and the Rational Offender

Erling EIDE
University of Oslo
Oslo, Norway

in cooperation with
Jørgen AASNESS
Terje SKJERPEN
Statistics Norway
Oslo, Norway

1994

NORTH-HOLLAND
AMSTERDAM • LAUSANNE • NEW YORK • OXFORD • SHANNON • TOKYO

ELSEVIER SCIENCE B.V.
Sara Burgerhartstraat 25
P.O. Box 211, 1000 AE Amsterdam, The Netherlands

ISBN: 0 444 82072 8

This book is printed on acid-free paper.

PRINTED IN THE NETHERLANDS

INTRODUCTION TO THE SERIES

This series consists of a number of hitherto unpublished studies, which are introduced by the editors in the belief that they represent fresh contributions to economic science.

The term "economic analysis" as used in the title of the series has been adopted because it covers both the activities of the theoretical economist and the research worker.

Although the analytical methods used by the various contributors are not the same, they are nevertheless conditioned by the common origin of their studies, namely theoretical problems encountered in practical research. Since for this reason, business cycle research and national accounting, research work on behalf of economic policy, and problems of planning are the main sources of the subjects dealt with, they necessarily determine the manner of approach adopted by the authors. Their methods tend to be "practical" in the sense of not being too far remote from application to actual economic conditions. In additon they are quantitative.

It is the hope of the editors that the publication of these studies will help to stimulate the exchange of scientific information and to reinforce international cooperation in the field of economics.

The Editors

Preface

Some of the more exciting fields of research, I think, are located on the borderline areas of traditional disciplines. I guess that is why, being an economist, I wrote my Ph.D. theses within engineering economics and now a book on crime as norm-guided rational behaviour. In crossing frontiers of disciplines one is especially vulnerable to charlatanism. I recognize the kind efforts of my colleagues Endre Stavang, Cecilie Høygård, and Per Ole Johansen who, reading various parts of early drafts, have tried to eliminate some of my misunderstandings.

Chapter 6 has Jørgen Aasness and Terje Skjerpen at the Research Department in Statistics Norway as co-authors. This chapter is based on a research project partly financed by The Research Council of Norway.

I recognize the assistance of Statistics Norway and Norwegian Social Science Data Services, which both provided data used in this book.

Erling Eide

Contents

Chapter 3
METHODOLOGICAL ISSUES OF EMPIRICAL MACRO STUDIES 87

Chapter 4
PREVIOUS CRIMINOMETRIC STUDIES 115

Chapter 1

INTRODUCTION

Crime is intriguing. Most of us deplore criminal acts, while at the same time being both sinners and common offenders. Some offenders are punished by sanctions, thus enduring the society's requirement for revenge, retribution, and general deterrence, or its hope of individual improvement. Leaving the deeper and more philosophical aspects of crime and punishment to Kant, Dostoyevskyi and others, the main theme of this book concerns the more mundane problem of the effect on crime of the benefits and costs of legal and illegal activities.

Theories of crime are abundant. Various mental, physical, developmental, economic, social, cultural, and other causes have been launched as explanations of why people offend. The subject became even more difficult when some sociologists of deviance claimed that the official crime statistics were simply a product of the agencies of social control. During the last 25 years economists have invaded the field using their all-embracing model of individual rational behaviour, where a criminal act is preferred and chosen if the total pay-off, including that of sanctions and other costs, is higher than that of legal alternatives. Empirical tests with increasing statistical rigour and refinement have been done on the basis of this model.

No single theory of crime encompasses all significant determinants of criminal behaviour. In Chapter 2 I develop a framework of norm-guided rational behaviour in order to place the various theories in relation to each other in a comprehensive, organized perspective. Each theory will in a sense be a special case of the "grand theory" expressed by the framework. Within this framework I present the "economic" model of crime, survey the empirical literature based on this model, discuss various theoretical criticisms of it, and offer some new evidence obtained by use of both traditional and more advanced statistical methods.

Although virtually all criminal legislation is pervaded by the belief that punishment has an abating effect on crime, neither theory nor empirical studies have resolved the question of whether, or to which degree, punishment deters. Certainly, several empirical studies over the last 20 years confirm the general prevention hypothesis. But methodological problems cast doubt on the results, and some criminologists are quite reluctant to believe in a significant deterrent effect of punishment at all.

Most scholars seem to agree that a complete lapse of the threat of punishment will be followed by a marked increase in crime. This was empirically confirmed by the substantial increases in crime during the police strikes in Liverpool in 1919 and in Montreal in 1969, and when Copenhagen was without police for some months during World War II. Moreover, occupying powers have demonstrated that extremely severe punishment may produce a marked reduction in the number of crimes. As far as moderate changes in the threat of punishment are concerned, however, the empirical basis for drawing definite conclusions about the effect on crime is disputed. The theoretical and empirical status of most other possible determinants of crime is also controversial.

The models surveyed, and those employed in my own empirical analyses, bear a strong resemblance to those used by economists in their econometric studies. Such models are as the whole only used by economists in their study of crime. This explains why, in the literature of criminology, models of this kind are named "the economists' model" or "the econometric model". Since this terminology gives the impression that narrow economic reasoning is the crucial element in the models, the choice of terms is not so fortunate. In fact, these models are based on a far more general theory of individual rational behaviour. True, such models are favoured by economists, but, as shown in Chapter 2, they are relevant also for behaviour in other areas. One could, somewhat imprecisely, say that a person acts rationally if he is able to assess correctly the various possible forms of behaviour and their consequences, and choosing on that basis the alternative that is best according to his own preferences. Punishment as well as socio-economic circumstances are relevant for this assessment. Furthermore, to the extent that the consequences of illegal activity are determined by society, society has a possibility to influence the amount of crime.

Changes in the consequences of various courses of action will not necessarily influence the behaviour of a given person. But for the population as a whole, it seems reasonable to assume that gradual changes in the consequences will for an increasing number of people result in changes of behaviour. The models of this study will be used to estimate the impact of such changes in the population as a whole.

To avoid wrong connotations in connection with terms like "the economists' model" or the "econometric model", I shall call the models used in this book for estimation and testing "criminometric models", thus indicating that the model 1) has a clear basis in criminological theory concerning which factors influence crime, 2) is expressed in a mathematical form, and 3) is defined so that statistical theory can be used in empirical tests and estimations.

As a point of departure a short survey of the main theories of crime is given in Chapter 2. Somewhat at variance with the common attitude of considering norms and rational choice as competitive explanations of criminal or law-abiding behaviour, various theories will be included in a rational choice framework where both binding and non-binding norms have their place. These theories are discussed within a framework that combines two very different, and weakly linked levels of analysis in much of modern sociology: Individuals, defined by their attitudes and personal characteristics on the one hand, and society, defined as a structure that rewards and penalizes those individuals on the other. Norms are introduced as a component of the individual's preferences, and the formation of these norms by certain social institutions is discussed. The chapter also contains a survey of some types of "economic models of crime", models that more aptly should be called "models of rational criminal behaviour". It is demonstrated that the theories are sufficiently plausible to warrant testing and eventually being used for estimation of effects on crime of punishment and other factors.

It has been argued that the rational choice theory fails as a predictive theory because people are subject to cognitive limitations, or because their actions are determined by social norms and not by want-maximizing behaviour. It has also been alleged that the simple rational choice theory is inadequate because people's behaviour is determined by procedural rationality, in which an individual is portrayed as a follower of rules established by history or social relations, or by expressive rationality, in which an individual, through symbolic acts, demonstrates to himself and others his self-conception and worth. The significance of these criticisms for the use of the rational choice assumption in empirical studies of crime will be given some attention.

The empirical part of this book concentrates on studies of crime based on macro data, i.e. on data where the observational unit is a police district, a region, a state, or a country. A main issue in Chapter 3 is to which extent such data can be combined with the theory of individual rational choice to estimate the effects on crime of various determinants. The chapter deals with several methodological problems of empirical macro studies of crime, such as, aggregation, identification of models, incapacitation, substitution between crimes, empirical measures of theoretical concepts, measurement errors, choice of estimation methods, etc.

In borderline studies like the present one it is especially interesting with literary surveys. Chapter 4 contains a rather comprehensive survey of empirical macro regression studies of crime, where a main object has been to determine as accurate as possible what are the empirical results so far of correlation and regression analyses. As most macro regression studies have their weak points, none of them can alone provide reliable evidence on the effects of determinants of crime. Surveying a wide variety of studies gives a better foundation for drawing conclusions about the effect of various determinants. In fact, I find that there is ample and consistent evidence on the effects of some factors, whereas those of others are still obscure. A Panel on Research on Deterrent and Incapacitative Effects appointed by the Governing Board of the US National Research Council concluded that: "Taken as a whole, the reported evidence consistently finds a negative association between crime rates and the risk of apprehension, conviction, or imprisonment." (Blumstein et al. (1978, p. 4)). The Panel adds (p. 5): "There are three primary obstacles to interpreting the finding of a negative association in analyses of natural variation as valid evidence that sanctions indeed deter crime: (1) the error in measuring crimes; (2) the confounding of incapacitation and deterrence; and (3) the possibility that the level of crime affects sanctions in addition to sanctions deterring crime, which is known as a simultaneous relationship." The Panel's report produced a beneficial caution against macro crime studies. However, the review of more recent studies in Chapter 4 reveals that some of the Panel's reasons for being reluctant to accept that deterrence works, now should be given less weight.

Despite some progress in empirical studies of crime, ameliorations of various sorts remain to be done. In the two following chapters I present the results of empirical studies based on data from police districts in Norway. The survey in Chapter 4 serves to explain my choices of empirical models, and to interpret and judge the estimates obtained. The two studies in Chapter 5 resemble some of those reviewed in Chapter 4, whereas Chapter 6 contains models and estimations that are believed to represent an improved approach. In the analysis of Chapter 6 the obstacles emphasised by the above mentioned Panel have been removed: Measurement errors are explicitly handled by introducing latent variables for crimes and clear-ups, incapacitation is a negligible nuisance for the data employed, and the problem of simultaneity (and identification) is largely solved by use of panel data. The LISREL procedure is used for estimation.

Borderline fields often suffer from a lack of understanding from scholars of adjacent disciplines. They speak different languages. A certain effort is made to make the present study accessible and relevant for both economists, criminologists, and sociologists in general. Although some elementary material is placed in appendices, a little indulgence and patience from experts in various fields is required in certain sections.

Hopefully, the present work will serve as a kind of cookery book for studies of crime with its general theoretical framework, review of empirical studies, methodological discussion, and specific recipes for theoretical and empirical research.

Chapter 2

THE DETERMINANTS OF CRIME

The main concerns of this book are to study to what extent criminal behaviour can be described and explained as individual, rational choice, and to what extent crime is dependent on the threat of punishment and various socioeconomic factors. Crime is defined as the behaviour condemned by society. Roughly, behaviour is regarded as rational when an individual considers the pros and cons of various possible actions in a given set of conditions, before choosing the alternative that best satisfies his desires.[1] Conditions, such as income and punishment, partly determine the pros and cons, or benefits and costs, and individual behaviour is therefore to some extent a result of conditions created by society. Thus, a change in crime may possibly be described and explained as a response to changing rewards and punishments created by the environment, a possibility tested in the empirical chapters below.

A topic of paramount importance is whether the model of rational choice is in conflict with, a substitute for, a supplement to, or a general framework for other theories of crime. In a seminal article about the economic approach to crime Becker (1968, p. 170) suggested "that a useful theory of criminal behaviour can dispense with special theories of anomie, psychological inadequacies, or inheritance of special traits and simply extend the economist's usual analysis of choice". Without countering this view, I would suggest that an even better use of the model of rational choice is to extend the model framework to

---

[1]Although it is possible, and for the discussion of some problems indeed necessary, to distinguish between rational choice and rational behaviour, the two terms are used interchangeably in this study.

include main features of various other theories.[2] This will make it easier both to judge the relevance of the model of rational choice and to interpret the empirical results obtained by employing it. The extended model framework is developed in section 2.1.

More specific theories of crime inspired by models of rational choice commonly used in economics are presented in section 2.2. Several objections to the models are discussed in relation to these theories. Although some criticism is clearly relevant, I still find it acceptable to base empirical work on the assumption of individual rational behaviour.[3] Furthermore, I will argue that the results of such studies are of interest even if this assumption is not accepted. A summary of the various models will make it clear under which conditions of attitude towards risk one obtains unequivocal predictions of changes in crime as a result of changes in the probability and severity of sanctions, in the benefits of crime, and in income.

2.1. The norm-guided, rational offender

An extended framework of rational choice is offered below. First, the traditional model, as usually employed in economics, is presented in section 2.1.1. This analytical tool is supplemented in the following sections by the introduction of individual norms, resulting in a model of norm-guided rational behaviour. Subsequently, some main theories of crime are discussed within this framework, theories running from biological, constitutional and acquired anomalies of the offender, via psychological deviations, to economic and social factors characterizing the offender himself or his environment. The various individual and environmental characteristics and properties having an effect on crime will be called determinants of crime. The overview of theories will form a basis for deciding which mechanisms and determinants of crime should be included in empirical analysis. As usual, we are faced with the problem that any theory specific enough to be testable will not explain very much, whereas any theory broad enough to explain a great deal will not be testable. A further purpose of this discussion is to assess the appropriateness of using macro data in analyzing crime as rational behaviour. What kind of information can macro data

---

[2] A similar approach is taken by Carr-Hill and Stern (1979, p. 13): "We want to emphasize that the two types of theory discussed here can be seen as complementary rather than conflicting. The economic approach isolates the importance of the probabilities and magnitude of reward and punishment, and shows how they can be treated formally ... The criminological approach takes these for granted and indicates how different groups might view and react to these probabilities, rewards, and punishments."

[3] A similar conclusion is drawn by Føllesdal (1982, p. 311) in his article on "The status of rationality assumptions in interpretation and in the explanation of action".

give about the relevance of these theories?

2.1.1. Rationally induced to crime[4]

Models of rational behaviour certainly have had some success in describing and explaining economic activities. Economic analyses are in fact almost exclusively based on the hypothesis of rational individual behaviour. In recent years similar analyses have been made to describe and explain as different phenomena as marriage, child-bearing, church attendance and suicide, - to name a few. The explanatory power of such models in these areas is debatable, but the challenge to traditional sociological approaches is obvious. It is true that sociological theories of human activity often include "functional" explanations, i.e. that certain activities serve required ends. Using economic terminology, such activity is "satisficing", it produces a requested result. But it does not necessarily maximize individual or group welfare, which most often is the goal in the theory of rational behaviour.

Rational choice, as usually conceived, is outcome-oriented: an individual, when confronted with several possible courses of action, chooses the one that he believes will give the best overall outcome. The results of possible courses of action are compared, and the best result dictates what course of action to take.

More specifically, rational choice involves four elements, see Fig. 2.1: A feasible set of courses of action (or activities), a structure of the environment or the situation, the opportunity set of outcomes, and an individual, subjective ranking of outcomes. The feasible set encompasses all courses of action which satisfy various constraints of behaviour, such as restrictions on working hours, and the person's physical abilities. The structure of the environment or the situation determines the outcome of various actions. Rational behaviour means to choose the element in the feasible set that produces the highest-ranked outcome. For simplicity, I include in the opportunity set of outcomes the various attributes of courses of action that may cause satisfaction or dissatisfaction of wants (but not of norms, which will be considered below), such as warmth and security. People may dislike working in a mine because of dirt and health risk, and like picking grapes

---

[4]In this section and the next I rely partly on a lucid discussion of "Social norms and economic theory" by Elster (1989). Elster writes (p. 99): "One of the most prominent persistent cleavages in the social sciences is the opposition between two lines of thought conveniently associated with Adam Smith and Emile Durkheim, between homo economicus and homo sociologicus. Of these, the former is supposed to be guided by instrumental rationality, while the behavior of the latter is dictated by social norms. The former is "pulled" by the prospect of future rewards, whereas the latter is "pushed" from behind by quasi-inertial forces ... The former adapts to changing circumstances, always on the lookout for improvements. The latter is insensitive to circumstances, sticking to prescribed behavior even if new and apparently better options become available. The former is easily caricatured as a self-contained, asocial atom, and the latter as the mindless plaything of social forces."

because of a warm and sensual atmosphere.

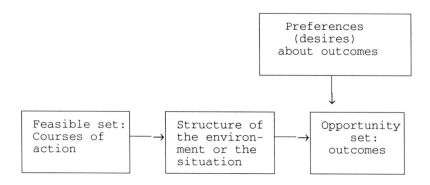

Fig. 2.1. Illustration of norm-free rational choice

If norms have no impact whatsoever on what course of action to choose, one may speak of norm-free rational behaviour. This is an extreme alternative, far from reality, and defended by nobody as a comprehensive description of how people behave in economic or other matters. To obtain a thorough explanation of the demand for high-heeled shoes or for churches, norms must be considered. Desires to be satisfied are not only of a narrow materialistic or psychic kind, but also include social acceptance, self-esteem, and other aspects of life in which norms are essential. Economists and others using the model of rational choice are certainly not ignorant of the importance of norms, but having insufficient insight into norms and norm formation, leave this domain to scholars in other disciplines. On the other hand, sociologists in general, and criminologists in particular, often neglect the problem of individual choice, and concentrate on social factors that seem to determine behaviour. They tend to link people's behaviour more directly to the environment or the situation without elaborating too much on individual preferences, feasible sets of courses of action, and opportunity sets of outcomes. This approach is somewhat unsatisfactory because no explanation of social life explains anything until it explains individual behaviour. However, to the extent that sociological studies reveal restrictions on the feasible sets of courses of action, they obviously add important information to the model of rational choice. Psychologists, and especially developmental psychologists, for their part, concentrate on the genetic or constitutional origins of norms, and on how norms are formed and developed by parents, teachers etc. A comprehensive explanation of crime must rely on knowledge from all these fields. Such a gargantuan undertaking is too much for the present author. A more modest approach, developed in the following, is to sketch how various determinants of crime are interlinked by extending Fig. 2.1 to include some main features of theories from different disciplines. This approach will produce a basis for design and evaluation of empirical macro studies of crime.

A well established application of the model of rational choice is found in consumer theory. Here, the feasible set of a consumer, i.e. the various baskets of goods he can buy, is constrained by his income, and by the prices of the goods available. Income and prices determine how much of the goods available can be bought. The outcomes are the effects of consuming goods in various proportions, e.g. warmth, joy, and health. These outcomes are ranked on the basis of a system of preferences that are genetically, socially or otherwise established. The preference structure represents the intensity of various desires, and the degree to which different outcomes satisfy these desires. If preferences - whatever they are - are stable over time, observed changes in the choice of courses of action can - and indeed within this model must - be explained by changes in the environment. At any time, the individual chooses the basket of goods that - given the environment - best satisfies his wants, cf Fig. 2.1.

In the theory of labour supply the feasible set consists of possible types of work that produce not only income, but also various psychic benefits and costs. These benefits and costs are an integrated part of the opportunity set: when a course of action is chosen, the outcome includes the attributes of the course of action itself. The ranking of alternatives is thus dependent not only on the "pure" outcomes, but also on the likes and dislikes for the courses of action producing these results. It is usually assumed that by their choices individuals reveal wealth equivalents of the psychic elements of actions, thus making an analysis similar to the one of consumer theory applicable.

Criminal activities may be part of the feasible set confronting an individual who has to decide how to use his time, labour force, and other resources. Crimes will produce outcomes including pecuniary as well as various physical and psychic elements, just as in the theory of labour supply. To the extent that the individual is capable of choosing according to the model of rational choice, wealth equivalents of the various elements can be revealed, and the theory of labour supply is at our disposal for analysis.[5] If a criminal act produces an outcome that is more desirable than what comes out of legal activity, the model of rational choice both prescribes that crime should be committed, and explains why

---

[5]To show the basis for the construction of rational choice models of crime, sketches of elementary consumer theory and supply of labour theory are given in Appendices 1 and 2 to this chapter.

crimes in fact are. Examples of such models are found in section 2.2 below.

Sanctions may deter people from committing crimes. Deterrence (or "mere" deterrence, cf 2.1.6) is the inhibiting effect of sanctions on the criminal activity of people at large. The possibility of punishment is an aspect of the environment that determines - in a probabilistic manner - the outcomes of particular courses of action. Some of these may become less attractive if they are made punishable (or punished more severely), and consequently, legal activities may be substituted for illegal ones. The hypothesis of the existence of deterrence can thus be derived from the general proposition of rational behaviour where incentives influence individual choice.

2.1.2. Norm-guided to crime

Some scholars find norms so important and binding that a rational choice approach is felt to be irrelevant or misleading, at least for some segments of our behaviour. Using our framework, norms are found to restrict the possible set of courses of action to the extent that there is not much to choose between. Courses of action are entirely determined by accepted norms, and behaviour changes only because norms, for some reason, change. Changes in the environment will have no effect upon behaviour (unless norms also are altered). Such changes might have a significant effect on outcomes, but as activities are determined by norms and not by evaluation of outcomes, rational choice is of no significance. Theories of anomie and of certain psychological inadequacies conducive to crime go a long way in this direction, although they do not seem to reduce the feasible set of courses of action to a single alternative.

Thus, we have two extreme approaches: norm-free rational behaviour, where emphasis is placed on how to satisfy one's desires by choosing (presumably preference neutral) actions that provide the relevant outcome, and binding norm-guided behaviour where strict adherence to the norms reduces the feasible set of courses of action to one or a few similar alternatives.

Only empirical studies can decide which, if any, of these two extremes gives an acceptable description of human behaviour. Evidence so far suggests that elements of both approaches have to be included in a comprehensive model. The present study is intended as a contribution to this research program. Although the study is based on the model of rational choice, the influence of norms on crime is also considered.

2.1.3. Rationally norm-guided to crime

The theory of rational behaviour does not exclude an analysis of how norms influence our activities. On the contrary, it offers a useful framework for a discussion of how a combination of norms and wants form a basis for our choice of actions. We have desires not only about outcomes, but also about adhering to norms. Together with wants (for outcomes) norms (about activities) can be considered as part of our preferences. Just as wants for various baskets of goods are more or less satisfied by various outcomes, so are norms by various courses of action, see Fig. 2.2. We prefer to adhere to norms, adherence gives satisfaction. But as we have many norms and many desires, one specific norm might not be the only guide for action. Thus, we have to strike a balance between various actions and outcomes, between norm adherence and want satisfaction. The preference structure represents the intensity of the various desires, and also the ordering of various competing norms and wants.

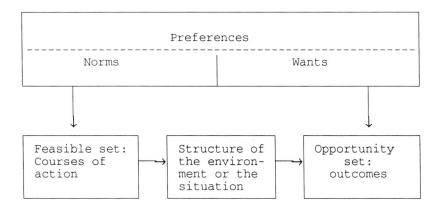

Fig. 2.2. Illustration of rational choice with norms

A norm might be important in the sense that a person, because of the desire for self-esteem, will feel quite uncomfortable or guilty by not adhering to it. But if an action that is not conform with the norm results in a "pure" outcome that is desired, the individual might well choose to break the norm. Confronted with several possible actions, the norm-breaking choice might simply be the best, all desires considered together. Thus, norms are not always binding. This is no news to Christians who (should) believe that we are all sinners.

Also, anybody who has ever driven a car can honestly say he has never "sinned". A given norm is not followed by everybody, and a given individual does not follow a norm under all circumstances.

As indicated in Fig. 2.2 preferences are constituted by norms and wants. Norms refer to morally based attitudes towards actions, whereas wants refer to attitudes towards outcomes and those aspects of the courses of action that are not norm relevant. (In the literature "tastes", "wants", "desires" and "preferences" are often used interchangeably, and norms are - explicitly or implicitly - included in these terms. For my purpose it is necessary to distinguish between wants and norms, and I will use "preferences" or "desires" to designate the combination of both. The reasonable possibility that wants depend on norms, and vice versa, will not be discussed.)

The proposition that our behaviour is determined by binding norms can formally be introduced into our framework in two ways. Either these norms delimit the feasible set of courses of action (to what is not binding), or they are given unlimited weight in the preference structure. If the opportunity set of outcomes is reduced to just one acceptable alternative, one may speak of binding norm-guided behaviour. Presumably, only norms that are firmly rooted in moral convictions can have such a binding effect.

Norm-free rational behaviour and binding norm-guided behaviour thus represent extreme alternatives that may be useful for some types of analysis, but they are generally incomplete. By combining the two, one obtains a comprehensive framework where both norms and traditional utility maximization have their place.

A further discussion of how behaviour is guided or determined by norms requires a distinction between internalized and non-internalized social norms. Social norms are norms that are shared with others.[6] Non-internalized norms exert their influence only through their effects on outcomes. Breaking these norms might cause unpleasant, informal reactions in the environment that changes the opportunity set of outcomes. An example might be a norm of sexual practice that is not internalized by an individual, but is despised and informally punished by others. Internalized norms work, in addition, through the person's own need for self-respect. Regardless of what others might do to him, feelings of anxiety, guilt, and shame accompany violation of internalized norms. Bad conscience emerges. This view of the effect of norms is at variance with the idea that "conscience" is fictitious: that

---

[6]It is possible to delimit a plentitude of types of norms, see e.g. Elster (1989a). There are moral norms based on more or less explicit ethical constructions; legal norms enforced by the judicial system, - norms that might coincide with or differ from social norms; habits, distinguishable from private norms in that violation does not generate self-blame or guilt; and finally, social norms, examples of which are consumption norms (e.g. manners of dress), norms against behaviour "contrary to nature" (e.g. incest and cannibalism), norms regulating the use of money (buying into a queue is non-U), norms of reciprocity (gift-giving), norms of retribution, work norms, norms of cooperation, and norms of distribution.

we refrain from bad actions only because of calculation of benefits and cost in want satisfaction. An example of the defectiveness of the latter idea is the working of the lie detector. The only way this machine can find out that we are lying, is by detecting our anxiety of merely uttering a lie. It does not help that our calculation tells us that we can conceal the truth: the calculation is based on the wrong supposition that we can lie without bad conscience.

Internalized norms might restrict the feasible set of courses of action (in exceptional cases perhaps to just one possible action); or adhering to them or violating them might involve sentiments that are "traded" against each other or against the satisfaction of outcomes. Non-internalized norms work through their effects on the satisfaction of wants. If, for instance, a man's sexual practice is disliked to such an extent that he is not invited to parties, the satisfaction of certain wants may be reduced.

Thus, an illegal act will be judged by an individual's preference structure along several dimensions. The act might be more or less desirable according to
a) individual norms (e.g. self-esteem),
b) internalized social norms,
c) psychic and physical attributes of the act itself,
d) "pure" outcomes (incl. risk of formal punishment, and informal reactions to breach of norms, such as being fired).

People thus adhere to norms because of pure individual desires (personal or internalized social norms), or because of actions and attitudes in the individual's environment, including punishment. Sometimes, the desire for the outcome of an illegal act is so intense that norms do not constitute a sufficient prevention. Behaviour is guided by norms, but rational choice requires infringement of them. Furthermore, many people have a conscience strong enough to prevent them from committing a crime in one situation, but not in another.

The term "norm-guided rational choice" will be used to designate behaviour where norms are vital, but where also rational evaluations of trade-offs between norms (concerning courses of action) and wants (concerning outcomes) have a significant influence on behaviour.[7]

A self-report study by Willcock and Stokes (1968) may serve as an illustration of the main elements of our framework. In this study 808 young males were asked what considerations would or would not prevent them from committing nine specified offence. The main results are reproduced in Table 2.1. Answers of type 1, "personal restraints", communicate an element of the preference structure of the youth. About half of them would

---

[7]When Becker proposes to dispense with these norms, he renounces of making use of the additional insight these norms might give us in designing empirical research and in interpreting the results.

stay law-abiding because of the bad conscience a crime would produce, and/or because the expected output was not tempting enough. The strength of norms and wants taken together is sufficient for crime not to be committed. Answers of type 2, "inability to execute deed itself", express some of the restrictions of the feasible sets of activities. (Some of the answers here might not represent real "inability to execute the deed", but just the person's consideration that the outcome would not satisfy any want.) Answers of type 3-7 represent the preventing effects of various aspects of informal and formal sanctions.

The table is an indication of the importance of norms and wants. This observation should not be taken as an argument against rational choice, which by no means reduces the relevance of preferences for various norms and wants. Rational choice is the mechanism by which a person, restricted by the environment, chooses among feasible courses of action. If sexual desire is overwhelming, norms against violence are weak, and the number of legal actions available for satisfaction are less than few, what could be more rational than rape?

This means that rational choice cannot predict behaviour without reference to some preference structure. Any action could in fact be explained as rational choice on the basis of a particular structure. What is then the relevance of rational choice? A feature of major interest for the present work is that it provides an explanation of why the environment may have an effect on individual behaviour. This quality makes it reasonable to base empirical research on the possibility that the environment counts, and that it has an effect on behaviour through the outcomes obtained. Some rapes are perhaps avoided because of the deterrent effect of severe sanctions.

The influence of the environment on norms provides another mechanism, also (shortly) discussed below, by which behaviour may be affected.

The premise of rational behaviour provides an explanation of actions that differ from what usually is called causal explanations. The police strike in Montreal in 1969, for instance, is considered to be the reason for the sharp increase in crime that year. Assuming rational behaviour one obtains (as will be further discussed in section 2.1.6) a deeper understanding of why more people chose to commit crimes when sanctions were less probable.

Table 2.1

Answers to question: "What sort of things hold you back, or worry about doing it?"[a]

Things which informants believed would hold them back, or worry about doing	Breaking into a lock-up shop %	Pick-ing up a wallet %	Breaking into a private house %	Taking unknown persons car %	Stealing from a large store %	Throwing stone at a street lamp %	Stealing from a coat %	Starting punch-up in a dance hall %	Stealing from a small shop %
1. *Personal restraints* (excl. physical inability) incl. reasons of conscience; consideration for the injured party, and the situation is not (sufficiently) a temptation	42.7	60.9	43.8	38.7	33.9	51.0	65.0	34.4	45.9
2. *Inability to execute deed itself* (excl. "being caught"), e.g. "can't drive a car", "afraid might get hurt/smash car/injure innocent people"; "can't fight", "might lose fight", "woudn't be able to get in", would miss street light anyway"	1.5	0.0	2.6	15.6	0.4	1.9	0.6	26.9	0.0
3. *Effect on parents/opinion of others/on own future*	9.9	3.4	6.1	3.5	7.4	3.7	5.9	7.7	5.3
4. *Difficulty of concealment - easily caught*	7.7	11.9	7.7	6.3	21.4	8.3	5.5	2.1	8.6
5. *The punishment/sentence*	5.3	1.3	4.7	8.4	4.1	2.1	1.4	4.2	4.5
6. *Miscellaneous and unspecified disadvantages of being caught not covered above (unspecified further)*, "scared of being caught for something so petty"	24.7	8.9	27.4	19.6	24.9	11.5	12.9	9.3	26.1
7. *Nothing would deter* (incl. "have done it, undeterred)	1.6	9.3	1.2	2.1	1.9	13.2	1.6	5.3	3.2
8. *Vague answers*, etc.	6.6	4.3	6.6	5.8	6.1	8.3	7.0	10.2	6.4

[a]Reproduced from Zimmring and Hawkins (1973, 328-9).

2.1.4. The limits of rational choice

The continuing discussions in literature about whether man is rational is a healthy warning not to uncritically base studies of crime on the assumption of rational behaviour. These discussions, however, stem partly from the fact that the notion of rationality is used to designate a host of various ideas. Elster (1983) distinguishes between more than 20 senses of the word (not all of which are in conflict). Føllesdal (1982) concentrates on four types of rationality that he considers to be of special interest in connection with interpretation and explanation of actions (p. 304): "They are (1) rationality as logical consistency, (2) rationality as well-foundedness of beliefs, (3) rationality as well-foundedness of values, and (4) rationality of action."

Types (1) and (2) both refer to beliefs: "Rationality as logical consistency is the requirement that a person's beliefs shall be logically consistent with one another." ... "Well-foundedness requires something more, namely that our beliefs be well supported by the available evidence." Rationality as well-foundedness of values requires that norms and values have a rational justification, for instance in the form of Rawls' (1972, 19-21) reflective equilibrium. Type (4), rationality of action, seems to coincide with what I call rational (norm-free or norm-guided) behaviour.

This distinction between various types of rationality makes it meaningful to talk about rational behaviour even if a person is not rational in the sense of Føllesdal's rationality types (1), (2), and (3). An individual may sometimes make his rational choice on the basis of (a) norms that are not consistent with other norms he has (but which are not evoked in the situation at hand), and (b) beliefs that are not in accordance with available evidence, and (c) norms that are not well-founded. Although one may be reluctant to accept that this man is wholly rational, one may nevertheless find that he is able to choose the action that best satisfies his preferences under the given norms and subjective beliefs, and thus acts rationally as far as his abilities permit. From a subjective point of view his choices are meaningful, and on this basis his activities can be explained and understood. This is more or less explicitly the position taken in the theories surveyed below where crime is explained as a result of maximization of expected utility. Becker (1968), for instance, bases his theory on the *subjective* probability of sanctions. In our empirical investigation in Chapter 6 we, in contrast to Becker (and most (all?) scholars working in his tradition), explicitly model the relation between subjective beliefs about crime and their observed counterparts.

The status of the four types of rationality discussed by Føllesdal depends on whether they are considered to be normative or descriptive. Mainly because of the limited cognitive and intellectual capacities of man, Føllesdal tends to consider his rationality types (2) and (3), concerning beliefs and values, respectively, and even type (4) concerning actions, as normative notions. Most of us do not conform to all these aspects of rationality, and as descriptions of how we actually are constituted they are inadequate. On the other hand, they may be considered as good rules of conduct. At least, rationality of action offers conditional imperatives, cf Elster (1986, p. 1). It tells us what to do in order to obtain our ends. Føllesdal (1982, p. 316) carries the argument further and suggests that people in fact strive to live according to these forms of rationality, - with more or less success:

"Man has rationality as a norm, as a second-order disposition of the following kind: once one becomes aware that one has fallen into irrationality, one will tend to adjust one's belief, attitudes and actions such as to make them rational.

... Studying man, we may assume that he is rational unless he cannot help being irrational, e.g. because his irrationality is hidden from his view, because the situation is too complex or because of other obstructions."

Thus, perfect rationality is never obtained, but as we aspire to be rational, and to some extent succeed, rationality assumptions, and especially rationality of action, should be the basis for our study of man's activities (p. 311):

"The decision theoretic pattern of explanation of action that I have just sketched is often regarded as the paradigm of rationality, the model of rational decision making. One always chooses what is best for one, or more accurately, what one believes to be the best for one.

When I am proposing this pattern as a basis for explaining actions and thereby for understanding them, it is because I know of no better theory. Some theory of action is, I think, necessary in order to get the enterprise started of explaining and understanding actions.".

The present study is based on this approach (although I read Føllesdal's article after most of the manuscript was finished). Rational behaviour is the centrepiece of explanation, whereas the several "causes" of crime discussed in various theories will be presented below as factors influencing the various elements of the rational choice model: norms, wants, beliefs, and the environment.

The limited success of man's endeavour to be rational diminishes the fruitfulness of the assumption of rational behaviour. However, a main asset of this assumption is that, by using it, one may predict changes in behaviour from changes in the environment, i.e. from changes in sanctions. If people have wrong beliefs about the environment, or if changes in the environment make people revise their norms, such predictions become intricate, or even impossible. People may have wrong beliefs about the feasible set of courses of action, about the environment, and about the correspondence between actions and outcomes, see Fig. 2.3. Both lack of information and lack of cognitive capacity may cause beliefs to be false. People may also have misconceptions about the degree to which desires will be satisfied by outcomes. Furthermore, if beliefs are affected by preferences, and vice versa, the rational choice theory either looses some of its firm basis, or becomes much more intricate.[8] In both theoretical and empirical analysis one has to assess the likely effects of these problems on the results obtained.

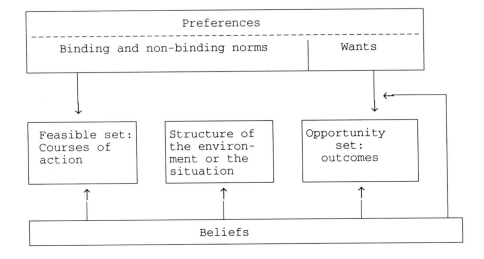

Fig. 2.3. Illustration of the role of beliefs for rational choice

Bounded rationality
Herbert Simon (1955 and 1957) introduced the term "bounded rationality" to designate the individual's behaviour when beliefs are distorted because of cognitive limitations. More and even costless information will not overcome this problem. People do not possess the ability to process all information needed to make rational choices. During the last decade or so many authors have elaborated on these problems. Laboratory experiments have often shown that people do not choose according to the axioms of rational choice.[9] The framing and

---

[8] See e.g. Elster (1990) for a more comprehensive discussion of how beliefs and preferences can be adjusted.

[9] A presentation of recent results and problems encountered is found in Cook and Levy, ed. (1990), where Jon Elster writes about "When rationality fails", Amos Tversky and Daniel Kaheman about "Rational choice and framing decisions", Mark J, Machina about "Choice under uncertainty: Problems solved and unsolved", just to mention a few.

transparency of the choice set (opportunity set of outcomes) seems to influence decisions.

Even if cognitive limitations do not prevail, it would be irrational for a person to gather and process all information needed to obtain correct beliefs in all details. Much time and use of various abilities would be required, and the feasible set of activities would in most cases be curtailed to such an extent that satisfaction of desires would be significantly reduced. In fact, rational behaviour requires an optimal degree of ignorance. Time and abilities should be allocated among belief production and other activities in order to obtain the highest possible satisfaction. But of course it is difficult, or perhaps impossible, for a person to know to what extent beliefs can be corrected by using more time and resources on information gathering. Search theory in economics has produced some interesting results in this domain, but so far only partial answers to the main question have been obtained.

A particular form of bounded rationality prevails if the individual is satisfied when obtaining a required end. A chosen course of action that grants this end is considered as sufficient. Behaviour is satisficing. Better courses of action might exist, but for lack of information or cognitive capabilities these are not considered. Satisficing behaviour does not imply that the individual is irresponsive to changes in the environment, in exogenous factors. It only means that as long as a given end is obtained, behaviour is not changed.

Unstable preferences and expressive crimes.

In rational choice theory it is usually assumed that preferences are stable.[10] This assumption secures that any change in behaviour can be ascribed to changes in the environment. Apparently preferences are not always stable. If I, a non-aggressive person, kicks a man that insulted me, one may easily think that I lost my mind, that I temporarily forgot, or set aside, my well established norms. But if my reaction to a similar insult in a similar situation always is the same, there is no instability in preferences. Also, it is not a sign of unstable norms to kill in self-defence. Instability, or change, in norms would be an issue only if I do not do it every time my life is threatened. In these cases, it would in principle be possible to correctly predict the reaction on the basis of stable preferences and a given environment. Instability of preferences would occur only when behaviour in similar situations differ.

Emotional arousal might temporarily change our feelings about the importance of a norm, for instance reduce our inhibitions, or make one outcome especially desirable. But if such emotions are incited by the environment, preferences can still be regarded as stable. Furthermore, our appetite for food and sex may certainly fluctuate during the day, but after

---

[10]Stigler, G. J. and G. S. Becker (1977) have most forcefully claimed that individual preferences are stable over time and fairly invariant among people. Elaborating on adaptive preferences, they ascribe addictions and habits to the accumulation of specific knowledge and skills.

being satisfied the desire steadily returns. Thus, although our wants can be temporarily satisfied, the striking characteristic of preferences is that they are stable.

Emotional arousal can, however, undermine the theory of rational choice. Anger or fascination can distort the individual's beliefs about the environment and outcomes, and thus generate non-optimal courses of action. This effect should not be mistaken for the fact that emotions also can shorten the individual's time horizon, or, more generally, increase his rate of time discount.

Our discussion of the stability of preferences does not imply that norms and wants cannot be formed by parents, schools, etc. This possibility will be considered in several sections below. The issue above is the stability of preferences in the short run. The lack of success in programs of rehabilitation of offenders is an indication that preferences are not easily changed, even in the long run.[11] The amount of advertising is often taken as an indication of the opposite. One should not ignore, however, that advertising to a large extent is concerned with various means of satisfying the same fundamental wants.

It has been argued that the rational choice framework might be relevant for certain property crimes, but not for violent crimes that are considered to be "expressive" and not "instrumental". Undoubtedly, the degree of "expressiveness" differs among crimes, but rationality does not require "instrumentality". Several empirical studies support this view. At least substantial elements of rationality are revealed in a study of mugging by Lejeune (1977), in a study of rape and homicide by Athens (1980), and in a study of spouse abuse by Dobash and Dobash (1984). Other empirical studies surveyed in Chapter 4 support the view that threat of punishment also has a preventive effect on "expressive" crime. Although the effect of punishment may differ among types of crime, evidence so far indicates that the rational choice framework is relevant for all types of crime, and that analyses rejecting a priori that some types of crime are deterrable are inadequate.

Changing norms and rational behaviour
In the economics of crime literature, as in most other economic literature, norms[12] are

---

[11] Another explanation of the lack of success is that the feasible set of courses of action is very restricted also after rehabilitation, and that crime turns out to be rational even if preferences have changed somewhat.

[12] It has been suggested that norms of behaviour merely are tools for maximizing utility. (See Coleman (1973), Coleman (1990), Axelrod (1984), Taylor (1987, [1976], and Ellickson (1991)). Norms may have been consciously introduced by certain groups for that purpose, or they have appeared as a result of interaction between individuals in search of maximum utility.

Elster (1989a) discusses several types of social norms, and presents examples apparently showing that social norms cannot always be said to contribute to individual satisfaction of outcomes. Elster's aim here seems to be to demonstrate that norms cannot always be considered as intricate tools of utility maximization. Of course he does not deny that in many cases norms are such tools.

On a few occasions in the present study I will discuss the possibility that norms are formed by the environment, given a somewhat superficial treatment. The attitude often taken, implicitly or explicitly, is that norms are fairly stable, and that effects on outcomes of changing circumstances can be discussed as if in fact they are. The common cet. par. assumption usually includes the supposition that norms do not change with changing environments, or for other reasons. The less norms are influenced by changing circumstances, the more such a supposition is acceptable. When norms adapt slowly to changes in the environment, and the problem at hand is of a short term character, the usual procedure may also be acceptable. Sociologists and psychologists tend to regard this assumption with more scepticism than economists. To evaluate some of the criticism raised against empirical studies in the economics of crime literature, I will in Chapter 4 come bak to the possibility that changing norms might be the reason why criminal behaviour changes.

The limits of rational choice and its use

The importance that because of distorted beliefs, unstable preferences, etc. should be attached to the critique of rational choice theory depends on what the theory is to be used for. If one demands that a theory shall explain every single act, the theory of rational choice would certainly be deficient. So would any other known theory. But in the sciences of human behaviour, the ambition of a theory must be kept lower. Any human act depends on a multitude of conditions that we never will be able to specify in detail. We have to stick to the common requirements to a theory: as general and as simple as possible. The desire for simplicity requires that some aspects of behaviour cannot explicitly be dealt with. It is a serious analytical flaw to think that the theory of rational choice is irrelevant because eventually some offenders are found to have wrong beliefs or to be irrational in some other fashion. If the theory gives an explanation of why the rest of the population abides or not to the law, it performs better than most theories.

In the case of bounded rationality it is often presumed that minor changes in the environment will not have any effect on behaviour. They will not be sufficient to dictate a change in chosen activities. It may well happen, however, that a "satisficing person" has approached the brink of accepting a new goal, and that a minor change in beliefs is enough for it to occur.

Bounded rationality implies that even if crime gives the best satisfaction of desires, law-abidingness may prevail: the person may be ignorant of feasible criminal acts, or of the

---

but I will not pursue the idea that norms are chosen in order to maximize utility. In the present framework this possibility would mean that "real" preferences are constituted only by tastes, whereas norms are a kind of pseudopreferences that in fact are means of satisfying the real ones. The mechanism would be that the norms, especially the social norms, affect the environment in order to widen, by alternatives that are higher preferred according to given tastes, the opportunity set of norm generating persons.

opportunities of crime. But if legal activities no longer meet the required end, illegal acts may be considered and undertaken. In a similar way, the precise amount of an increase in the threat of punishment may be misconceived, but what is believed may still be enough for illegal activities to appear as less attractive than legal ones.

The main theoretical problem with this kind of incomplete rationality is that one cannot predict the effect of marginal changes in the environment on individual behaviour. In macro studies, however, the problem is to some extent lessened. The trick is to assume - quite reasonably in my view - that in a large population some individuals with satisficing behaviour will usually be on the brink of choosing other courses of actions. Furthermore, a change in the environment may perhaps go unnoticed by some of these individuals on the brink, while others among them will register the change, and choose other activities than before. On the macro level, then, one would expect an effect even of minor changes in the environment. This conclusion is supported by the following supposition: If a satisficing activity gradually is made more and more unattractive by some change in the environment, it is wholly incredible that most people would not sooner or later turn to other courses of action. It is unreasonable to expect that everybody would wait until the greatest degree of unattractiveness is reached. Gradual changes in behaviour is what would be expected. If this is accepted, it is an empirical question to reveal the precise marginal macro effects on behaviour of changes in the environment, and it will be meaningful to estimate these effects.

It would be a misconception of theory as such to demand exact explanation and prediction of human behaviour in all circumstances. In order to be simple and tractable, a theory can never be expected to give more than an approximate or average representation of the real world. Furthermore, even if satisficing is common, utility maximization may be an acceptable approximation to reality.

This means that our model of norm-guided rational behaviour may still be valid as a guide for studies of the behaviour of large populations. It is then an empirical question to what extent rational choice can explain and predict differences and changes in crime. To be specific: even if some people do not react to changes in the probability of clear-up because they have not observed the change or do not attach any significance to the change, others might. For society it would *perhaps* be best to predict the result for each and every individual, but it is also interesting to know the macro effect. The norm-guided rational choice model with deficient beliefs cannot fully explain the behaviour of a given person, but can still be valid as a description of the mechanism by which some people react to changes in exogenous factors.

A special problem arising within the norm-guided rational choice framework is that the environment may affect behaviour not only through direct influence on outcomes, but also via norms. Thus, an observed effect of the risk of punishment is not necessarily a sign of rational choice, but of norm formation. This mechanism does not undermine the rational choice approach, but seriously hampers the possibility of empirical testing. If both mechanisms are at work simultaneously, it can be difficult, or even impossible, to distinguish between the two. Attempts to separate these two effects of the environment, and especially of sanctions, should be pursued in designing empirical tests and in interpreting results.

The limits of rationality bring up the question of skipping the whole theory of rational choice, and merely estimate, for instance, the correlation between the clear-up probability and crime. The obvious reason for not doing so is that scientific explanations require clarifications of the mechanisms by which phenomena occur. The theory of norm-guided rational choice, at variance with some sociological theories, provides such an explanation. Changing behaviour on the macro level can be explained by individuals who react either fully rationally to changes in the environment, or at least in a satisficing manner. All behaviour being individual behaviour, theories of crime not including explanations of what determines individual choice, will lack propositions about the mechanisms by which criminal acts occur.

2.1.5. Motivation

In our framework the common term "motivation" covers any element in the preference structure that has a significant impact on behaviour. Individual choice can be determined by a desire to adhere to certain norms or by a desire to satisfy some wants. Norms can be divided into "shoulds" and "should nots". The strength of motivation depends on several factors. The motivation not to kill is strong because the norm of not killing is general, it appeals to moral feelings, it is just (in the sense that we think people have a right to live), it is important, it is legitimate, and it has a high legal status. The norm of not taking more than one bottle of liquor into a country without paying tax is not strong for the "opposite" reasons. Motivation can be enhanced by missionary zeal, anger and outrage, and expectations of adherence in the individual's subculture. Motivation can also be rooted in the desire to satisfy wants. Pleasure seeking, personality needs, etc. can be main determinants of a certain behaviour. Motivation is thus a subset of determinants that are considered to be of importance in explaining crime. Often, the term is used only for norms and wants that presumably explain criminal behaviour, not law-abidingness.

To some people norms, such as the commandment not to kill, may be so strong that all other motivation, including the fright of punishment, is of no significance. The feasible set of courses of action will never include murder. This corresponds to a (partially) lexicographic preference structure. In general, several motives seem to be at work at the same time. Stealing may be motivated by the urge to satisfying wants, counter-balanced by the norm (motive) of not doing so, and by the want (motive) of avoiding punishment.

If motivation is strong, and the threat of punishment low, one cannot expect moderate changes in punishment to have a significant effect on crime. But if the degree of motivation differs among individuals, one would expect that some will be affected by a threat of punishment. In large populations many people will desire the death of some other person. Binding norms may prevent some killings. In other cases even capital punishment does not efficiently deter. It is utterly unreasonable, however, that these two simple possibilities are the only ones. More compelling is the supposition that although homicide may be considered, a combination of non-binding norms and sanctions prevents it. Only empirical research can decide if changes in sanctions, for instance from capital to less severe punishment, have any effect on the number of homicides.

By extracting certain motives from the preference structure, one runs the risk of neglecting important elements of the latter. In the present study norms and wants are included in a more general approach, and motives as a special category are only occasionally considered.

2.1.6. The preventive effect of sanctions

A main theme of this study will be the effect of formal sanctions on crime. The presumed deterrent effect is here of special interest. The effect of threatening people by unpleasant formal sanctions, inflicting on them pain, loss or harm, is in literature usually called "simple" deterrence or "mere" deterrence. Punishment may also have an effect on crime by informing people about social norms, or through individual norm formation. The whole bundle of these effects is denoted as general prevention, in contrast to individual prevention which constitutes the effect of punishment on the person punished.[13]

Some sanctions are informal, applied by family members, friends, neighbours, employers, and people at large. Others are formal, applied by the Criminal Justice System (CJS). This study concentrates on formal sanction.

Formal sanctions may prevent crime through several mechanisms[14], which can be

---

[13]See Andenæs (1975) or Andenæs (1989) on the various effects of sanctions.

[14]Gibbs (1975, p. 92-3) maintains that there are several ways in which punishment might prevent crime without involving notions of deterrence: "... incapacitation, surveillance, enculturation, reformation, normative validation, retribution, stigmatisation, normative insulation, and habituation." Most of these effects are easily

located within our model framework. Incarceration will diminish the offenders' possibilities of committing new crimes. The feasible set of actions of some individuals will be reduced.

Formal sanctions may alert people at large, and thereby produce better protection against offenders. The costs of crime will increase by this change in the environment, and the amount of crime may decrease.

Formal sanctions may also change the beliefs of people as to the consequences of offending. The effect of changes in sanctions depends on how beliefs about sanctions are established and changed. Information about sanctions can be obtained through personal experience, by contact with people having experience with the criminal justice system, through mass media, and by the more general cultural surrounding.[15]

If beliefs generally are wrong, but not systematically so, the risk of punishment will have no influence on crime, since there is no systematic relationship between the real world and beliefs about it. If empirical research reveals no link between punishment and crime, we here have a possible explanation. If, on the other hand punishment is shown to have an effect, the supposition that beliefs generally are grossly wrong, is not supported.

Furthermore, formal sanctions may involve unpleasant consequences, for instance incarceration and stigmatization, that change the opportunity set of outcomes. Sanctions against offenders are part of the environment that determine the outcomes of various courses of action. People at large show no appetite for unpleasantness, and do their best to avoid sanctions. To maintain that sanctions have no effect on crime is thus intuitively unreasonable. Quite another question is the degree to which minor changes may have an effect - a main issue below.

Formal sanctions may also influence the informal sanctions, with similar effects.

In addition, it has been suggested that sanctions help to create law-abiding habits, and that habits make the theory of rational choice less important. The idea is that habits make the "calculation" of which outcome is the best irrelevant. People do not balance benefits and costs for all possible actions at every second. They act according to habits. It is, however, difficult to see how habits are established if not by choosing a way of life on the basis of acquired norms and available outcomes. The fact that we do not repeat the balancing at every second can itself be a result of rational behaviour: repetition of similar considerations of benefits and costs would be a waste of resources. The crucial question is if habits produce "mistakes" in the sense that we act otherwise than a new evaluation of

---

ordered within our framework, and will be considered in various sections. Gibbs reserved the concept of deterrence to denote instances where someone refrains from committing a crime because of the fear of punishment.

[15]Zimring and Hawkins (1973, 156) suggest that "...the communication of legal threats is analogous to the advertising function in that it must compete for attention, must convey information, and must, if it is to serve its purpose, persuade."

costs and benefits would suggest. Undoubtedly, this can occasionally happen. But once having decided that stealing is not your way of life, it is farfetched to surmise that another consideration would give a different result.

Formal sanctions may also establish individual norms or reinforce norms already existing. A decrease in the severity or in the probability of punishment may on the other hand weaken individual norms against crime. People may internalize what they regard as a more lenient condemnation of certain acts. Crime may seem less wrong, and conscience will have less bite.

In discussing the general preventing effects of formal sanctions it is often asserted that sanctions work only under certain circumstances. As already mentioned, sanctions might work through various mechanisms, and various conditions might be pertinent to some people, but not to others. Only certain main qualifications will be discussed here. They do not wreck our framework, but add flesh to it.

According to our model of norm-guided rational behaviour norms may be so solid that formal sanctions have no additional effects. Some commandments might be considered so binding that certain courses of action are not feasible. Or conventional ties make the costs of informal sanctions so high that formal sanctions make no difference. The rewards of a crime may also be far higher than the costs. In that case, even severe sanctions will not prevent crime. The existence of criminal peer influence might be an example. If norms are formed by people who per se consider crime acceptable, or even desirable, severe punishment will not have enough weight to prevent crime. It may also happen that changes in sanctions are not discovered, and consequently beliefs, and thereby actions, are not changed. For a given offender there is therefore no guarantee that a particular sanction will be strong enough to counteract the rewards of a particular crime.

When considering a particular crime, these qualifications of the effect of formal sanctions may be relevant as an explanation of behaviour. On a macro level they are less relevant. The reason is as follows: In a large population conditions for some people may be such that certain crimes will never be committed regardless of formal sanctions. On the other hand, some crimes will be committed no matter what sanctions are introduced. Between these extremes there are people for whom increases in sanctions (when noticed) might tilt the balance in favour of law-abidingness. When benefits and costs (excluding sanctions) are almost equal, even mild sentences might have an effect. It is a goal of empirical research to reveal this change in behaviour. The criticism of the rational choice framework does not seem to be of a kind that undermines the use of our theory for this purpose.

According to some of the theories of crime discussed below, individual preferences for certain outcomes are so strong that the risk of punishment, or other aspects of the environment, have no effect. This may apply to some kinds of sexual crimes, pyromania, etc. If punishment is shown not to have any effect on crime, strong desires for certain outcomes might be the explanation. According to the model of rational choice, the stronger the motivation, cet.par., the more severe the threat of punishment has to be in order to be effective. But this possibility does not invalidate an empirical test of deterrence. Even if courses of action are not significantly changed by the risk of punishment, behaviour can still be rational. The degree of deterrence is an empirical question. Table 2.1, although not containing any information about the marginal effect of changes in formal sanctions, indicates that such sanctions can indeed prevent crime. The most surprising result of this table is perhaps that only a very small proportion of those interviewed declare that nothing would deter.

This preliminary discussion of sanctions reveals that our norm-guided rational choice framework seems suitable to the further study of the deterrent effects of the probability and severity of punishment. A fuller assessment of the fruitfulness of the framework depends on how various existing theories of crime fit into it. In the following subsections, theories emphasizing various constitutional factors, as well as the environment, are considered.

2.1.7. Constitutional and acquired characteristics

Criminal statistics and many investigations indicate that people with certain characteristics are more crime prone than others. Apparently, gender, age, race etc. are related to crime. Our framework of norm-guided rational choice can assist in understanding these relationships. Variation in crime between individuals can presumably be explained by differences in norms and wants, in feasible activities, and in the environment. It will be argued that individual differences in crime proneness do not eliminate the choice situation for each individual, but add supplementary explanation of behaviour.

Born to crime
More than a hundred years ago the young Italian specialist in mental diseases, Cesare Lombroso, by his publishing of *"L'Uomo delinquente"* (*The criminal man*, 1876, 1976), brought about a shift in criminology from a legalistic preoccupation with crime to a scientific study of criminals. He contended that real criminals are a special type of people - biological throwbacks to a primitive stage of human evolution. He admitted, however, that not all criminals were born to it, and in later works he also analyzed social causes of crime. Other biological and genetic factors than those studied by Lombroso, such as organic brain injuries, endocrinal abnormalities or chromosomal aberrations have also been postulated as

causes of crime.

Lombroso's famous contention was tested by Lange (1929), who compared criminal activities of identical twins (what else do these poor people do, except being studied?) and of other twins. He found that even in cases where identical twins had been separated at an early age, their criminal careers were astonishingly similar. Such a similarity was not evident in other twins.

The same, though somewhat less evident, distinction was also found by Christiansen (see Hurwitz og Christiansen (1968-71): Kriminologi, pp. 112-118). Andenæs (1989, p. 42) concludes a discussion of these and other studies by asserting that there is a clear difference between the two groups of twins as regards the more serious types of crime, but less so for minor crimes. Wilson and Herrnstein (1985), reviewing mainly the same studies, obtain similar conclusions. Referring to more recent studies of anthropometric measurements of delinquents and control groups, these authors also find that offenders tend to be constitutionally distinctive. They do not suggest, however, that a certain physique causes people to breach the law, but rather that a particular body type is associated with temperamental traits that predispose people to offending. Some of these traits are considered in subsections below. These authors further link the asserted constitutional factors to psychological traits that may be relevant for the understanding of individual choices between legal and illegal activities.[16]

The studies of twins have been criticized for not attaching enough importance to the possibility that the similarities in the criminal activity of identical twins might be caused by society's similar reactions to people with identical appearance. In a study of Norwegian twins by Dalgard and Kringlen (1976), this possibility made the authors conclude that it is impossible to judge definitely the importance of biological and genetic factors to crime. Biological factors might be essential for some crimes, especially some violent crimes and crimes of seemingly motiveless nature. Their effects on crime in general, however, is so far not substantiated by empirical research.

Even if biological factors have an effect on crime, the norm-guided rational choice framework is relevant to the extent that the "lombrosian offender" recognizes that several courses of action are possible, and that the threat of punishment makes some of the illegal ones less attractive. Biological characteristics or deficiencies might produce unusual norm structures, create abnormal wants, delimit the feasible set of courses of action, generate

---

[16]"The average offender tends to be constitutionally distinctive, though not extremely or abnormally so. The biological factors whose traces we see in faces, physiques, and correlations with the behaviour of parents and siblings are predispositions toward crime that are expressed as psychological traits and activated by circumstances. It is likely that the psychological traits involve intelligence and personality, and that the activating events include certain experiences within the family, in school, and in the community at large,..." Wilson and Herrnstein (1985), p. 102-3.

special responses from people in the environment, and distort beliefs. Nevertheless, room may be left for rational choice. Sanctions, and changes in sanctions, may well have an effect, albeit modest, on the behaviour of some of these individuals. Except in a very few cases, existing evidence does not support the view that sanctions have no effect whatsoever. Empirical research is therefore needed in order to reveal the degree of deterrence also for this group of people (if they at all exist).

Psychologically disposed to crime

Another type of explanation is that criminal behaviour is a result of mental illness or psychological deviation. In our framework these problems may create particular norm structures where common norms are absent, or are given little weight compared with other desires. Punishment may even be just what is desired. Mental illness might also reduce the feasible set of courses of action, especially legal activities. It also generates reactions from people in the environment that reduce the attractiveness of some activities and outcomes. In addition, strong desires (motivations) for certain courses of action and for certain "pure" outcomes may be decisive for the person's choices. Furthermore, wrong beliefs may reduce the possibility of choosing activities that in fact would best satisfy desires. The problem of wrong beliefs and bounded rationality can be accentuated.

All these effects of mental illness might lead to criminal behaviour, but even here rational choice, or bounded rationality, cannot be excluded, at least not in the less serious cases of mental illness. Even people that are mentally ill usually try to avoid punishment, a sign that sanctions are considered to be a nuisance. More important for a macro study of crime, mental illness does not seem to be responsible for a large proportion of crimes. Kleptomania may be a symptom of compulsive neurosis, but only a minor part of all thefts can be ascribed to kleptomania. Libel may be related to persecution mania, and sexual deviations may lead to sexual offenses, but these crimes are also committed by "normal" people. Similar considerations are apparently relevant for other illnesses and crimes as well.

Descriptive analyses of offenders have been attempted by psychologists using psycho-diagnostic tests, but few general conclusions as to the causes of crime have appeared. At a descriptive level, however, psychological studies have offered a basis for describing offenders as types. Offenders are sometimes found to be impulsive, non-reflective and immature. But so are many law-abiding individuals.

Further studies of the personality of offenders and non-offenders would presumably illuminate individual differences in crime. A person's personality summarizes characteristic traits and attitudes, and thus reveals aspects of the profile of norms and wants, i.e. the types and strengths of wants and the prevalence and importance of norms. Differences in personality will delimit different feasible sets of courses of action, and ascribe different benefits and costs to given results. According to our framework of norm-guided rational choice, we would expect that people with, for instance, shallow inhibitions against crime, would tend to offend more than average. So far only a few empirical studies can substantiate this presumption.[17]

Time discount and impulsiveness

People prefer to have their wants satisfied sooner rather than later. The balancing between the present and the future can be expressed through the rate of time discount: future events are given less weight than the present ones. Consequently, a delayed sanction implies a lower cost than an immediate one.

This discount rate differs among people: some are patient, others impulsive. Their personalities, congenital or formed by experience or education, differ. For very high discount rates, sanctions will presumably have to be exceptionally harsh in order to outweigh the immediate benefit of a crime.

Crimes differ as to when benefits and costs occur. For violent crimes, the benefits (sexual satisfaction, enjoyment of vengeance, etc.) usually occur at once, whereas the costs (bad conscience, formal and informal sanctions, etc.) come in the future. One would therefore expect impulsive people with a high rate of time discount to be over-represented among violent offenders.

Recent research suggests that the rising crime rates in many countries during the last decades perhaps are partially caused by a shortening of the time horizon of at-risk persons.[18] Why this may be so, is still obscure.

In our norm-guided rational choice framework the various benefits and costs must be adjusted by rates of time discount in order to obtain a comprehensive model. It has been suggested that the urge to commit a crime sometimes is so strong that an indefinitely high rate is required to represent a person's evaluation of the present against the future, and that

---

[17]Encyclopedia Britannica (1984, p.269) concludes a discussion of psychological studies of crime by stating that: "[a] number of studies have indicated no significant difference between the personality traits of prisoners and nonprisoners, and no definable personality makeup of delinquents compared to nondelinquents. Some accumulated evidence does suggest that the traits of aggressiveness and feelings of inadequacy are common features in delinquent personality. But beyond this, there is really no agreement on what psychological factors differentiate criminals from noncriminals, and the reason for this could be that there is no great difference between the two groups." On the other hand, Wilson and Herrnstein (1985, p. 173) state that: "People who break the law are often psychologically atypical. This is not to say that they are necessarily sick (although some are), or that atypicality of any sort characterizes every single lawbreaker. Rather, the evidence says that populations of offenders differ statistically in various respects from populations of nonoffenders." And further (p. 217) "Compared to nonoffenders and occasional offenders [persons who are markedly more likely than others to commit predatory crimes] are more impulsive (they cannot or will not defer gratification) and they are less socialized (they display little regard for the feelings of others)."

[18]See e.g. Wilson and Herrnstein (1985, p. 422).

benefits and cost occurring in the future therefore are irrelevant. For most crimes, however, it is hard to imagine that no sanction, no matter how immediate and severe, has no effect on the offender.

Gender

If the framework of norm-guided rational choice can be used to explain criminal behaviour, it should also reveal why women commit fewer crimes than men. Is gender an autonomous determinant of crime, or is gender just correlated with other elements in our framework? If women commit crimes for the same reasons as men, why do they commit fewer of them?

First of all, the preference structure of men and women may differ. Women may genetically be disposed to having more crime averse norms, or by tradition acquire such norms. They may, for instance, fear informal sanctions more than men, as they spend more of their time among family members and in a closer circle of acquaintances. Their wants may be less strong, and thus easier to satisfy by legal means. Women may further be less self-reliant, more obedient, and more responsive to conformity pressure than men. The psychic costs of breaking rules will therefore be relatively high, and legal activities preferred. Genetic factors may also cause the feasible set of actions to differ. Lack of physical abilities may restrict women from committing certain crimes, or at least the outcomes will not be attractive. Burglary and robbery are presumably less rewarding for women than for men. Furthermore, the daily life of most women might hinder criminal activity, cf the routine activity approach discussed below. They may have fewer opportunities, as they tend to stay at home taking care of children.

After reviewing several theories and empirical investigations on the effect of gender on crime, Wilson and Herrnstein (1985) go a long way in attributing the gender gap to biology. They conclude (p. 124) that: "... our best guess centers on the difference in aggression and perhaps other drives that flow into the definition of sex roles".[19] The fact that shop-lifting is at least as common among women as among men, indicates that abilities and opportunities may account for a major part of the gender gap, and that biological differences are relevant primarily for violent crimes.

The gender factor seems to fit well into our framework. The various explanations are

---

[19]They continue (p. 124-5) "[M]ales and females ... diverge sharply in antisocial and criminal behavior in the years of early adolescence, just as the primary and secondary reinforcers of adulthood emerge and begin to shape the full range of differences in sex roles. Just as the gender gap in crime has survived the changes of recent decades, so also have the major sex roles, and most probably for similar reasons. The underpinning of the sexual divisions of labor in human society, from the family to commerce and industry to government, may not be rigidly fixed in genes, but their roots go so deep into the biological substratum that beyond certain limits they are hard to change."

linked to norms and norm formation, wants, abilities, opportunities, and evaluation of punishment. Norm-guided rational choice is a perspective general enough to discuss and evaluate the gender gap.

Age

In many countries about 2/3 of those arrested are below 25 years. Crime increases with age from early adolescence to a peak some years later, and thereafter decreases steadily. The peak is reached at somewhat different ages for various types of crime, but the main development is the same for all.[20]

The explanations of why age affects crime are numerous. In their self-report study, Rowe and Tittle (1977) investigated many of the existing suggestions by controlling for several socio-demographic factors, such as family size, home life, education, and occupation. They also questioned their subjects on their moral commitments, on their fear of punishment, and on the extent of their need of the outputs of various offence. Although some of these variables appeared to have a certain influence on crime, age remained a significant determinant.

Genetic factors and mental illness can hardly be held responsible for the significance of age. But socialization and acquisition of norms may take time, and may depend on life's requirements at various ages. Juvenile norms may thus account for a significant part of youth delinquency. Most of the variables studied by Rowe and Tittle, and by others, fit well into our framework. Young people's opposition to parents and elders implies an antagonism, or at least less attachment, to common norms of grown-ups.

But the effect of the environment should not be underestimated. The feasible set of courses of action may for quite a few young people not include many legal income generating activities, whereas the opportunities for crime may be high for young people not tied to work and family most of the day. Also, the costs of punishment might be low when no legal income, and perhaps no status, is at risk. Furthermore, unemployment, low pay, and small savings make it more difficult to satisfy wants by legal means.

Even if the age factor has a separate effect on crime in addition to these elements, the norm-guided rational choice perspective appears to be relevant. Juvenile norms, crime prone feasible sets of actions, low sanction costs, and want-satisfying results of crime underscore our approach. Furthermore, no empirical study seems to indicate that opportunities do not count for young people, or that they are not worried about punishment.

---

[20]See e.g. Wilson and Herrnstein (1985, p. 126-47) for a review of research.

Intelligence[21]

Large bodies of data have consistently shown that offenders in the United States and in Great Britain have an average IQ of about 90. The IQ scores are found to be especially low for violent offenders, whereas forgery, bribery, embezzlement, etc. is associated with IQ-scores not very different from the average of the population. Controlling for socioeconomic, racial, cultural, and other variables have reduced the difference in IQ-scores between offenders and non-offenders, but not eliminated it. Within the group of offenders IQ scores are found to be especially low for violent offenders. Note that most of these studies are based on traditional IQ tests; other measures of intelligence might have given different results.

It has been suggested that registered crime and IQ-scores are correlated because dumb persons tend to be more easily caught and convicted than more intelligent ones. The suggestion is supported by self-reports that mostly show a rather weak, if any, association between crime and IQ scores. These reports, however, are probably biased by the fact that unintelligent persons tend not to cooperate in self-report studies. They become under-represented, and the possible association between crime and IQ-scores is thus reduced.

Within our framework of norm-guided rational behaviour intelligence may be related to crime through various mechanisms. Firstly, low intelligence may hamper the understanding, learning and internalization of norms. This suggestion is hardly supported by a study of Gordon (1975), which reveals that delinquents and non-delinquents roughly agree about which actions are "good" and which are "bad". Gordon finds, however, that the depth of disapproval for the "bad" actions was much shallower for the delinquents. This result supports the idea of our general framework that norms should be allowed to have different weights within the preference structure of various individuals. It also supports the view that if norms against crime are weak, the keeper of those norms tend to be more delinquent than average.

Secondly, across various groups, the average IQ was found to be associated with the expressed level of disapprobation of "bad" actions. As an explanation of this association, it has been suggested that low IQ tends to result in bad academic performance at school, which again tends to produce antisocial feelings and low commitment to common norms. As concluded by Wilson and Herrnstein (1985, p. 171): "The less one disapproves of an offense, the more reward one gains from it, other things being equal. If less intelligent people fail to see what is wrong with their offenses, or merely fail to see quite how wrong their offenses are, the scale for them will tip more often toward crime."

---

[21]This subsection relies heavily on section "6 Intelligence" in Wilson and Herrnstein (1985).

Race

Crime statistics suggest that race is a determinant of crime. The correlation may, however, be the result of covariation between race and various (other) determinants of crime. Possibly, minorities are not very committed to the norms established by the majority. Differences in opportunities, and thereby in outcomes of various activities, are presumably also of importance. Furthermore, studies in the US consistently show that the average IQ of blacks is about 11 to 15 percent lower than that of whites. To the extent that intelligence (as measured by the IQ tests) is related to crime, we have also here a possible explanation of why crime and race are related. To which extent there is a place for race after controlling for other determinants seems to be an unresolved question.

Class

Virtually all investigations of the effect of class on crime show that crime is more common the lower the social and economic status. This is so not only for property crimes, but also for violent crimes. (See Chapter 4 for some of the evidence.) It is difficult to explain this relationship between crime and socio-economic status. A high social status might imply loyalty to the existing system of norms, and high costs of sanctions. On the other hand, low status people have little to lose, and would, therefore, be anxious not to lose the little they have of social respectability. Those very high up in the hierarchy may have much to lose by sanctions, but as they anyhow have plenty of resources of various kinds, the threat may well not be very frightening. Furthermore, there is an ambiguity as to cause and effect. Low status may perhaps cause crime, but crime may also cause low status, for instance by loss of job or respectability.

Bad living conditions might produce mental illnesses related to certain types of crime, and low status might hamper the socialization of children and thus be conducive to the formation of crime-prone norms. Unsatisfactory upbringing is often assumed to give rise to individual value structures (preferences) where crime is more or less accepted. The formation of norms is of course extremely intricate, and so far little is known about this process. The family structure and its values are presumably of importance. However, only a minority of young people exposed to slums, low income, divorced parents etc. become serious criminals, and most low income people seem to be just as law-abiding or law-violating as others. In designing empirical studies, and in interpreting their results, it is a demanding task to distinguish between norm formation and deterrence. Sanctions might work through both mechanisms.

Drugs

A large proportion of crimes are committed under influence of alcohol, heroin, or other drugs. A high consumption of drugs will have both an immediate and a more long term effect. The immediate effect is presumably a change in individual preferences. Some norms are felt to be less important, inhibitions are weakened, and aggressive wants strengthened. The user becomes more impulsive, and thus more attracted to the immediate rewards of an act and less concerned with the delayed sanctions. Over the years, a high consumption will change the opportunities for legal versus illegal activities. Drug abuse may be caused by a combination of constitutional traits and opportunities. Its continuation is often possible only by extensive property crimes. Wrong beliefs about consequences of various courses of action may also be a result of alcohol or drug abuse, and thus contribute to the choice of criminal acts.

Summing up

This short overview of some relationships between crime and certain individual characteristics shows that gender, age, race, etc. represent rather superficial "explanations" of crime, and that a deeper understanding must be sought in variations in norms and wants, in abilities, and in the opportunities, rewards and costs determined by the environment. Variation in crime among individuals may be caused by differences in all these elements of the norm-guided rational choice framework.

A characteristic feature of the usual models of rational choice is the assumption that preferences are stable, and even equal among individuals. What is assumed to change is the environment, and the change in behaviour is explained as a reaction to a changing environment without invoking special norms or wants. Of course, a deeper insight into preferences would give a fuller understanding of behaviour, but such knowledge is not necessary to reveal the immediate cause of a change in behaviour, and to predict this change.

As detailed descriptions of individual preferences cannot usually be obtained, various characteristics of an individual's personality have been suggested as parts of a more comprehensive explanation of criminal behaviour. Personality characteristics such as self-control, responsibility, impulsiveness, authoritarianism, risk attitude, achievement orientation, and future orientation have been proposed. Until recently there was little evidence of the precise effect of these personality attributes either on crime or on the effect of sanctions.[22] Wilson and Herrnstein (1985, p. 27), however, state that "[t]here is

---

[22]Most surveys and textbooks of criminology conclude similarly on this issue. Zimring and Hawkins (1973, 117): "Yet it must be admitted that our present knowledge about differences in human personality and their bearing on criminal behaviour is very limited". Sutherland and Cressey (1970, 8th ed., 170): "Research studies conducted by scholars representing different schools of thought have found no trait of personality to be very closely associated with criminal or delinquent behavior. No consistent statistically significant differences between personality traits of delinquents and personality traits of nondelinquents have been found".

mounting evidence that, on the average, offenders differ from non-offenders in physique, intelligence, and personality. Some of these differences may not themselves be a cause of crime but only a visible indicator of some other factor that contributes to crime." In particular, there are examples of individual crimes where sexual deviance, neurosis and other personal characteristics obviously have been vital. This does not imply that these crimes could not have been deterred by more certain and/or by more severe punishment. It is important here to remember the distinction between causes of crime and causes of non deterrence. A strong sexual drive and a low level of inhibition may certainly make rape more probable, but rational choice is thereby not eliminated. Sanctions, however, must possibly be severe to counteract the other elements.

2.1.8. Environmentally directed to crime

Our model of rational choice suggests that variation in the environment affecting outcomes of individual activities may have a rather direct effect on crime.[23] Differences in crime between individuals and over time may thus, at least partially, be explained as the result of rational behaviour for given preferences under various conditions.[24] This approach can be regarded as a special case within our "grand theory" of norm-guided rational choice. This special theory will be presented in more detail in section 2.2.

The last decade or two has witnessed a growing interest in situational factors that may influence crime. A kind of survey is offered by the routine activity approach (see e.g. Cohen and Felson (1979)) which provides a long list of situational factors affecting crime. This approach emphasizes that predatory offence require the combination of an offender, a target, and the absence of a guardian. Variation in the occurrence of this combination, generated by differences in daily routines, will cause crime rates to differ. If the development of the society grants more opportunities for offenders to consider unguarded targets, crime will increase. "Opportunity makes the thief". Furthermore, changes in the values, inertia, visibility and access of the targets will affect the number of crimes.

---

[23]Adam Smith, well known for his individualistic approach to human behaviour, was not blind to the possible importance of circumstances in explaining crime. In his "Lectures on justice, police, revenue and arms" (1763, pp. 155-6) he argues that "[n]othing tends so much to corrupt mankind as dependency, while independency still increases the honesty of the people. The establishment of commerce and manufactures, which brings this independency, is the best police for preventing crimes. The common people have better wages in this way than in any other, and in consequence of this a general probity of manners takes place through the whole country. Nobody will be so mad as to expose himself upon the highway, when he can make better bread in an honest and industrious manner".

[24]"Note that the ecologist would say that the environment is causing the criminal act, whereas the economist would say that the criminal is acting, taking his environment into account." Chapman (1976, p. 50).

Technological development may either promote criminal behaviour (e.g. through lighter loot), or hamper it (e.g. through better electrical supervision). The routine activity approach can be regarded as a special case of rational choice. The situation determines the benefits and costs of various courses of action, and crime is assumed to be increased by the benefits and reduced by the costs.

Criminal statistics also indicate that the environment affects crime. More offence are, for instance, committed in urban than in rural areas, and in certain ghettos crime rates are extremely high. However, regional differences in crime can have many causes. Individuals with genetic characteristics conducive to crime might to a greater extent than other people move to towns. Urban life might produce mental illness and a psychological disposition that contribute to crime. Social and economic conditions in urban areas might produce less crime averse norms than those of the countryside. Lack of opportunities might in more serious cases result in a situation where differential association or social anomie leads to substitution or evasion of common norms.

The extent of informal social control may also affect crime. If there is variation in the effort of family members, teachers, neighbours, etc. in controlling or stimulating the activities of young people, differences in crime rates may occur. Various types of households, and the extent and quality of family life could here be of importance.

Apparently, there are a great number of environmental factors affecting crime rather directly by determining the outcomes of various courses of action. In empirical analysis it is a great challenge to separate the various mechanisms. In a macro study, it is obvious that only some major effects can be estimated.

In addition to the effect of the environment on the outcomes of various courses of action, the environment may also influence crime through the formation of norms and wants. Theories emphasizing these mechanisms can be regarded as special cases of the "grand theory". In Fig. 2.4 some of the main psychological and sociological theories are schematically included into our framework. The theories (or better: groups of theories) of ethical learning, culture conflict, anomie, and cultural deviance all cover various mechanisms by which norms (and to some extent wants) are determined by the environment or the particular situation of the individual. The figure illustrates that the same aspects of the environment might have an effect on crime both directly through outcomes, or indirectly through formation of norms and wants.

Ethical learning and maladjustment
The proposed mechanisms of ethical learning are numerous, and, in many cases, somewhat

vague.[25] An individual's acquisition of norms depends both on his responsiveness to conditioning and on the efficiency of various training methods. Of special interest for the present study is the possibility that sanctions not only determine some of the costs of crime, but also the norms that guide individual behaviour to legal or illegal behaviour. Social norms are possibly learnt and internalized by the general use of sanctions in society.

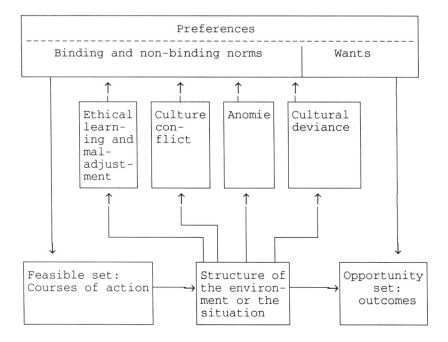

Fig. 2.4. Illustration of some main theories of crime

The efficiency of conditioning hinges presumably on characteristics of the environment. Psycho-analytic and psychological concepts of maladjustment, for instance, emphasize the significance of bad upbringing in unstable homes in creating crime-prone norms. After a long period where a reformist spirit among many criminologists has directed attention to social phenomena that presumably cause crime, and that possibly can be altered (such as class structure, race prejudice, gangs, police attitudes, etc.), the role of the family now

[25]See Eysenck (1957) and Trasler (1962).

seems to have regained a more prominent position in criminology. Andenæs (1989, p. 31) maintains that unfortunate family and upbringing conditions are far more common among recidivists than among first time offenders. Since a large part of property crimes are committed by a group of recidivists, the family seems to be an important clue to the understanding of crime. Precise effects of family life, useful for an empirical macro study of crime, do not seem to be available.

The effects of schooling on crime are equally uncertain. Many studies show that delinquents tend to obtain poor results in school. A possible reason for this might be a common cause, for instance an impulsive personality. The benefits of schooling lie in the future. Impulsive individuals tend to discount future rewards heavily and choose actions that produce more immediate satisfaction of wants. Impulsiveness may in a similar manner make the immediate benefits of crime more tempting than its remote costs, and also more tempting than the distant benefits of law-abidingness. The association between crime and poor results in school may also occur because a feeling of inferiority among low-intelligence pupils can generate an hostility against authorities, and an indifference to common norms. The latter explanation implies that schooling has an effect on the norm profile of the children.

Broken homes and abusive parents are often considered to affect children's norms in a way that generates delinquency. The observed correlation between serious family problems and delinquency[26] may, however, be the result of a common cause, such as poverty. It has also been suggested that family problems can be caused by difficult children, and also, that child abuse and family problems on the one hand, and poverty on the other, both are caused by impulsive and violent parents that find it as difficult to hold a job as they find it easy to abuse a child.

Culture conflict

The theory of culture conflict[27] has been developed from the suggestion that when one group imposes its own code of conduct on another by force, members of the latter will not easily internalize these norms, and they will not feel obliged to abide by them.[28] The amount of crime in a society will then to some extent depend on the existence of minorities with norms different from those underlying the formal system of sanctions. Immigrants

---

[26]See e.g. Wilson and Herrnstein (1985), section 9, for a review of literature.

[27]See Sellin (1938), and Downes (1966)

[28]Referring to the "Report of the National Advisory Commission of Civil Disorder, Greenwich and Wadyski (1973, p. 143) argues as follows: "It appears that many black persons regard law as an instrument that has historically been used to suppress them and thus they feel alienated from the law."

might constitute such a crime-prone group, working-class youth another[29]. This theory is a special case in the sense that it neglects the choice problem that still remains for these individuals. They, too, have a feasible set of actions, including legal activities, and an opportunity set of outcomes from which an optimal alternative can be chosen. The theory of culture conflict may explain that minorities tend to put less weight than average on ruling codes of conduct, but it neglects the fact that most crime in most countries is committed by the "ruling majority". It seems to be an unsettled empirical question to what extent a somewhat higher crime rate among certain minorities is the result of differences in norms (and perhaps wants) or in feasible sets of actions and in environments. The problem is not made easier by the possibility that crime and clear-up rates among minorities are especially high because of a more intense supervision by the police. Furthermore, it has been observed that among certain minorities, e.g. among Chinese in some countries, crime is lower than average. Low crime reporting and informal sanctions within these minorities might explain these low crime rates, but one is left with the question of why minorities differ.

Anomie

The theory of anomie suggests that a sudden deterioration of an individual's economic or social condition, or a permanent desperate situation, will make it impossible for normally law-abiding people to satisfy legitimate wants. Two main solutions to the frustrating situation are provided: either satisfying wants by illegal activities, or acquiring crime prone norms (or both).[30] One observes that the first solution is well within the framework of rational choice; Sudden or permanent poverty can make crime attractive on the basis of rational choice without changes in norms. The second solution represents the special case when the environment has an effect on crime only through norm formation. Little attention is here given to various benefits and costs of crime and non-crime, for instance to sanctions. Consequently, crime committed by "ordinary" people cannot be explained by this theory.

Another possible effect of deteriorating economic and social conditions is that unattainable outputs are considered to be "sour grapes" (see Elster 1983). This mechanism, although not in accordance with the usual rational choice assumption of constant preferences, will help to keep the person law-abiding.

---

[29] An example illustrating the difficulty with this explanation is the low crime rate among Chinese immigrants in the US; they may, however, from the very beginning have had individual norms in line with US laws and regulations - or be more scared by the social stigma of being arrested and convicted than people at large.

[30] See e.g. Durkheim (1966), Merton (1957), and Cloward and Ohlin (1961).

Cultural deviance

The theories of cultural deviance emphasize that living in a criminal neighbourhood will make a person both learn criminal techniques and acquire attitudes, motives and drives common to offenders.[31] Both norms and efficiency in obtaining wanted outcomes through crime are affected. A more specific version of this theory is the theory of differential association, which states that criminal attitudes, motives, drives, and rationalizations are formed by gang peers, who also teach techniques of committing crimes. Wilson and Herrnstein (1985, p. 293) maintain that "... scarcely any of these theories [of differential association] is supported by adequate empirical data." They also suggest that delinquency is not an effect of gang life, but that boys join gangs because they already are delinquents: Birds of a feather flock together.

Unemployment

Unemployment is also regarded as a cause of crime. Unemployment reduces the feasible set of actions, and offending may become the best alternative according to given preferences. The reduction in crime in many countries during the Great Depression does not support this view, but countervailing forces might have been at work at that time. In circumstances when crime and unemployment are positively correlated, a third common factor may be at work. Both low intelligence and impulsiveness may cause problems on the labour market, and make crime more attractive. Crime may also cause unemployment because offenders have less time to seek ordinary work. Unemployment may further have a crime-promoting effect on norms; unemployment may be considered as unjust, and contribute to a reduction in respect for social norms. On the other hand, a reduction in unemployment is usually associated with an increase in wealth, and thus in the amount of goods that can be stolen. As a whole, the relationship between unemployment and crime seems to be intricate, and empirical studies cannot be expected to give acute answers.

2.1.9. Crime as a product of agencies of social control

When speaking about crime it is usually with reference to what society has decided to be illegal acts. Crime is what society determines to be crime through legislation and the practice of the system of criminal justice. Thus the delineation between what is legal and what is illegal to some extent determines the amount of crime in society. Acts that some people might find quite moral, like stealing from the rich or shooting an occupier, are

---

[31]See Sutherland and Cressey (1966).

defined as crime, whereas immoral acts, like being unfaithful to ones spouse or slandering a friend, are not. This observation warns us not automatically to severely condemn all illegal acts, as well as not accept all legal ones, but it does not undermine our effort to study what is called crime on the basis of rational choice. Rationality in this sense is a general approach that presumably can help explaining both criminal and non-criminal acts, irrespective of how they are delineated.

The task of explaining changing crime rates, however, becomes more difficult. An increase in these rates may be the result not only of changing behaviour, but also of the definition of crime, of the reporting of various acts (that have become criminal) to the police, and of the use of resources and the choice of activities in the agencies of social control.

2.1.10. Summing up

The reasons why people are more or less law-abiding are numerous. Certain individuals may have more crime prone (or less crime averse) norms than others. The special norm structure may be a result of genetic, biological or psychological characteristics, an effect of lack of socialization, or a consequence of cultural conflict, cultural deviance, or anomie. Inherited or acquired abilities may restrict legal activities more than illegal ones. None of these explanations, however, deny the possibility of rational choice, even if other special factors are considered to be more important. None of the theories dismiss rational choice as one of the factors determining crime, and the theories that tend to ignore rational choice appear to concentrate only on segments of crime, such as arson and rape. Rational choice seems to be everywhere present[32], although sharing the explanation of crime with other theories. Fig. 2.4 may be regarded as a specification of the proposition by the Nobel Prize Winner Niko Tinbergen (who should not be confused with J. Tinbergen who has won the Nobel Memorial Prize in economics) that four levels of analysis should be put together: the biological (genetical), the developmental (how an individual is socialized), the situational (how the environment elicit behaviour), and the adaptive (how a person responds to the benefits and costs of alternative courses of action).

Many theories of crime seem to exaggerate the differences between offenders and others, and also the differences among the offenders themselves. Crime is frequently seen as pathological, evil, abnormal, or irrational, and irredeemably alien to ordinary behaviour.

---

[32]Various studies emphasize the relevance of rational choice for behaviour as different as suicide (Hamermesh and Soss 1974), church attendance (Azzi and Ehrenberg 1975), alcoholism (Bigelow 1973), psychosis (Ayllon and Azrin 1965) and a range of crimes (Cornish and Clarke, eds. 1986).

Although genetically or socially acquired personality traits indisputably may contribute to crime, evidence suggests that crime is usually non-pathological and commonplace. The degree of reasoning may vary from person to person (offenders and non-offenders alike), but elimination of rational choice as a possible hypothesis would be farfetched. Furthermore, situational characteristics seem to be at least as pertinent to crime as the offenders' and non-offenders' personal characteristics.

As a main finding of their comprehensive survey of a large body of studies of crime Wilson and Herrnstein (1985, p. 291) emphasize that "[t]he great majority of persons who commit crimes at high rates begin their criminal careers at quite early ages". They further contend (p. 311) that "most of the variation among individuals in criminality can be accounted for by personal traits, family socialization, and (perhaps) school experiences, and this is especially true for variation in [the rates of crime for each person]." Even these conclusions do not prevent the environment, and especially sanctions, from having a substantial effect on crime. The authors also seem to have reached their conclusions without considering most of the rational choice based econometric studies of crime that will be reviewed in Chapter 4.

The short overview of theories of criminal behaviour shows that a whole series of "causes" may be involved, and that recorded differences in crime between regions, gender, races, drug abuse, etc. might be related to more fundamental explanations of crime, involving norms, wants, opportunities and circumstances. The intricacy of relationships shows the difficulty involved in developing models of behaviour including all interesting mechanisms, and some modesty in ambition is obviously warranted.

The norm-guided rational choice model, comprising personal norms and wants, feasible sets of activities, environmental characteristics, and individual outcomes, provides a suitable framework for discussing various theories of crime, including characteristics of individuals and circumstances.[33] The framework allows for a simultaneous consideration of many possible determinants of crime. The abstract model is a means of gaining insight into the elements of rational behaviour, and it permits filling bits of information into a broader context.

In the present study the major use of our theoretical framework will be to help designing econometric macro studies of crime, and to evaluate to what extent such studies can explain why crime varies among regions and over time. To carry out an evaluation of this kind it would be recommendable to know why individual crime rates differ. We have seen that individual norms and wants apparently count for a major part of these differences. For the

---

[33] A similar view is expressed by Cornish and Clarke (1986, 10) when discussing their "rational choice perspective".

full understanding and predicting of behaviour, it is therefore essential to know how preferences have become what they are, and to what extent they eventually change over time. Although many possible explanations of the source and formation of norms are given, little firm evidence exists on the quantitative aspect of these relationships. Assuming rational choice one may in principle deduce the effect on crime of the environment even if individual preferences are not known. One must, however, assume something about the preferences. Some relationship between outcomes and satisfaction has to be stated. Usually it is claimed that people prefer more wealth to less. This relationship is considered more in detail in section 2.2 below. The other common assumption is that preferences are stable (or at least almost so for the time period studied).[34] With these assumptions, changes in individual behaviour can be explained as rational choices made within a changing environment. The relevance of this explanation will of course depend on how the stated assumptions are regarded, and of how well behaviour is predicted by this procedure.

An additional challenge is to find empirical measures representing relevant theoretical terms. Fully to solve these problems is an unattainable goal. It is nevertheless useful to employ our model of norm-guided rational behaviour as a framework for the evaluation of specific theoretical models of crime (Section 2.2), for discussing methodological issues of macro studies (Chapter 3), for evaluating previous empirical studies (Chapter 4), and as a guide for further empirical work (Chapters 5 and 6). The aim is to offer a more systematic treatment of possible causes of crime than what is common in many traditional sociological studies, and in studies based on the assumption of rational behaviour.

---

[34]Becker (1976, p. 5) simplifies his analysis in stating that "[s]ince economists generally have had little to contribute, especially in recent times, to the understanding of how preferences are formed, preferences are assumed not to change substantially over time, nor to be very different between wealthy and poor persons, or even between persons in different societies and cultures." And, as an argument of stability (p. 5): "The preferences that are assumed to be stable do not refer to market goods and services, like oranges, automobiles, or medical care, but to underlying objects of choice that are produced by each household using market goods and services, their own time, and other inputs. These underlying preferences are defined over fundamental aspects of life, such as health, prestige, sensual pleasure, benevolence, or envy, that do not always bear a stable relation to market goods and services. ... The assumption of stable preferences provides a stable foundation for generating predictions about responses to various changes, and prevents the analyst from succumbing to the temptation of simply postulating the required shift in preferences to 'explain' all apparent contradictions to his predictions."

2.2. Rational crime behaviour - expected utility models

2.2.1. The "economic" theory of crime

In models of criminal behaviour developed by economists, it is commonly assumed that people somehow calculate or estimate what actions - some of which are illegal - produce the highest welfare or utility. Maximization of utility implies balancing benefits against costs, where both benefits and costs may include wealth equivalents of various physical and psychic elements associated with different actions. When choosing among possible actions, an individual is assumed to consider the risk of punishment as a kind of cost in addition to other costs (and benefits) associated with illegal activity. Thus, the theory of general deterrence is regarded to be but a special case of the general theory of rational behaviour under uncertainty.[35]

In these models, preferences are typically represented by a well-defined utility function giving utility as a function of wealth or income. Wealth is usually composed of an initial or exogenous component and various benefits and costs of legal and illegal activities corresponding to the outputs of these activities. Uncertainty is usually dealt with by assuming that people maximize *expected* utility, an approach followed in all the models discussed below. The method is appealing because it follows from the von Neumann-Morgenstern axioms of individual behaviour that for a long time have been regarded as reasonable.[36] However, many laboratory experiments have given results in conflict with these axioms. Not only the outcomes, but also the context, or the "framing", of the various actions in the feasible set seems to have an effect on what is chosen.[37] The consequence is that choices become inconsistent: people (or at least some of them) do not choose in accordance with maximization of expected utility. In fact, experiments demonstrate that

---

[35]Ehrlich (1973, 523): "In spite of the diversity of activities defined as illegal, all such activities share some common properties which form the subject matter of our analytical and empirical investigation. Any violation of the law can be conceived of as yielding a potential increase in the offender's pecuniary wealth, his psychic well-being, or both. In violating the law one also risks a reduction in one's wealth or well-being, for conviction entails paying a penalty (a monetary fine, probation, the discounted value of time spent in prison and related psychic disadvantages, net of any direct benefits received), acquiring a criminal record (and thus reducing earning opportunities in legitimate activities), and other disadvantages. As an alternative to violating the law one may also engage in legal wealth or consumption generating activity, which may also be subject to specific risks. The net gain in both activities is thus subject to uncertainty. A simple model of choice between legal and illegal activity can be formulated within the framework of the usual economic theory of choice under uncertainty".

[36]See e.g. Gravelle and Rees (1981, Ch. 19).

[37]See Tversky et al. (1990) for a summary and discussion of many of their findings, and of those of some other authors.

common axioms in the theory of choice is frequently violated.[38] As a result, several non-expected utility procedures, excluding or weakening some of the violated axioms, have been developed. These methods have, to my knowledge, not been applied to illegal activities.

Although the expected utility approach has been severely hit by many experiments, it has not lost all interest. It may still be regarded as a suitable approximate description of individual behaviour. The fact that some experiments reveal that individuals often do not choose in accordance with maximization of expected utility does not mean that this approach is irrelevant or wrong with respect to choices between legal and illegal activities. But our belief in maximization of expected utility is certainly weaker now than some years ago.

The models of expected utility presented below will demonstrate how psychic and other non-monetary attributes of legal and illegal actions can be included in a maximization framework. The models will also be used to illustrate how individual concerns about norms can be included in the analysis of utility maximization. These topics will be equally relevant also when utility is dealt with by other procedures than maximization of its expected value.

It is natural to start this short survey of economic models of crime by presenting, in section 2.2.2, the main points of Becker's (1968) seminal work on "Crime and punishment", although the first attempts to study crime as rational behaviour date back at least to Beccaria (1971, [1764]) and Bentham (1843, 1864)[39]. Several types of economic models of crime have later been developed, and will be presented below.[40] The simplest one is very similar to models of portfolio choice, where a person's wealth is allocated between various risky and non-risky projects. In the economics of crime version of this model the illegal alternatives are considered as risky mainly because of uncertainty about punishment. This type of model is presented in section 2.2.3. In a somewhat different type of model the individual allocates his time (and not his wealth or income) between various activities. Two versions of this model, differing from each other by the assumption of fixed or non-fixed leisure time, are presented in sections 2.2.4. A generalisation of this type of

---

[38]Fishburn (1987, p. 47) concludes an investigation of a long series of experiments as follows: "Virtually any axiom of preference or principle of choice can be violated by suitable framing in experiments on preference judgements and choice behavior. Moreover, even when special effects due to framing are minimized, systematic and persistent violations of some traditional axioms are observed. This has been the case most notably for violations of the independence axiom and for the preference reversal phenomenon."

[39]"... the profit of the crime is the force which urges man to delinquency: the pain of the punishment is the force employed to restrain him from it. If the first of these forces be the greater, the crime will be committed; if the second, the crime will not be committed." Bentham (1843, 399).

[40]Other surveys of economic models of crime are found in Heineke ed. (1978), Bleyleveld (1980), Pyle (1983) and Schmidt and Witte (1984).

model, where several types of sanctions are considered simultaneously, is also included. Finally, in section 2.2.5, a labour supply model of crime, where legal and illegal activities do not influence utility through monetized psychic gains and losses, but directly as arguments in the utility function, is presented. All these models draw on the theory of supply and the theory of behaviour towards risk. Two Appendices are added to this chapter to remind the reader of some notions and results of these theories, and in a third Appendix the analytic derivation of the comparative static effects on crime of various changes in the environment is given. The main results are summarized in section 2.2.6, and the inclusion of norms into models of maximization of expected utility is discussed in section 2.2.7.

2.2.2. Becker's model

The main purpose of Becker's essay is not to present a theory of criminal behaviour, but to analyze how to minimize the social loss of crime. He defines total social loss in terms of real income as the sum of
   - the net direct damage of the offence (harm to society minus gain to the offender),
   - the social cost of obtaining a certain probability of punishment,
   - the social cost of punishment to society (including that of the offender).
All these cost elements[41] depend on the number of offence committed.

In order to analyze the minimization of total social loss w.r.t. the probability and the severity of punishment Becker introduces a "supply of offense function", where the number of offence depend on these two parameters. The establishment of a such a function requires a discussion of theories of criminal behaviour in order to determine the effect on crime of the probability and severity of punishment. Becker reacts to existing theories, and suggests "that a useful theory of criminal behaviour can dispense with special theories of anomie, psychological inadequacies, or inheritance of special traits and simply extend the economist's usual analysis of choice" (1968, 171) as developed in utility theory.

The basic assumption of this theory is that an individual acts as if he is a rational utility maximiser.[42] Moreover, as the total outcome of a criminal act is uncertain, proper account has to be taken of uncertainty. Becker employs the usual assumption that people act as if

---

[41]Becker does not discuss how the cost elements should be determined. He assumes that society somehow has reached a consensus on the question of evaluation. However, his conclusions are valid for any costs. One may, for instance, choose whether to include or not the offender's psychic cost of being punished.

[42]See e.g. Gravelle and Rees (1981, Ch. 19) for a demonstration of why behaviour in accordance with certain rationality axioms is equivalent to utility maximization.

they were maximizing expected utility[43], and that utility is a positive function of wealth. As stated in section 2.1.9, assumptions of this kind are required in order to deduce the behavioral responses to changes in the environment (in this case in benefits and costs of crime).

Becker subsequently develops what he considers to be a general theory of individual behaviour, both criminal and non-criminal. As a rational utility maximiser in a situation where an offence is an optional risky act, an individual will take into account the probability of being caught, and various costs and benefits associated with the act. Whether the offence will be committed or not depends on the individual's perception of these factors[44], as well as on his attitude towards risk. As supplement to this theory, traditional explanations of criminal behaviour might be added, a possibility not pursued by Becker. The source and formation of the preferences represented by the utility function might have been discussed, as well as the assumed constancy of these preferences.

The utility expected from committing an offence is defined as:

$$E[U] = PU(Y\text{-}f) + (1\text{-}P)U(Y),$$

where

$U(\cdot)$ is the individual's von Neumann-Morgenstern utility function
$E[U]$ is the individual's expected utility
P is the subjective probability of being caught and convicted
Y is the monetary plus psychic income (i.e. the monetary equivalent[45]) from an offence
f is the monetary equivalent of the punishment.

The individual will commit the offence if $E[U]$ is positive, and he will not if $E[U]$ is negative. It is easily seen that changes in both the probability and the severity of convictions might change the individual's behaviour; but for some values of the parameters, and for some forms of the utility function, the changes in the probability and/or the severity have to be substantial for a change to occur.

A slightly modified version of Becker's model will be used in the following analysis.

---

[43]They are assumed to act in accordance with the von Neumann-Morgenstern axioms of choice under risk, see Appendix 2 to this chapter for an introduction to this theory.

[44]The possibility that the individual's beliefs about these factors are wrong, does not ruin the model as a theory of *subjective* rational behaviour.

[45]It is thus assumed that the individual is able to compare monetary and nonmonetary benefits of crime, and furthermore to consider an "index of benefits" Y.

Instead of considering the income and punishment equivalents of an offence separated from other income, as Becker does, the individual's initial wealth or income position will be taken as a point of reference. Furthermore, it will be assumed that the offender might retain some gain from the offence in case of conviction, which apparently will not happen in Becker's analysis. Without changing the main aspects and conclusions, these changes will render Becker's analysis somewhat more general, and more in line with subsequent models in this chapter. As attitude towards risk presumably is dependent on the wealth or the income of the individual, some problems cannot be analyzed in a satisfactory manner without referring to a wealth or income situation.

Following Brown and Reynolds (1973) the individual's present wealth is W_o, which gives the utility $U[W_o]$ if no offence is committed. A possible offence will give a gain G, whereas the loss will be L if caught and convicted, the probability of which is P. The expected utility for a person committing such an offence will be

$$E[U] = PU(W_o\text{-}L) + (1\text{-}P)U(W_o\text{+}G). \tag{2.1}$$

Assuming that the individual maximizes expected utility, he will prefer to commit an offence rather than not if $E[U] > U[W_o]$. As above, his choice will depend on all the parameters of (2.1), and also on his attitude towards risk. His situation is depicted in Fig. 2.5 which shows the utility as a function of wealth for a risk avoiding person (convex utility function). If choosing not to commit an offence the level of wealth will be W_o, which gives a utility $U(W_o)$. Committing a crime will give a utility $U(W_o\text{-}L)$ if caught and a utility $U(W_o\text{+}G)$ if not. The expected utility will be equal to these utility levels only when $P = 1$ or $P = 0$, respectively. For intermediate values of P, the expected utility will be somewhere between these levels: the higher the value of P, the closer the expected utility will be to $U(W_o\text{-}L)$. The expected values of wealth are found along the straight line AB. The offence will not be undertaken unless the offence gives an expected utility at least as high as that of the certain alternative W_o. The expected wealth must be at least W^* for this to occur.

It is because of risk avoidance that $W_o < W^*$. A risk neutral person, whose utility function would have been represented by a straight line, would have (just) accepted a fair gamble, i.e. a gamble where the expected wealth is equal to a certain outcome. For a risk lover we would have $W_o > W^*$, i.e. even if the expected wealth obtained by committing an offence is lower than the certain level of wealth without the offence, the individual could nevertheless prefer crime for certain values of the parameters.

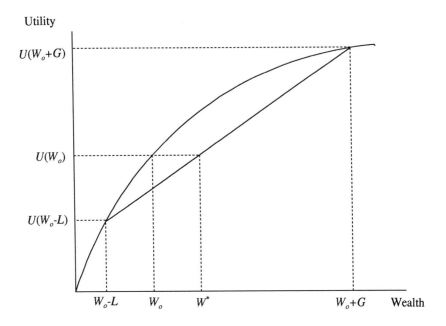

Fig. 2.5. Risk aversion and criminal behaviour

How would an individual respond to changes in these parameters? From (2.1) we obtain:

$$\partial E[U]/\partial P = U(W_o-L) - U(W_o+G), \qquad (2.2)$$

and

$$\partial E[U]/\partial L = - PU'(W_o-L). \qquad (2.3)$$

Given the usual assumption of $U'>0$[46], one observes that an increase in the probability of punishment (as conceived by the individual) will reduce the expected utility. If an offence initially is a preferred act, increases in P and/or L therefore might deter the commitment. These main results are for comparison recorded in Table 2.3 of section 2.2.6 together with similar results for other models. (The result that an increase in L has a negative effect on crime is in Table 2.3 noted in the column "Shift, loss function". The shift parameter β is relevant only for some other models.) Becker's results are independent of the absolute risk aversion, the increase or decrease of which is crucial for many of the results obtained in the other models presented below.

Becker asserts that the number of crimes committed by an individual in a given period is a decreasing function of both the probability of being punished and of the severity of this punishment. The precise relationship here is not explicitly dealt with. The determination of the number of crimes is not analyzed. Formally, all crimes that produce a positive expected utility will be committed. Thus, the number of crimes committed by an individual are restricted only by the number of such opportunities. Although the functional relationship might differ from one person to the other, an increase in the probability or severity of punishment will tend to reduce the number of crimes committed by some individuals in a society. For simplicity Becker then considers a supply of offence function for the society as a whole, where the total number of crimes are a function of the average values of the probability and the severity of punishment.

Becker also asserts that the number of crimes committed by an individual might depend on his "intelligence, age, education, previous offence history, wealth, family upbringing, etc.", and that such characteristics consequently are of importance for the average individual and for society as a whole, but he does not elaborate upon these elements. This will be done at several occations below.

2.2.3. A portfolio choice model of crime (Heineke's model I)

Inspired by models of portfolio choice and by the seminal paper by Becker (1968), Allingham and Sandmo (1972), Kolm (1973), and Singh (1973) have constructed models for a special type of crime - that of tax evasion. Heineke's (1978) slightly elaborated

---

[46]Cf the argument by Brennan (1990) that the rational choice theory can predict actions only when it includes substantive claims concerning the content of the actor's preferences. In the present model the choice of arguments in the utility function, and the derivatives of the utility function with respect to these arguments, seems to be an example of what Brennan considers to be required.

version of their simple type of model is presented here.[47] This model gives strong conclusions as to how the probability and the severity of punishment influence crime. In later sections, where somewhat more general models are presented, it will be demonstrated that as far as the severity of punishment is concerned, such strong conclusions do not appear.

Consider an individual with an exogenous income (or wealth) W_o confronted with the problem of deciding what proportion χ of this income to allocate to an illegal activity with risky outcome. (See Table 2.2 for symbols used.) Assume that the individual's preferences can be represented by a von Neumann-Morgenstern utility function $U(W)$.[48]

Suppose that there are gains to the illegal activity represented by the gain function $G(\chi;\alpha)$. Here α is a shift parameter that may be used later to express changes in the gains that might be obtained. If there are psychic gains to crime, these are supposed to be included in G. It is assumed that the gain function is non-negative, that it has the value zero when there is no illegal activity, and that it is increasing with the proportion of income allocated to illegal activity (see assumptions of Table 2.2).

Similarly, it is assumed that there is a loss (e.g. a fine) $F(\chi;\beta)$ if the illegal behaviour is unsuccessful. β is a shift parameter that will be used to analyze changes in the severity of punishment. It is assumed that the loss function is non-negative, has the value of zero when there is no illegal activity, and that it is increasing with the proportion of income allocated to illegal activity. The loss function is also assumed to include psychic losses that might prevail if the illegal activity is unsuccessful.[49]

It is further assumed that there are only two possible results of the individual's choice: success or failure.[50] If the criminal activity is successful, the income is

$$W_s = W_o + G(\chi;\alpha). \tag{2.4}$$

At variance with Becker's model where the income of crime (Y) is a parameter, the income of criminal activity here is a function of the proportion of the exogenous wealth (or

[47]This is Heinekes Model I, which is also found in Schmidt and Witte (1984).

[48]Sufficient axioms for preferences to be represented by a von Neumann-Morgenstern utility function is given e.g. in Gravelle and Rees (1981, Ch. 19).

[49]Monetization of psychic gains and losses of crime is possible if a person is able to choose consistently between alternatives that include both psychic and monetary gains. If an activity (legal or illegal) results in a monetary gain M_0 and an additional psychic gain, and if the individual is able to determine a sum M making him indifferent between the activity and this sum, i.e. $U(M_0$, psychic gain$) = U(M)$, then $M - M_0$ is the monetized value of the psychic gain. This value might obviously differ from one person to another. Rational choice involving psychic gains and losses does not imply that an individual explicitly determines the monetary value of a psychic gain or loss, but that he is able to choose consistently between alternatives involving such elements.

[50]A model with partial success is discussed in Block and Heineke (1975).

income) allocated to illegal activity. If the criminal activity is unsuccessful, the income becomes

$$W_u = W_o + G(\chi;\alpha) - F(\chi;\beta). \tag{2.5}$$

Assuming that there is a probability P that the criminal endeavour is unsuccessful the individual's expected utility is

$$EU[W] = (1 - P)U(W_s) + PU(W_u). \tag{2.6}$$

Table 2.2
Symbols used in portfolio model of crime

Symbols	Definitions	Assumptions
W_o	Exogenous income (or wealth)	
W	Actual income (or wealth)	
$U(W)$	The individual's von Neumann-Morgenstern utility function	$U_W > 0$, $U_{WW} < 0$
χ	Proportion of W_o to be allocated to illegal activity	$0 \leq \chi \leq 1$
$F(\chi;\beta)$	Monetary penalty if the illegal endeavour is unsuccessful. β is a shift parameter	$F(\cdot) \geq 0$ $F_\chi > 0$ $F(0;\beta) = 0$
$G(\chi;\alpha)$	Monetary gain if illegal endeavour is successful. α is a shift parameter	$G(\cdot) \geq 0$ $G_\chi > 0$ $G(0;\alpha) = 0$
P	Probability that the illegal endeavour is unsuccessful	
W_s	The individual's income if illegal endeavour is successful. $W_s = W_o + G(\chi;\alpha)$	
W_u	The individual's income if the illegal endeavour is unsuccessful. $W_u = W_o + G(\chi;\alpha) - F(\chi;\beta)$	

This expected utility is a function of χ, and it is assumed that the individual picks the value of χ that maximises the expected utility. Differentiating (2.6) w.r.t. χ gives the 1. order necessary conditions of maximum utility.[51]

$$(1 - P)U_s G_\chi + PU_u(G_\chi - F_\chi) = 0, \tag{2.7}$$

from which the optimal value χ^o can be found.

Disregarding possible "corner" solutions (for $\chi = 0$ or $\chi = 1$) it is now possible to find the individual's response (change in the optimal value χ^o) to changes in the parameters P, W_o, α and β of the model. It turns out that for both risk averse and risk-loving people[52]

$$\partial\chi^o/\partial P < 0, \tag{2.8}$$

which means that the higher the probability of the illegal endeavour being unsuccessful, the lower the amount allocated to this kind of activity.

The effects of changes in the other parameters depend on the individual's attitude toward risk. For the common assumption of decreasing absolute risk aversion (i.e. $R>0$ and $dR/dW \equiv r < 0$), we obtain

$$\partial\chi^o/\partial W_o > 0, \tag{2.9}$$

which means that an individual will allocate a larger proportion of his income to illegal endeavour the higher his income (or wealth). The higher the income the lower the absolute risk aversion, and the higher proportion of the income is exposed to the given constant risk. This result is at variance with the idea that misery creates a situation where crime is a rational reaction. If misery causes crime, it must according to this model be through norm formation, or some other mechanism, and not come as a result of rational choice. The same sign as in (2.9) is obtained also for increasing absolute risk preference ($R<0$ and $r>0$), whereas the opposite sign is obtained for the two other cases of non-neutral attitude towards risk. In the case of risk neutrality the effect is nil.

A positive shift in the loss function (increased severity of sanctions) will have similar effects for illegal activities as a wage decrease will have for legal activities in labour supply models, see Appendix C to this chapter. Two effects occur: a substitution effect and an income effect. In labour supply models the substitution effect consists of a reduction in

---

[51]It is assumed that all functions possess continuous derivatives of sufficient order to permit the analysis, and that internal maxima exist.

[52]The arithmetics are given in Appendix C to this chapter.

labour supply because more leisure is preferred when work becomes less rewarding. The income effect consists of a change in activities because the reduced reward has the effect of a change in income. The substitution effect of a more severe punishment (higher β) will consist of less crime. The result of the income effect will depend on individual attitude towards risk. For a risk averter the reduced reward (or "income") will have similar effects as those obtained by changes in W_o, cf (2.9), and the total effect of a shift in β will be

$$\partial \chi^o / \partial \beta < 0. \tag{2.10}$$

For a risk lover the two effects have opposite signs, and the total effect on crime of a change in β is indeterminate.
The result in (2.10) is in accordance with the deterrence hypothesis: an increase in the severity of punishment deters. This holds for the commonly accepted assumption of risk aversion, but for a risk lover the result is indeterminate.

Decreasing absolute risk aversion also gives

$$\partial \chi^o / \partial \alpha > 0, \tag{2.11}$$

which means that an increase in the returns to illegal activity increases the proportion of income allocated to these activities. The same result is obtained in the case of increasing absolute risk preference, whereas the total effect is indeterminate for the two remaining cases of non-neutral attitude towards risk.

The inequalities (2.8) and (2.10) show that in this model both the probability and the severity of punishment deter crime for a risk averse person under the given assumptions. But for risk lovers, the effect of the severity of punishment is uncertain. The effects of changes in gains of crime and in exogenous income depends on whether there is decrease or increase in the risk aversion or risk preference. These results, and others obtained in Appendix C, are summarized in Table 2.3 of section 2.2.6, where the present model is called Portfolio Model.

2.2.4. Portfolio models of time allocation

In the time allocation models of crime, analogously to the supply of labour models, the individual is assumed to allocate his time (rather than his wealth or income) between legal and illegal activities. It turns out that some of the results depend on whether leisure time is assumed to be fixed or not. Both alternatives are discussed in subsequent sections.

Time allocation model with non-fixed leisure time

An individual can spend his time on legal or illegal activities as well as on leisure. Let the amount of time spent on legal activities be t_L and that of illegal activities t_I. As was done in the previous model, the net gains to time spent on illegal activities are represented by the function $G(t_I,\alpha)$. The loss if the criminal act is unsuccessful is given by the function $F(t_I,\beta)$, and the net gains to time spent on legal activities are given by the function $L(t_L,\delta)$, where δ is a shift parameter.

If the criminal activity is successful (undetected), income is[53]

$$W_s = W_o + L(t_L,\delta) + G(t_I,\alpha). \tag{2.12}$$

If the criminal activity is unsuccessful (detected), the income is

$$W_u = W_o + L(t_L,\delta) + G(t_I,\alpha) - F(t_I,\beta). \tag{2.13}$$

The function L measures the monetary and non-monetary benefits and costs that depend on t_L. Other benefits and costs of legal work, for instance the value of having a job, is supposed to be included as parameters in the L-function. Similar assumptions are introduced also for the G- and F-functions. This implies that the monetary value of the time spent on illegal activities is independent on the exogenous income (or wealth) and on the time spent on legal activities. It is also independent of the benefits and costs of legal and illegal activities (that are included as parameters in the L- and G-functions). Using the same probability assumption as above, i.e. a fixed probability that the criminal activity is detected, the individual's expected utility is given by

$$E[U(W)] = (1 - P)U(W_s) + PU(W_u). \tag{2.14}$$

It is assumed that the individual chooses the values of t_L and t_I that maximise the expected utility.

Two versions of this model have been discussed in literature. In the simplest one the maximization of expected utility w.r.t. t_L and t_I is performed without restrictions on these time variables. (Heineke (1978), Model II). In a somewhat less general version expected utility is maximised subject to the constraint that (t_L+t_I) equals some specified quantity. Implicitly, leisure time is constant.

---

[53]For ease of comparison I use the same symbols as in the previous model, although the definitions are somewhat different.

In the unconstrained version of the model an interesting characteristic appears. It turns out that the optimal values of the time variables are determined recursively. Mathematically this result is obtained because the derivative of (2.14) w.r.t. t_L is independent of t_I. (See Appendix C to this chapter for details.) This means that the individual allocates his time to legal activities until net marginal returns are zero. Then time is allocated to illegal activity, also until net marginal returns are zero, but here the choice depends upon the value of t_L already chosen. The recursivity of the system contributes to rather clear-cut conclusions about how changes in the parameters affect the optimal values of the time variables.

The main results of how the parameters of the model influence the time allocation are summarised in Table 2.3. It turns out that the optimal value of t_L is independent of P, W_o, α and β, but that a positive shift in the income function increases time allocated to legal activity. The line for t_I shows that an increase in the probability that criminal activity is unsuccessful reduces criminal activity, whereas the effect of increases in the severity of punishment, in exogenous income and in the gains to crime depends on the attitude towards risk. These qualitative results are identical to those of the previous more simple models (see first and second line of the table). The similarity in results shows what a more detailed study of the two models will make evident: that the special formulation of time allocation in this model, where psychic benefits and costs are monetized, and where there is a high degree of independence between the types of activities, results in the time allocation model being essentially a kind of portfolio choice model.

A perhaps unexpected result is that an increase in returns to legal activity increases time allocated to both types of activities for some attitudes towards risk. Such an increase in total time allocated to these two types of activities is possible because an inner solution has been assumed. Somewhat different results are obtained if it is assumed that leisure time is fixed, so that the remaining number of hours per day has to be split between legal and illegal activities.

Ehrlich's model
Several authors have studied the latter type of model, which is similar to the model discussed in the previous section, but with the additional restriction that time allocated to leisure is fixed (and thus independent of returns and costs for legal and illegal activities). This restriction is used e.g. in Ehrlich (1973). The assumption of a fixed leisure time obviously requires that the time allocated to legal and illegal activity changes in opposite direction (and with equal amounts), but other effects of changes in parameters are also different from the previous model.

Although Becker mentions that crime takes time, he does not explicitly consider crime as a problem of time allocation. Ehrlich did just that in formulating the theoretical basis for several empirical studies of crime in the US. He assumes that the time t that can be devoted to legitimate and illegitimate activities is fixed, which implies that time allocated to leisure and consumption also is fixed. If t_l is the time devoted to illegitimate activity, $t - t_l$ is the time devoted to legitimate activity, both of which can be zero.

In other respects the theory is quite similar to that of Becker: An individual is assumed to choose between criminal and non criminal activity in a one period situation where only two states of the world can occur: in state (a) the offender is punished, in state (b) he is not. The ordinary state-preference theory is applied.

Using the same symbols as above, and excluding the shift parameters, we obtain, cf (2.12) and (2.13):

$$W_s = W_0 + L(t\text{-}t_l) + G(t_l) \tag{2.15}$$
$$W_u = W_0 + L(t\text{-}t_l) + G(t_l) - F(t_l). \tag{2.16}$$

It is assumed that returns increase with time devoted to the respective activities, but at diminishing rates: $dL/dt_L = L_{tL} > 0$, $dG/dt_I = G_{tI} > 0$, $d^2L/dt_L^2 = L_{tLtL} < 0$, and $d^2G/dt_I^2 = G_{tItI} < 0$. The punishment is assumed to increase with t_I, $F_I > 0$, and at an increasing rate, $F_{II} > 0$. These assumptions are sufficient (but not necessary) for diminishing marginal returns to be obtained in both states of the world. This will imply a concave transformation curve, as the one in Fig. 2.6.

Denoting the probability of being punished P, and the probability of not being punished $1\text{-}P$, the individual's expected utility is

$$E[U] = PU[W_0 + L(t\text{-}t_l) + G(t_l) - F(t_l)]$$
$$+ (1 - P)U[W_0 + L(t\text{-}t_l) + G(t_l)]. \tag{2.17}$$

The individual is assumed to behave as if he was interested in maximizing the expected utility of a one-period consumption prospect. P is assumed to be independent of t_l and t_L. As t is fixed, the individual has only one choice variable. The value of t_l that maximizes the expected utility is determined by the first order condition

$$dE[U]/dt_l = PU_u[-L_{tl} + G_{tl} - F_{tl}] + (1\text{-}P)U_s[-L_{tl} + G_{tl}] = 0. \tag{2.18}$$

The first order condition for an interior solution is

$$\frac{G_{tl} - L_{tL}}{G_{tl} - L_{tL} - F_{tl}} = -\frac{PU_u}{(1 - P)U_s}. \tag{2.19}$$

Given the probabilities of being in either state (a) or state (b), the term on the right-hand side represents the individual's marginal rate of substitution of wealth between these two states. This term expresses the slope of an indifference curve in the (W_s, W_u)-space. Differentiation of (2.17) gives in fact

$$dE[U] = PU_u(dW_u) + (1 - P)U_s(dW_s),$$

and setting $dE[U] = 0$, we obtain

$$\frac{dW_s}{dW_u}\bigg|_{dE[U]=0} = -\frac{PU_u}{(1 - P)U_s}.$$

An indifference curve for the case of risk aversion[54] is drawn in Fig. 2.6, where the wealth obtained in the two states are measured along the axes. The special case where the individual commits no crimes, and therefore $W_s = W_u$, is given by the 45° line from the origin.

The term on the left-hand side of (2.19) represents the marginal rate at which W_u can be transformed into W_s by reallocating time from legitimate to illegitimate activities. Point A represents an outcome that is certain, where the individual specializes in legitimate activities, and where $W_u = W_s$. Increasing t_l from zero will produce a movement along the transformation curve: W_u is substituted for W_s according to

$$\frac{dW_s}{dW_u}\bigg|_{t=const.} = \frac{G_{tl} - L_{tL}}{G_{tl} - L_{tL} - F_{tl}} \tag{2.20}$$

until point C, which represents specialization in illegitimate activities, is reached. Here we have $W_u = W_0 + G(t) - F(t)$, and $W_s = W_0 + G(t)$. We shall assume that $F(t) < W_0 + G(t)$, which implies $W_u > 0$. The transformation curve is not defined to the left of C.

---

[54]It can be shown that the indifference curves are convex for risk averters and concave for risk lovers, see e.g. Anderson (1976, 14-16). Similarly, it can be shown that diminishing marginal returns give a concave transformation curve, as in Fig. 2.6, whereas increasing marginal returns give a convex transformation curve.

Usual assumptions about the utility function (cf Table 2.2) will give convex indifference curves with negative slopes, as shown in Fig. 2.6. The assumptions about the functions in (2.15) and (2.16) give a concave transformation curve. One of the end points of this curve will always be a point A on the 45° line, but the slope and position will depend on the various elements of (2.20).

The alternative depicted in Fig. 2.6 is the one where W_u and W_s moves in opposite directions along the transformation curve, i.e. where the curve has a negative slope. This is when $G_{tl} > L_{tL}$ and $F_{tl} > G_{tl} - L_{tL}$.

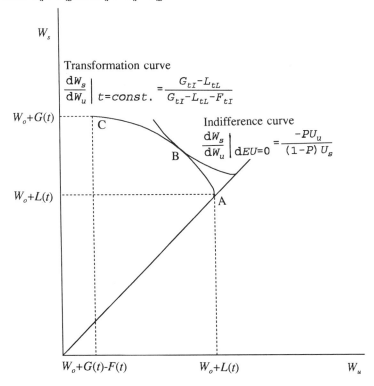

Fig. 2.6. Determination of activity mix

Under the given conditions an individual will participate in illegitimate activities if

$$\frac{dE[U]}{dt_l}\bigg|_{t=0} > 0. \tag{2.21}$$

At A, where $t_l = 0$, we have $W_u = W_s$ so that $U_u = U_s$. From (2.19) and (2.21) we then obtain

$$
\frac{G_{tl} - L_{tL}}{G_{tl} - L_{tL} - F_{tl}} > - \frac{P}{1 - P}, \tag{2.22}
$$

which can be simplified to $G_{tl} - L_{tL} > PF_{tl}$, i.e. that for crime to occur the marginal differential reward from offence must be higher than the expected value of punishment. This conclusion does not depend on the characteristics of the utility function. In this case the tangency point B represents the highest possible expected utility. When some of the parameters of the model are changed, generally the position of the curves changes, and consequently point B. It is demonstrated that some effects depend on whether we have risk aversion or risk preference, and on whether there are increasing or decreasing marginal returns. The analytic derivation of the changes are given in Appendix C to this chapter, and the results are reproduced in Table 2.3 (labour supply model with fixed leisure).

Positive slopes are obtained in two situations. If $L_{tL} > G_{tl}$, the transformation curve will go from A and down to the left. With the given indifference curve it is obvious that utility cannot be increased by offending. This also conforms with common sense: the differential reward, $L_{tL} - G_{tl}$, must be positive for anybody running the risk of being punished.

The slope of the transformation curve is positive also if $F_{tl} < G_{tl} - L_{tL}$. The curve then starts at A and slopes upwards to the right. In this case the punishment is so small that the individual will specialize in crime. Even if punishment is certain, the expected punishment will be lower than the marginal differential reward.

Several sanctions model
The portfolio model of time allocation with non-fixed leisure time has been somewhat extended by Wolpin (1978a) and by Schmidt and Witte (1984), who have introduced four possible criminal justice states[55] (and also a distinction between individual employment or non-employment). The four criminal justice states are: (1) not apprehended, (2) arrested but not convicted (3), convicted and fined, and (4) convicted and freedom restricted. The probabilities of these states are: the probability of arrest P_a, the probability of conviction given arrest $P_{c/a}$, and the probability of restricted freedom given conviction $P_{j/c}$.

---

[55]Schmidt and Witte can not have been aware of the study of Wolpin, whose model (without certain details) is presented here.

The income levels of the eight states are similar to (2.15) and (2.16). In half of the states there is no labour income component, and the loss functions differ between the four criminal justice states. The psychic gains and losses are assumed to be monetized and included in the gain and loss functions.

The individual's expected utility is given by

$$E[U(W)] = \sum_{i=1}^{8} P_i U(W_i) ,$$

(2.23)

where $i = 1, 2, ...,8$ refers to the eight states with corresponding probabilities and incomes. The individual is assumed to choose the amount of time used for legal and illegal activities to maximize expected utility.

The analysis is performed under the assumption that the constraints are not binding, i.e that the individual prefers to allocate some time to all three activities (crime, work, and leisure). Mathematically this amounts to an unconstrained maximization of (2.23). The first order conditions show that the individual first allocates time to legal activity until the marginal gain equals marginal cost for that activity. This result is the same as in the corresponding portfolio model with one single type of punishment. When time allocated to the labour market is decided, the individual allocates time to illegal activity until expected net marginal utility of such activity becomes zero. This is when the expected increase in utility from an increase in illegal activity is equal to the expected decrease in utility from the corresponding penalty.

In the same manner as for the previous models one may find how the optimal allocations of time respond to changes in the environment. Now three probabilities must be considered, in addition to the expected unemployment rate. The other parameters to study are the same as above. Some of the results are summarized in Table 2.3.

The recursive nature of the model implies that the time allocated to legal activity is unaffected by changes in all parameters except the returns to legal activity itself. On the other hand, the time allocated to illegal activity depends on all the parameters that characterize the environment.

Not surprisingly, an increase in the expected probability of apprehension decreases time allocated to illegal activity. Similar conclusions for the conditional probabilities of conviction and of restrictions on freedom cannot be derived without further assumptions about the marginal gains to illegal activity net of the marginal costs of criminal justice sanctions for all criminal justice outcomes. There is little a priori evidence on these net gains, but reasonable assumptions will lead to the same conclusions as for the expected probability of apprehension.[56]

The effect of a change in non-labour income is essentially the same as in the previous models.

The effect of a change in the gains to illegal activity depends, as in the previous models, on the effect of exogenous income. If the assumptions toward risk are such that $\partial t_I / \partial W_0 > 0$, we will also have $\partial t_I / \partial \alpha > 0$.

The effect of a change in the shift parameter of the loss functions (the same parameter has been used for all the three loss functions), is slightly more ambiguous than in the previous models. In these models an increase in the penalty leads to a decrease in time allocated to illegal activity if the individual is risk averse. In the present model also some restrictions on the net marginal returns to crime in different states are required to obtain the same result.

Also a change in returns to legal activity has a more ambiguous result in the present model than in the previous ones. If the individual is risk neutral, we will have $\partial t_I / \partial \delta = 0$. But even in the case of decreasing absolute risk aversion the effect of more severe penalties is ambiguous, although reasonable assumptions imply less illegal activity.

Somewhat surprisingly, illegal activity will decrease with increasing unemployment under the standard assumptions of decreasing absolute risk aversion. The explanation is that unemployment implies a lower income, and therefore a higher risk aversion, and then again a lower expected utility of crime. Under risk neutrality time allocated to illegal activity is not affected by a change in the expected employment rate.

2.2.5. Models with non-monetized attributes to illegal activity

If one is not willing to accept the assumption that all psychic factors associated with legal and illegal activities can be monetized[57], one has to use utility functions where time allocations and their attributes are introduced explicitly. Block and Heineke (1973, 1975) have studied a model where the individual's utility function is represented by $Z(t_L, t_I, S, W)$, where S is a vector of attributes of the penalty. To simplify the interpretation, S is assumed to be the length of sentence if convicted. The individual's problem is to maximize

$$(1-P)Z(t_L, t_I, 0, W_s) + PZ(t_L, t_I, S, W_u)$$

[56]See Schmidt and Witte (1984, p. 186) for the assumptions giving this result.

[57]Monetization implicitly takes place if an individual, having to choose between actions involving such gains and losses, acts according to certain axioms.

subject to $t_L + t_I + t^* = 24$, where t^* is leisure time.

Following the same procedure as for the previous models (finding the first order necessary conditions for an internal maximum, and computing the derivative of t_I w.r.t. the parameters of the model) one obtains considerably less unambiguous results than for the other models. Unless one is willing to make much stronger assumptions about individual preferences, it is not possible to decide whether criminal activity will decrease or increase as a result of changes in the probability of being unsuccessful, in returns to legal and to illegal activity, and in exogenous income, cf the last line of Table 2.3.

Block and Heineke (1973, 1975) have shown that changes in legal and illegal remuneration lead to changes in illegal activity that are composed of stochastic counterparts of the substitution and income effects of traditional supply and demand theory. But the similarity is not close. Even if one assumes that illegal activity is inferior (i.e. that such activity is decreasing with income), it is not possible to sign the relevant terms. Increasing the penalty, for instance, will not unambiguously deter crime.

Witte (1980, p. 59) and Schmidt and Witte (1984) have also studied a model where time is an explicit argument in the utility function. Witte posits the utility function

$$U = U(t_L, t_I, t_{CL}, t_{CI}, W),$$

where t_L is time spent in legal income-generating activity (work), t_I is time spent in illegal income-generating activity (theft, etc.), t_{CL} is time spent in legal consumption activities, and t_{CI} is time spent in illegal consumption activities (drug use, assaultive activities, etc.). Thus, these time allocations are separate arguments in the utility function in addition to the income generated in the first two activities. This income is included in W. This utility function is combined with the main features of the several sanctions model discussed above, and the optimal allocation of time can as usual be obtained by the 1. order conditions of maximum utility. This model is somewhat less general than the one analyzed by Block and Heineke, but similar inconclusive results are obtained.

2.2.6. Summary of comparative static model results

For various models discussed above Table 2.3 summarizes the comparative static results of the effects on the supply of crime of changes in the probability and severity of punishment, in gains to crime, and in exogenous income and income from legal activity. The possible deterrent effect of sanctions is given by expressions analogous to the familiar Slutsky substitution and wealth effects. The existence of deterrent effects is therefore uncertain, and has to be determined empirically.

The labour supply models with non-monetized attributes (last line) give inconclusive effects for changes in all parameters. For the other models the effects are to a large extent clear, and can be summed up as follows:

An increase in the probability of failure (clear-up or arrest) has, regardless of the sign of the attitude towards risk, a negative effect on the supply of crime. This correspondence constitutes a certain support for the probability part of the deterrence hypothesis.

The effect of an increase in the conviction rate, given arrest $(P_{c/a})$, is indeterminate without further assumptions, and the same holds true for an increase in the probability of restriction of freedom given conviction (not included in Table 2.3). However, reasonable assumptions will produce the same conclusions as for the unconditional probability of failure.

An increase in the severity of punishment, i.e. a positive shift in β, has for any attitude towards risk in Beckers's model, and for risk averters in three of the least general portfolio models of time allocation, a negative effect on the supply of crime. For risk neutral people the same effect occurs only in the two simplest models, whereas the effect is nil for the portfolio model of time allocation with non-fixed leisure time. For risk lovers the effect is uncertain, and depends on the values of the derivatives of the various functions of gains and losses. For the group of models as a whole the severity part of the deterrence hypothesis thus hinges upon the question of attitude towards risk. Contrary to widespread belief, not all economic models of crime do unconditionally support the severity part of deterrence hypothesis.

Furthermore, Table 2.3 reveals that a positive shift in the loss function in the several-sanctions-model and in the labour supply model with non-monetized attributes can cause an increase in crime for any attitude towards risk. In the latter model, the restriction necessary to generate this effect is that the income effects are greater than the substitution effects

An increase in the gains to crime has a positive effect upon crime in all the portfolio models of time allocation for the cases of decreasing risk aversion, increasing risk preference, and risk neutrality, whereas the effect is uncertain for other attitudes towards risk.

The effect of an increase in exogenous income is positive in the cases of decreasing risk aversion and increasing risk preference, nil in the case of risk neutrality, and negative for other attitudes towards risk.

The results are less certain for a positive shift in the income function. Here, decreasing risk aversion and increasing risk preference also result in a positive effect on crime in the two portfolio models with a single sanction, but for the several sanctions model the effect

Table 2.3.
How costs and benefits affect the supply of criminal endeavour[a]

Models	Probabilities of failure			Exogenous income					Shift, gain function, α					Shift, loss function, β					Shift, income function, δ				
	P	P_a	P_{c/a}	R>0 r<0 r>0	R=0	R<0 r<0 r>0			R>0 r<0 r>0	R=0	R<0 r<0 r>0			R>0 r<0 r>0	R=0	R<0 r<0 r>0			R>0 r<0 r>0	R=0	R<0 r<0 r>0		
Becker's model	−													− −	− −	− −			− −	− −	− +		
Portfolio model[c]	−		+	− +	0	− +			− +	+	+ +			− −	− −	− − b			− −	+ 0	+ +		
Portfolio model of time allocation, leisure non-fixed[d]																							
t_L	0		0 +	0 0	0 0	0 0			0 + b	0 +	0 + b			0 −	0 −	0 b −			0 +	0 +	+ +		
t_r	−		− +	+ −	0 0	0 +			− +	− +	− +			+ −	− −	− − b			− −	+ −	− −		
Portfolio model of time allocation, leisure fixed[e]																							
t_L	+		− +	+ +	0 0	− +			− + b	− +	− +			+ +	+ +	+ + b			− +	b b	b b		
t_r	−			+ −	0 0	+ −			b b	b b	b b			− −	− −	− − b			+ +	b b	− +		
Portfolio model of time allocation, several sanctions[f]																							
t_L	0 0_b		0 +	0 +	0 0	0 +			0 + b	0 +	0 + b			0 b	0 b	0 b			+ b	b b	+ b		
t_r	−		−	0 −	0 0	0 +			b b	b b	b b			b	b	b			b b	b b	b b		
Labour supply model with non-monetized attributes[g]																							
t_r	b	b	b	b	b	b			b	b	b			b	b	b			b	b	b		

[a]See sections 2.2.2 for derivation of results.
[b]Further restrictions necessary to obtain sign.
[c]Model discussed by Allingham and Sandmo (1972), Kolm (1973), Singh (1973), and Heineke (1978, model I).
[d]Model discussed by Heineke (1978, model II).
[e]Model discussed by Ehrlich (1973), and Heineke (1978, model II).
[f]Model discussed by Wolpin (1978), and Schmidt and Witte (1984).
[g]Model discussed by Block and Heineke (1975), Heineke (1987), and Schmidt and Witte (1984).

is uncertain. The effect is still nil in the case of risk neutrality, whereas only the model with non-fixed leisure time gives an unambiguous (negative) result for other attitudes toward risk.

As a whole one may conclude that the effects of changes in the environment depend on the individual's attitude towards risk. If one is willing to stick to the rather common assumption that decreasing absolute risk aversion prevails, and also that psychic effects can be monetized, and that there is just one type of sanctions, the effects are clear: Crime is deterred by increases in the probability and in the severity of punishment, and enhanced by increases in exogenous income, and in gains from both legal and illegal activities. The reason why increases in various incomes and gains increases crime, is that punishment in the case of decreasing absolute risk aversion produces a smaller reduction in expected (total) income. For risk neutral people an increase in the probability or severity of punishment and a decrease in the gains to crime will reduce the supply of crime, whereas changes in exogenous income, and in the remuneration of legal activity have no effect. Here, changes in the latter income components do not change the bite of punishment.

2.2.7. The utility of norms

According to the discussion in section 2.1 norms may be regarded either as restrictions on the set of feasible actions or as factors altering the overall evaluation of various courses of action and their outcomes. The first alternative is relevant when individual or internalized norms are so strict that certain actions are out of question regardless of how various wants may be satisfied by illegal acts. The norm "thoug shalt not kill" may be an example; but probably not the norm that "you shall respect regulations such as individual import quotas". In the latter case a reward of, say, 1 Million dollar for a bottle of whisky, would presumably transform many of us from law-abiders to offenders. The shame or loss of self-respect of a minor breach of import regulations will, by some, be balanced against the satisfaction of wants that the act will involve or allow.

Bad conscience etc. can easily be included in most of the models of utility maximization considered above. In the portfolio choice model the cost of crime may be extended to include an element of psychic uneasiness of norm infringement. Formally, one may introduce an extra term in equation (2.5), say the function $N = N(\chi)$, which, for instance, is given the value N^* if $\chi > 0$ and the value 0 if $\chi = 0$. The comparative static analysis of the model will be analogous to the one already discussed, and a change in N^* will have the same qualitative effect as a change in the exogenous income W_o. (The comparative static results deal with internal solutions. Possible corner solutions must be considered separately in both models.) If the psychic uneasiness increases with the value of χ, and also depends on the formal sanctions represented by β, we have $N=N(\chi;\beta)$ with $N_\chi>0$ and, conventionally, $N_\beta>0$. Except for a possible discontinuity at $\chi=0$, the N-function is formally identical to the punishment function F, and the handling of it is similar. This approach is a response to the critique of the models in section 2.1 that they do not allow for formal sanctions to have an effect on crime through norms. The N-function appears to be exactly what has been found to be missing. If more severe sanctions have the effect of strengthening norms, the uneasiness of infringement of them will increase, and this is what the N-function represents. The psychic uneasiness of norm infringement can be introduced in a similar manner also in the other models of maximization of expected utility.

It can be shown that the qualitative results summarized in Table 2.2 still hold when the N-function is included. As far as the signs of the effects of changes in the parameters are concerned, the N-function is of importance mainly for the cases when the signs are indeterminate.

The procedure of allocating a certain monetary value to the infringement of a norm may seem unfamiliar. If, however, a person is able to make consistent choices among various actions involving norm infringement, there will implicitly be a monetary equivalent. Let us take the amateur whisky smuggler as an example. If he at every trip will take with him a bottle extra if a friend pays him 1 million $ for it, but never take a bottle if the reward is only 10 $, the monetary equivalent of norm infringement lies somewhere between these amounts. By gradually reducing the interval one may find (perhaps through an interview) a more exact level of the monetary equivalent. In practice, a precise value will seldom be reached, but the point here is that there is a level exact enough to make our analysis relevant. If the person's preferences are unstable, i.e. that the psychic uneasiness of norm infringement is not (approximately) constant, we run into the same difficulties as when wants are variable. Norms do not represent a particular problem in this respect. One may, however, presume that norms are more stable than wants, and that they consequently pose a lesser problem as far as stability of preferences are concerned.

The inclusion of norms into our analysis makes it evident that we cannot know by which mechanism formal sanctions eventually work: by deterrence or by norm formation. The problem is well known in the literature, and has here been given a formal representation.

The interesting conclusion for the present study is that the inclusion of the mechanism of norm formation does not essentially alter the results obtained in the models of utility maximization. On the other hand it is if possible even clearer than before, that one should be careful not to assign an eventual effect on crime of differences in formal sanctions to deterrence (alone).

2.2.8. Rational crime behaviour - non-expected utility models

Laboratory experiments have shown that people often do not behave according to the hypothesis of maximizing expected utility where the preference function is linear in the probabilities. Various alternative forms of preference functions that are non-linear in the probabilities have been proposed (Karmarkar (1978), Kahneman and Tverski (1979), Machina (1982), Chew (1983), and others), see Machina (1987) and Fishburn (1987) for surveys. Whereas participants in laboratory experiments usually are asked to choose between *legal* alternatives, Lattimore et al. (1992) offer burglaries as a possible risky prospect. Also for this type of activity the preference functions seem to be non-linear. This does not mean that crime is not sensitive to changes in the probability of sanctions, only that crime may be less (or more) sensitive than what simple expected utility maximization implies.

Appendix A to Chapter 2

Consumer demand and labour supply

Legal work being a main source of income for most people, there is a close relationship between the theory of consumption and the theory of labour supply (supply of legal work). A sketch of the main ideas of the simple theory of consumer demand is therefore a useful starting point for explaining this relationship somewhat more precisely.

Let us assume that an individual in a given period has to his disposal an income, W. This sum may be spent on m types of goods. The unit price of good no. i is p_i and the quantity that the individual chooses to buy and consume is q_i. The prices $p_1,..., p_m$ are assumed to be fixed, whereas the quantities $q_1,..., q_m$ are chosen by the individual, with due respect to the budget constraint:

$$\sum_{i=1}^{m} p_i q_i \leq W. \tag{2A.1}$$

The choice depends upon the consumer's preferences for various goods. These preferences are represented by a utility function:

$$U = U(q_1, q_2,...q_m), \tag{2A.2}$$

which says that the individual's "utility" or level of satisfaction depends on the consumption levels of the relevant goods. Every possible bundle of goods gives rise to a certain level of satisfaction or utility. It is further assumed that the consumer picks the bundle of goods that yields the highest level of utility within his budget constraint.

Mathematically the problem is simple: Find the non-negative q's that maximize (2A.2) subject to the budget constraint (2A.1). The utility function (2A.2) is unobservable, and it has been claimed that it is useless or even meaningless to construct theories based on the assumption that the consumer maximizes something that presumably does not exist. It has been demonstrated, however, that testable implications about the consumer's choices can be deduced, and many empirical tests give results in accordance with the theoretical construct. Even if a utility function does not exist, consumers often act "as if" they maximise utility with respect to budget constraints.

Above it is assumed that the consumer considers the prices and the income as given. In general other values of these parameters would give other bundles of goods. This dependence is expressed by a demand function for each good:

$$q_i = f_i(p_1, p_2,...,p_m, W), \quad i = 1, 2,..., m. \tag{2A.3}$$

In economics as well as in criminology, it is interesting to study how people react to changes in the environment. In our simple consumer demand model the environment is represented solely by the individual's income and the prices of goods. Analytically, the environment is changed by introducing other values of these parameters. The result of small changes in the prices are found by partial derivation of the demand functions:

$$\partial q_i/\partial p_i = \partial f_i(p_1, p_2,..., p_m, W)/\partial p_i, \quad i=1,2,...,m \tag{2A.4}$$

One would perhaps expect that the higher the price of good i, the lower the demand for this good. But one cannot be sure. The effect of a higher price can be split into two components: the consumer may want to change the purchase of good i 1) because it has become more expensive, and 2) because the price increase is equivalent to a decrease in the consumer's income. The first effect is called the substitution effect and the second the income effect. Both effects are in a sense hypothetical: they are artificial constructs helpful to understanding the change in demand. The substitution effect is obtained by changing the income at the same time as the price of good i, so that the utility level remains unchanged. But as this change in income is "artificial", one has to subtract the partial effect of it in order to get the final effect on the consumption of good i of a change in p_i. It can be proved mathematically that (2A.4) can be expressed as the sum of these effects, i.e. that:

$$\frac{\partial q_i}{\partial p_i} = \left[\frac{\partial q_i}{\partial p_i}\right]_{U=const.} - q_i \left[\frac{\partial q_i}{\partial W}\right]_{prices=const.} \tag{2A.5}$$

where the first term on the right hand side is the substitution effect and the other the income effect.

The income effect is a product of two terms. The term in brackets shows how the demand for the good changes as a consequence of a change in income when all prices are kept constant. The income effect is obtained by multiplying this partial derivative with the old quantity q_i. The higher this quantity is, the heavier this good weighs in the consumer's budget, and the more important the income effect of a price change of this good becomes.

Theoretically it has been proved that the substitution effect is positive. The last term of (2A.5) may have either sign. Empirical studies show that a partial increase in income may lead either to a higher or to a lower demand for a certain good. High negative values are not very common, though.

If $\partial q_i/\partial W > 0$ the good is said to be *normal*. In that case the last term of (2A.4) (including the negative sign) will be negative. Both terms on the right hand side are then negative, and we get the unequivocal result that a higher price of the good will lead to a reduction in demand for that good.

If $\partial q_i/\partial W < 0$, the good is said to be inferior. If the two terms on the right hand side of (2A.4) are of opposite signs, and the income effect greater than the substitution effect, the result is that an increase in the price of the good will lead to a greater demand. This result is more likely the greater the old quantity bought was. For goods that do not count heavily in a person's budget, this will seldom happen.

Thus the conclusion is drawn that an increase in the price of a good will lead to a decrease in demand except for the rather uncommon occurrence of an inferior good that also makes up for a substantial part of the consumer's expenses.

By assuming that the individual earns a fixed wage w per hour of work, and that he is free to choose the number H of hours to work per day, the present model can easily be generalized to include variable labour income in addition to a fixed income component. If the fixed income component is called I', the new budget constraint becomes:

$$\sum_{i=1}^{m} p_i q_i \leq I' + wH. \qquad (2A.6)$$

Theoretically, a person could work up to 24 hours a day, but a shorter workaday is generally chosen. His attitude towards work can be included as an argument in the utility function. This is usually done by considering the leisure time, $L = 24 - H$, along with the quantities consumed:

$$U = U(q_1, q_2,..., q_m, L). \qquad (2A.7)$$

Using the definition of leisure time the budget constraint becomes:

$$\sum_{i=1}^{m} p_i q_i + wL \leq I' + 24w, \qquad (2A.8)$$

which can be interpreted as follows: The value of the consumption of goods and leisure cannot exceed the sum of the constant income and the maximal possible earned income. Leisure is valued at its opportunity cost, i.e. an hour of leisure is an hour of work income, w, forgone. Maximizing (2A.7) w.r.t. consumed quantities and leisure time under condition (2A.8) will give demand functions similar to (2A.3). Among these is the demand function for leisure:

$$L = L(p_1, p_2, ...,p_m, I', w). \qquad (2A.9)$$

This model makes it possible to analyze the consequences of changes in the wage rate. Of special interest is how leisure time changes as a result of a change in w. It can be shown that $\delta L/\delta w$, analogously with the previous model, can be broken down into a substitution effect and an income effect. The substitution effect is unambiguously negative: If w is increased, and at the same time I' is changed so that the total income remains constant, the person will choose to work more, which gives less leisure. However, with the income component held constant, an increase in the wage rate makes the person richer, and he can afford more goods and also more leisure. If leisure is a normal good, (which is very probable for a person assumed to have the possibility of choosing the number of hours to work), he will then increase leisure time and work fewer hours. Compared with the previous model the result in this case is more ambiguous. The substitution effect and the income effect are here of opposite signs for a normal good. If the wage rate increases, the substitution effect makes the individual work more, whereas the income effect makes him work less. Leisure becomes more expensive, but he is in a better position to afford it.

Appendix B to Chapter 2

Behaviour towards risk

This appendix contains a summary of some aspects of the economic theory of uncertainty relevant for the choice between criminal and non-criminal behaviour. Everyday life consists of a flow of choices between alternatives with uncertain outcomes. Sometimes the uncertainty may be considered to be rather small, and therefore disregarded. Sometimes the uncertainty obviously is of greater importance, but disregarded for analytical reasons. As for crime, uncertainty about the consequences of a criminal act is essential. In the following the economists' traditional way of handling uncertainty is presented. An example may be clarifying.

Assume that a person has an amount of, say, $100 that either can be kept with certainty or used in some prospect involving risk. Let one alternative consist of a bet with a flip of a coin where a "head" gives a complete loss of the initial sum of $100, whereas a "tail" doubles the sum. The expected income of this prospect (= the sum of probability times amount of dollars of both outcomes) is equal to $100. As the other alternative the person may buy a lottery ticket of $1 which gives a return of $150 with a probability 0.01 and nothing with probability 0.99. The expected income of this prospect is $99.50. The prospects are summarized in Table 2B.1.

Table 2B.1
Examples of prospects

Prospect No.	Outcomes				Expected income $E[W]$
	$	Probability	$	Probability	
1	100	1.0			100
2	0	0.5	200	0.5	100
3	99	0.99	149	0.01	99.50

If our person is only interested in expected income, the third prospect will not be chosen. But as people in fact buy lottery tickets that are unfair, as in our example, one cannot disregard this alternative. Some people "take the risk", at least in certain situations. Again if we assume that our person is interested only in the expected income, he will be indifferent to the choice between the fist two prospects. In that case he is considered to be neutral toward risk. If, however, the first prospect is chosen, the person clearly prefers[58] the sure prospect to the risky prospect, as the expected income is the same for both.

These various attitudes towards uncertainty can be more precisely expressed by using the utility function:

$$U = U(W), \tag{2B.1}$$

which is found by substituting the q_i's in (2A.2) by those of (2A.3) and assuming that the prices are constant.

The first and second order derivative of this function will be used to characterize the person's attitude toward uncertainty. The first order derivative, $U' = dU/dW$, is called the marginal utility of income. It is uncontroversial to assume that $U' > 0$.

A more general approach than assuming that people seek to maximize expected income is to assume that they choose the alternative that maximises expected utility, $E[U(W)]$[59]. These two approaches will be compared below. It is shown that the attitude towards risk and the choices made are fundamentally related to the sign of $U'' = d^2U/dW^2$.

Let us first consider the analytically easiest case, where $U'' = 0$. Here marginal utility is constant, and the utility function is of the form $U = a + bW$, where a and b are constants. A graph of this function is drawn in Fig. 2B.1.a.

Assume that there are two possible outcomes, W_1 and W_2, with probabilities P_1 and $1-P_1$ respectively. The expected income is then

$$E[W] = P_1W_1 + (1 - P_1)W_2, \tag{2B.2}$$

whereas the expected utility is

$$E[U(W)] = P_1U_1 + (1 - P_1)U_2$$
$$= P_1(a + Bw_1) + (1 - P_1)(a + Bw_2) = a + Be[W].$$

Furthermore

$$U[E(W)] = a + Be[W],$$

---

[58]No distinction between preference and choice is made in this appendix.

[59]During the last 3-4 decades this assumption has been rather common in studies of risk. In recent years, however, laboratory experiments and other observations have shown that people's attitude towards risk is perhaps more intricate. For a good survey of problems involved in the hypothesis of maximization of expected utility, see Machina (1987).

which implies that in this case the expected utility of income is equal to the utility of expected income. It is of no significance then whether the person maximize expected income or expected utility: the same choice will be made.

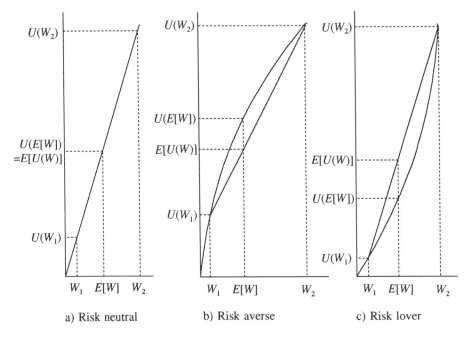

a) Risk neutral   b) Risk averse   c) Risk lover

Fig. 2B.1 Attitudes towards risk

The first two prospects in our example have the same expected value, see Table 2B.2. Their expected utilities are also equal. The person is therefore indifferent to those prospects in both alternatives. He is said to be *risk neutral*.

Let us next consider the case where $U'' < 0$, see Fig. 2B.1 b). The marginal utility of income is here decreasing as income is increasing. This case has an intuitive appeal: an extra dollar will presumably add more satisfaction to a poor person than to a rich one. (But see below about buyers of lottery tickets!) The figure clearly shows that $U(E[W]) > E[U(W)]$. The utility of the expected value $E[W]$ (with probability 1) is greater than the expected value of the utility $U(W)$. The person prefers the "sure thing" $E[W]$ to the expected value of the utility of the two outcomes. In this case, with $U'' < 0$, the person is said to be risk averse. Among outcomes with equal expected income, the person prefers the certain one (or the one least risky).

An example of a utility function with $U'' < 0$ is $U = \sqrt{W}$. The values obtained by using this function on our three prospects are given in Table 2B.2. The utility of the expected income is still the same for the two first prospects, whereas the expected utility is higher for the sure prospect than for the uncertain one. An individual with such a utility function dislikes uncertainty. Third prospect is also preferred to the second. Even if the expected income is lower for the latter, the uncertainty is so much greater for the former that the latter is preferred.

Table 2B.2
Examples of utility functions and prospects

Prospect No.	$U''=0$ $U=a+Bw$		$U''<0$ $U=\sqrt{W}$		$U''>0$ $U=W^2$	
	$U(E[W])$	$E[U(W)]$	$U(E[W])$	$E[U(W)]$	$U(E[W])$	$E[U(W)]$
1	a+100b	a+100b	10	10	10000	10000
2	a+100b	a+100b	10	7.07	10000	20000
3	a+99.5b	a+99.5b	9	9.97	9900	9925

The individual's valuation of certainty is expressed by $U(E[W]) - E[U(W)]$. This difference is called a risk premium. A look at Fig 2B.1.b will indicate that this risk premium depends on the curvature of the utility function; a strong risk aversion corresponds to a marked curvature. The common measure of risk aversion is

$$R(W) = - U''(W)/U'(W), \qquad (2B.3)$$

which is called the *Arrow-Pratt measure of absolute risk aversion*. Pratt (1964) has shown that this measure is approximately proportional to the risk premium.

Remains the case in which $U'' > 0$, see Fig 2B.1.c. Here, the marginal utility of income increases with income. In this case $E[U(W)] > U(E[W])$, which means that the individual prefers a risky alternative to a sure thing. He is willing to pay for a risky alternative - which is exactly what is done when a lottery ticket is bought. The person is said to be *risk-loving*.

Table 2B.2 shows the result for our three prospects for the utility function $U = W^2$. Prospect no. 2, which is most risky, is the one giving the greatest expected utility.

It is commonly assumed that people are not risk lovers. The whole insurance business is taken as an indication, and there are others. But even if most people in most circumstances display a risk averse behaviour, one cannot know for certain. The purchase of lottery tickets has been mentioned. People have argued that such tickets are bought not for the buying of risk, but for the excitement or the moral obligation of participation. But think of a situation where you are almost broke and crash your car, and that your mother-in-law is the only person who can lend you money to buy a new one. It is embarrassing to ask for a loan, - the purchase of some lottery tickets might appear a preferable solution. If you gain you will be happy, and if you loose and you nevertheless have to borrow, the embarrassment will be on a par with before. Even if risk loving behaviour is uncommon, it has to be regarded as a possibility - also when studying crime.

Appendix C to Chapter 2

I. Comparative static results of the portfolio choice model of crime

The individual's reaction to changes in the parameters of the model is found by implicit derivation of (2.7), which gives

$$\partial \chi^o / \partial W_o = - [(1 - P)U_{ss}G_\chi + PU_{uu}(G_\chi - F_\chi)]/J^o \tag{2C.1}$$

$$\partial \chi^o / \partial \alpha = - G_{\chi\alpha}(\partial EU/\partial W_o)/J^o + G_\alpha(\partial \chi^o / \partial W_o) \tag{2C.2}$$

$$\partial \chi^o / \partial \beta = P[(G_\chi - F_\chi)U_{uu}F_\beta + U_u F_{\chi\beta}]/J^o \tag{2C.3}$$

$$\partial \chi^o / \partial P = [U_s G_\chi - U_u(G_\chi - F_\chi)]/J^o. \tag{2C.4}$$

It is conventionally assumed that

$$G_\alpha > 0; \; G_{\chi\alpha} > 0; \; F_\beta > 0; \; F_{\chi\beta} > 0.$$

In the equations above J^o represents the Jacobian associated with the equilibrium condition (2.4). A necessary 2. order condition for maximal expected utility is that

$$J^o = (1 - P)U_{ss}G_\chi^2 + PU_{uu}(G_\chi - F_\chi)^2 + (1 - P)U_s G_{\chi\chi} + PU_u(G_{\chi\chi} - F_{\chi\chi}) \tag{2C.5}$$

is negative.

Substituting (2B.2) into (2C.1) one obtains

$$\partial \chi^o / \partial W_o = [R(W_s)(1 - P)U_s G_\chi + R(W_u)PU_u(G_\chi - F_\chi)]/J^o$$
$$= [R(W_s)A + R(W_u)B]/J^o,$$

where $R(W_s) = - U_{ss}/U_s$, etc. Now $A > 0$, $B < 0$, and from the first order condition of an internal maximum we have $A = - B$.

In the case of risk neutrality we easily obtain

$$\partial \chi^o / \partial W_o = 0, \; \partial \chi^o / \partial \alpha > 0, \; \partial \chi^o / \partial \beta < 0.$$

From the assumption of decreasing absolute risk aversion we have $R(W_u) > R(W_s)$, which implies that the numerator is negative and $\partial\chi^0/\partial W_o > 0$. Hereby, the last expression of (2C.2) is positive and we get $\partial\chi^0/\partial\alpha > 0$. The same effects are obtained in the case of increasing absolute risk preference ($R<0$ and $r>0$).

In the case of decreasing absolute risk preference[60] the sign of $\partial\chi^0/\partial\beta$ depends on the values of some of the derivatives of the gain and the loss function as well as on the degree of the absolute risk preference.

Since $(G_\chi - F_\chi) < 0$ by the 1. order condition (2.7), risk aversion implies $\partial\chi^0/\partial\beta < 0$. In the cases of risk preference the sign of $\partial\chi^0/\partial\alpha$ becomes indeterminate.

The sign of (2C.4) is found by manipulating (2.7) into

$$U_sG_\chi = P[U_sG_\chi - U_u(G_\chi - F_\chi)],$$

which has the same sign as the numerator of (2C.4). We then easily get $\partial\chi^0/\partial P < 0$ for any attitude towards risk.

II. Comparative static results of the simple time allocation model with non-fixed leisure time

The highest expected utility is found by maximising (2.14) w.r.t. t_L and t_I. Necessary conditions for an internal maximum are

$$(1 - P)U_sL_{tL} + PU_uL_{tL} = 0$$

$$(1 - P)U_sG_{tI} + PU_u(G_{tI} - F_{tI}) = 0, \tag{2C.6}$$

where subscripts are used to denote derivatives, i.e. $L_{tL} = \partial L/\partial t_L$, etc. The first condition requires $L_{tL} = 0$, which gives the optimal value t_L^o. This value is independent of P, W_o, α and β, implying that the time allocated to legal activity is independent of other income, of the probability of criminal endeavour being unsuccessful, and of costs and gains of illegal activity. On the other hand, the optimal value t_I^o obtained from (2C.6) depends on the time allocated to legal activity.

Let J_2^o symbolize the Jacobian associated with the system (2C.6) evaluated at t_I^o and t_L^o, and let D_{ij}, i,j = 1,2 be the elements of this determinant. Implicit derivation of the second

---

[60]Risk preference is barely discussed by Ehrlich (1973) and Heineke (1978).

equation of (2C.6) gives:

$$\partial t_l/\partial P = D_{ll}[U_s G_{tl} - U_u(G_{tl} - F_{tl})]/J^o_2. \qquad (2C.7)$$

Rewriting the second first order condition of (2C.6) similarly to what was done in section II above, one observes that the expression in the brackets of (2C.7) is positive. By assumption, D_{ll} is positive and the Jacobian negative, and we get

$$\partial t_l/\partial P < 0.$$

An increase in the probability of being detected leads to a decrease in criminal activity, regardless of the attitude toward risk. We further have

$$\partial t_l/\partial W_o = - D_{ll}[(1 - P)U_{ss}G_{tl} + PU_{uu}(G_{tl} - F_{tl})]/J^o_2. \qquad (2C.8)$$

As above, we obtain $\partial t_l/\partial W_o = D_{ll}[R(W_s)A + R(W_u)B]/J_2^o$, where $A>0$, $B<0$ and from the first order condition $A=-B$.

If the person is risk averse and displays decreasing absolute risk aversion, or risk loving and displays increasing absolute risk preference, the expression in brackets is positive, and we get

$$\partial t_l/\partial W_o > 0,$$

which means that the individual allocates more time to illegal activities the higher the non-labour income. In the case of increasing absolute risk aversion or decreasing absolute risk preference the opposite effect is obtained.

$$\partial t_l/\partial \alpha = - D_{ll}(\partial EU/\partial W_o)G_{2\alpha}/J^o_2 + G_\alpha(\partial t_l/\partial W_o). \qquad (2C.9)$$

The first expression on the right hand side is positive. The second is positive, as just demonstrated, in the case of decreasing absolute risk aversion, or increasing absolute risk preference, and negative otherwise. Thus, in the case of decreasing absolute risk aversion and increasing absolute risk preference we get

$$\partial t_l/\partial \alpha > 0,$$

which means that more time is allocated to illegal activities if returns to such activities are increased. In the other cases of non-neutral attitude towards risk the sign is indeterminate. The first term on the right hand side of (2C.9) expresses the direct effect of an increase in gains to crime, whereas the second expresses the income effect.

$$\partial t_I/\partial\beta = PD_{II}[F_\beta U_{uu}(G_{tI} - F_{tI}) + U_u F_{2\beta}]/J^o{}_2. \qquad (2C.10)$$

Assuming conventionally $F_\beta > 0$ and $F_{2\beta} > 0$ we obtain

$$\partial t_I/\partial\beta < 0,$$

for risk averse people, which means that more severe penalties deter crime. For risk lovers the two terms in the brackets of (2C.10) have opposite signs, and the effect of a change in β depends on the values of the various factors of these terms. We further obtain

$$\partial t_I/\partial\delta = L_\delta(\partial t_I/\partial W_o) \qquad (2C.11)$$

$$\partial t_I/\partial\delta = -D_{22}(\partial EU/\partial W_o)L_{I\delta}/J^o. \qquad (2C.12)$$

Both of these equations have the same sign as $\partial t_I/\partial W_o$, i.e. they are both positive for decreasing risk aversion and increasing risk preference, and negative for the two other cases of non-neutral attitude towards risk.

For risk neutral people we obtain $\partial t_I/\partial W_o = \partial t_I/\partial\delta = 0$, $\partial t_I/\partial\alpha > 0$, $\partial t_I/\partial\beta < 0$, and $\partial t_I/\partial\delta > 0$.

III. Portfolio model of time allocation, leisure time fixed

The assumption of a fixed leisure time has as a consequence that the system (2C.6) is changed to

$$(1 - P)U_s(- L_{tL} + G_{tI}) + PU_u(- L_{tL} + G_{tI} - F_{tI}) = 0, \qquad (2C.13)$$

which has an internal solution for $L_{tL} < G_{tI}$ and $G_{tI} - L_{tL} < F_{tI}$. Then

$$\partial t_I/\partial P = [U_s(- L_{tL} + G_{tI}) - U_u(- L_{tL} + G_{tI} - F_{tI})]/J^o{}_3 \qquad (2C.14)$$

$$\partial t_I/\partial W^o = [(1 - P)U_{ss}(- L_{tL} + G_{tI}) + PU_{uu}(- L_{tL} + G_{tI} - F_{tI})]/J^o{}_3 \qquad (2C.15)$$

$$\partial t_l / \partial \alpha = - (\partial EU / \partial W^o) G_{2\alpha} / J^o{}_3 + G_\alpha (\partial t_l / \partial W^o) \tag{2C.16}$$

$$\partial t_l / \partial \beta = P[U_{uu} F_{2\beta}(- L_{tL} + G_{tl} - F_{tl}) + F_\beta U_{uu}] / J^o{}_3 \tag{2C.17}$$

$$\partial t_L / \partial \lambda = - (\partial EU / \partial W_o) L_{l\delta} / J^o{}_3 - L_\delta (\partial t_l / \partial W_o), \tag{2C.18}$$

where $J^o{}_3$ is the determinant of the Jacobian associated with equation (2C.13), evaluated at equilibrium. Comparison of (2C.14) - (2C.17) with the corresponding relations for the model with non-fixed leisure time shows that for decreasing absolute risk aversion, increasing absolute risk preference, and risk neutrality the signs of the expressions are the same. This means that changes in the four parameters in these cases lead to the same qualitative changes in illegal activity in both models. In the two other cases of non-neutral attitude towards risk the effects of changes in the parameters are ambiguous in both models. As leisure time is fixed, the effects upon legal activities for any attitude toward risk will be the opposite of those on illegal activities.

Chapter 3

METHODOLOGICAL ISSUES OF EMPIRICAL MACRO STUDIES

3.1. Introduction

Empirical macro studies of crime, based on cross section or time series data for e.g. police districts, usually have as purpose either to test a specific theory of crime or investigate to which extent various theories can account for variation between observational units. The aim of these studies are not to explain why some persons become criminals, but to uncover what determines the amount of crime in society.

According to Chapter 2 variation in crime may at the individual level be a result of differences in feasible courses of actions, in benefits and costs of legal and illegal activities, in constitutional traits that determines preferences (norms and wants), in the environment's formation of preferences, and in the person's beliefs about these elements. At the macro level crime will vary among observational units to the extent that there are differences in the distribution of individuals with various characteristics and environments.

The literature of criminology offers three major kinds of research design for estimating the magnitude and statistical significance of the effects of deterrence and of various other incentives or disincentives to crime: experiments, quasi-experiments, and analysis of non-experimental variation in crime and its determinants. Experiments are for obvious reasons scarce. Quasi-experiments can be undertaken when there is an abrupt change in the law (e.g. substitution of fines for imprisonment) or in the enforcement policy (e.g. a distinct intensification of traffic control). In a way quasi-experiments are easy to carry out if all determinants of crime except sanctions are regarded as constant. With that assumption, however, one runs the risk of neglecting that the change in statutes or policy may be caused by - or cause - a change in norms, and that a change in behaviour may be due to a change in norms. (The same problem is of course also present in analyses of non-experimental changes in crime.) Quasi-experiments are further restricted to events of sudden changes in statutes of enforcement policy, and they are not suitable when investigating effects on crime of other aspects of the environment. Studies of non-experimental variation thus seem to constitute the main source of knowledge of the effects of the whole spectrum - or at least a substantial part - of the determinants of crime.

Theories of crime cannot be included into empirical macro studies unless some quantification of its elements is possible. The elements of the traditional rational choice approach, such as benefits and costs of legal and illegal acts, are presumably easier to quantify than those of ethical learning, cognitive dissonance, etc.

Several methodological problems were considered in Chapter 2, especially the relevance for crime of the model of individual, rational choice and of maximizing behaviour under uncertainty. This chapter is reserved for problems encountered in empirical macro analyses of crime in the Becker/Ehrlich tradition, where data consist of non-experimental variation in crime and its determinants. Objections to such analyses have been many and occasionally fierce.[1] Parts of the criticism are highly relevant and deserve thorough consideration. In section 3.2 I will discuss the possibility of deducing a macro function of crime supply on the basis of individual supply-of-crime functions, followed by a section treating the macro crime effects of changes in individual costs and benefits. In section 3.4 I will comment upon the problem of identification of macro models of crime, and especially identification of the crime generation equation. The possibility that imprisonment causes crime to decrease because of incapacitation and not because of deterrence will be considered in section 3.5. The jump from models of individual rational behaviour to models representing the behaviour of groups of individuals in police districts or states is a formidable one. The choice of mathematical representation of macro relations is crucial, and is considered in section 3.6. The well-known problem of under-reporting, together with other problems of measurement errors, are considered in section 3.7. The following section (3.8) consists of a discussion of which empirical macro variables that can be found to represent the various determinants of crime on the individual level. Errors of specification caused by unsatisfactory macro variables are discussed in section 3.9, and related problems of interpretation in section 3.10. A particular empirical problem is whether to study total or separate categories of crime, and in this connection the question of substitutability of

[1]See e.g. Blumstein et al. (1978), Orsagh (1979), Brier and Fienberg (1980), Prisching (1982), Cameron (1988).

crimes arises. These questions are discussed in section 3.11. The chapter is concluded by a summing up of the methodological problems. In Chapter 4 previous empirical studies will be reviewed partly on the basis of comments in the present chapter.

3.2. From micro to macro

Although the theory of rational choice presented in Chapter 2 is a theory of individual criminal behaviour, most empirical studies are based on aggregate data.[2] There are good reasons to analyze criminal behaviour on the individual level instead of on the macro level. In the first place it is at best controversial to posit that behaviour is anything but individual. Second, a substantial theory of individual behaviour (surveyed in Chapter 2) has been developed, in contrast to the more ad hoc reasoning often underlying macro studies. Third, the identification problem (see section 3.3) is less serious when individual behaviour is studied: it can reasonably be assumed that the probability and severity of punishment is determined without being influenced by the actions of a given individual. Thus, the deterrence variables can be considered to be exogenous to the individual's choices, and the problem of simultaneity inherent in macro studies is absent. These aspects are of course not particular to studies of crime, but to studies of social phenomena at large.

Testing of specific theories, like those of section 2.2, seems to require very strict assumptions. These theories produce unequivocal effects for changes in parameters only for given (stable) preferences. To test these results in a macro study, one is compelled to consider the observational unit as a "representative individual" and to assume that the preference structure is the same for all "individuals". When investigating to what extent various theories account for variation in crime, one can rely on less strict assumptions. When examining, for instance, the effect of punishment on crime, one need not necessarily distinguish between the preventive effect through norm formation and the preventive effect through deterrence. One may determine the total effect, without trying to split it.

A study of variation in crime and its determinants between districts or over time can of course not reveal the effects of causes of crime that in fact do not differ between observational units. Norms are presumably important determinants of crime, but if norms are equal, or if they are distributed equally within each observational unit their effects upon crime cannot be traced. A similar problem arises when differences in norms exist, but when

---

[2]See Manski in Heineke (1978, 87-88), Witte (1980, 57), Sjøquist (1973, 441), and Ehrlich (1973, 534) for discussions of various aspects of the jump from micro to macro. Aggregation problems do not appear to be any different in criminometrics than in other areas of econometrics, and analysis of such problems is omitted here.

no empirical measures or characteristics of norms are available. Most, if not all, of the theories of crime discussed in Chapter 2 are affected by these difficulties of empirical macro studies. However, if one has good reasons to assume that norms in fact do not differ, one may conclude that an observed effect of sanctions on crime must have obtained through one of the other mechanisms discussed in Chapter 2.

Empirical studies on the individual level have, however, their own difficulties. The main problem is lack of data: One needs information on the environment of each person, and preferably also individual perceptions of the probability and severity of sanctions. Furthermore, the theory of Chapter 2 does not explain how often a person will commit a crime, only that changes in the environment has an effect on the costs and benefits of crime, factors that are of importance for the choice between legal and illegal behaviour. Efforts to establish formal explanations of individual crime rates have resulted in rather complicated, although not intractable, models[3].

A problem common to both micro and macro studies of crime is to establish the correct relation between the time or the resources allocated to illegal activity and the number of crimes committed. The models of individual behaviour under uncertainty discussed in Chapter 2 imply that time, or other resources, allocated to crime, depend on punishment as well as on benefits and costs of legal and illegal activities; they do not answer the question of how many crimes a person will commit in a given period. Assuming, however, that the number of crimes is an increasing function of time or resources allocated to illegal activity, the portfolio models of time allocation, for instance, imply that we will have an individual supply-of-crime function

$$c_i = f_i(p_i, s_i, w_s, w_u, w_0), \tag{3.1}$$

where c_i is the number of crimes committed by person i in a given period, p_i and s_i are the probability and the severity of punishment, respectively, w_s and w_u are the net benefits of a successful and an unsuccessful crime, respectively, and w_0 is exogenous income (or wealth). Table 2.3 shows the signs of the marginal effects of these variables, signs that will apply also to the present equation. According to the specific model of individual rational choice under uncertainty (discussed in section 2.2), and the underlying, more general, theory of individual, rational behaviour (discussed in section 2.1), the individual supply-of-crime function may contain other explanatory variables, representing the person's norms, wants, abilities, and socio-economic situation.

There are two main procedures to establish the bridge between micro and macro. The

---

[3]See e.g. Manski (1978), and Witte (1980).

first is to assume that all individuals are identical, i.e. have equal tastes and norms, and equal evaluation of costs and benefits (that are the same for everybody). Then equation (3.1) can be regarded also as an aggregate supply function, except for a change in scale.

In the second procedure, individual behaviour is assumed to be adequately described by the model of rational choice, but preferences, abilities, and environments differ among individuals. If Becker's model is adequate, the aggregate effect of a change in sanctions is straightforward. A decrease in actual probability or severity of punishment, accurately observed by everybody, will make crime more attractive. The change will not necessarily change the behaviour of a given individual, perhaps not even a majority of individuals: the change may just not be big enough to substitute an illegal activity for a legal one, or the person has already specialized in legal activities, cf section 2.2.4. In a large population, however, it is highly probable that at least some individuals are just on the brink of committing an illegal act before the decrease in punishment, and the decrease is just sufficient for it to happen. Gradual decreases in punishment will thus produce changes here and there in the population, and a noticeable change in the aggregate crime rate will take place.[4]

The result may be approximated by

$$C = F(P, S, W_s, W_u, W_0),\tag{3.2}$$

where the variables are mean values of the corresponding variables of (3.1). Equation (3.2) may be interpreted as the criminal behaviour (crime supply) of an "average individual".

The aggregate relationship is not equally simple for the other models in section 2.2. From Table 2.3 it is seen that a given change in legal or illegal sanctions, or in exogenous income (or wealth) may increase the criminal activity of some individuals, and decrease it for others. The effect depends on the attitude towards risk, and in some instances on the relative strengths of the various mechanisms involved. The aggregate effect will then depend on the composition of individuals in the population, and their characteristics.

If one is willing to assume that everybody has the same attitude towards risk, the aggregate effect of a change in some of the variables becomes less uncertain. Table 2.3 shows, for instance, that in the case of decreasing absolute risk aversion (a frequently used assumption in economics), the effect of changes in explanatory variables is unambiguous, and equal, for most models. Unfortunately, one may suspect many offenders not to be risk averters, but risk lovers.

---

[4]This analysis resembles text book investment theory, where an increase in the interest rate will make more investment projects profitable.

Thus, even if an explanatory factor moves in the same direction for everybody, the aggregate effect on crime is uncertain. Nevertheless, the models of section 2.2 give some guidance as to what kind of results we may expect from macro studies. All, but one of them, regardless of individual attitudes towards risk, predict an increase in crime as a result of decreasing probability of punishment. A similar effect would therefore also be expected on the aggregate level.

If an aggregate study does not show a significant effect of punishment on crime, a general rejection of subjective rational crime behaviour is not necessarily warranted. The result might be due to violation of the assumption that beliefs are correct or other auxiliary hypotheses that are introduced in various studies.

In interpreting macro studies one must keep in mind that differences in average values of characteristics between districts do not necessarily affect every individual. If crime and unemployment are found to be correlated, one cannot be sure that it is the jobless who have become offenders.

3.3. Macro effects of individual costs and benefits

The discussion in Chapter 2 has documented that reactions to changes in costs and benefits of crime may vary among individuals. The macro effect will therefore depend on the distribution of preferences and individual costs and benefits in the population.

The simplest effect to analyze seems to be that of changes in the probability of punishment. The comparative static results of section 2.2 show that the probability of punishment is inversely related to crime, except for the labour supply model with non-monetized attributes, where the relationship is more ambiguous. The effect of the severity of punishment, represented by the crime loss function, is ambiguous for risk lovers in most models, and also for other attitudes towards risk in the model with non-monetized attributes. If the income effect is greater than the substitution effect, crime will be directly related to the severity of punishment. Assuming that also benefits and costs of legal activities are risky, even more ambiguous results are obtained, cf Cameron (1987). If punishment has an effect on norms, an additional ambiguity is added. Furthermore, harsh punishment may generate less household protection expenditures, which again may counterbalance the possible deterrent effect of punishment, cf Shogh (1973). If, then, there is a significant proportion of risk lovers in the population, and/or if the income effect often is greater than the substitution effect, and/or the effects of legal activities are risky, and/or household protection expenditures are inversely related to the severity of punishment, an increase in the severity of punishment may well cause crime to increase on the macro level.

If, however, in spite of these crime increasing effects, macro studies show that crime is reduced when punishment becomes more severe, there is all the more reason to believe in a deterrent and/or a norm formation effect of punishment.

The supposition that punishment has a deterrent effect on the aggregate level is further supported by the observation that a complete lack of sanctions in a community produces much crime (cf effects of police strikes in Copenhagen), whereas crime is greatly reduced by extremely harsh punishment. A gradual development from one of these extremes to the other should then produce a gradual change in the crime rate, and the mechanism outlined above provides an explanation why. However, an adverse mechanism may also be at work. An increase in sanctions may lead persons committing crimes to resist apprehension more strongly, thus inciting further crimes. But if analyses show that crime decreases when punishment becomes more severe, the latter mechanism is not given support.

Wrong beliefs about changes in punishment are often mentioned as a critique against the model of rational choice. The objection loses some of its force in an aggregated framework. It may well be that some persons do not observe a given change, and also that they have been mistaken in their beliefs. But the gradual change from very lenient to very harsh punishment will certainly be observed by at least a part of the population, and behaviour will change as already explained. It is possible, however, that minor changes in sanctions at some levels of punishment will not produce significant aggregate changes, either because beliefs are wrong or because the balance between legal and illegal actions is not changed for a great majority of individuals. It is up to empirical analyses to determine the actual effect of changes in sanctions. Again, if crime decreases when sanctions become more certain or more severe, the changes in punishment must have been observed by part of the population. In chapter 6 we introduce latent variables to represent *beliefs* about the probability of sanctions.

3.4. Identification

An aggregate crime rate is determined within a system whose actors include offenders, victims and non-victims, and the various parts of the criminal justice system. The interplay of these actors at the macro level is intricate, - here as in other fields. The empirical problem of sorting out the various relationships becomes acute if crimes and clear-ups both depend on each other, and furthermore on the same set of other variables. It is then impossible to disentangle the various effects that determine the level of both: the equations representing the various functional relationships cannot be identified. If one finds that the crime rates and the probabilities of punishment are negatively associated, one cannot distinguish between the possibility that higher probabilities of punishment cause lower crime rates, or the possibility that higher crime rates cause lower probabilities of punishment (because of police overloading).

The question of identification[5] can conveniently be discussed by use of the following typical criminometric[6] model:

$$C_t = a + bP_t + \Sigma c_j Z_{jt} + \gamma_t \tag{3.3}$$
$$P_t = d + eC_t + fR_t + \Sigma g_k Z_{kt} + \pi_t, \tag{3.4}$$

where

C_t = crime rate in period t (= X_t/N_t, where X_t = No. of crimes, and N_t = population),
P_t = probability of punishment in period t (= Y_t/X_t, where Y_t = No. of clear-ups),
R_t = resources per capita of the Criminal Justice System (CJS) in period t,
Z_{jt}, Z_{kt} = socioeconomic factors in period t,
a, b, c_j, d, e, f, g_k = constants,
γ_t, π_t = stochastic error terms.

Equation (3.3) states that the crime rate is a linear function of the probability of punishment, and various socioeconomic factors. It is hypothesized that an increase in the probability of punishment will deter crime. Equation (3.4) states that the probability of punishment is a linear function of the crime rate, the per capita resources of the CJS, and various socioeconomic factors. It is hypothesized that a higher crime rate will cause the probability of punishment to decrease since the police input will be stretched thinly over crimes[7], whereas more resources (especially police resources) per capita will have the opposite effect.

The model has two endogenous variables, and according to common identification rules estimation of (3.3) requires that at least one restriction can correctly be imposed on that equation. The common type of restriction is an a priori knowledge that one of the variables of the model has no direct effect on the crime rate. A socioeconomic variable having an

---

[5] Most introductory textbooks in econometrics explain the problem of identification of statistical models, e.g. Stewart and Wallis (1981), or Johnston (1984). An excellent (and somewhat distressing) discussion of the (im)possibility of identifying the crime function is given by Fisher and Nagin (1978).

[6] I use the term "criminometric model" to designate what is usually called "econometric model of crime", cf "cliometric model", "psychometric model", etc.

[7] In addition to this resource saturation effect, the "limits to punishment" hypothesis also implies a negative effect of crime on sanctions. According to this hypothesis society is willing to deliver only a given amount of punishment. If crime in one year (or in one district) is high, the probability of punishment (or other sanction variables) will be low.

effect on the probability of punishment, but not on the crime rate, would suffice. Fisher and Nagin (1978) declare that they know of no such socioeconomic variable.[8] When some authors for instance include total population in (3.4), but not in (3.3), Fisher and Nagin argue that the total population of a jurisdiction might have an effect on the crime rate just as well as on the probability of punishment. At the then prevailing state of knowledge (in 1978) they rejected that socioeconomic variables could be used as valid identification restrictions. As for our model above, their position would imply that the same Zs must be included in both equations. The remaining possibility is then the characteristics of the CJS itself. Model (3.3)-(3.4) assumes that the resources of the CJS can be used to identify the crime function: R_t is included in (3.4) but not in (3.3), which means that resources may have an effect on the probability of punishment, but not directly on the crime rate. Fisher and Nagin are reluctant to accept this assumption. They argue that crime can be directly affected by the amount of resources. If for instance, because of higher police expenditures, police are seen more often in the streets, the pure presence may independently deter or prevent crimes. The variable R_t should therefore be included also in (3.3), and the assumed identification is not obtained.

Even if exclusion of R_t in (3.3) is accepted, correct identification is obtained only if R_t is truly exogenous to the system, or predetermined by a process that can be adequately taken care of in an extended version of the model. True exogeneity means that R_t does not depend on the endogenous variables, i.e. the crime rate or the probability of punishment, of any previous period. This independence is not very likely. Finally, one must consider the possibility that R_t depends on the crime rate and the probability of punishment of previous periods in a way that can be adequately modelled. In this case correct estimation hinges upon correct specification of the behaviour of the stochastic terms γ_t and π_t. The most restrictive assumption is that each of these terms is uncorrelated over time. Then, standard estimation techniques will give consistent estimates. If, however, γ_t is correlated with γ_{t-1}, and if R_t depends on C_{t-1}, which again depends on γ_{t-1}, then R_t will be correlated with γ_t. In this case standard estimation techniques will not give consistent estimates unless the behaviour of the stochastic terms over time is adequately modelled. The simplest way to do this is to assume that γ_t follows a first order autoregressive process, characterized by

$$\gamma_t = \rho\gamma_{t-1} + w_t,$$

---

[8] "Currently we simply do not have a sufficiently well-developed and validated theory of the socioeconomic factors affecting crime and sanctions plausibly to assume that some SES [socioeconomic] factor can be excluded from the crime-generating model but included elsewhere in the system." Fisher and Nagin (1978, 379)

where ρ is a parameter and w_t is a non-serially correlated disturbance term. Another possibility is to assume an autoregressive process of order m:

$$Y_t = \sum_1^m \rho_j Y_{t-j} + w_t.$$

Although not impossible, an adequate choice of process is difficult. For a given set of data, it might, however, be acceptable to assume a first order autoregressive process if there is good reason to believe that this year's resources in the CJS depends on last year's crime rate.

In cross section studies true exogeneity of R_t (where t here denotes a jurisdiction instead of a time period) is often improbable: the resources of the CJS of a jurisdiction will most often depend on the crime rate or probability of punishment of that jurisdiction. In cross section studies it is further very unlikely that adequate specification of auto-correlation over jurisdictions can be specified.

In some studies an equation describing the granting behaviour of the society is added, e.g.

$$R_t = h + iC_t + \Sigma r_t Z_{lt} + \varepsilon_t, \tag{3.5}$$

where it is assumed that a higher crime rate will produce more resources for the CJS. This equation can help identify the crime function only if it contains socioeconomic variables that can be excluded from the crime function. In some studies (3.5) is substituted for (3.4), and R_t is included directly in the crime function. Identification is of course not further enhanced by this procedure.

Disregarding the possibility of correct modelling of auto-correlation, identification of (3.3) then hinges upon the existence of variables that influence the probability of punishment or the allocation of resources, but not the crime rate. If such variables do not exist, i.e. if data are generated by a process that in fact leaves the crime rate unidentified, no technical refinement can surmount this obstacle.

Fisher and Nagin (1978) have not explicitly discussed a means of identification employed by Phillips and Votey (1975). The authors presume that efficient resource allocation in crime prevention requires a response to input price changes, especially changes in wages for police officers. If wages are exogenous to the enforcement sector, and vary between districts or over years, they are good candidates for identifying the crime supply function: Including these wages as a determinant of crime in the crime supply function would be rather farfetched.

The identification problem becomes less difficult, however, in studies of particular types of crime. It is arguable that a crime function of larceny might be estimated by the method of ordinary least squares, because simultaneity can safely be disregarded: changes in the crime rate of larceny have such a small effect on resource utilization in the CJS that the probability of punishment is not affected. But another problem arises: that of crime substitution. An increase in the probability of punishment of larceny may substitute robbery for larceny, and an increase in the probability of punishment for robbery may produce the opposite substitution. The estimated coefficients of the crime function for larceny may thus be biased.

Fisher and Nagin (1978) also discuss other models with various types of sanctions (instead of the probability of punishment), and models with several types of sanctions and/or several types of crimes. As a rule they find that the identification problem is more difficult in these models than in those considered above. If one tries to estimate substitution effects in a multi-crime-type, multi-sanction model, the identification problem becomes acute.

The problem of identification in macro crime studies does not seem to be qualitatively different from identification problems of macro studies in other areas. Although identification is considered to be an important question in most macro studies, it seems that this problem is regarded as especially serious in evaluations of what is usually called the economics of crime literature. In other areas macro studies are accepted as important sources of knowledge, even sometimes exclusively so, despite serious identification problems, whereas in the economics of crime literature it is not uncommon that macro studies are considered to be almost worthless. It is difficult to avoid the conclusion that either the judgement of macro studies of crime is too harsh or similar studies in other areas are accepted too uncritically.[9]

Although one has to agree with Fisher and Nagin in their judgement of each and every model they have considered, I find the identification restrictions of some studies, if not satisfactory to the degree that common statistical tests can be relied on, at least good enough to produce results that can be regarded as valuable pieces of information. If, for instance, a series of studies using different questionable - but not wholly implausible - identification restrictions, gives almost the same estimates of the effects of punishment, I would have some confidence in these results. The probability of accidental accordance of results, although not possible to estimate exactly, cannot be high. As empirical knowledge can never be certain, agreement in results from various, not completely satisfactory, investigations is perhaps the best we can aim at. It is, therefore, of interest to examine and

---

[9]Sims (1980) asserts that macroeconomic models cannot usually be identified by exogenous variables, essentially for the same reasons as those put forward against macro crime studies.

compare the results obtained in different empirical studies, an exercise pursued in Chapter 4 below.

Furthermore, considering several studies jointly can give additional information. In cross section studies long run differences in the level of crime will generally dominate short run fluctuations. Deterrence effects of variation in sanctions between jurisdictions will, given the relative unimportance of resource saturation (or congestion), tend to be underestimated. In time series studies, resource saturation will have a greater impact, and deterrence will tend to be overestimated. Taken together, upper and lower bounds of the deterrence effects may be obtained.

Even if identification of the crime supply function and the sanction function is impossible, and the estimation of the individual coefficients of (3.3)-(3.4) cannot be obtained, macro studies are not useless. Estimation of reduced-form models including (possibly a large number of) predetermined and exogenous variables is still possible, and the results can be used in forecasting the development of crime.

In Chapter 6 we employ a new method to identify a model of crime.

3.5. Incapacitation

Incapacitation is the effect of isolating an offender from the rest of the society, thereby preventing him from committing crimes in that society. The empirical studies reviewed in Chapter 4 reveal that crime is negatively correlated with the severity of punishment (prison sentence length or time served). It has been suggested that this correlation is due to incapacitation and not (only) to deterrence. The question is then how much crime the people who are imprisoned would have committed if free. The effect of incapacitation on crime is higher: a) the higher the proportion of offenders imprisoned, b) the longer the sentences, and c) the higher the average intensity of crime (no. of crimes per unit of time) of the people incarcerated[10]. If the rate of imprisonment per crime is low, and the individual crime rate is low too, the percentage increase in prison population needed in order to achieve a given percentage in crime is large. On the other hand, even if the number of man years in prison is low in a country, incapacitation can be significant if the people imprisoned (for limited periods) are responsible for most crimes. In countries where punishment is lenient, and offenders seldom are imprisoned, however, incapacitation cannot have a significant effect on crime. Furthermore, in almost all countries, only a minority of crimes are punished, and only a small proportion of known offenders are imprisoned. It has

---

[10]See e.g. Cohen (1978).

also been suggested that if an offender is imprisoned, another person will commit some of the same crimes that the imprisoned offender would have committed if free. This is especially relevant for gang crime.

Most macro studies of deterrence do not explicitly take incapacitation into account. To the extent that these studies refer to high sentencing countries where most crimes are committed by people receiving prison sentences, the confounding of deterrence and incapacitation can lead to serious misinterpretation of results.

As will be explained in Chapter 5, incapacitation cannot be said to have greatly influenced the Norwegian data used in our empirical studies.

3.6. Model selection and mathematical specification[11]

All theories of crime are vague with regard to the mathematical relationship between dependent and independent variables. The lack of theoretical basis suggests that the choice of functional form should be as general as possible, but not so general that it becomes intractable. Linear functions, and functions that are linear in the natural logarithms of the variables (by some called log-log functions, but here called log-linear functions) are natural choices because of simplicity of estimation, and also because of relative ease of identification.

In section 3.3 linear functions are used to discuss identification. If there are diminishing returns to police resources, then an increase in the proportion of clear-ups generated by a given increase in resources would diminish as resources increase relative to the number of crimes. A log-linear specification allows for this possibility. Postulating

$$P_t = C_t^\alpha R_t^\beta Z_t^\gamma, \tag{3.6}$$

decreasing returns of police resources for $0 < \beta < 1$ at any level of the other variables is obtained. Ehrlich (1973, p. 537) explains that a mean supply-of-offence function of the form (3.6) may be derived by integrating individual supply-of-offence functions of the same form, i.e.

---

[11]Leamer (1983) presents provocative examples from economics in general (especially cross section analyses) of what he considers as misleading studies. His discussion of model selection and mathematical specification is relevant also for studies of crime.

$$p_{ti} = c_{ti}^{\alpha_i} r_{ti}^{\beta_i} z_{ti}^{\gamma_i},$$
(3.7)

if the elasticities α_{ti}, β_{ti}, and γ_{ti} are the same for all individuals i. The variables entering (3.6) would then be the geometric means of the corresponding variables entering (3.7).[12]

3.7. Measurement errors

A substantial part of all crimes is not registered by the police. Extensive self-report and victimization studies have been designed in order to determine the extent of under-reporting. The results are strikingly diverse.[13] The "dark figure" of crime has long generated a widespread pessimism regarding the usefulness of employing crime statistics for research purposes. Lack of knowledge about how these report rates are established make all empirical studies based on official statistics suspect. However, the problem of under-reporting is not damaging to empirical research if the rate at which actual or "true"[14] crimes are reported are constant across regions (in cross section studies) or over the years (in time series studies), or if the differences or changes are known. The effects upon registered crime of various determinants can in any case be estimated, and the effects upon the "true" crime rate can be found to the extent that the relationship between "true" and reported crime rates are known. Although an assumption of an exact functional relationship between "true" and registered crime rates can be questioned, no one seems to argue that the differences and changes in registered crime rates is a result of differences and changes in report rates only. Cohen, Felson, and Land (1980, 96), for instance, conclude that victimization studies to which people often refer in criticizing studies based on registered crime rates, have resulted in "the consensus among criminologists who have studied this problem ... that increases in report rates, taken by themselves, have not been sufficiently

[12]Ehrlich also explains that (3.4) under certain conditions (3.4) could be specified in terms of arithmetic rather than geometric means.

[13]See Hindelang (1976) and Nettler (1978) for reviews of victimization studies. Examples of results: According to a 1973 survey in the US 44 percent of crimes against persons and 85 percent of crimes against business were reported to the police (US Department of Justice (1975, 233). Referring to national victimization surveys in the US for the period 1973-76 Cohen, Felson and Land (1980, 96) suggest that about 69 % of automobile thefts, 53 % of robberies, and 48 % of household burglaries are reported to the police. Schneider (1979) reports that only 1 in 10 crimes are reported in England and Wales, and 1 in 3 in the US. In a self-report study by Erickson and Empey (1963) it is found that only about 2 % of the offences admitted by a sample of 180 boys was detected by the police.

[14]Most sociologists of deviance would deny the relevance or existence of such an entity as a "true" crime rate.

large to account for all, or even most, of the variance in reported index property crime rates since 1960". Furthermore, self-report studies have their own weaknesses of registration[15], and cannot easily be used to demonstrate the degree of weakness of criminal statistics.

Every theory of social phenomena involving individual behaviour is affected by the fact that the agents' beliefs can be wrong. The problem is especially acute when the agents have to consider various uncertain events when the degree of uncertainty is not known. Presumably, the true risk of sanction is not known to the individual. Empirical studies suggest that people tend to overestimate the average risk, while at the same time believing that the risk they themselves run is lower than average. Offenders, however, seem to be better informed. Wilson and Herrnstein (1985, p. 392) refer to a study where over two thousand inmates of jails and prisons in California, Michigan, and Texas were interviewed about their criminal careers. The study revealed a close correspondence between the actual and perceived risk of imprisonment in Michigan and Texas, but somewhat less so in California. The study further corroborated the theoretical result that an increase in the probability of imprisonment will decrease crime.[16]

Deficient data is a common problem in social sciences. The consequence is usually not that the data are without value, only that ambitions must be accommodated to facts. The pessimism of earlier days of using official crime statistics seems, in part, to have been based on the misunderstanding that very "noisy" data represent a roadblock to research. The presumption that crime may be determined by a variety of causes, does not hinder estimation of the eventual deterrent effect of sanctions[17], only that the estimates may become rather imprecise. One may even argue that the more causes there are, the easier it is to specify the error term of the supply-of-crime function (e.g. as normally distributed).

It is also true that the noisier the data, the more one needs to utilize the implications of optimization hypotheses. By postulating rational choice, it is possible to construct models which can be used to extract structural relationships from data containing effects of a large variety of causes. This is not an argument for rational choice to be the one and only

---

[15]Cf a conclusion by Christie (1968, 6): "This leads us to the point where it has to be admitted that our present studies on self-reported crime have the same principal weakness as the official crime statistics. We have exchanged the official system of registration for some social scientist's system of registration"

[16]"...the rate at which Texas convicts committed robberies was significantly lower and the chances of going to prison for a crime in Texas significantly higher than they were in either California or Michigan. The reason became apparent from the inmates' answers to the following question: 'Do you think you could do the same crime(s) again without getting caught?' Even though the California inmates had committed more serious crimes than those in Texas, they were over twice as likely to believe that if they continued they could get away with it. The Texas inmates committed the fewest serious crimes and were least likely to believe they could get away with it." Wilson and Herrnstein (1985, p. 392).

[17]Phillips and Votey (1981, p. 145-7) have demonstrated for certain specifications of the supply-of-crime function that the parameter estimates are unbiased.

acceptable basis for research, only that it is especially useful when data are so cloudy that other procedures seem inappropriate.

If registration varies between police districts (or over the years within some districts) a spurious negative correlation will appear between the crime rate and punishment variables. (See e.g. Blumstein et al., eds., 1978). Differences in registration may occur because some police departments do not register all uncleared crimes reported to them in order to be regarded as efficient, or, on the contrary, they may register with great zeal anything that can possibly be considered illegal in order to generate a low clear-up proportion that can be used as and argument for higher grants. The reason for spurious negative correlation is that the number of crimes appears both in the numerator of the crime rate (X_t/N_t) and in the denominator of the clear-up proportion (Y_t/X_t), see (3.3). Given two districts with identical population and criminal behaviour, but with different registration habits, the district with high registration will have a high crime rate and a low clear-up proportion, and vice versa for the district with low registration. Taken together the two districts will show a spurious, negative correlation between the crime rate and the clear-up proportion, a correlation that easily can be mistaken for deterrence. The negative correlation will occur only if there is a difference between jurisdictions in the proportion of crimes registered. If only half of the crimes are registered everywhere, identical jurisdictions will all have the same observed crime rate and clear-up proportion.

A similar measurement error may occur in relation to equation (3.4), where a high crime rate $(C_t = X_t/N_t)$ is assumed to have a negative effect on the clear-up proportion $(P_t = Y_t/X_t)$. A spurious negative correlation due to measurement errors, will tend to make the estimate of the coefficient negative. By misinterpretation this result can be taken as a corroboration of the assumption that a high crime rate stretches police thinly, and therefore reduces the clear-up proportion.

On the other hand, if more police resources per capita increase the proportion of crimes that are registered[18], there will in (3.4) be a spurious negative correlation between the clear-up proportion and the number of policemen per capita. The sign of the estimated coefficient, f, can therefore be negative, and not positive as a positive effect of police on clear-ups would suggest.

As a whole the measurement errors can, by use of inadequate estimation techniques, corroborate deterrence, but reject the hypothesis that more police have an effect on the clear-up proportion. However, measurement errors are a real obstacle to estimation only if each function is estimated separately (e.g. by use of the method of ordinary least squares). If simultaneity is allowed for, if for instance the model (3.3)-(3.4) is adequately estimated

---

[18]See e.g. Greenwood and Wadycki (1973) and Willis (1983) for evidence of this registration bias.

by the method of two stages least squares, the recorded probability of punishment (P_t) is not assumed to be independent of variations in the unobservable factors affecting crime (γ_t), including variations in crime reporting.

3.8. Macro variables corresponding to individual determinants

The model of norm-guided rational behaviour suggests that an individual's choice between legal and illegal activities depends on his norms and wants, his abilities, the situation or environment in which he lives, and his beliefs about the achievable outcomes and about the satisfaction produced by the various acts and outcomes. Differences in one of these factors between any two individuals may, cet. par., make one person law-abiding, and the other not. Better opportunities for theft for the latter may be sufficient to make the difference; or perhaps not, if norms or other factors are strong enough to prevent it. For whole regions or countries one may presume that if the opportunities of theft is better in one population than in another, the number of thefts will, cet. par., be higher in the first one. Some of those who are on the brink of stealing, will become thieves because of better opportunities.

A main challenge in macro studies of crime is to find variables corresponding to the various individual determinants that characterize norms and wants, abilities, environments, and beliefs - either distributions of these determinants over the individuals of each region, or averages and other characteristic summaries of these distributions. If the determinants of crime in macro studies do not differ among observational units, the effects of these determinants cannot be found. Non-inclusion of such determinants will, however, not hinder estimation of the effects of other determinants of crime.

A problem of its own is that in existing theories the determinants of crime themselves are sometimes rather imprecise, and further specifications are necessary before corresponding macro variables can be found. Although personality traits, norms and wants certainly have an effect on crime, it seems difficult to specify which precise aspects of norms and wants can be considered as determinants of crime. High ethical standards will presumably foster a law-abiding behaviour, either by inhibiting certain crimes entirely, or by producing psychic costs of criminal acts that will make crime less tempting, but the concepts characterizing these individual ethical standards are perhaps not well defined. Particular wants may foster certain expressive crimes, but it may be difficult to obtain precise specifications of these wants.

A related problem is the difficulty of observing and measuring the empirical counterparts of certain determinants. Although one can imagine that a given person under no circumstance can commit a murder, it may be difficult to "measure" this quality. What is the characteristic of the individual that can tell us that he will never commit such a crime, and how can we "measure" his "murder-attitude"? Interviews might solve the problem, cf Table 2.1; but who would admit the possibility of becoming a murderer? Psychometric studies might supply relevant data, but on the macro level the best one can hope for at the moment seems to be rather crude proxies, such as attitudes towards law and order.

The attitude towards risk appears to be important for how people react to sanctions and to opportunities for legal and illegal income. It seems rather safe to assume that there is no great difference between regions or over time in the distribution of risk attitude. Although possibly important, this determinant of crime will not produce any variation in crime between districts or over time. One might suggest, however, that the environment may have an influence on this aspect of individual attitudes, and also that the attitude towards risk to some extent determines who will migrate to other regions, and thus form more or less crime-prone subgroups. But as no theory about the relationships between aspects of the environment and individual risk attitudes has appeared, any formal test or estimate is impossible.

The model of norm-guided rational behaviour, and the specific theoretical models of Chapter 2, suggest a certain classification of variables that can be used in empirical studies. I will distinguish between norm variables (representing desires for various courses of action), want (or taste) variables (representing preferences for various outcomes), ability variables (representing intellectual, psychic and physical characteristics), punishment variables (representing the probability and severity of punishment), individual economic variables (representing legal and illegal income opportunities), and environmental variables (other than punishment and economic variables). The norm and want variables will mostly correspond to the determinants of crime discussed in section 2.1.7 (constitutional and acquired characteristics), the punishment variables to those of section 2.1.6 (the preventive effects of sanctions), and the income and other environmental variables to those of section 2.1.8. A survey of variables used in various empirical studies of crime is given in four tables in section 4.7 below. In the present section I will discuss what kind of variables that may correspond to the determinants of crime considered in the framework of norm-guided rational choice.

Macro variables corresponding to possible differences in norms are difficult to imagine. Interviews of samples of population may be used, but are hardly available. One may be restricted to employ variables that presumably represent the ethical standards of people in general, like adherence to religious or ideological organisations. If satisfactory macro variables are not available, it is necessary to assume that norms and wants are equally distributed among regions or over time. Such an assumption seems rather innocuous for time series studies of shorter periods, or for cross section studies where the units of observation are culturally similar. In international comparisons the assumption is more suspect.

The situational and environmental determinants of crime are many. Considering first those determinants that have a direct effect on outcomes (and not indirectly via norms), there is a main distinction to be made between the benefit of crime, the opportunity cost of crime, and the cost of crime.

The (gross) benefit of crime includes the pecuniary gain from crime, and the eventual positive psychic experience of the criminal act. The more there is to steal, the higher the loot from theft, robbery and burglary. Therefore, a suitable proxy of the pecuniary gain could be a measure of the value of objects that can be stolen. A measure of the value of removable property would be a candidate, but such a measure is seldom available. A proxy that measures the psychic experience of crime seems difficult to imagine. Presumably, there is no difference among individuals in various regions in this respect, and changes over time are probably too small to explain any change in crime over a few years. Consequently, the psychic experience of crime cannot be examined in macro studies; its effect, if any, will be constant.

The opportunity cost of crime consists of the net benefit (gross benefit minus cost) of the legal activity forgone while planning, performing and concealing the criminal act. The lower an individual's level of income, the lower is his opportunity cost of engaging in illegal activity. Possible macro variables are averages of various legal incomes, for instance average wage rates for groups that are known to be crime-prone (if any). Unemployment reduces the opportunity cost because legal income foregone for some people is reduced, and the rate of unemployment may thus be a relevant variable. Formal unemployment does not necessarily reduce the opportunity cost to nil, because leisure time may be valued positively, or time may be used to repair one's house or car, but an increase in unemployment will nevertheless reduce the opportunity cost of crime for some individuals.

It can be argued, and rightly so, that income and unemployment do represent not only some of the opportunity costs of crime, but also some of the benefits of crime. The higher the income in an area, the higher (presumably) the loot from robbery, burglary and larceny. Unemployment removes some persons from work activity, and therefore reduces their risk of being victims in locations outside their residential neighbourhoods. The benefit of crime (in terms of robberies etc.) is thus reduced. It can also be argued that overtime work and leisure activities are reduced during recessions, and that people also for that reason spend more time in less exposed neighbourhoods. Furthermore, people at home also serve as guardians and informal controllers, thus increasing the cost of crime to potential offenders. An increase in unemployment will thus reduce the opportunity cost of crime, reduce the benefit of crime, and increase the cost for crime. The first mechanism implies a direct relationship between unemployment and crime, whereas the latter two both imply an inverse relationship.

The cost of crime includes all formal and informal sanctions, as well as pecuniary cost arising from lawsuits (lost income and any lawyer's fee). The formal sanctions include fines, various forms of incarceration, etc. The more severe these sanctions are, the higher the cost (with the possible exception that some criminals seek severe punishment). Variables representing these costs of crime might then be the length (and possibly type) of incarceration, and the size of fines.

The informal sanctions include any personal inconveniences connected with arrest, suit, and conviction. The sanctions related to the social stigma caused by arrest and formal sanctions must be added. Investigations indicate that formal sanctions constitute a rather modest part of the combined formal and informal punishment. The nuisance associated with appearing in court, and the reactions of employer, family and friends, seem to mean much more than formal sanctions[19]. To what extent the cost of these informal sanctions is fixed, or depends on the length of sentence or the size of fine, is not known. Presumably there is both a fixed element, and a variable element that increases with the severity of the formal sanction. Macro variables representing these elements are not easy to imagine. However, if they do not vary between regions or over time they cannot be responsible for observed variation in crime. If there is a difference, the informal sanctions are presumably stronger in smaller towns, or in the countryside, where information about arrests and convictions probably are more easily and widely spread. The degree of urbanization might perhaps be used to represent this effect. Among the costs of crime is also the legal (and illegal) net benefits foregone while incarcerated. Relevant variables will be the same as those already discussed, but the mechanisms by which they may have an effect on crime are different. Estimated effects of these variables must thus be evaluated with extra caution.

The common discounting of time (which means that we put a higher value on how we spend the next year than on how we spend the year thereafter) implies that the individual cost of incarceration increases less than proportionally with the length of sentence. If next year's costs are valued 10 % lower than an equal amount this year, the fifth year of incarceration will be regarded only about as half as bad as the first year. Offenders may have high discount rates, but as there is no information on the eventual differences in these rates among observational units on the macro level, this determinant can hardly be explicitly included.

Possible macro variables corresponding to individual probabilities of punishment are the proportions of crime that lead to arrest, clear-up, conviction, fine, imprisonment, etc. The

---

[19]See Carr-Hill and Stone (1979), p. 27-8 with further references.

measurement error of these formal sanctions were discussed in section 3.7. Variables corresponding to the probabilities of informal sanctions are hardly obtainable.

As explained in section 2.1.7, individual characteristics (Lombrosian constitution, psychological disposition, impulsiveness, gender, age, intelligence, race, class adherence, and drug abuse) to a large extent represent rather superficial "explanations" of crime. In part, these determinants occupy their positions in criminology in part because they are easily measured and correlated with crime, not because they represent fundamental causes of crime. The more basic determinants are found in norms, wants, abilities, opportunities, benefits and costs. Some of these determinants are correlated with gender, age, race, etc., thereby causing correlation with crime. Macro studies should as far as possible include the more fundamental determinants, but as these often are difficult to measure, one is obliged to use more superficial proxies as control variables. As these characteristics, such as age and gender, often are correlated with more than one fundamental cause of crime, the interpretation of empirical results is difficult.

If, in a macro study, opportunities, benefits, and costs of legal and illegal activities are appropriately treated, the effects on crime of the individual characteristics discussed above will reflect variation in norms, wants, abilities, and beliefs. How to distinguish among these latter determinants is, however, a demanding task.

Some of the individual characteristics discussed, especially "Lombrosian constitution" and various psychological dispositions to crime, are quite difficult to define. The illness or deviance might take the form of norm changes (so that illegal actions are more easily accepted), of changes in preferences that reflect the weights given to actions and outcomes, or just of wrong beliefs. Nobody seems to have seriously suggested, however, that we here have an explanation for a substantial part of total crime. If there is variation (in time or between districts) in the proportion of crimes committed for such reasons, relevant determinants would nevertheless be warranted. The omission of such determinants seem rather innocuous, though.

If the illness or deviance is caused by the environment, the relevant functional relationships should be included in macro crime studies. There are hypotheses suggesting that urbanization, ruptured families, etc. might cause the illnesses and deviances in question. The relationships are rather vague, and precise determinants are not easily found.

Although gender is a significant determinant of crime, there is often no point in including this factor in macro studies. It is usually the case that the proportion of women does not vary between observational units; thus its importance cannot be revealed, and nothing significant is added by including it.

In some countries statistics show that race might be a factor of importance in explaining crime. The proportion of various races often differ among regions and over time, and such variables are therefore warranted as control variables. Here too, if opportunities, benefits, and costs are adequately represented, a remaining race effect would indicate differences in norms, wants, abilities and beliefs.

As crimes are mostly committed by young men, measures of the age composition of the population should be included as control variables. Here too, if opportunities, benefits and costs of legal and illegal activities are adequately represented, any effect of age variables must reflect differences in norms, wants, abilities, or beliefs. Teenagers and young adults are at greater risk of property crime victimization than are older adults. Measures of age composition will thus also reflect the age of the victims. Hindelang (1976, 278) has found, however, that the 15-24 age range is more offender related than victim related.

Various IQ tests may be regarded as satisfactory measures of intelligence. There is no indication that the distribution of IQs in large populations differ among regions or over time. The inclusion of determinants representing intelligence is therefore hardly warranted in macro studies.

As class is a somewhat vague concept, people's feelings about class adherence is not easily obtainable. The proportion of individuals belonging to certain socioeconomic groups may be used as a proxy.

The proportion of registered abusers of alcohol and other drugs may indicate the amount of abuse. Per capita consumption of alcohol and drugs are perhaps next best determinants.

As demonstrated in section 2.1.8 the environment may influence norms and wants, and thereby crime. Ethical learning and maladjustment, culture conflict, anomie, cultural deviance, unemployment, etc. may produce more crime prone preferences.

Unsatisfactory upbringing may reduce the internalization of social norms, and thereby diminish the psychic cost of committing crimes. Precise features of upbringing that produce this result are difficult to imagine. The number of broken homes could be a proxy, and has been used in various (mostly non-crime) studies.

Variation in norms rooted in cultural differences can possibly be represented by the proportion of population belonging to the relevant cultural subgroups. However, there will always be a question to what degree norms and membership in subgroups correlate.

A difficult economic and social situation might cause differential association or social anomie that will generate weak respect for common norms. Relative poverty, and not absolute poverty, is probably here the driving force. General measures of income inequality in society, or the proportion of population with income far below average, may be relevant factors that produce the change in norms.

At several points in this discussion of empirical measures it has become evident that a given measure might reflect different mechanisms at the same time. This complication does not require that the measure not be employed, but caution has to be exercised in interpreting the results.

3.9. Errors of specification

In macro studies it is impossible to include the different variables representing all the various determinants of crime, and the functions to be estimated will easily be wrongly specified. In order to assess the seriousness of this omission it is necessary to consider whether the omitted determinants are correlated with the included predetermined variables or not. Determinants that are not correlated with the included predetermined variables will influence the crime rate in the crime function, and thus contribute to the error term. An increase in the error term will make tests less precise, but if the error term still has a known distribution, the estimates of included variables will not be biased. If tests show that some variables are statistically significant, the specification error does not undermine this result. But the specification error might, because of the larger error terms, make it impossible to reject some null-hypotheses, and thus make us believe that some of the included variables which appear not to be significant in fact are. More serious is the problem with omitted determinants that are correlated with the included predetermined variables, since estimates then will be biased.

These problems do not arise if there in fact is no variation over time (in time series studies) or between districts (in cross section studies) in these determinants. In order to test hypotheses by use of statistical methods, variation in data is of course a prerequisite. But if for some reason a determinant of crime has to be excluded, lack of variability in this determinant is just what we should hope for. These determinants will of course be of importance for the total amount of crime, but their influence will be included only in a constant term to be estimated, and will not have any influence on the other estimated coefficients. Determinants that according to previous discussion are likely to be omitted are those representing Lombrosian characteristics, psychic traits, impulsiveness, and intelligence. If some people are born to be criminals, one could reasonably assume that the proportion of such individuals is approximately constant over time. It is somewhat less certain that there are no differences between districts as to this proportion. One might imagine that these individuals have another migration history than other people, and if talents are hereditary, concentrations of these might differ between districts. If this Lombrosian theory is relevant, it is possible that such constitutional characteristics are correlated with several other determinants of crime, e.g. other personality deviations, low economic and social status, and high alcohol consumption. If these latter determinants are included in a particular study, their estimated effects may be biased because of the omission of determinants they are correlated with. The same type of problem occurs if various omitted crime related psychic traits are correlated with included determinants.

There is ample evidence that most cleared up crimes are committed by people who on average are somewhat less intelligent and more impulsive than people at large. Lack of variation among observational units makes it futile to include intelligence and impulsiveness in macro studies, but here too there is a risk of bias in estimates of included determinants.

3.10. Problems of interpretation

The discussion of determinants needed in macro studies has revealed that several relevant determinants may each represent various theories of crime, resulting in demanding tasks of interpretation of empirical results.

Most of the individual characteristics discussed above (Lombrosian constitution, psychological disposition, impulsiveness, gender, age, intelligence, race, class adherence, and drug abuse) cover each several explanations of crime. In a particular study one may be satisfied by using these determinants only as simple control variables without investigating what kind of mechanisms that lie behind. It would be more interesting to dig deeper and question to what extent each variable represent differences in norms, wants, abilities, opportunities, benefits, costs, and beliefs. Realistically, this far more demanding task can not be carried out. But the mere attempt is useful. One might discover, for instance, that the race factor is reduced to differences in opportunities and not in norms and abilities.

Various measures of income may represent both benefits of crime (loot), opportunity cost of crime (legal income forgone while planning and committing crime), and cost of crime (income forgone while incarcerated, etc.). According to the first mechanism higher income will produce more crime, whereas the two others will produce less. In a particular study it will not be possible to predict which of these effects that are strongest, and one would expect various studies to give different results. Conclusions as to the effect of income differences must be draw with extra caution.

In addition, theories of differential association and anomie are also rooted in the economic situation of people. Here, however, the focus is on income inequality. Inequality will make crime the best opportunity either directly, or indirectly by forming more crime prone norms. Great care should be taken in order not to confound the effects of various measures of income.

A possible means of differentiating between the two latter types of effects may reside in the different time perspectives of the two mechanisms. Norm formation is probably slow compared to the direct effect on behaviour of changing economic opportunities. A change in the proportion of poor people from one year to the next would probably have a smaller effect on crime through norm formation than through economic outcomes. If inequality or poverty is found to be significant in explaining crime in a time series study, one could tentatively interpret the result as a corroboration of the hypothesis that economic opportunities have a direct effect on crime through rational choice. In cross section studies one should be more cautious. In a district with e.g. extreme poverty, norm formation can have had time to develop over many years, and it will be more uncertain which mechanism is at work.

Urbanization is a multidimensional concept that may include many determinants of crime. Urbanization will certainly have an impact on opportunities, and on benefits and costs of legal and illegal activities. If these factors are appropriately included otherwise, the effect of urbanization will go through formation of norms, wants, abilities, and beliefs. In any particular study using urbanization as an explanatory variable it will be a problem to sort out which mechanisms that are at work.

Another determinant of crime that may represent several mechanisms is the ruptured family. Broken homes may reduce the socialization of children. Increasing inequality or poverty resulting form broken homes may have the same direct or indirect effects on crime as discussed above. Broken homes may also, according to the routine activity approach, produce better opportunities of crime because more homes become unguarded and more people are travelling in risky locations. Here, too, caution in interpretation will be warranted.

3.11. All crimes or special crimes

In empirical studies of crime one is faced with the problem of investigating either the total amount of crime or the amount of particular types of crime. Problems of identification (cf section 3.4) suggest that some priority should be given to studies of total crime. Such studies will, however, be obscured by changes in the composition of crime. If, for instance, deterrence works in such a way that more severe sanctions produce fewer serious crimes, but an equal increase in less serious crimes, no effect will appear. The statistical tests of the effect of deterrence will then be tougher.

A related problem stems from the fact that the rate of non-reporting of criminal acts varies across crime cateories; the proportion of unreported homicides is surely lower than that of unreported larcenies. A change in the composition of crime, leaving the total amount unchanged, will then produce a change in the total number of reported crimes. In studies of total crime there will then be a risk of biased estimates.

Crime statistics usually specify dozens of crime categories. The complete list of explanatory variables will differ among categories, and the total number of determinants of crime will be quite large. In empirical studies of total crime only the more general determinants can be included. The impact of other variables on one particular category of crime, has to be omitted, and their impact will be included in the error terms. If the variation in the composition of crime is insignificant, and the omitted variables are not correlated with those included, no serious problem of estimation will arise.

In studies of specific types of crime there is a risk of exaggerating the deterrent effect of punishment. An increase in punishment of the type of crime studied may produce only a substitution of crime and not a decrease in the total amount of crime. Burglary, for instance, may increase when robbery is sanctioned more severely. Similarly, geographical spillovers may keep crime constant, although an increase in punishment in one area may have a local deterrent effect. A problem studying specific types of crime is the practice among the police to register only the most serious offence of criminal episodes consisting of multiple crimes. An event may be registered as a rape, although in fact this offence was preceded by a burglary that eventually developed into a more serious crime. The number of less serious crimes are therefore underestimated.

Studies of total crime and special crime have both their weak aspects. Problems of identification, substitution, and spillover effects are most serious in studies of special crime, whereas changes in the composition of crime, and special aspects of particular types of crime causes problems mainly in studies of total crime.

3.12. Summing up

The methodological problems of macro studies of crime discussed above may be felt overwhelming, and quite detrimental to such studies. However, these problems are not very different from those commonly encountered in other macro studies of social phenomena. One is then faced with the question of either abandoning most macro studies of social phenomena, or systematically elaborating on these problems in order to reduce or eliminate their weak spots. Obviously, I follow the second strategy.

Many of the problems discussed in this chapter reduce the value of the empirical results that may be obtained, but without making them irrelevant. The jump from micro to macro, incapacitation, model selection and specification of variables, etc. constitute serious problems, but non of them represent insurmountable obstacles to gaining knowledge from macro studies.

All methods available to the criminological researcher have significant weaknesses. The great emphasis in this chapter put on problems in macro studies should not automatically lead to the easy conclusions that studies based on individual data are less flawed, and that macro studies should be abandoned. At least, a more systematic comparison is required before such conclusions eventully can be reached.

The most intriguing of the problems discussed seems to be that of identification. I have argued that this problem is not detrimental if it turns out that studies with different restrictions of identification give similar results. In addition, Chapter 6 contains a study based on panel data, where the problem of identification is solved. I regard that chapter as an example of how to proceed to gain more knowledge by empirical macro studies.

Chapter 4

PREVIOUS CRIMINOMETRIC STUDIES

The purpose of this chapter is to make an assessment of the contributions of criminometric[1] studies to the analysis of crime in general, and to the question of deterrence in particular. Many authors have tried to estimate the magnitude and statistical significance of deterrence, but the discussion in previous chapters has made it clear that one may question what has in fact been estimated. I intend to pinpoint some of the weak points of these studies in order to design my own empirical analysis so as to avoid as far as possible such weaknesses.[2] Most of the methodological questions raised have been given a general treatment in Chapter 3. The problems encountered are not particular to crime studies, but are appearing in many empirical studies of society. By some, these problems are regarded as detrimental to the type of studies reviewed below. Criminometric studies seem to be

---

[1]I shall call these studies criminometric, analogous to cliometric studies, psychometric studies, etc. They are usually called econometric studies, which is understandable given the similarity with empirical studies in economics, and the profession of most of the authors. But this classification can be misleading. The subject matter is crime, and although economic factors are significant in the study of crime, they are not exclusive.

[2]Several reviews of empirical studies of crime have been published. The most comprehensive bibliography on general deterrence research seems to be Beyleveld (1980). In his index 568 works are listed, most of which are given an annotated presentation. Beyleveld also offers comprehensive summary comments on subgroups of publications. In addition to several investigations of correlations between crime and deterrence variables he reviews 35 cross-sectional and 31 time-series econometric studies of crime. A thorough review of the empirical evidence of general deterrence is also given by Nagin (1978), who comments on 24 correlation and econometric studies, all but two also covered by Bleyleveld. Taylor (1978) concentrates upon six major econometric studies, whereas Pyle (1983) reviews the same studies and about 15 others. A shorter, but somewhat more up to date review is Cameron (1988). Reviews of certain parts of the literature are found in Fisher and Nagin (1978), Klein, Forst and Filatov (1978), Nagin (1978), Passell and Taylor (1977), Peck (1976) and Vandaele (1978). Assessments of empirical deterrence studies are of course also found in Andenaes (1974a, 1975, and 1989), Zimring and Hawkins (1973), and several others.

more harshly judged than similar empirical studies in other fields. Whether evaluations are too soft in other areas, or too strong in ours, is debatable. Although I, too, share the concerns about the weaknesses of both theory, estimation techniques, and data - concerns that are sufficient to make one sceptical about the results of each and every particular study seen in isolation - I shall conclude that the totality of studies corroborate the model of rational behaviour in general, and the theory of deterrence in particular.

The purpose is not to present a comprehensive study of all criminometric deterrence studies, but to present a selection representing the great variety of models and data. A particular emphasis is given to some recent studies that have not been surveyed in previous reviews.

The present review comprises studies from the US, Canada, England and Wales, Australia, India, Finland and Sweden, and also an international comparison. It includes studies based on quite different models, equation specifications and estimation techniques, and it includes studies utilizing data from states down to municipalities and campuses. Since theory and data cannot at the present time (and forever?) accurately determine the eventual deterrent effect of punishment, it is important to investigate to which degree different studies produce more or less similar results. If they do, despite weaknesses that possibly differ from study to study, one can perhaps obtain some evidence as to whether crime depends either on certainty and severity of punishment, on characteristics of the environment or individual characteristics, or on all these determinants.

In sections 4.1 - 4.6 I present empirical studies most of which, more or less explicitly, are based on the model of rational behaviour. The presentation includes sketches of model specifications and empirical measures (proxies) of the theoretical variables of the models. The emphasis will be on the supply of crime function, although most models employed also contain a police production function (explaining the probability of punishment), and/or a police expenditure (or manpower) function (explaining the amount of resources or manpower allocated to the police). Mentioned are also estimation techniques and data employed. Most studies reviewed include punishment and economic variables, and also some (other) environmental variables. In a few studies certain socioeconomic variables employed are also declared to be taste (norm and want?) variables.

Section 4.1 contains a very brief summary of some studies of correlations between crime and punishment (and some other) variables from about 1970. The bulk of criminometric studies consists of cross section regression analyses. Some of them are presented in section 4.2-4.4. In the first of these sections one will find "general" studies covering many types of regional areas, estimation techniques, and types of crime. A few of them address special questions, such as the effect of police "aggressiveness" in patrolling, or the influence of income differentials. The extent of substitution between crimes, i.e. to which extent a change in the probability and severity of punishment of one type of crime has an effect on the amount of other types of crime, is analysed in three studies presented in section 4.3. In section 4.4 I review a few studies of particular types of crime, especially property crimes and hijacking. Five studies based on time series are presented in section 4.5. In order to evaluate the macro studies in a somewhat broader context, some studies using data on individuals are presented in section 4.6. A summary of the results obtained in all these studies is given in section 4.7. The effects of the deterrence variables, and of the cost and income variables are given special emphasis. This section gives a rather self-contained summing up of the main results of the individual studies, and should be sufficient for readers who are not interested in methodological features of each of them. In order to evaluate the results on a somewhat broader basis a short summary of some empirical crime studies based on hypotheses like routine activity, stability of punishment, and situational opportunity is given in section 4.8. These studies, and the theories on which they are based, will help to draw better conclusions from the studies reviewed. In a final section I give an overview of the various empirical measures that have been used as proxies for the theoretical variables of our model of rational crime behaviour. This overview will guide the choice of empirical measures in studies presented in Chapters 5-6, and help in evaluating the results.

4.1. Simple correlation studies

Many studies of correlation between crime rates and punishment appeared in the late sixties and early seventies. Using data from 1960 on states in the US Gibbs (1975) concludes that both the certainty and the severity of imprisonment have a negative effect on homicide rates. Similar negative effects are also found by Gray and Martin (1969) who use the same data to estimate linear and logarithmic relationships between crime and punishment variables. Tittle (1969) obtains negative correlations between estimates of the certainty of punishment and offence rates for seven major felonies in the states of the US about 1960, whereas those between the estimated severity of punishment and the same offence rates are mainly positive. Chiricos and Waldo (1970) examine the deterrence hypothesis for each of the major index crimes in the US for three separate years. The certainty of punishment appears to have a negative effect on crime, whereas its severity has, if any, a positive effect. As a whole the authors conclude that their analysis provides little evidence of deterrence. Using data for 1971 Tittle and Rowe (1974) have calculated correlations between arrest clear-up ratios and crime rates for total crimes in municipalities and counties in Florida. They locate a critical level at about 30 percent for the clear-up ratio to have an effect on crime. Below this level there is no link between the clear-up ratio and the crime rate, whereas a negative relationship is obtained above this level. Correlation studies have also been performed by Bean and Cushing (1971), Bailey and Smith (1972), Logan (1972), Anthunes and Hunt (1973), Erickson and Gibbs (1973, 1975 and 1976), and Bailey, Davis and Gray (1974), Logan (1975).

With very few exceptions simple correlation coefficients of all the above mentioned studies indicate a negative association between the certainty of arrest and the crime rate for different crime categories. But crime rates do not generally vary with the severity of imprisonment, although there are some exceptions for homicide and a couple of other crime categories. These conclusions are in accordance with the theoretical results of our expected utility models summarized in Table 2.3. The probability of punishment has a negative effect on crime in all these models but one, whereas the effect of the severity of punishment for most models is uncertain.

A necessary condition for interpreting the results of these correlation studies as estimates of deterrence is, of course, that there is a one-way causation from punishment to crime, and none in the opposite direction. Simple correlation studies are also open to the criticism that a third factor may be related to both crime and punishment, and thus be responsible for the correlation that mistakenly is interpreted as deterrence. However, in most cases the main conclusions remain when these correlations are controlled for other deterrence variables and also for some socio-economic variables. A notable change occurs when the severity of imprisonment is controlled for the effect of certainty of imprisonment, cf. Logan (1972a) and Bailey and Smith (1972). The effect of severity on crime then changes from no significant influence to a negative influence.

4.2. Cross section regression analyses

The cross section criminometric studies are mostly based on various specifications of the general model

$$C = f(P, S, Z_j), \tag{4.1}$$
$$P = g(C, R, Z_k), \tag{4.2}$$
$$R = h(C, Z_l), \tag{4.3}$$

where
C = crime rate (= X/N, where X = No. of crimes, and N = population),

P = probability of punishment (= Y/X, where Y = No. of clear-ups),
S = severity of punishment,
R = resources per capita of the Criminal Justice System (CJS),
Z_j, Z_k, Z_l = socioeconomic factors,
cf (3.3)-(3.4), and (3.5). We shall call (4.1) the crime function (by some called the crime supply function), (4.2) the clear-up function (by some called the production function of law enforcement activity), and (4.3) the demand function for law enforcement activity.

The expected effects of the various variables on the crime rate, and the measures that can be used to represent them, are discussed in section 3.8, and the empirical measures employed in the studies reviewed are given in Tables 4.4 to 4.7. In some studies resources allocated to the CJS are considered to be exogenous, and consequently (4.3) is not included. In others, the probability of punishment is also considered to be exogenous, and only (4.1) is estimated. With a couple of exceptions, only linear and log-linear specifications are employed. The regression techniques[3] used are given in Table 4.1, where we for most studies reviewed also find the estimated effects on the crime rate of punishment variables. In Table 4.2 the effects of various socioeconomic variables are presented.

Among the first simultaneous regression analyses in this field we find Ehrlich (1972), Phillips and Votey (1972), and Orsagh (1973). Orsagh focuses especially on the possibility of simultaneous equation bias, and he estimates, applying the method of two stages least squares (2SLS) a two equation model similar to (4.1)-(4.2), where the crime rate is a function of the conviction ratio, and vice versa. A few socioeconomic variables are added, mainly for identification purposes. He finds that the conviction ratio has a significant negative effect on crime.

In a multivariate analysis of the deterrent effect of arrest and convictions on crime rates for Indian states and federal territories, Bailey (1978) finds that the arrest ratio (arrests divided by reported crimes) has a negative effect upon the offense rate for rape, theft, and burglary, and for most years also for homicide and robbery. As for the conviction ratio (convictions divided by reported crimes) both positive and negative effects on crime are revealed.

The first major empirical study appearing after Becker's theoretical article was the one by Ehrlich (1973). He studied seven types of crimes in the US based on data for all states from 1940, 1950, and 1960. Elaborating on the theory of Becker and others Ehrlich comes up with a log-linear specification of (4.1)-(4.3), where the two deterrence variables both refer to imprisonments.

---

[3]We use the following abbreviations: OLS = ordinary least squares, 2SLS = two stages least squares, 3SLS = three stages least squares, FIML = full information maximum likelihood.

Table 4.1
Elasticities of crime rates w.r.t. punishment variables[1,2]

Study, data, year	OLS				2SLS/3SLS/FIML			
		Cert.		Sev.[6]		Cert.		Sev.
	P_A[3]	P_C[4]	$P_{C/A}$[5]		P_A	P_C	$P_{C/A}$	
Ehrlich (1973)[7] US States 1960								
Murder		-.341*		-.140		-.852		-.087
Rape		-.578*		-.188		-.896*		-.399*
Assault		-.275*		-.180		-.724*		-.979*
Robbery		-.853*		-.223		-1.303*		-.372*
Burglary		-.534*		-.900*		-.724*		-1.127*
Larceny		-.133*		-.263*		-.371*		-.602
Auto theft		-.247*		-.174		-.407*		-.246
Crimes against pers.		-.550*		-.349*		-.803*		-.495*
Property crimes		-.508*		-.621*		-.796*		-.915*
All offences		-.526*		-.585*		-.991*		-1.123*
1950 All offences		-.566*		-.474*				
1940 All offences		-.653*		-.289*				
Forst (1976) US States 1970								
All offences (Ehrlich's model)						-.65†		-.62†
All offences						-.02†		-.01†
Vandaele (1978) US States 1960								
Murder						-2.440		.488
Rape						-1.270*		-.450
Assault						-.925*		-1.140*
Robbery						-1.674*		-.528
Burglary						-.776*		-.826*
Larceny						-1.018		-1.370
Auto theft						-.791*		-.289
Crimes against pers.						-1.150*		-.425*
Property crimes						-.899*		-.739*
All offences						-1.113*		-.885*
Phillips and Votey (1975) Counties, Calif.								
All offences		-.622 (7.81)		-.347 (2.13)		-.610 (4.32)		-.342 (2.04)

(Cont.)

Table 4.1 (cont.)
Elasticities of crime rates w.r.t. punishment variables[1,2]

Study, data, year	P_A[3]	P_C[4]	$P_{C/A}$[5]	P_A	P_C	$P_{C/A}$	Sev.
			OLS	Sev.[6]		2SLS/3SLS/FIML	Sev.
		Cert.			Cert.		
Myers (1980) US Cities							
Robbery	-.144	-.883		-.639	-.382	-.878	-.571
	(1.525)	(13.92)		(5.114)	(1.741)	(12.73)	(4.091)
Burglary	-.117	-.498		-.413	.500	-.486	-.422
	(1.409)	(7.297)		(4.055)	(1.757)	(5.395)	(3.166)
Larceny	-.258	-.402		-.201	-.397	-.471	-.247
	(2.856)	(6.691)		(1.943)	(2.433)	(7.868)	(2.310)
Auto theft	-.590	-.013		-.013	-.948	-.012	-.017
	(5.453)	(-.778)		(.638)	(4.108)	(.185)	(.969)
Mathur (1978) US cities 1970							
Murder					-.094		-.145
Robbery					-1.58[b]		-.654[b]
Burglary					-.256[b]		-.270[b]
Assault					-.910[b]		-.605[b]
Rape					-1.10		-.410
Auto theft					-.505[b]		-.327[b]
Larceny					.486[b]		-.392[b]
Swimmer (1974) US Cities							
Murder				-.005			-.005
Robbery				-.062[c]			-.066[c]
Burglary				-.296[b]			-.341[b]
Assault				-.199[b]			-.199[b]
Rape				-.016			-.015
Auto theft				-.173			-.137
Larceny				-.187			-.235
Chapman (1976) California, towns, 1960&1970							
Property crimes[9]				-.93[A]			
Murder assault				-.09			
Sjøquist (1973) US municipalities 1968							
Prop.crimes[10]							
Regression 1	-.342[A]			-.212			
Regression 2		-.354[A]		-.292[B]			
Regression 3			-.678[A]	-.467[B]			
Regression 4	-.365[A]		-.267	-.285[B]			

(Cont.)

Table 4.1 (cont.)
Elasticities of crime rates w.r.t. punishment variables[1,2]

| Study, year, data | OLS | | | | 2SLS/3SLS/FIML[13] | | | |
| | | Cert | | Sev.[6] | | Cert | | Sev. |
	P_A[3]	P_C[4]	$P_{C/A}$[5]		P_A	P_C	$P_{C/A}$	
Mathieson & Passell (1976), NY Precincts, 1971								
Homicide	-.743			-1.96				
	(6.19)			(3.74)				
Robbery	-1.06			-2.95				
	(4.21)			(4.08)				
Thaler (1977), NY, Rochester 1972								
Property cr.[11]				-.0006				
				(.165)				
Property cr.[12]				-.0017				
				(2.24)				
Avio & Clark (1978)10 Ontario, 1971								
Robbery					-.831	-.697	-.036	
					(1.880)	(1.747)	-.935	
Burglary					-1.020	-1.008	-.174	
					(4.950)	(1.552)	(.959)	
Theft					-.782	.575	-.012	
					(4.112)	(.884)	(.315)	
Fraud					.588	-1.989	.076	
					(1.071)	(1.650)	.614	
Carr-Hill & Stern (1979) Engl. & Wales, All offences								
1961 urban	-.75[a]			-.14[d]	-.97[b]			-.12[c]
1966 urban	-.29[b]			-.17[c]	-.79[d]			-.28[a]
1971 pooled	-.62[b]			-.30[d]	-.80[d]			-.10
1961 urban		-.59[a]		-.27[a]		-1.00[b]		-.34[b]
1966 urban		-.43[a]		-.18[c]		-.84[b]		-.27[b]
1971 pooled		-.95[a]		-.42[b]		-.69[d]		-.36[b]
Willis (1983) Engl. & Wales, 1981								
Theft off.	-.776		-.452	-.298				
Violence off.	-.054	-1.319		-.016				
Sexual off.	-1.021		-.132	-.014				
Schuller (1986) Sweden								
All offences	-.28				-.50			
	(3.40)				(2.2)			

(Cont.)

Table 4.1 (cont.)
Elasticities of crime rates w.r.t. punishment variables

| Study, year, data | OLS | | | | 2SLS/3SLS/FIML[13] | | |
	P_A^3	Cert. P_C^4	$P_{C/A}^5$	Sev.	Cert. P_A	P_C	Sev. $P_{C/A}$
Holtman & Yap (1975) US							
Burglary						$-.81^b$	$-.22$
Robbery						$-.25$	$-.16$
Larceny						$.14$	$-.12$
Furlong & Mehey (1981), Montreal							
Robbery					$-.62$ (2.86)		
Burglary					$-.71$ (5.15)		
Theft					$-.92$ (1.80)		
Prop. crime					$-.58$ (1.80)		
All offences					$-.59$ (2.26)		
Danziger & Wheeler (1975) US							
Aggr. assault		$-.077$					
Robbery		$-.166$					
Burglary		$-.742^B$					
(1975)US SMSAs							
Aggr. assault		$-.077$					
Robbery		$-.510^B$		$.148$			
Burglary		$-.480^B$	$-.220$	$-.491^B$			
Heineke (1978) Substitution SMAS (pooled)							
Burglary					$-.343$†		$-.272$†
Robbery					$-.834$†		$-.569$†
Larceny					-1.137†		$-.914$†
Sesnowitz & Hexter 1982 US States							
Robbery						-1.62 (4.28)	$-.708$ (1.45)
Burglary						$-.62$ (3.92)	$-.59$ (2.13)
Blumstein & Nagin (1977) US States Draft evasion							
Linear f.		-1.62 (2.59)		$.078^{14}$ .58			
Logistic f.		$-.123$ (1.82)		$.10^{14}$ (.77)			

Notes: see next page.

Notes:

[1] The estimated coefficients of this table are all elasticities of the crime rate w.r.t the deterrent variables, except those of Thaler. These elacticities can be interpreted as showing the effect on the crime rate of a 1% change in the independent variable associated with the coefficient.

[2] t-values are printed in petit

[3] P_A=probability of arrest

[4] P_C=probability of conviction

[5] $P_{C/A}$=Probability of conviction given arrest

[6] Severity=mean length of imprisonment

[7] Only some of the results are reported here.

[8] Severity is measured by the fraction of commitments consisting of state imprisonment, probation with jail, and straight probation.

[9] Theft, auto theft, burglary, and robbery

[10] Robbery , burglary, and larceny

[11] Arrest clear-up ratio

[12] Police clear-up ratio

[13] FIML is used in Carr-Hill and Stone, 2SLS elsewhere

[14] Expected sentence

[a] Significant at the 1 % level, two-tailed test

[b] Significant at the 5 % level, two-tailed test

[c] Significant at the 10 % level, two-tailed test

[d] Significant at the 20 % level, two-tailed test

[A] Significant at the 1 % level, one-tailed test

[B] Significant at the 5 % level, one-tailed test

[C] Significant at the 10 % level, one-tailed test

*Estimated values at least twice of t-values or of standard errors

†Significance level or t-statistic not reported.

The main results concerning the impact of the deterrent variables on crime by use of the OLS and 2SLS methods are summarized in Table 4.1. The certainty variable (the probability of imprisonment) has a significantly negative effect on all types of crime, also for the cases not reported here. The coefficient of the severity variable is also negative for all cases, and significant in about half of them. These results are consistent with the deterrence hypothesis, and lend support to the model of rational criminal behaviour.

It is worth noticing that for most cases the certainty coefficient is higher than the severity coefficient, which also is in accordance with the theory. For rape, assault, burglary, and for the group of all crimes against the person, the difference between these coefficients is regarded as significant. These results are in agreement with the opinions of most criminal experts, as well as with the theoretical model of rational behaviour if potential criminals prefer risk. However, for burglary and larceny, and for assault in the 2SLS regression, the severity coefficient has a higher absolute value than the probability coefficient.

As explained in section 3.7, measurement errors may create a spurious negative correlation between the crime rate and the clear-up rate, a correlation that mistakenly may be interpreted as deterrence in an OLS estimation. On the other hand, if sanctions have an effect on crime, and crime has an effect on clear-ups, the estimation of the crime function by OLS tends to produce a simultaneity bias that shows up as a too low effect of the probability of punishment on crime. The 2SLS estimates of the certainty coefficients are about twice as high in absolute value as those of the OLS estimates. If society reacts to higher crime rates by producing a higher probability of being imprisoned, then the difference in results is as expected: The simultaneous estimation isolates the deterrent effect from the above mentioned positive effect of crime on the probability of imprisonment in the criminal justice system. Ehrlich does not report estimates of this latter impact.

It is also of interest to note that the deterrent effects do not seem to be less for crimes against the person than for other crimes - except that the severity of punishment does not have any significant impact on murder.

The main results for some of the sosioeconomic variables are given in Table 4.2.

The hypotheses that crime is positively related to income and to income differentials are strongly supported by the OLS estimates, almost all of which are significantly positive. The 2SLS estimates are less conclusive, although all estimates are positive, and those for property crimes as a group and for all crimes together significantly so. For murder, however, none of the estimates are significantly different from zero. The elasticities accociated with crimes against the person are not found to be lower than those associated with crimes against property.

Ehrlich regards his measure of income differential as a proxy for legal income, chosen for "statistical reasons". It is somewhat surprising that both income measures have

Table 4.2
Elacticities of crime rates w.r.t. socioeconomic variables[1,2]

Study	Legal income opport.	Income diffe- rential	Gain to crime	Unem- ploy- ment	Non- white propor.	Popula- tion density	Propor- tion of youth
Ehrlich (1973)[D]							
2SLS, 1960							
Murder		1.109	.175		.534		
Rape		.459	.409		.072		
Assault		1.707	1.650		.465		
Robbery		1.279	1.689		.334*		
Burglary		2.000*	1.384*		.250*		
Larceny		1.792	2.229		.142*		
Auto theft		2.057*	2.608		.102		
Crimes							
against pers.		.587	.328		.376*		
Property							
crimes		2.132*	1.883*		.243*		
All offences		1.775*	1.292*		.265*		
OLS, 1960							
Murder		1.364	.417		.553*		
Rape		.894	1.222*		.154*		
Assault		1.470*	2.094*		.677*		
Robbery		1.841*	2.909*		.376*		
Burglary		2.045*	1.797*		.227*		
Larceny		1.621*	2.689*		.132*		
Auto theft		1.898*	2.893*		.115*		
Crimes							
against pers.		.915*	1.046*		.490*		
All offences		1.801*	2.065*		.207*		
Forst (1976)[D]							
2SLS, 1970							
All offenses		.40	.60	.11	-.007	.71	.63
		(1.93)	(1.51)	(.21)	(1.51)	(2.17)	(1.45)
Vandaele (1978)[D]							
2SLS, 1960							
Murder		1.031*	.500	-.257	.539*		.977
Rape		-.073	.457	.344	.117		1.594*
Assault		1.809	2.332*	-.597	.334*		1.566
Robbery		1.669*	2.094*	-.878*	.252*		..
Burglary		1.644*	1.031*	.050	.290*		..
Larceny		1.905*	2.421*	.141	.126		..
Auto theft		1.649*	1.933*	-.187	.147*		..
All offences		1.625*	1.235*	-.127	.277*		
Myers (1980)[E]							
US Cities							
OLS							
Robbery	-.038		-.118				
	(.106)		(1.408)				
Burglary	-.779		-.103				
	(2.816)		(1.002)				
Larceny	-.766		-.355				
	(2.481)		(3.303)				
Auto theft	-.610		-.043				
	(1.393)		(.208)				

(Cont.)

Table 4.2 (cont.)
Elasticities of crime rates w.r.t. socioeconomic variables[1,2]

Study	Legal income opport.	Income diffe-rential	Gain to crime	Unemploy-ment	Non-white propor.	Popula-tion density	Propor-tion of youth
Myers (cont.)							
2SLS							
Robbery	-.037		-.116				
	(.105)		(1.386)				
Burglary	-.750		-.107				
	(2.621)		(1.005)				
Larceny	-.532		-.256				
	(1.682)		(2.309)				
Auto theft	-.627		-.061				
	(1.412)		(-.298)				
Swimmer (1974)[F]							
US cities, 2SLS							
Murder	-.107[a]	.017		.016	.045[b]		.016
Rape	-.025	-.004		-.088	.038[b]		.003
Assault	.008	.016		.028	.037[a]		-.066[a]
Robbery	-.007	.052[b]		.048	.029[a]		-.026
Burglary	-.008	.036[a]		.015	.006		.001
Larceny	.008	.026[d]		.016	.000		.006
Auto theft	-.007	.044[a]		.025	-.004		.026[a]
Mathur (1978)[F]							
US cities 1970							
Murder	-5.39[D]	-2.43[c]		.042[d]	.051[b]		
Robbery	-6.15[D]	2.29[d]		-.007	.044[b]		
Burglary	-6.37[D]	1.54[c]		.037[c]	.013[b]		
Assault	-4.96[D]	-.89		.009	.032[b]		
Rape	-9.77[D]	1.02		.009	.037[b]		
Auto theft	-5.78[D]	.09		.093[c]	.018[b]		
Larceny	-6.57[D]	-1.20		.135[b]	.013[b]		
Chapman (1976)[F]							
California, towns							
1960&1970							
Property cr.[3]	.26[A]			1.80[A]	.09[A]		
Murder,assault				1.15[B]	.2[A]		
Sjøquist (1973)[G]							
US munici-palities 1968							
Prop. crimes[4]							
Regression 1	.142		.167		.126[A]	.051	
Regression 2	.205		.071		.140[A]	.087	
Regression 3	.349		-.111		.121[A]	.208	
Regression 4	.200		.088		.142[A]	.077	
Mathieson &							
Passell[E] (1976),							
NY Precincts,							
1971							
Homicide	-3.30		.061				
	(5.17)		(.35)				
Robbery	-1.75		.499				
	(2.49)		(2.94)				

(Cont.)

Table 4.2 (cont.)
Elasticities of crime rates w.r.t. socioeconomic variables[1,2]

Study	Legal income opport	Income differential	Gain to crime	Unemployment	Non-white propor.	Population density	Proportion of youth
Thaler (1977), NY, Rochester 1972							
Property cr.[4]		-.0003 (.86)					
Property cr.[4]		-.0002 (.59)					
Avio & Clark (1978)[E,7] Ontario, 1971							
Robbery			3.110 (2.891)	.856 (1.603)	.076 (.582)		2.322 (1.225)
Burglary			.153 (.236)	.761 (2.290)	.144 (1.957)		3.191 (2.678)
Theft			.980 (2.139)	.671 (2.401)	-.033 (-.515)		1.195 (1.179)
Fraud			1.957 (2.534)	.173 (.445)	.003 (.031)		1.534 (.938)
Carr-Hill & Stern (1979) Engl. & Wales							
All offences							
OLS							
Clear-ups							
1961 urban			.13[b]				-.03
1966 urban			.14[b]				.49[a]
1971 pooled			.09[b]				.04
Convictions							
1961 urban			.19[a]				-.03
1966 urban			.14[a]				.50[a]
1971 pooled			.17[a]				.36
2SLS (or FIML?)							
Clear-ups							
1961 urban			.15[a]				-.01
1966 urban			.17[a]				.53[a]
1971 pooled			.09[b]				.07
Convictions							
1961 urban			.21[a]				-.18
1966 urban			.15[a]				.51[a]
1971 pooled			.17[b]				.36
Willis (1983)[I], Engl. & Wales, 1981							
Theft off.	.483		.069	.197*		.109*	
Violence off.			-.043	.194*		.047	
Sexual off.			-.161	.132		.075	

(Cont.)

Table 4.2 (cont.)
Elasticities of crime rates w.r.t. socioeconomic variables[1,2]

Study	Legal income opport.	Income differential	Gain to crime	Unemployment	Non-white propor.	Population density	Proportion of youth
Schuller (1986)[E]							
Sweden							
All offences							
OLS	-.07			-.09			.55
	(.42)			(2.07)			(2.30)
3SLS	-.05			-.08			.23
	(.26)			(1.71)			(.94)
Holtman & Yap							
(1978)[E], US States							
Burglary	-1.69[b]	1.05[c]	3.71[b]	.19	.21[b]		
Robbery	.16	2.92[b]	5.12[b]	-1.02[b]	.32[b]		
Larceny	-1.98[b]	1.75[b]	4.65[b]	.41[c]	.10		
Danziger &							
Wheeler (1975)							
US SMSAa							
Aggr. assault		-.716		-.115	.531	-.047	.217
		(.54)		(.329)	(4.37)	(.28)	(.404)
Robbery		-1.290		-.037	.312	.295	(-.872)
		(1.05)		(.12)	(2.87)	(1.92)	1.76
Burglary		-1.172		-.049	.148	-.034	-.376
		(1.37)		(.219)	(1.82)	(.32)	(1.08)
Heineke (1978)[I]							
Substitution							
SMSA (pooled)							
Burglary	-.079*		2.051				
Robbery	-.194*		1.947				
Larceny	-.012*		1.565				

[1]The estimated coefficients of this table, except those of Swimmer and Thaler, are all elasticites of the crime rate w.r.t. income, taste, and other socioeconomic variables. These elacticities can be interpreted as showing the effect on the crime rate of a 1% change in the independent variable associated with the coefficient.

[2]t-values are printed in petit.

[3]Theft, auto theft, burglary, and robbery.

[4]Robbery , burglary, and larceny.

[5]Arrest clear-up ratio.

[6]Police clear-up ratio.

[7]Non-white=indian.

[a]Significant at the 1 % level, two-tailed test.

[b]Significant at the 5 % level, two-tailed test.

[c]Significant at the 10 % level, two-tailed test.

[d]Significant at the 20 % level, two-tailed test.

*Estimated values at least twice of t-value or of standard error.

[D]As proxy for gain to crime: median family income.

As proxy for legal income opportunity:

[E]Median family income;

[F]Median income;

[G]Annual labour income;

[H]Mean family income;

[I]Mean income per tax unit;

[J]Mean income per capita.

significant effects upon crime. Ehrlich explains this result by assuming that violent crimes are "time-intensive consumption activities" competing with income-generating legal and illegal activities. An increase in the income differential reduces the cost (income foregone) that accompanies this kind of consumption, resulting in an increase in violent crime. If, however, an increase in the income differential creates cultural deviance or anomie, this increase in violent crime may be explained by changes in norms (less allegiance to the social contract) and wants (hatred, malevolence). This is a pertinent example of how a given empirical study may be taken as corroboration of different theories.

In the 2SLS regression the non-white estimate is significantly positive except for murder, rape, and assault.

In a separate regression analysis Ehrlich introduces three more variables in his supply-of-crime relation: unemployment rates and labour-force participation for males in the age estimated coefficients of the variables are found to be significant, and the other estimates do not change noticeably through the inclusion of these variables. A possible reason for these results might be lack of variation across municipalities in the data on the three additional variables.

Ehrlich's study has been thoroughly scrutinized by several authors, some of whom have given harsh evaluations of his work. Forst (1976) has repeated Ehrlich's study of all offences (index crimes) by using 1970 data instead of 1960 data. The results, included in Tables 4.1 and 4.2, show a more moderate effect on crime of all explanatory variables. Forst suggests that the difference may come from an increased court leniency during the 1960s, or from an even less accurate measure of the true crime rate in 1960 than it was in 1970, cf section 3.7 above.

Forst's main concern, however, is different. He suggests that the effect on crime of some of the explanatory variables in Ehrlich's crime function is spurious. Especially, he maintains that the effect of the probability of imprisonment and the average prison terms reflect the effect of variables not included in the crime function, variables correlated with that probability. He then adds seven variables, two of which are population migration and population density. These two are considered to "reflect characteristics of potential victims". (This perspective is further elaborated in the routine activity approach discussed in section 4.8.1 below.)

Using 1970 data in estimating a model somewhat different from Ehrlich's, Forst finds, as expected, that both migration and density of population have a significant positive effect on crime, while the probability of imprisonment and average sentence are found to be statistically insignificant.

However, in explaining further the reasons for introducing the migration and density variables, Forst mainly emphasizes that the "probability of successful crime commission" is higher the more there is of migration in an area and the more densely populated it is.[4] If Forst by "probability of successful crime commission" means "probability of not being punished", he may in fact have introduced two other proxies for the subjective probability of punishment. One may presume that offenders, when evaluating the probability of punishment, do not look into statistics, but assess the particular environment of the considered crime. If high migration and high population density reduce the probability of being detected, apprehended, and imprisoned, Forst's two variables may just reflect the risk evaluation of the offenders. Considering crime as individual rational choice implies that it is not the registered risk, but the individual's own subjective assessment of the probabilities of being arrested, convicted or jailed that counts. This assessment is certainly based on information from various sources, and official statistics may perhaps not be an important one. This does not mean that the probability of punishment is unimportant, only that Forst may have found better proxies than Ehrlich. Forst concludes (p. 490): "The evidence suggests strongly that Ehrlich's crime-deterrence variables are, to a large degree, substitutes for demographic factors that are real determinants of crime but that are not included in Ehrlich's "supply-of offences" equation". One may, however, ask what is meant by "real determinants of crime". High migration and density of population may, in addition to probability of punishment, also reflect economic conditions (better income opportunities for illegal behaviour?), tastes (more intense wants for certain outcomes?), or norms (more permissive?). These various interpretations are not arguments against the use of the two variables in estimating a crime function, just a warning against easy interpretations.

Forst also finds both the proportion of households that are not husband-wife households and a measure of income dispersion to have significant positive effects on crime (at a 10% significance level). The proportions of males, youth, non-whites and unemployed seem to be of less, or no importance in explaining cross-state differences in crime.

Forst has estimated his model both when the variables are included multiplicatively and when they are included additively. Forst finds that the latter form performs slightly better. It is interesting to note that this form gives lower estimates of the punishment variables than the former.

Nagin (1987) suggests that incapacitating effects might be confounded with deterrence

---

[4]"I used population migration ... and density ... variables because I see them as reflecting the potential vulnerability of a victim population. It seems reasonable to expect that places with higher rates of population migration and density are more vulnerable, because, there, randomly selected residents are less likely to know one another; since a higher proportion of people there than elsewhere are strangers, any particular stranger is likely to be less closely monitored than in a neighborhood where persons are more familiar with one another. I expect, therefore, a priori, that criminals perceive a higher probability of successful crime commission in a place with either high population migration or high density, other things being equal, than in a place with a low rate of either." (Forst, 481-2).

in Ehrlich's study. Using a method of estimation of the effect of incapacitation developed by Shinnar and Shinnar (1975) on Ehrlich's 1960 data, the estimates of the effects on crime of the probability and the severity of imprisonment are found to be almost halved.

In a thorough revision of Ehrlich's study Vandaele (1978) reveals several inaccuracies and errors in both data and results. As a whole, however, the corrected estimates confirm (or at least do not contradict) Ehrlich's results. Vandaele's estimates of the elasticities of crime rates with respect to punishment variables are at most about 10% lower in absolute values than those reproduced in Table 4.1.

More fascinating is Vandeale's investigation into how sensitive Ehrlich's results are to exclusion of outliers and to changes in model specifications. He concludes (p. 280) that "with the exception of the instability in both the murder and assault crime equation, the results obtained within the framework of Ehrlich's model are not sensitive to modifications in the identification or the [U.S.] states included in the analysis".

Brier and Fienberg (1980) present a long list of objections to Ehrlich's study. Most of these objections are relevant for macro studies of crime in general, and I have dealt with them in various sections of this book, especially in Chapters 2 and 3.

Pogue (1975) has studied the effect of police expenditures on crime rates employing data for Standard Metropolitan Statistical Areas (SMASs) in the U.S. for the years 1962, 1967 and 1968. His theoretical model consists of a specification of (4.1)-(4.3), and he includes 12 exogenous, environmental variables in estimating linear and log-linear specifications of his model by 2SLS.

The clear-up ratios are found to have a negative effect on each of the seven felony crimes, and also on total crime, where 66 SMSAs are included. The magnitudes of the coefficents, however, vary. Pogue presents the figures for the log-linear specification, but reports that the linear specification gave similar results.

In a separate estimation a sentence severity index is also included: the difference between the sentences actually given for each type of crime by the US District Court(s) in the SMSA and the sentences that would have been given if the District Court had given the same sentence for each type of crime that on average was given by all District Courts. The coefficients of this variable are reported to be significantly positive for all crimes except burglary and grand larceny (where they are insignificant). The other coefficients, however, are largely unaffected by this severity variable. Pogue remarks that his result on the effect of the severity of punishment on crime is in contrast to the deterrent effects obtained by Gibbs (1969), Tittle (1969), and Gray and Martin (1969). He adds, however, that "further comparison and reconciliation of these results is difficult because the studies employ different measures of severity, units of observation and control (environmental) variables.".

The results support the hypotheses that crime rates are directly (positively) related to per capita income, poverty (percentage of households with income below $3000), proportion of youth, (percentage of population aged 12-17 and 18-24)), and city size (total population of SMSA). The results further show that the proportion of whites has a negative effect on crime. The author also finds that the population density has a negative effect, but this conclusion is hardly supported by his publicised estimates. Unemployment rates and education levels appear to have little systematic impact on crime rates.

Greenwood and Wadycki (1973 and 1975) estimate crime functions for crimes against property and crimes against persons where the crime rates are assumed to be functions of per capita police employees and some sociodemographic variables. The per capita police employees are assumed to be functions of the expenditures on police which again are postulated to be functions of the crime rates, per capita property taxes, and median income.

A 3SLS procedure was followed utilizing FBI data from 1960 on 199 SMSAs in the US.

The results show that the per capita police employees exerted a significant positive influence on both aforementioned crime rates, a fact the authors find expresses the crime detection effect of the police. The possible crime prevention effect is not present, or is too small, to outweigh the detection effect. Population density is found to have no significant effect on crime, a result at variance with what is argued in traditional criminological work. Neither the anonymity nor the target argument of population density is thus corroborated. The results indicate a slight positive effect of poverty (measured by the percentage of families with annual income below $3000), higher for crimes against persons than for crimes against property. The value of owner-occupied housing, assumed to reflect the benefits to the lawbreaker of committing crimes against property, obtains the expected positive effect on such crime. An increase in crime rates induces an increase in police expenditures, which again induces an increase in the per capita police employees. Taxes and mean income also have a significant positive effect on police expenditures.

In a study of crime in 50 counties in California in 1966 Phillips and Votey (1975) emphasize the construction of supply and demand functions for law enforcement personnel as a basis for specifying (4.3).[5] Estimating a log linear version of (4.1)-(4.3) they find that the conviction ratio has the expected sign and is highly significant. Severe sentences also have a negative and significant effect on crime. Mild sentences have the same sign, but the coefficients are not significantly different from zero.

Phillips and Votey introduce twelve variables in order to characterize the demographic and socioeconomic features of the counties which could hypothetically be associated with

---

[5]This article is reproduced in a slightly different form, and with a more elaborate conclusion, in Phillips & Votey (1981), together with some other studies of crime. This book is a treat for those who prefer equations explained graphically and in detail.

the incidence of crime. A principal component analysis of these variables leads to the inclusion of just one principal component in the crime function, an index interpreted as representing frustrated economic ambition. This index assigns high positive weights to the percentage of population unemployed, the population of males 18-24 years old in the labour force, and population density. This index is found to be highly significant. But it is noteworthy that the other socioeconomic indices in the preliminary regression analysis are found not to be significant: urban and ethnic variables do not play a prominent role, and the authors conclude that measures of economic conditions are more important than purely demographic measures.

On the question of identification Phillips and Votey (1981, 257) state that "[i]t would be farfetched to argue that the extent of economic opportunities in the general economy has much to do with police ability to make arrests and procure convictions" (the index of socioeconomic factors is excluded from the specification of (4.2)) "or that the level of police manpower should have an effect in determining offenses independent of their impact through the probability of arrests" (the criminal justice personel per capita is excluded from the specification of (4.1)). The real sceptics would perhaps hesitate to join the authors on this point.

The degree of underreporting of crime has been investigated through victimization studies by Ennis (1967), Skogan (1974), Sparks et al. (1977), Hindelang and Gottfredson (1976), Dodge et al. (1976), and others. Two views regarding nonreporting of crimes have emerged.

The first view is sometimes presented as economic or utilitarian (Myers Jr. 1980, p. 24): A crime is reported to the police only if the sum of monetary and psychic costs and benefits to the victim is positive. Victims might choose not to report because reporting is time-consuming, because of beliefs that reporting will not result in recovery of stolen or damaged property, because of beliefs that the offender will not be punished, or because of anxiety of retaliation by the offender or by arrest of innocents. Reporting will presumably be higher the higher the value of the property stolen or damaged, and the higher the possible recovery. One would expect such costs and benefits to depend on income and on different social and demographic attributes of the individuals.

The other view is related to the characteristics of the incident: the degree of reporting depends on the seriousness of the crime, the victim's relationship to the offender, and the degree of completion of the crime.

Also the incident-specific view depends on the victim's assessment of the total costs and benefits of reporting, and on his choice being rational in the sense discussed in this book. What is regarded as important factors for the choice is, however, different for the two views.

In addition, costs and benefits may determine to which extent reported crimes are officially registered by the police.

Empirical studies of these views give weak and somewhat conflicting results. Dodge et al. (1976) find nonreporting dependent on age, race, and sex, but statistical tests of these results are not given. Hindelang and Gottfredson (1976) find that income has a slight positive effect on reporting. Skogan (1976) and Sparks et al. (1977) do not find such relationships. They report results corroborating the incident-specific view.

Myers Jr. (1980) estimates supply-of-offences functions for four crime categories for cities in the U.S. using corrected crime rates obtained from victimization studies instead of official crime rates. The corrected crime rates are found by estimating a logit function where the odds in favour of reporting are a function of various variables representing hypothesized costs and benefits of reporting. Explanatory variables of the supply of offence functions are the average values of the stolen goods of robbery, burglary, larceny and auto theft, the probability of arrest, the arrest ratio, the probability of punishment (measured by the number of court commitments to prison per offence of relevant crime category), average length of sentence served, mean family income, and public assistance income for families. Almost all coefficients on punishment variables were found to be negative, and a majority of them significantly so. Comparing estimates using official and corrected crime rates, Myers Jr. concludes that for robbery, burglary, and auto theft, "correction for underreporting leads to revised coefficient estimates differing from the original estimates by only about 5 to 15%."

Both average income and welfare benefits are found to have consistently negative, and in most cases significant, effects upon the four types of crime.

Myers Jr. (1982) has also used victimization data in a study based on a mean-variance specification of the crime supply function. "Offenders are assumed to face two income-earning activities, work and crime, both receiving uncertain returns. For returns independently, identically, and normally distributed, or for identical utility functions quadratic in income, it can be shown that the urban supply of crime will be a function of the expected rate of return to crime, $E(r_c)$, the expected rate of return to work, $E(r_w)$, the variances of returns to crime and work, $Var(r_c)$, $Var(r_w)$, and the covariance of returns to crime and work, $Cov(r_c, r_w)$."[6] By introducing variances of the returns into his model specification, Myers Jr. is relating his empirical work more closely to the theoretical portfolio choice models of section 2.2 than what is common in criminometric work.[7] The linear specification of the crime function

---

[6]Myers Jr. (1982, p.150).

[7]Cf Appendix C to Chapter 2.

$$C = Ae(r_c) + Be(r_w)Cvar(r_c) + Dvar(r_w) + Ecov(r_c, r_w),$$

together with a law enforcement equation, is estimated for four types of crime by 2SLS, using data for US cities.

Negative estimates of c are obtained, a result that is in accordance with theory if people are risk averse: increased risk in crime reduces participation in crime. The estimated effects of increased expected returns to crime and to work are either insignificant or differ between types of crime.

The effect on crime of more or less "aggressiveness" in police activity is given special emphasis in a study by Wilson and Boland (1978). Utilizing 1975 data on robberies in 35 large US cities they estimate by 2SLS a four equation model including a robbery crime rate equation. The coefficient on the robbery arrest ratio in this equation is found to be negative, and significantly so. The percentage of non-whites and the population density is found to be directly and significantly related to the robbery ratio. A proxy for "police aggressiveness", moving citations per patrol unit, is found to have a highly significant positive effect on the robbery arrest ratio, and thus on the crime ratio. Similar significant results are not obtained for burglary and auto theft using 1975 data, whereas 1970 data give results more in line with the robbery results for 1975.

Swimmer (1974) estimates a specification of (4.1) and (4.3) for the seven FBI felonies using data for all cities in the US with 100,000 or more residents in 1960. Police expenditure (but not the probability of arrest or conviction) is an explanatory variable in the crime function, whereas the crime rate is an explanatory variable in the police expenditure function. Swimmer uses a semilogarthmic specification of the crime function, i.e. the log of the crime rate is assumed to be a linear function of the explanatory variables.

Both OLS and 2SLS are employed, and, in accordance with statistical theory, the negative effect of police expenditure on crime is higher for 2SLS than for OLS. The former method gives significant negative estimates of this effect for a majority of types of crime.

The expected sentence (which in this study lumps together the probability and severity of punishment) is found to have a negative effect upon crime, and significantly so for aggravated assault, robbery and burglary (see Table 4.1), whereas the unemployment rate, the proportion of youth, the north-south dummy, and median income, do not have significant effects (see Table 4.2). The percentage of poor and rich families, assumed to measure the gain from economic crimes, is highly significant in all property crime equations (except larceny where it is significant only at 20 percent).

Mathur (1978) uses the same data as Swimmer to estimate a specification of (4.1)-(4.3). Separate estimates are obtained for each of the seven FBI felonies by use of the 2SLS technique. Mathur finds that for most types of crime both certainty and severity of punishment have negative and statistically significant effects upon crime for 1960 and 1970. The proportion of non-whites is found to have a consistent and significant positive effect. Unemployment mostly has a positive effect, but significantly so only in 1960. The estimates for median income, the Gini coefficient for income inequality, median years of schooling, and percentage of white-collar inhabitants are inconclusive.

The estimation of the police production function reveals that for 1960 police expenditures have mixed (insignificant or significant positive or negative) effects on the probabilities of arrest for different crimes, whereas in 1970 the effects are negative for all cases except murder. For murder the relationship is significantly positive for both years. Mathur explains (p. 465) that "this result could mean either that when police departments devote most of their efforts towards solving murders, it could decrease the probability of apprehension and punishment for other crimes in spite of the increase in police expenditure; or that increased expenditure results in more reported crimes as opposed to admissions in prisons thereby causing the certainty index to fall for most crimes."

The certainty of punishment for all crimes, except grand larceny in 1970, varies inversely with crime rates for both years, and the coefficients are statistically significant in the majority of cases. For almost all cases the severity is found to have a negative effect upon certainty, perhaps reflecting that the juries tend to find the defendant guilty of a lesser offence when severe punishment is involved.

Chapman (1976) estimates a three equation model using pooled cross-section data for the years 1960 and 1970 from 147 towns in California. The equations are specified in a linear form, and the whole model is estimated by use of the 2SLS method. The arrest rate is found to have a negative effect on both property crimes and violent crimes, but significantly so only on the former type. The employment variable is found to have a negative and significant effect upon both types of crime, whereas the percent of non-whites has a significant positive effect.

On the basis of a model of criminal behaviour similar to that of Becker, Sjoquist (1973) has estimated crime functions for a cross section of 53 medium sized municipalities in the US using data from 1968.

Only property crimes are studied: the dependent variable is the per capita number of reported robberies, burglaries, and larcenies over $50. Three different variables representing the probability of punishment are studied: the probability of arrest, P_A, the probability of conviction, P_C, and the probability of conviction given arrest, $P_{C/A}$. Being a conditional probability, the latter measure would be expected to have a smaller impact on crime than the others. The severity variable used is average prison sentence served. Sjoquist uses a log linear crime function, which was estimated by use of OLS. Ten regressions were performed for various combinations of the deterrent and other variables. The results for the deterrent variables for four of these regressions are given in Table 4.1. For all regressions the coefficients for these variables are in accordance with the theoretical model: All signs are as expected, but not all estimates are statistically significant.

The estimated coefficients for the annual sales per establishment are positive in three of the regressions and negative in one, and none of them are significantly different from zero. The result probably reflects the fact that this variable is a rather crude measure of the gain to criminal activity.

The estimated coefficients for legal income are positive in all four regressions, although not significant. This result does not support the hypothesis that a higher legal average income will stimulate legal activity at the expense of illegal. Sjoquist suggests that average income could be a measure of the gain to illegal activity as well, and that the sign of the estimate could go both ways. The mean school years is found to have a positive impact on crime, although not highly significant. Furthermore, the coefficient on the density of population is found to be positive, but not significantly different from zero. The coefficients on the unemployment rate are significantly positive for all alternatives, whereas the proportion of low income families obtains mixed coefficients. The non-white coefficients are significantly positive in all regressions, also in those where the unemployment rate and the proportion of low income families are included.

Mathieson and Passell (1976) estimate a log linear specification of (4.1)-(4.3) using data on homicide and robbery for New York City police precincts.

The probability of arrest appears to have a negative and highly significant effect on both homicide and robbery applying both OLS and 2SLS. The median income has the expected negative impact on crime in all four cases, and significantly so in three.[8] As expected, the proportion of rich families (availability of high income victims) has a positive effect in all four cases, but significant (at 1%) only in one.

Thaler (1977) estimates by 2SLS a four-equation model of property crime (robbery, burglary, and larceny) utilizing 1970 data from 89 census tracts in Rochester, New York.

---

[8]The authors comment on these results as follows (p.89-90): "First, that the negative elasticity of homicide with respect to median income is generated by a rational response (whatever the motive) to the costs associated with punishment - *ceteris paribus*, the opportunity cost of prison is less for a poor man than for a rich person. Equally plausible is the possibility that crimes of passion are not explained by the variables in the equation, but the incidence of death resulting from assault depends upon the availability of lethal weapons. Poor neighborhoods have substantially higher crime incidence, and it is likely that a higher percentage of poor people possess handguns for self-defense.

Similarly one could explain the negative elasticity of homicide with respect to the probability of apprehension either in strictly rational terms or as an accidental correlation based on misspecification. In neighborhoods where there are many homicides per capita, the arrest/crime ratio is generally low. This may be because the possibility of apprehension genuinely deters murder, or it may be that the police devote fewer resources to solving murders in low-income neighborhoods (where crime rates are high) than in high-income neighborhoods (where crime rates are low)."

In addition to (4.1)-(4.3), he includes an equation expressing the proportion of criminals of each tract as a function of sociodemographic variables. As a proxy for the number of criminals the number of arrestees living in each tract is employed.

Thaler uses two different certainty measures in separate estimations: the police clear-up ratio and the arrest clear-up ratio. The former, which is used by most police departments, is obtained by including not only those crimes that are the direct causes of the arrests, but also other crimes confessed by the arrested persons. The latter is obtained by considering only those crimes for which the arrests are the direct causes. The police clear-up ratio will thus be higher than the arrest clear-up ratio.

Thaler finds that the (proxy for the) number of criminals is strongly related to the offence rate, whereas the police presence does not appear to have any significant influence on property crime. The police clear-up ratio has a negative and significant effect on the offence rate, whereas the arrest clear-up ratio is statistically insignificant.

Thaler also finds some support for the view that "the effect of more police is to increase the reporting of crime more than it deters the commission of crime".

McPheters (1978) has estimated a two equation model of total crime utilizing FBI 1975 data of crime on American campuses. A 2SLS procedure is used to estimate a crime rate function and a function explaining security expenditures on the campuses. The only deterrent variable in the crime rate function is the security expenditures, whereas the rest of the variables represent characteristics of the campuses and their environments.

A striking result is the positive and highly significant relationship between security expenditures and crime rate. The author suggests that this unexpected result might be explained, not only by a lack of deterrent effect of security activity, but also by a willingness to report more crimes to a well-equipped security force, and because such a force discovers more crime than forces with fewer resources.

Employing census data for up to 37 areas in Ontario, Avio and Clark (1978) estimate a log linear specification of (4.1)-(4.3) for four types of property crimes. The results show that the clear-up ratio has a negative and significant effect on robbery, break and enter, and theft, whereas the effect on fraud is insignificant (and positive). The conviction ratio, conditional upon arrest, also has a negative effect on three of the property crimes, but the estimates are not significant. The same holds true for the expected sentence length. The rate of unemployment, considered to express the opportunity cost of crime, has as expected a positive and mostly significant effect on crime. A similar result is obtained for the average income, considered to be proxy for the "victim stock" and thus capturing the expected gains from property crimes.

As a measure of the severity of punishment, Avio and Clark use the length of the sentences of offenders convicted during the period, rather than that of released offenders, which has been used in several other studies. Although the authors find their own measure superior, no significant effect on crime is obtained.

The problem of possible spill-overs of crime from areas with high to those with low clear-up ratio are studied by including into each crime supply equation the minimum clear-up ratio among contiguous neighbouring areas. The coefficients for these variables are all insignificant. This result is slightly at variance with that of Mehay (1977) who reports a statistically significant but "relatively minor" effect of spill-overs between police districts in Los Angeles. It seems reasonable, however, that spillover is more prominent in an urban area like Los Angeles than in a vast state like Ontario.

In an attempt to test the hypothesis that crime categories may be substitutes or complements, clear-up ratios for various property crimes were sequentially included in each supply equation. None of the cross-elasticities are found to be statistically significant.

In an earlier study employing pooled time-series cross section data for Canadian provinces Avio and Clark (1976) found support for the hypothesis that the certainty of punishment has a negative effect on crime. No consistent effect of the expected sentence length was found.

In a comprehensive monograph Carr-Hill and Stern (1979) have used data for police districts in England and Wales in cross section studies of total recorded crime for the years 1961, 1966, and 1971. The data differ sharply from those used in many US studies in that they also include a large number of thefts of low property value. In constructing their model the authors have made extensive references to various theories of crime, including theories of labelling, of deterrence/incentives, and to "traditional" criminology. Finding it impossible to include all desirable aspects of crime in their model, they end up with three relations: one determining the recorded number of offences as a function of deterrence/incentive factors and labelling habits of the society (especially of the police), another determining the proportion of offences solved as a function of offences, police resources and police work load, and a third determining the number of police officers as a function of offences, detection rate, and some social characteristics of the police districts. Labelling habits are modelled by introducing the proportions of young males and of working class in the crime function, assuming that members of these groups run a greater risk than others to be reported and registered as criminals for acts that are equally common to all. High proportions of these groups are expected to give high recorded offence rates.

It is clear that both the detection rate and the severity of punishment affect the recorded offence in the direction predicted by deterrence theories. The effect of the proportion of young people on the recorded offence rate was not uniform over the years, being negative (significant at 20%) in 1961, positive (significant at 5%) in 1966 and not significant in 1971. When explaining these results the authors refer to changing relationships (antagonism) between the police and young people during the period. The proportion of working class people mostly has a positive and significant effect on the recorded offence rate for all data sets. This result may corroborate either the labelling theory or the traditional explanation that the workers are more criminogenic than others. Discussing the results, the authors do not consider explicitly the possibility that the proportion of working class people might reflect income differences that again might be an incentive to crime.

A rather unexpected result is that for most data sets more police tend to have a negative effect on the clear-up ratio. (The effect on the conviction ratio is less uniform.) An explanation of this result might be that more offences, especially offences difficult to clear up, will be reported if there are many police officers around. More police officers might also deter offences that are relatively easy to detect, thus reducing the recorded detection rate. These effects work in opposite direction of the assumed "creating effect", where more police officers make it possible to record more of the minor offences that are easy to detect, and that are not recorded when police officers are scarce. The combination of these, and possibly other effects, might explain why more police do not produce more recorded detection.

The total ratable value is found to have a positive and highly significant effect on the offence rate for almost all data sets.

Carr-Hill and Stern also present the reduced form of the estimated model. This form makes it possible to assess the effects of changes in the exogenous variables on the recorded offence rate, the recorded detection rate and the size of the police force. Assuming that the model is an acceptable representation of how society functions, it is only through the exogenous variables that the three above mentioned endogenous variables can be affected. Surprisingly, many studies do not present the reduced form solution, although policy issues often are discussed.

Willis (1983) has estimated crime functions for theft, violent offences, and sexual offences for police districts in England and Wales utilizing data from 1981. Compared with the study of Carr-Hill and Stern (1974), who analysed "all indictable offences" taken together, Willis has also incorporated more economic factors and has used more recent data. For all three categories of offences the coefficients on the clear-up rate, the conviction rate, and the combined imprisonment/custodial sentence rate are found to be negative, but significantly so only in some of the cases. Willis finds support for the hypothesis that unemployment reflects low opportunity costs of engaging in all three categories of illegal activities. A further reported result is that both the amount of unrecovered property and the ratable value of property of an area have no significant effect upon crime. Willis finds the population density to have a positive and significant effect on theft and violent offences, but remarks that density is a kind of "an aggregate proxy variable for all environmental pollutants".

In a comprehensive study of crime in Sweden Schuller (1986) has estimated crime models using both cross section and time series data. In the cross section part he uses average data from 1975 and 1976 on 278 municipalities to estimate a log linear specification of (4.1)-(4.3). As estimating techniques 3SLS, 2SLS, SURE, and OLS are used, all producing the same signs for the coefficients discussed here.

As expected by Schuller, the effect on crime of the clear-up probability is found to be significantly negative. The coefficients on income and on the proportion of people living in separate houses are also negative, and that of the proportion of population on welfare programmes (a poverty variable) positive, but only the latter two are significantly different from zero. The demographic variables also have the expected effects: crime is positively related to the proportion of the population that has moved into the municipality recently (a variable indicating the degree of social control), the population of the biggest town in the municipality, and the proportion of population 10-24 years old.

Using data from the same municipalities and years, Sandelin and Skogh (1986) obtain more or less similar results. In addition, they find that church attendance (representing "moral attitudes" has a negative effect on crime.

Furlong and Mehay (1981) estimate for various types of crime a specification of (4.1)-(4.3) using data from 38 police districts in Montreal in Canada. The effect of the clear-up rate on crime is found to be negative for all crime categories (robbery, burglary, theft, property crimes in all, and all crimes) studied. The same holds true for the proportion of young males, and also for the spill-over effect showing that some offenders are attracted by higher gains to crime in adjacent districts. Unexpectedly, the unemployment rate has a positive effect. The effects of the other variables differ somewhat between crime categories, and are partly statistically insignificant.

Using both aggregate and individual recidivism data from counties in North Carolina Trumbull (1989) emphasizes the complementarity of such studies. Aggregate data may be employed to analyse general deterrence, whereas individual data on recidivism[9] may be used to analyse special deterrence. Using a Hausmann specification test Trumbull finds that the data rejects the hypothesis that there is simultaneity between the crime rate and police and arrest variables, and OLS is therefore appropriate.

Trumbull finds highly significant negative effects on crime of the probabilities of arrest, of conviction, of imprisonment, and of the length of sentence. Police employment per

---

[9]According to Trumbull the only individual data available are data on people who have been in prison. In section 4.6 below, where also Trumbull's results on special deterrence are presented, I review some studies of breach of tax laws that perhaps can be considered as studies of general deterrence. In addition, self-reports may also be used to study general deterrence.

capita has a significant positive effect on crime, possibly reflecting a more complete recording of crime when manpower is relatively affluent. High population density and urbanization is also found to increase crime, as well as the proportion of non-whites, whereas unemployment unexpectedly has the opposite effect. Per capita income, and the proportion of youth do not have statistically significant effects.

Danziger and Wheeler (1975) have tested the hypothesis that increasing inequality is accompanied by more crime. Using US data for the period 1949-1970 they estimate, in a time series OLS regression, crime functions for burglary, aggravated assault and robbery. Similar functions are also estimated by use of 1960 data for 57 large US SMSAs.

Danziger and Wheeler assume that crime arises from utility maximization of rational individuals when utility functions are interdependent. They "hypothesize that the relative level of legitimate returns is an essential argument" in the economic calculus of costs and benefits of legal and illegal activities. They posit that an individual's utility is not a function of his income, but of 1) the distance between this income and the average income of a reference group, and 2) a measure of relative income inequality across the entire income distribution. An increase in the first measure (the absolute income gap) will reduce utility. Two reactions are possible: the individual will work more in order to reduce the gap, or "strike out at the system by resorting to illegal activities" (p. 116). The latter solution may be accompanied by "feelings of malice and envy, if the poor come to view the system as 'rigged' against them" (p.117). This is apparently a kind of cultural deviance, anomie, or differential association caused by low relative income, and resulting in more crime prone norms.

Danziger and Wheeler further suggest that "[i]n addition to economic conditions, an individual's allegiance to societal norms can motivate malevolence. It is assumed that all individuals are distributed across some 'social contract tolerance index'", which is a function of variables expressing "the socioeconomic or psychological background of the individual - his taste for risk, his level of education, his peer group relations, the cohesiveness of his neighbourhood and stability of his family, his age, local labor market conditions, etc." (p. 117). These variables apparently include factors characterizing preferences (taste for risk), abilities (level of education), opportunities for legal income, norm forming environment, etc. It is thus slightly odd to group all these factors in a single index. It is probably done because the authors want to stress that these factors may produce a deviant attitude towards society. But they then disregard several other mechanisms that the same factors may represent.

The crime function, estimated by use of times series data, contains, in addition to the two income inequality measures, three punishment variables (the probabilities of being charged, found guilty, and imprisoned), and two variables originating in the social contract tolerance index (age 15-24 years, and unemployment). For all three types of crime the signs of the two inequality variables are positive, as expected, and those of the   punishment variables negative, also as expected. The authors find that youth is positively associated with crime, whereas the effect of unemployment is regarded as uncertain. The estimates of the youth effect, however, are not statistically significant, except in regressions where one of the inequality measures are *not* included (because of multicollinearity). It is interesting to note that removing the income gap variable from the crime equation makes youth a significant, and important factor. This indicates that young people commit crimes mainly because their income is relatively low.

The cross-section regression confirms the hypothesis that a greater degree of relative income inequality leads to higher crime rates, but coefficient on the income gap here has the wrong sign, although not significant. The effects of youth and unemployment mostly are not significant.

4.3. Substitution

Changes in benefits and costs of committing a particular type of crime might have effects on other types of crime. If, for instance, the probability of being convicted for robbery increases, some robbers might shift to burglary. One crime is substituted for another, just as people buy more apples instead of oranges when the price of oranges goes up. Such substitution effects between crimes have been estimated in a few empirical studies. Ehrlich was possibly the first. He found that burglary and theft were substitutes and that burglary and robbery were complements.[10]

It has become almost a rule that estimated crime supply equations include variables representing gains and losses to the crime in question and gains in legal activity. Variables representing gains and losses to other types of crime are rarely included. Heineke's (1978, Chapter 5) study of property crimes of SMSAs in the US is one of the rare exceptions. Employing methods developed to estimate systems of demand functions, Heineke derives a system of activity supply and commodity demand equations consistent with utility maximizing behaviour. Crime functions for burglary, robbery and larceny are included, and data from about ten SMSAs for the years 1967-72 are used for estimation. The method requires specification of individual preference functions. The transcendental logarithmic

---

[10]Spill-over effects can also be considered as a kind of substitution: differences in gains and costs of crime between districts may cause crime to be high in districts where crime is most profitable, see studies by Avio and Clark (1976), and Furlong and Mehay (1981) discussed above.

(nonhomothetic) function is chosen after the more simple homothetic and the linear logarithmic (additive) functional forms are rejected by a log likelihood test.

Heineke finds that increases in the probability and severity of punishment of each crime decrease that crime, whereas increases in gains (value of stolen goods) increase crime. The cross elasticities (showing the effect on the aggregate supply of each crime by increases in the probability of conviction, in mean sentence, and in gains to *other* crimes) are, as expected, much smaller, and in many cases also statistically insignificant. The main result is that the conviction ratio and mean sentence for larceny have negative effects on robbery (and not positive as one might expect), and the conviction ratio and mean sentence for robbery have a negative effect on larceny. For burglary similar results are not obtained. Problems of methodology and data hamper precise conclusions as to these cross effects, and one should be careful not to conclude that the property crimes studied are complements and not substitutes. More convincing is a further result that increases in exogenous wealth and remuneration to legal activity will decrease crime.

Holtman and Yap (1978) estimate crime equations for burglary, robbery, and larceny, where each equation contains probability and severity variables for all three types of crime. Thus, they are able to estimate substitution effects, i.e. effects on one type of crime of a change in the cost (probability and severity of punishment) of committing another type of crime. They apply data from 1970 on 43 U.S. states, and employ 2SLS on equations that are linear in logarithms. The probability measure used is, for each type of offence, the number of offenders imprisoned as a percentage of the number of offences, and the severity measure is the average time served.

For burglary the "own" probability has a significant negative effect, whereas the two other probabilities have significant positive effects. For robbery the "own" probability has no significant (negative) effect, whereas the imprisonment probability for burglary has a significant negative effect, and the imprisonment probability for larceny has a positive effect. Also for larceny the "own" probability is not significant (but positive), the same is true for the imprisonment probability of robbery, whereas the imprisonment probability of burglary is significantly negative. The average time served has the expected negative effect in all cases, but the estimates are not statistically significant.

Cameron (1987) has studied substitution between offence categories by estimating crime functions for robbery, theft and burglary where in each relation the probabilities of arrest for each of the three offences are included as explanatory variables.

Cameron finds that the own-effects of the arrest rates are significantly negative for robbery, insignificant for theft and significantly positive for burglary. The same arrest rates have mostly positive and significant effects on the other two types of offences. Furthermore, youth, unemployment and density all have positive and, in a majority of cases, significant effects on the offence rates.

Cameron reports experimentation with various functional forms. A log-likelihood test has shown that a simple linear form is superior to the log-linear specification.

As a whole the estimated substitution effects of the punishment variables vary in these studies. Of the 18 estimated coefficients expressing the degree of substitution between burglary, robbery and larceny there are 7 that are significantly positive (indicating substitutability), and 3 that are significantly negative (indicating complementarity). They are mostly negative in Heineke's study, and positive in those of Cameron, and of Holtman and Yap. Complementarity can in this field have a special explanation different from the one in economics: A high probability of punishment for burglary may reduce the number of intended burglaries. But an action that is planned as a burglary may result in robbery or larceny, and be registered as the latter. If the number of intended burglaries is reduced, so may also the number of registered robberies or larcenies. The most interesting result of the studies of substitution is thus that a certain number of statistically significant effects are found, a result that further corroborates the type of model applied in criminometrics.

4.4. Individual types of crime

Crime functions for individual categories of offences have been estimated separately on the assumption that the police does not substitute their resources between various types of crime, or that criminals are not engaged in substitution.

Studies of individual types of crime are interesting especially to the extent that modelling is based on particular knowledge of factors determining the type of crime in question. The vast literature on homicide and capital punishment will not be discussed here. The evidence is debated, and the methodological issues depend on the high standards of statistical significance required in studies that may be used as arguments for introducing and maintaining capital punishment.[11]

Studies of separate crimes are included in many of the contributions discussed above. Worth mentioning is also a study by Sesnowitz and Hexter (1982) who use data for 31 states in the US to estimate crime functions for robbery and burglary. In addition to measures of probability and severity of punishment they include as explanatory variables i.a. insurance claims as a proxy for gains to crime. The conviction rate and the average

---

[11]Contributions to the analysis of capital punishment are i.a. Ehrlich (1973), (1975b) and (1977), Bowers and Pierce (1975), Passell (1975), Peck (1976), Blumstein et al. (1978), Ehrlich and Gibbons (1977), Brier and Fienberg (1980), Hoenack and Weiler (1980), Layson (1985), Ehrlich and Brower (1987), Kloeck (1987) and Grogger (1990).

prison time are found to have statistically negative effects on both types of crime, whereas the opposite effect is found for insurance claims.

Landes (1978) analyses hijacking of US aircrafts utilizing data for the period 1961 to 1976. He finds highly significant and substantial effects on hijacking of the probability of apprehension, of the probability of incarceration given apprehension, and of the sentence length. All these deterrence variables increased substantially during the middle of the period, and a sharp decline in hijacking followed. Landes finds that mandatory screening of passengers and luggage contributed to the decline. However, removing the years of such screening in his regression analysis, the estimated effects of the deterrence elasticities remain more or less the same.

In a study of draft evasion in the US, Blumstein and Nagin (1977) escape four of the main problems encountered in criminometric studies: (1) As draft evaders are likely to be well informed about possible sanctions because of the authorities policy of pressuring the individual to submit for induction rather than face prosecution, the problem of wrong beliefs cannot be detrimental. (2) As draft evasion occurs only when there is a refusal to comply with an induction order, and virtually every refusal to comply is followed by an indictment, data are relatively free from error in reporting and recording. (3) As draft evasion can happen only once, there is no danger of confounding incapacitation effects with deterrence effects. (4) Simultaneity problems caused by over-taxing of the Criminal Justice system are unlikely because draft evasion cases are given priority in the relatively well staffed federal courts.

Using data for two years for US states, Blumstein and Nagin estimate both a linear and a logistic crime function including as explanatory variables the probability of conviction and the *expected* sentence. For both mathematical specifications the probability of conviction is found to have a negative effect on crime, whereas the expected sentence is found not to be significant. The authors consider their results to provide "an important statistical confirmation of the existence of a deterrent effect" (p. 270). It is interesting to note that in this study, where some of the common problems of criminometric studies are avoided, the impact of the probability of conviction on crime is found to be greater than what is found in most other studies. The remaining socioeconomic variables are found not to be significant, except for the median income, which has a positive effect on the rate of draft evasion.

An interesting feature of the study is the estimation of the double effect of the probability of conviction. Introduced as a separate variable, this probability is considered to reveal the stigma effect of being convicted. Included also into the expected sentence (sentence multiplied by the probability of conviction) its significance for the severity of the formal punishment is added. The estimates referred to above embrace both effects, of which the stigma effect accounts for more than 90% of the total of the two. This result supports what is found in other studies: the formal sanction has a modest effect on crime compared to the stigma effect of being arrested and convicted, cf e.g. Willcock and Stokes (1968), and Table 2.1.

4.5. Time-series studies

Among the many criminometric time series studies I have chosen to consider studies from various parts of the world: Cloninger and Sartorius (1979), Houston; Wolpin (1978), England and Wales; Schuller (1986), Sweden; Winthers (1984), Australia; Wahlroos (1981), Finland; and Wolpin (1980), an international comparison.

Utilizing data for the period 1960 to 1976 Cloninger and Sartorius (1979) have analyzed homicide and auto theft in the city of Houston in the US. The crime rates of each of these felonies are postulated to be functions of the respective arrest rates, conviction rates, and the mean sentence length. For both crime categories the (predicted) arrest rate, and the conviction rate have negative and highly significant effects on crime. Also the mean sentence length is found to have a negative effect, but not a significant one. The estimated coefficients, based on the six different police input measures, are quite similar for all six regressions.

The estimated elasticities (coefficients of the log linear equations) corroborate the hypothesis by Becker that the criminal activity is progressively less sensitive to probability of arrest, probability of punishment, and severity of punishment, in that order.

In a time-series study of crime utilizing data for England and Wales for the period 1894 to 1967 Wolpin (1978a) has estimated separate crime functions for larceny, burglary, robbery, auto theft, malicious wounding, felonious wounding, all offences against the person, and all offences together. A log-linear specification, including several environmental variables, was estimated by OLS. All estimated coefficients on the probability variables are found to be negative for all crime categories, most of them with rather high t-values. The estimates for the length of sentence, however, are erratic in both signs and statistical significance, possibly as a result of its weak relationship to time served (as opposed to time imposed by the court).

Young males are found to be positively related to property crimes, whereas the opposite is true for the proportion of individuals aged 15 and over attending school. Unemployment is found to have a negative effect on crime overall and especially on non-violent property crimes. The estimates for the degree of urbanization, the real per capita gross domestic product, and the real weekly wage in manufacturing industries are erratic both in signs and statistical significance. The time trend appears to be positive, but not in all cases significantly so. In a separate analysis where the time trend was deleted, the deterrent variables were basically unaltered.

Although Wolpin finds that his results mildly conform to the deterrence hypothesis, he has studied the possible effect of incapacitation on crime rates by comparing the impact of non-incapacitating punishments to that of imprisonment. For offences overall, and for all offences against the person, Wolpin finds that a marginal increase in imprisonment has about the same effect upon the crime rate as a similar increase in non-incapacitating punishment. Assuming for the sake of argument that imprisonment only has a capacitating and not a deterrent effect, deterrence and incapacitation are found to have equal effect upon crime. For robbery, auto theft, and felonious wounding the deterrent effects are found to be higher than the incapacitative effect.

Wolpin also used the 2SLS method to estimate a supply-of-offences function for crimes overall. The results are similar to those obtained by OLS, and this conformity suggests that simultaneity bias may be of little importance for the OLS estimates of each crime category.

In his time series study, using Swedish data from 1966-82, Schuller (1986) has estimated a two equation model consisting of a crime function and a clear-up function. In his base model the crime rate is a function only of the clear-up probability and the average time served in prison, and the clear-up probability is a function of resources allocated to the criminal justice system and the work load of this system. Added to this base model (only one or two at a time because of the small number of degrees of freedom) are various socioeconomic variables.

Both the clear-up probability and the average time in prison are found to have a significant negative effect on crime. Unemployment, and the proportion of the population on welfare programmes, have positive effects, whereas the effects of mean income and consumption of alcohol are not significant. Schuller finds it surprising that the proportion of people under 15 years has a significant negative effect on crime, referring to the many young people engaged in various criminal activity. Would it not be equally surprising if an increase in this proportion of the population (including also the not very crime active children under ten years old) caused an increase in the level of crime.

Withers (1984) has analyzed the determinants of homicide, rape, violent crime, property crime, and total crime in the seven Australian territories and states utilizing data for 13 years from 1963 on.

Withers finds that both the committal rate and the imprisonment rate have negative and highly significant effects on property crime and on total crime (which is mostly composed of property crime). The imprisonment rate also has a similar effect on rape, whereas the effects of these deterrent variables are insignificant for other violent crimes. Considering the prison population and the frequency of offences by ex-prisoners Withers concludes that the major effect of imprisonment comes through deterrence and not through incapacitation. Both median income and low income share are found to have positive and significant effects on property crime and violent crime. The estimated coefficients are positive also for homicide and rape, but significant only for rape in the case of median income. Male youth unemployment, education, and television viewing do not appear to have significant effects, whereas male youth population has a positive effect.

The main mathematical specification is log-linear, but Withers reports that the major results were not sensitive to re-estimation by use of linear, log-complement, semi-logarithmic and tobit specifications.

Wahlroos (1981) employs a two equation model, closely resembling the first two equations of Ehrlich's model, in a time-series study (1948-75) of larceny and robbery in Finland. Including first only three socioeconomic variables, the apprehension rate is found to have a negative effect on both types of crime, whereas an index of the severity of punishment has a significant negative effect on larceny only. The 2SLS methods gives higher absolute estimates of all these effects than the OLS method. The estimates are quite sensitive to the inclusion of additional socioeconomic variables, however, indicating serious multicollinearity between some variables.

The purpose of Wolpin's (1980) paper "is to ascertain the extent to which deterrence, environment, and "culture" can be considered responsible for the observed variance in the propensity for criminal behaviour across countries. It is based on time-series observations on robberies from 1955 to 1971 for three countries: England, Japan and the United States as represented by California. The differential impacts on the per-capita robbery rate of the certainty and severity of punishment and of economic and demographic characteristics are estimated. Culture is defined to be the set of unmeasured crime determinants that permanently differ across countries and its effect is captured by country-specific dummy variables." During the period of observation the robbery rate has trebled in California, increased sevenfold in England, and been reduced by more than a half in Japan.

The robbery rate is assumed to be a function of the clear-up rate, the conviction rate, the probation rate, the imprisonment rate, the median time served for those imprisoned, and some environment variables. A set of sanction equations expresses the dependence of the deterrence variables on the environment and dummy variables. Assumptions are introduced to permit consistent estimation of both types of equations by a generalized least squares procedure.

All deterrence variables are found to have negative and highly significant effects on crime. The proportion of males aged 10 to 25 years and the unemployment rate have equally significant positive effects. Increases in the real per-capita gross domestic product are found first to reduce the robbery rate and later on to increase it. The culture dummy variable has a negative impact on crime in the UK and a not significant positive impact in Japan compared to that of California.

4.6. Studies using data on individuals

Although the theoretical models of individual, rational criminal behaviour have been known for some time, empirical tests of these models by use of data on individuals are few. The main obstacle seems to be lack of suitable data. What we have are mainly self-reports on criminal activity and records of criminal activity compiled by the criminal justice system. The most serious problem with these data seems to be that they often do not constitute representative samples of the population, but are biased in the sense that only convicted persons are included. It is hardly possible to test a general theory of rational criminal behaviour by studying only one special subgroup of the population.[12] A related problem is that most available data sources include information only about choices made, and not about those available, but not chosen. It is difficult, if not impossible, to test a theory of rational choice if the choice set in this way is limited.[13] On the other hand, these data are often appropriate for studying special deterrence, but that is not the subject of this book.

The first four of the nine studies discussed below use data on released prisoners, the fifth uses a sample of minority youth, whereas the remaining studies use samples of tax returns.

On the basis of the theoretical model sketched in section 2.2.5 Witte (1980) and Schmidt and Witte (1984) have estimated a crime function where the arrest rate (or alternatively the conviction rate) is a function of the following factors: the probabilities of conviction given arrest, of jail given conviction, and of being employed; the returns to time spent in the labour market; the sanctions imposed if arrested and/or jailed; and several socioeconomic variables that are considered to represent tastes. The model is tested by use of individual data on post-release activities of a random sample of 641 men who were in prison in North Carolina in 1969 or 1971. Empirical measures of the probability of arrest, of gains to illegal activity, and cost of conviction are not found. Maximum likelihood regressions were run with and without the following taste variables: age, age squared, age at first arrest, number of arrests before incarceration in 1969 or 1971, number on convictions before incarceration in 1969 or 1971, number of rule violations during prison term, and dummy variables for

---

[12]Remember the story about the (biased group of) war pilots sitting at the bar telling their stories, and concluding that after all things usually turn out well.

[13]See, however, Manski (1978, 91-93) for a discussion og "choice based sampling".

race, serious alcohol problems, drug use, supervision when released, and marital status. The coefficients on the probability of conviction given arrest, the probability of incarceration given conviction, and the individual historical average sentence length (a proxy for the severity of punishment) were all found to be negative in all four regressions, but only half of them significantly so at a level of significance of at least 0.10. Being non-white, and having supervision have significant negative effects on crime, whereas serious problems with alcohol, drug use and rule violation in prison have positive (and mostly significant) effects. Schmidt and Witte find their results "generally consistent with earlier results that were obtained using aggregate data". Only the coefficients on initial wealth and on unemployment have unexpected, but not significant, negative signs.

Myers Jr. (1983) presents maximum likelihood estimates of coefficients of a logistic model of recidivism using a sample of 2127 individuals released from US Federal prisons during 1972. He has included somewhat fewer variables than Witte, and the studies differ on several points. Like Witte he finds that severity of punishment has a significant negative effect on crime. Somewhat surprisingly he finds that the certainty of punishment, measured by the ratio of previous prison commitments to previous convictions has a positive effect: as this probability increases, the probability of recidivism also increases.

Trumbull has estimated a crime model employing both aggregate (see section 4.2) and individual data. Aggregate data are used to study general deterrence, whereas recidivism and special deterrence are analyzed by use of data on 2186 offenders released from prisons in North Carolina in the first quarter of 1981 and surveyed during a follow-up period of eighteen months. Using a Tobit estimation procedure Trumbull finds that none of the deterrence variables (probabilities of arrest, conviction and imprisonment, and length of sentence) are statistically significant. Trumbull finds this result natural, since the sample consists only of individuals who, whatever the probability and severity of punishment, have chosen to engage in illegitimate activities. However, the effect of an offender's own previous sentence length has a significant negative effect on crime, a result that corroborates the hypothesis of special deterrence. Higher earnings on the first job after release has a negative effect on crime. Quite unexpectedly, so has unemployment. Other statistically significant results: recidivism is increased if the individual has a high number of previous convictions and a high number of rule violations while in prison; it is decreased if the age at release is high, and if imprisonment was due to felony commitment.

Viscusi (1986) uses an approach common in labour economics in the studies of hazardous jobs to estimate the risk/reward trade-off for illegal activities. In labour markets increasing health risks are often rewarded by some amounts of money in addition to non-risk wages. Treating the probability and severity of punishment in the same manner as the probability and severity of injury are treated in analyses of hazardous jobs, Viscusi is able to estimate the effects of changes in these variables. A 1979-80 survey of 2358 inner-city minority youths from Boston, Chicago, and Philadelphia constitutes the data employed. Several personal characteristics, and factors describing crime-related background, labour market, etc. are included. Viscusi finds that the premiums obtained for criminal risks are strong and quite robust. In his framework this is interpreted as a corroboration of the deterrence hypothesis: "The findings here suggest that the threat of criminal sanctions does not simply pass the usual test of statistical significance but is a dominant determinant of crime income" (p.339). Viscusi also reports that increased legitimate job prospects reduces crime.

Most empirical studies of our model of rational behaviour where individual data are used, are analyses of tax returns supplemented by audit information. Our model suggests that the amount of tax evasion depends upon the expected costs and benefits of this kind of cheating compared to alternative costs and benefits for legal and other illegal activities. Relevant factors should be the increase in income if evasion is successful (which depends upon the marginal tax rates), the probability of being discovered, and the following fine.

Clotfelter (1983) has utilized data from 47 000 individual tax returns for 1969 collected as part of the Taxpayer Compliance Measurement Program of the Internal Revenue Service of the US. The amount evaded, as assessed through auditing, has been regressed on the marginal tax rate, income categories, and several demographic and environmental variables. He finds that the marginal tax rate has a positive and highly significant effect on tax evasion, a result that might be taken to support the hypothesis that the higher the benefit of illegal activity, the more such activity there will be. The estimated elasticity of underreporting with respect to after-tax income is found to be positive, a result that corroborates the hypothesis of decreasing absolute risk aversion. Clotfelter also finds that underreporting is lower for wages than for business activities. This result might be explained by the higher probability of being discovered for wage underreporting, a result in accordance with the model of rational choice.

Witte and Woodbury (1985) have also analyzed data from the same program as used by Clotfelter. They find that the probability of audit has a negative effect on tax evasion, and that non-compliance is greatest at very low and very high income levels.

Slemrod (1985), using a somewhat different method of study of 23 111 tax returns collected by the Internal Revenue Service in 1977, did not obtain the same effects of increases in marginal tax rates as those obtained by Clotfelter. Slemrod was not able to distinguish the effects of increases in income from those of increases in marginal tax rates. He concludes, however, that "the tendency for tax evasion increases for higher income, higher tax households."

Klepper and Nagin (1989) have studied the non-compliance to tax laws using line item data obtained from approximately 50,000 individual tax returns included in the Taxpayer Compliance Measurement Program of 1982. They allow for the possibility that the probability of detection is partly determined by the individual's choice of how much not to declare, and on which line to do it. They conclude that their "findings suggest that compliance behaviour conforms closely to the incentives and deterrents created by the enforcement environment", and that marked variations in compliance levels across line items "appear to be systematically related to the difficulty of establishing non-compliance and the penalties for detected non-compliance". They also find that taxpayers appear to allocate their non-compliance across line items to minimize expected penalties.

As a whole, the studies of tax cheating using individual data produce results in accordance with the main predictions of the model of rational criminal behaviour. Both the probability and the severity of punishment have been found to have negative effects upon crime.

Most empirical studies using individual data are based on surveys of released prisoners or of taxpayers. A variety of statistical approaches and data sets have been employed. As a whole the empirical results are in accordance with the main predictions of the model of rational behaviour: The more probable or the more severe sanctions are, the lower the crime rate will be.

4.7. Summary and interpretation of empirical results

In this section I summarize the main results of the studies reviewed above. The purpose is to offer an overview of what kind of knowledge criminometric studies have given us so far. In each subsection I will first consider to what extent the results, in terms of statistically significant estimates, reject or not our model of rational individual behaviour, including individual utility maximization. In addition, I will investigate the possibility that the results have not been produced by the mechanisms of this theory, but by phenomena explained in other theories, such as differential association, anomie, etc. For instance, one may suggest that the negative association between the crime rate and the probability of punishment is a result, not of deterrence, but of norm formation. It is well known that any social phenomenon can be "explained" by un unlimited number of theories. The search for explanations that can substitute or supplement our main theory will, however, be restricted to main hypotheses found in the literature of criminology.

The emphasis in this summary will be on the impact on crime of punishment variables (4.7.1), and of economic variables (4.7.2), whereas the effects of variables representing norms, tastes, abilities, and various aspects of the environment will only be shortly mentioned (4.7.3). The reason for the rather superficial discussion of the latter variables is the rather vague arguments in many studies for introducing such variables, and the meagre amount of knowledge obtained.

4.7.1. Effects of punishment variables

Almost *all correlation studies and cross section regression analyses* show a clear negative association between punishment variables and the crime rate. A survey of the various empirical measures of the certainty and severity of punishment employed is given in section 4.9, Table 4.4. The main results of most of the cross section analyses are gathered in Table 4.1 above. (Some analyses are excluded because the empirical results are not easily comparable to the remaining ones.) Almost without exception the coefficients of the punishment variables (which in all cases are the elasticities of the crime rates w.r.t the punishment variables) are negative, and in most of the cases significantly so.[14] This result is further corroborated by results of studies not included in Table 4.1, e.g. the one by Wilson and Boland (1978).

The results are further condensed in Table 4.3, where the range of variation of the estimates, the number of negative and positive estimates, and the median of the estimated values are given. All statistically significant estimates of each study in Table 4.1 are included. This condensed presentation is composed of results from very different studies, and the estimates refer to various types of crime and data sets. Too much significance should therefore not be attached to these numbers. However, I believe that they give an interesting summary of the results obtained: As a whole these studies corroborate the hypothesis that there is a negative relationship between the crime rate and the probability and severity of punishment. Furthermore, the estimated elasticities have rather high values.

The *studies of substitution among property crimes* (section 4.3) can be regarded as a further corroboration of the theory of deterrence: differences in punishment variables of one type of crime tend to have significant effects on other types of crime. The significant estimates are mostly positive, indicating that a high probability of punishment of one type of property crime tends to increase another type of property crime.

A couple of *studies of individual types of crime* (robbery, burglary and highjacking)

---

[14]These results confirm a conclusion obtained by Blumstein et al. (1978, p. 4) on the basis of studies known in the late 1970-ies: "Taken as a whole, the reported evidence consistently finds a negative association between crime rates and the risk of apprehension, conviction, or imprisonment.". They add: "The Panel's task is to assess the degree to which the observed association is found *because* the higher sanction levels reduced the amount of crime committed.".

Table 4.3
Summary of estimates of punishment variables[a]

Punishment variable/ estimation technique	Range of variation of elasticities	Number of estimates Pos.	Neg.	Median
Probability of arrest,				
OLS	[-1.06, -.054]	11	0	-.342
2SLS	[-2.95, -.0006]	11	1	-.71
Probability of conviction,				
OLS	[-1.62, .43]	21	1	-.55
2SLS/3SLS/FIML	[-1.674, .486]	32	1	-.84
Probability of conviction given arrest,				
OLS	[-.132, -.132]	1	0	-.132
Mean length of imprisonment,				
OLS	[-.900, -.005]	16	0	-.474
2SLS	[-1.140, .392]	25	1	-.425

[a]Includes only results that for OLS are statistically significant at 5 % or better in a two-tailed test, or at 1 % or better in a one-tailed test, or that for other methods have asymptotic t-values higher than 2. This corresponds to the cases symbolized a, b, A, or * in Table 4.6.

show that for these data too, high values of the probability and severity of punishment decrease the number of crimes.

Five time-series *studies from various countries* give rather firm additional support to the existence of a negative relationship between crime and punishment. The variables representing the probability of punishment all have a negative, and mostly statistically significant effect on crime. The variables representing the severity of punishment also mostly have a negative and significant effect. Several studies of recidivism and of taxpayer behaviour where *individual data* are applied, also reveal a similar negative association between crime and the probability and severity of punishment.

As a whole, criminometric studies clearly indicate a negative association between crime and the probability and severity of punishment. The result may be regarded as a rather firm corroboration of the deterrence explanation in the theory of rational behaviour: an increase in the probability or severity of punishment will decrease the expected utility of criminal acts, and thereby the level of crime. It should be noted, however, that in a few studies the effect of an increase in the severity of punishment is not statistically different from zero. Recalling that the models of utility maximization discussed in section 2.2, for some assumptions of attitude towards risk, predict a positive or zero association between crime and the severity of punishment, the results of these few empirical studies are not surprising. Variation in the attitude towards risk among different populations can well produce different effects of the severity of punishment.

But what about competing explanations? Let us first look at the effects of variation in the probability of punishment. It will be remembered that all the theoretical models discussed in Chapter 2 predict a negative effect on crime of the probability of punishment, and that this relationship holds for any of the types of attitude towards risk considered.

But does the probability of punishment work through deterrence, or through the indirect mechanism of norm formation? An example of norm formation might be the following: a type of crime that almost never is cleared up will easily be considered as not very serious. A low clear-up rate can well be regarded as a society's signal that the crime in question is not very condemnable, and individual norms may adjust accordingly. The psychic costs of illegal activity will be less, and the level of crime will increase.

Can criminometric studies distinguish between the two mechanisms? In cross section studies one can imagine that people living in regions where the clear-up probability is low tend to consider crime as less serious than do people in other regions. If such differences in norm formation exist, they are probably more predominant the longer the distance between the regions that are compared, for instance in international comparisons, or in studies of states in the US. But in the review of this chapter the negative relationship between the crime rate and the clear-up probability is obtained also when data represent counties of only one state (Chapman (1976), Avio and Clark (1978), and Trumbull (1989), or of police districts in a metropolitan area (Mathieson and Passell (1976), Thaler (1977), and Furlong and Mehay (1981)). One may still find it possible to obtain significant differences in norm formation due to differences in clear-up probabilities - large enough to cause significant differences in crime - in these rather small geographical areas. It is, however, more difficult to accept that differences in the probability of committing a property crime will have a significant effect on people's norms about other property crimes (section 4.3). It is equally difficult to understand how a low probability of clear-up of not declaring one type of income, could have a significant effect on people's norms about how much to declare of other incomes (section 4.6). Without denying the possibility that norms about crime to some extent depend on the probability of punishment, the studies reviewed in sum clearly corroborate the hypothesis that there is a pure deterrent effect of this probability.

Another possible uncertainty about the evaluation of results is that there might exist an underlying phenomenon, unknown and/or not studied, a phenomenon that at the same time produces a low crime rate and a high probability of punishment. Individual norms may create such a relationship. If people in one region appreciate each others' welfare more than on average, they will both have a relatively strong aversion against criminal infringements against others, and a high interest in clearing up crimes in order to decrease crime in general. If such differences in norms exist, they must be rooted in cultural differences of some kind. Possibly, such differences can develop if regions are situated far from each other, or if distance in time is substantial. For the smaller regions in some of the studies reviewed, such differences seem to be unrealistic.

Even if the importance of each mechanism is regarded as uncertain, the estimates obtained in various studies are still of interest. Not only from a political point of view, but also from a scholarly one, it may be useful to know that the probability of punishment has a certain negative effect on crime, notwithstanding the mechanism(s) involved.

Our evaluation of the effect of the probability of punishment is to a large extent relevant also for the *severity of punishment*. The predictions of the models of section 2.2 are here less uniform. For certain probable attitudes towards risk, especially for decreasing risk aversion, many of the theories predict a negative relationship between crime and the severity of punishment, and such a relationship is at least not excluded for other attitudes. Most of the results of the cross-section studies in Tables 4.1 are in accordance with this theoretical prediction. The same holds true for the time-series studies in section 4.5, and also for the studies in section 4.6 when data on individuals are employed.

Here, too, one may ask what mechanism is at work. Does the severity of punishment have a significant direct effect on the cost of crime, or does it work indirectly through norm formation? If crimes are punished very leniently, they are possibly not considered as serious, and people's crime aversion might be negligible. As discussed with regard to the probability of punishment, it is difficult, however, to understand that norm formation will vary among districts situated close to each other. In a world where everybody receives news about punishment in various districts and regions, and where mobility is high, it is improbable that the severity of punishment in one's own district has a predominant effect on norms. The effect on crime of variation in the severity of punishment found in studies using data from rather small areas within a region, can therefore hardly be explained by a norm formation mechanism.

The question of whether increased severity in the form of more imprisonment produces an incapacitation effect that may explain the negative association between crime and the severity of punishment is seriously discussed in rather few of the studies reviewed.[15] Withers (section 4.5) finds that the major effect of imprisonment is deterrence, and not

---

[15]Cohen (1978) offers a theoretical study of incapacitation, illustrated by use of data from other studies. She recognizes the differences of opinion about the incapaciation effects, and proposes a refined research program.

incapacitation.

It has been suggested that the theory of special deterrence might explain differences in norm formation. In regions where the probability of punishment is high, a large proportion of those committing crime will be acquainted with the criminal justice system. If special deterrence works for these individuals, norms will tend to change in the direction of crime aversion (in addition to the possibility that better knowledge of actual punishment will make people understand that punishment represents a higher direct cost of crime than previously believed). Such an effect will eventually be the opposite of what is sometimes asserted: that contact with the criminal justice system creates offenders because of labelling, because of closer contact with other offenders while in prison, because of increasing differential association, or because the cost of crime is less for a person who already has lost some social standing through a first clear-up. The four studies of recidivists in section 4.6 reveal a negative association between the crime rate and the severity of punishment. This result indicates that special deterrence, with its negative association between crime and punishment, has a greater effect on crime than the various other consequences of punishment just mentioned, where the association is predicted to be positive. Whether it is beliefs or norms that have changed, is difficult to say. The result is anyhow at variance with common opinions among many academics. Special deterrence may have a limited quantitative effect, but great enough to more than outweigh the crime increasing impact of labelling, differential association, and other factors associated with imprisonment.

One may question whether it is the norm formation effect of special deterrence that also causes the differences in crime between districts. In a world where people move, and presumably do not change their norms overnight, it would be surprising, however, if the district specific norms should have the overwhelming negative effect on crime that is obtained in most of the studies reviewed.

It is also interesting to note that the median values of the OLS-estimates are lower than those obtained by other methods, - just as statistical theory predicts in case of simultaneity, cf Table 4.3. A similar result is obtained in a time-series study by Wahlroos (section 4.4), whereas Wolpin (section 4.5), also in a time-series study, obtains almost equal results by using OLS and 2SLS. On the other hand, the differences are not large enough to make OLS studies irrelevant even if simultaneity obtains. Furthermore, if OLS produces significant negative estimates one may be rather certain that methods where simultaneity is treated more correctly, would give even higher negative estimates.

As a whole, it seems that our model of individual utility maximization, including punishment variables representing deterrence, is the best explanation of which mechanism causes the negative relationship between the crime rate and the probability and severity of punishment. Other mechanisms may, however, in some instances, contribute to this relationship. Of course, this conclusion does not repudiate that norms are important in decisions whether to behave illegally or not, only that norms do not seem to be very important for understanding the variation in crime between districts and over (not very long periods of) time.

4.7.2. Effects of income variables

In accordance with the models of individual utility maximization of section 2.2 most of the criminometric studies reviewed contain income variables representing some of the benefits and costs of legal and/or illegal activities. The main results are summarized in Table 4.2, where, for instance, the legal income opportunity column shows estimated coefficients (elasticities) of variables representing legal income opportunities.

Benefits of legal activities
Looking first at the benefits of legal activities, it is evident that various proxies are applied: median family income (Schuller, Holtman and Yap, Mathieson and Passell), median income (Swimmer, Chapman, and Mathur), labour income to manufacturing workers (Sjoquist), mean family income (Myers, Avio and Clark), mean income per tax unit (Willis, Heineke), and mean income per capita (Trumbull). No systematic relationship seems to appear between the income measures applied and the estimates obtained. Although the hypothesis that an increase in legal income opportunities decreases crime is not rejected in most of the studies (Myers, Mathur, Schuller, Holtman and Yap, Heineke, and Mathieson and Passell), other studies would not reject the "opposite" hypothesis that an increase in legal income opportunities would increase crime (Chapman, Sjoquist, Avio and Clark, and Willis). This ambiguity in results might be due to the fact that the income measures used represent benefits not only of legal activities, but also of illegal ones: Higher legal incomes (mostly wages) tend to make work more attractive than crime, but to the extent that higher legal income in a region produces a greater number of more profitable targets for crime, the same empirical income measure may be positively correlated with criminal activity. If both mechanisms are at work simultaneously, and their relative strength not universally constant, it is not surprising that the results of various studies differ. The theory is not necessarily deficient, but the methods applied do not distinguish between the two mechanisms. The main problem is that the incomes of legal and illegal activities are highly correlated, and that it is difficult (or impossible?) to find empirical measures that with precision can distinguish between their effects. The impact of income is further obfuscated by the fact that private security measures increase with income, while higher income probably reduces

the marginal utility of each piece of property.

Gains to crime

The estimates in the column of gains to crime for Ehrlich's study illustrate our discussion. Ehrlich uses median family income as a measure of gains to crime, the same measure that Schuller, Holtman and Yap, and Mathieson and Passell apply as a measure of *legal* income opportunities. Ehrlich obtains a positive relationship between this income measure and crime, but it is questionable if it is the effect of gains to crime that is estimated.

In other studies the results for gains to crime are equally ambiguous, perhaps because of the different proxies used. A survey of empirical measures of gains to crime is given in section 4.9, Table 4.5. The results obtained by Ehrlich, Mathieson and Passell, Carr-Hill and Stern, Holtman and Yap, and possibly Heineke, indicate a direct relationship between the crime rate and opportunities of crime, whereas Myers Jr.'s indicates an inverse relationship. The estimates of Sjoquist and of Willis are of both signs in each study, and mostly not significant. The proxies producing a positive relationship are median family income (Ehrlich, and Holtman and Yap), and total ratable value per acre (Carr-Hill and Stern), whereas the only one producing a negative relationship is the average value of stolen goods (Myers Jr.). Proxies giving more ambiguous results are yearly sales per retail establishment (Sjoquist), and ratable value of the property in the area per capita (Willis).

Income differentials

The effects of income differentials on crime rates are also not unambiguous. Ehrlich, Forst, and Vandaele (percentage of families below one-half of median income), Swimmer (percentage of families with incomes of less than $ 3,000 or greater than $ 10,000), Danziger and Wheeler (distance between income and average income of reference group), and Holtman and Yap find them to be positive, whereas Mathur (Gini coefficient) obtains both positive and negative effects. Those estimates that are significant, however, are mostly positive. This result is in accordance with the theory of rational behaviour. A large income differential may indicate that crime is a comparatively rewarding activity for the very low income group (that may find a lot to steal from the very rich). Holding average income constant, the higher the percentage of families with very low and very high incomes, the higher the potential gains from crime. But the estimates may perhaps also reflect a mechanism from the theory of differential association: people who see no possibility of obtaining the general material standard of the society develop crime prone norms.

In studies including appropriate variables for both legal and illegal activities, and in addition a variable of income differential, a significant effect of the latter might reasonably be regarded as an effect of differential association (or something similar), and not of income opportunities. The study of Holtman and Yap is the only one including variables of both legal and illegal income opportunities in addition to one of income differential. They obtain significant estimates of the expected signs for all three variables.

Unemployment
Unemployment is usually included in criminometric studies as a proxy for (lack of) legal income opportunities. Unemployment will make crime more attractive if the alternative is a life in poverty. The estimates of the effect of unemployment on crime, however, are positive in some studies, and negative in others. An explanation given in Carr-Hill and Stern to the latter result is that unemployed fathers stay at home and keep an eye on their delinquent sons. Another explanation of the differences in results might be the variability in unemployment insurance schemes. In some places unemployment insurance is only slightly below ordinary legal income, and in addition, some of the formally unemployed receive income from short term jobs. According to our theory, crime will then not increase when unemployment increases, and even a decrease may occur. But if unemployment hits people without such income opportunities, crime will increase. Here, too, differential association may develop, but the studies reviewed do not give much support to this possibility.

Summary
As a whole it seems that the variables chosen to measure the opportunities of legal and illegal activities are not appropriate. A reason might be that average or median income measure both legal end illegal income opportunities (including monetary equivalents of psychic elements), whereas the other proxies of what can be gained from criminal activity are bad measures for the real gains to crime.

4.7.3. Effects of norm and taste variables

In most studies various sociodemographic variables have been included. Unfortunately, the reasons for including many of these variables are often not discussed. An explanation, for instance, of exactly how differences in preferences for legal and illegal activities may vary between groups of people are often lacking. The various choices of empirical measures probably reflect the availability of data. Of the many variables used, only race, age, and population density are considered here. A short survey of other variables employed are given in section 4.9, Table 4.12.

Race

The estimated coefficients on the proportion of non-whites in the population are almost without exception positive in the ten studies where this variable is included. The same conclusion is obtained in Wilson and Boland (1974). Even so, it is difficult to decide whether this result reflects differences in norms, in tastes, in abilities, or in income opportunities. It will also be recalled that IQ and race is correlated, and that the empirical results may reflect variation in IQ.

Age

In the three studies where the proportion of youth is included, and where the estimates are statistically significant, a positive effect on crime seems to occur. Considering that most crimes are committed by young people, one would have expected even stronger results. Several explanations might be offered: Perhaps there is not enough variability in the proportion of youth between statistical units to produce precise estimates. Also possible, crime among young people is not a consequence of their preferences (lack of socialization, etc.), but of their meagre legal income opportunities that possibly is adequately represented by other variables. Young people are perhaps not different, just poorer.

Population density

Four of the studies in Table 4.2 have included population density as an explanatory variable. All the statistically significant coefficients are positive. A significant positive effect is also found by Wilson and Boland (1978), whereas no significant effect is found by Greenwood and Wadycki (1973). Population density may reflect various phenomena, such as differences in social control, psychic diseases, etc. The studies reviewed are hardly suitable for a discussion of which of these mechanisms may be at work.

The traditional factors like the proportion of non-whites and youth, and population density perform according to expectations.

4.7.4. The deterrent effect of the police

Some studies use police expenditures or the number of police officers as possible deterrent variables instead of measures of probability and/or severity of punishment. Most of these studies show that police activity has a negligible, and sometimes positive, effect on crime. Such results have tempted some authors to dismiss deterrence as an efficient means against crime. (See e.g. Buck et al. (1985) referring to the studies of Greenwood and Wadycki (1973), Zipin et al. (1974), and Furlong and Mehay (1981).) However, it is quite misleading when Buck et al. (p. 245) writes that "... a common failure of the literature on the economics of crime is the inability to accept the deterrence hypothesis. More often than not, in spite of increasingly elaborate Becker-type models, increasingly sophisticated econometric techniques, and increasingly detailed data sets, there appears to be a positive relationship between enforcement and the incidence of crime; that increased enforcement does not deter criminals is a common conclusion in empirical literature." This statement is even more surprising when confronted with Furlong and Mehay's own conclusion: "Our results not only confirm the strength of the deterrent effect of the apprehension probability as measured by police clearances, but also demonstrate that the latter are a major output of police activities."

It will also be recalled that if an increase in police expenditures gives an increase in *registered* crime without a corresponding increase in clear-ups, a spurious negative correlation between police expenditures and clear-up rate will result. This effect might be large enough to eliminate the deterrence effect of police activity and thus explain the empirical results mentioned above. This possibility is substantiated by the study of Greenwood and Wadycki (1973), where the number of police per capita is found to have a significant positive effect on crime. The authors ascribe this result to the detecting activity of the police. Swimmer finds the effect on the crime rate of the total expenditure on police per capita to be negative for most crimes, but not significantly so.

To some extent situational variables are also included in other studies reviewed. Chapman (1976), for instance, finds that the female participation rate in the labour market, a proxy for the proportion of unguarded homes, has a significant effect on crime.

4.7.5. Criticism of criminometric studies

Undervaluation of the effect of norms
In our framework of norm-guided rational behaviour the possibility that norms depend on the environment is included, although not thoroughly discussed. Few would deny that such a relationship exists, cf Fig. 2.4, but as norms presumably change slowly by this mechanism, one can obtain much knowledge from empirical research disregarding it. Even without knowing anything about people's preferences we can estimate rather accurately how their consumption of beef depends on incomes and prices. It would have been interesting to know how their preferences about beef are formed, but their reaction to changes in the environment is of interest too. Although preferences for smoking (probably) depend on advertising (i.e. on an aspect of the environment), we may still estimate how sales of cigarettes depend on the price. (But if price changes also work through preference

formation - e.g. more expensive cigarettes make them more (or less) attractive - our conclusions may be erroneous.) If, then, empirical studies are tailored such that changes in the norms due to changes in the environment are not likely to occur, the simplified framework of Fig. 2.2 is relevant.

Empirical research should therefore include variables representing the effect of the environment on the *outcomes*, i.e. punishment and other gains and losses to legal and illegal activities, and preferences, i.e. norms and tastes.

Not all these determinants have to be included in an empirical study. Only those factors that change with time (in a time series study) or across districts (in a cross section study) should be considered. Only such factors will have a recognizable effect on crime. Determinants that do not change, will exert their influence through estimated constants.

Various operationalisations
One argument against empirical macro analyses of crime is that they operationalise the theoretical variables differently, thus showing that the theoretical models are not easily testable and the results difficult to compare. This objection is certainly relevant, but the consequence is not necessarily that such analyses should not be undertaken. Problems of operationalisation cannot discard a theory as irrelevant, but require that various kinds of operationalisations must be scrutinized.

Under such circumstances one might also expect that it will be quite difficult to reach a conclusion as to when a theory has been really subjected to a test. But if various operationalisations produce similar results, there is an indication that the theory is robust to such differences. Then, one might even conclude that the theory is quite good, even if each and every formal test of significance is of limited value.

The studies reviewed above reveal quite consistent results as far as the sign of effects of the punishment variables are concerned. The insensitivity of these results to various operationalisations is comforting. The effects of income variables are less consistent, a result that might either imply that economic factors do not have a uniform effect on crime or that some, or all, of the operationalisations tried are unsuitable.

Various mathematical specifications and statistical techniques
In several studies both linear and log-linear specifications have been tried, and also some other mathematical forms. Many authors report that they have not obtained substantially different results with different specifications. One reason for this unexpected conformity might be that the variation in data is too small for "thresholds" to cause problems. In addition, this variation is probably not important enough to cause the specifications to lose their value as workable approximations. Perhaps here is an example of what is sometimes

observed in economics: If a relationship between some variables is really strong, any reasonable operationalisation, mathematical specification, and choice of data will reveal the relationship. The precision of the estimates will of course differ among the various alternatives.

In the studies where both OLS and 2SLS have been used on the same data the absolute values of the estimated coefficients are higher for the latter method. This is what would be expected in case of simultaneity bias. On the other hand, the estimates obtained by the two methods do not seem to be substantially different, a result that suggests that the simultaneity bias is not so important as to make OLS regressions without value.

Publication bias

Prisching (1982, p.173) has suggested that publication bias might give the distorted impression that deterrence works. Publication bias is a general problem in empirical work, and criminometric studies are not excluded. It is not obvious, however, that a possible publication bias will work in the direction assumed by Prisching. Firstly, many of the studies discussed above include results where economic variables did not have the effect on crime expected from the theory of rational choice. Of course, there might still be a publication bias in favour of this theory, but why are the reported deterrence effects more consistent than the effects of purely economic variables? Secondly, is there really an empirical underpinning of the assumption that it is easier to get results in accordance with the general opinion published? Would not a reviewer or an editor find the opposite empirical result at least as interesting? These two objections to Prischings' remark of course do not make his point irrelevant, but show that the question remains unanswered.

Related to the assertion of publication bias is the allegation that economists believe in deterrence, and that their investigations therefore are unreliable.[16] This allegation runs against the table-talk joke that if you ask three economists for advice you get at least four different replies. More important, after the works of Block, Heineke, Lind, and others in the 1970ies, it is clear that models of crime inspired by economic theory do not predict unequivocal effects of changes in the severity of punishment (although the effects of changes in the probability of punishment is clear). After the publication of these studies nobody can be sure that more severe punishment has a deterrent effect. On the other hand, the empirical studies reviewed above - studies that permit equally both positive and negative effects on crime of punishment variables - give a strong support for the view that increases in the probability and in the severity of punishment both will cause a decrease

---

[16]Dijkstra (1991) summarizes a critical paper thus: "A simple lemma is derived to support the claim that regression models can be manipulated to a very large extent, by simply adding one regressor one can obtain essentially every set of desired regression coefficients and predictions as well as t-values and standard errors."

in crime.

4.8. Empirical studies of other theories of crime

Although I consider the model of rational behaviour the encompassing theory of illegal behaviour, other theories may, as explained in Chapter 2, contribute to a deeper understanding of crime. In empirical work the various theories might suggest inclusion of particular control variables. They may also provide valuable insight in assessing the results of empirical studies. Perhaps the variables we find to be significant do not reflect the associations we presume, but something else that is elucidated in another theory. Of particular interest is the fact that for almost all estimated crime functions discussed above, there is a great and highly significant constant for which an explanation is lacking.

A few empirical studies based on special theories of crime will be reviewed in brief to see if they may shed additional light on results obtained so far.

4.8.1. Routine activity

Cohen and Felson (1979) suggest that "[m]ost criminal acts require convergence in space and time of *likely offenders, suitable targets, and absence of capable guardians against crime*" (p. 588). They present data indicating that the development of daily routines and economic development over time have increased the amount of targets, and reduced the presence of guardians, thus increasing the number of occasions where the prerequisites of crime prevail. In a regression analysis, crime is assumed to be a function of an index representing the proportion of unguarded homes and of persons at risk of victimization. The proportions of youth and unemployed are included as control variables. Using US data for the period 1947-74 they find that for five different types of crime their index is positively related to crime. The effects of their control variables are not significant.

The result that crime and the proportion of unguarded homes are positively associated is consistent with the assumption that a lower probability of clear-up will increase crime. The routine activity approach provides an explanation of why the probability of clear-up has decreased because of more unguarded targets. The theory focuses on the number of opportunities for crime with low clear-up probabilities. Thus, it concentrates on a section of our framework of norm-guided rational behaviour; more precisely on the evolution of the environment that increases the benefits of crime, and reduces its costs. Disregarding other elements in our framework, the routine activity approach can be considered as a specific theory within this broader framework, or perhaps just as adding flesh to the more common rational behaviour.

4.8.2. Situational opportunity

Cohen, Felson, and Land (1980) have elaborated on the routine activity approach, and tested a model based partly on the theory that the situational opportunity of crime is a major determinant of robbery, burglary, and auto theft. According to this theory the opportunity is higher the more property targets there are, and the less these targets are guarded. For each crime category the crime rate is postulated to be a function of the crime rate of the previous year, the residential population density ratio, the unemployment rate, and the proportion of the population aged 15 to 24 years. The residential population density ratio is measured by an index representing the proportion of people staying at home guarding their property. A high unemployment rate is expected to reduce the crime rate also because more people will stay at home or perform activities in the neighbourhood. The opportunity of burglary is further operationalised by a proxy for the stock of consumer durables, and similarly the number of autos per capita is included in the auto theft equation.

The equations for each of the three crime categories were estimated in the log-linear form. (The authors report that a linear form performed less well.) Stochastic difference equations, where the crime rates were lagged one year, were obtained. Data from the FBI Uniform Crime Report for the period 1947 to 1977 were used in OLS regression calculations.

For all three equations large constant terms were found, indicating that crime would be substantial even with substantial changes in the explanatory variables. The estimated coefficients of the lagged crime rates were positive and highly significant for robbery and auto theft, but insignificant for burglary. Moreover, the estimated values of the coefficients were quite high for both the former categories. The estimated index of residential population density were found to have the expected "guardian" effect. The unemployment rate had the expected (by the authors) negative effect on robbery and auto theft, but a positive effect on burglary. The proportion of youth had the expected positive effect for all categories of crime. The proxy for consumer durables was found to have a positive effect on burglary, whereas the number of autos per capita did not have a similar effect on auto theft, probably because of collinearity.

Like the related routine activity approach, the theory of situational opportunity focuses on aspects of the environment that increase the benefits of crime (amount of targets), and reduce its costs (probability of clear-up). This approach can further be considered as a specific theory within our broader framework, or just as adding flesh to the more common rational behaviour.

4.8.3. Victimization studies

The existence of a substantial "dark number" of crime has fostered a certain interest in using victimization studies to obtain more reliable data. But survey data have their own deficiencies. The problem of characterizing an event as a (particular type of) crime or not is probably less serious for the police, who may have information from various sources, than for an interviewer who has to rely on the explanation of one person. The memory of the offended person is presumably also better at the time of reporting to the police than when the interview takes place.

Data as a whole being scarce, it is still interesting to use data from victimization studies to estimate criminometric models. In estimating a rather simple model Wilson and Boland (1976) used the number of robberies recounted to Census Bureau interviewers in 26 large U.S. cities as a measure of the robbery crime rate. They found the same strong negative association between crime and punishment as those using the Federal Bureau of Investigation crime reports. Myers Jr. used data on victimization in order to correct crime rates. Although the true offence rates are substantially higher than the reported ones (on average twice as high for robbery and burglary, 3.4 times higher for larceny, and about 37% higher for auto theft) the elasticities of the sanction variables estimated by Myers Jr. do not differ more than 5 to 15% between the two cases of corrected and non-corrected crime rates. Other victimization studies give similar results, and they do not seem to invalidate the conclusions drawn in section 4.7.

As a whole, the studies of routine activity, situational opportunity, and victimization do not contradict the qualitative results obtained in the empirical studies reviewed. These three approaches to the study of crime focus on different factors that together fill in relevant knowledge.

4.9. Overview of empirical measures of determinants of crime

In section 3.8 an effort was made to specify macro variables corresponding to individual determinants of crime, i.e. to factors representing individual norms and wants, abilities, the situation or environment, beliefs about attainable outcomes, and about the satisfaction the various acts and outcomes will produce. A distinction was made between norm variables (representing desires for various courses of action), taste variables (representing wants or tastes for various outcomes), ability variables, punishment variables (representing the probability and severity of punishment), economic variables (representing legal and illegal income opportunities), and environmental variables (other than punishment and economic variables). The norm, taste and ability variables correspond mostly to constitutional and acquired individual characteristics, the punishment variables to the preventive effects of formal sanctions, economic variables to gains and losses of various activities, and other environmental variables to various factors that contribute to the outcomes of activities. Tables 4.4-4.7 give a survey of macro variables used to represent such variables in various studies. I have added some measures used in studies not discussed, and also some alternatives that should be considered as alternative proxies for the theoretical concepts.

This survey shows the great diversity in the empirical measures that have been used. This diversity cannot exclusively - not even mainly - be explained by a corresponding diversity in problems that have been discussed and in hypotheses that have been tested. The reason for the use of different empirical measures seem partly to be lack of good theory, but first and foremost lack of more suitable data.

Table 4.4 shows that several measures of punishment variables have been employed. When only one type of sanctions is included, one would expect that the effect assigned to this variable in fact includes effects of punishment variables correlated with the one included. More satisfying is to use several sanctions simultaneously, as proposed and employed by Witte. Few authors mention the possibility that differences in punishment in time and space may have an effect on norms in addition to that on simple outcomes of illegal activities. Often it is assumed, implicitly or explicitly, that the distribution of norms within an observational unit is equal and constant for all units.

Despite the variety of empirical measures used, the summary in section 4.7 of the effects on crime of punishment variables corroborates the hypothesis of general prevention. It was further argued that simple deterrence is a main mechanism at work. These results, being obtained for a variety of empirical measures, constitute a strong support for such an interpretation of the studies as a whole.

Table 4.5 includes empirical measures representing possible material gains to crime. High income, skewed income distribution, and much real capital indicate that there is a lot to gain from crime. The worth of movables, of trade, of number of capital items, such as cars and cabins are added as possible measures.

Of particular concern is the fact that different authors in a few instances have used the same empirical measure as an indicator of different theoretical variables. In some studies average income is used as a measure of the gain of illegal activities, whereas in other studies the same measure is used to indicate the gains to legal activities.

Table 4.4

Empirical punishment variables (as a cost of crime)

Punishment variables	Studies where used
Severity:	
Capital punishment	Ehrlich (1975), Passell (1975)
Average sentence length handed down	Avio and Clark (1978)
Average sentence length	Sjoquist (1973)
Median number of months served	Mathur (1973)
Jail	Antunes & Hunt (1973); Ehrlich (1972);
Fine	
Prosecution suspended	
Proportion of convicted Offenders given custodial treatment	Carr-Hill & Stern (1973)
Probability:	
Clear-up ratio	
Apprehension	
Arrest ratio	Chapman (1976); Mathieson & Passell (1976); Bailey (1978); Greenberg, Kessler & Logan (1979); Hoenach, Kurdle & Sjoquist (1978);
Suspended prosecution	
Charges per offence	Avio and Clark (1978)
Conviction	Sjoquist (1973)
Conv. ratio given arrest	Sjoquist (1973)
Conviction per charge	Avio and Clark (1978)
Fine	Wolpin (1978)
Jail	Antunes & Hunt (1973); Ehrlich (1972), Mathur (1977)
Capital punishment	Hoenach, Kurdle & Sjøquist (1978)
Expected sentence	Swimmer (1974)

Table. 4.5
Variables representing material gains from crime[a]

Variables	Studies where used
Average income	Reynolds (1971); Ehrlich (1973); McPheters & Strong (1974); Forst (1977)
Average income of highest quartile in income distribution	Fleisher (1966)
Gini coefficient of income distribution	Mathur (1978)
Real capital (do)	Carr-Hill & Stern (1973)
Worth of movables (total, per inh. or per sq.km)	
Worth of retail trade (do) Wealth (do)	
No. of cabines (do)	
No. of cars (do)	
Consumer expenditures in year t-2 for durable goods other than automobiles	Cohen, Felson, and Land (1980)
Automobiles per cap.	Cohen, Felson, and Land (1980)
Median family income	Forst (1976)
Value of owner-occupied housing	Greenwood and Wadycki (1973)
Yearly sales per retail establishment	Sjøquist (1973)
Percentage of rich and poor families	Swimmer (1974)
Proportion of families with income greater than $ 25.000	Mathieson and Passell (1974)
Pr. square mile No. of owned houses No. of TV Population Average rental price of housing	Avio and Clark (1978) (in preliminary analysis only)

[a]Value of property available as booty for offenders.

Table 4.6

Variables representing loss of legal income

Indicator	Studies where used
Average income	Grieson (1972), Beasely & Antunes (1974), Swimmer (1974), Chapman (1973)
Average income for next to lowest quartile in income distribution	Fleisher (1966)
Average income, manufacture	Sjøquist (1973)
Proportion of families with income less than median	Ehrlich (1973)
Proportion of families with income between median income and poverty limit	Forst (1977)
Median income	Swimmer (1974), Mathur (1978)
Median family income	Mathieson and Passell (1978)
Unemployment rate	Swimmer (1974), Mathur (1987), Avio and Clark (1978)
Unemployment rate, men	Fleischer (1966)
Unemployment rate, age groups	Phillips & Votey (1972), Ehrlich (1973)
Lagged unemployment rate	Hoch (1974)
Proportion of population with work income	Ehrlich (1975), Forst (1977)
Proportion of population without work income	Phillips & Votey (1972), Forst (1976)

Table 4.6 includes variables representing loss of legal income, loss that can be interpreted as a cost of illegal activities. Here, high incomes are considered as incomes foregone if engaged in illegal activities. Unemployment measures indicate the extent to which there is no loss of legal income for an offender.

Table 4.7 contains a sample of socioeconomic and demographic variables employed in various criminometric studies. The exact theoretical motivation for including them is often sparsely explained. They may represent aspects of the environment as well as individual tastes and norms. Variables expressing race proportions are often considered as reflecting income opportunities. They may perhaps also reflect differences in norms or tastes. The same holds true for the proportion of youth. The exact reason for including the proportion of males is rather obscure, except that men are responsible for most crimes.

Some gains and losses are of a kind that cannot easily be represented by quantitative or qualitative variables. This is the case for psychic benefits and psychic costs. In criminometric studies variables representing psychic benefits and costs are lacking. These elements can be significant: Carr-Hill and Stone report that in a group of youth, formal punishment itself was felt less serious than reactions to the offence from family, girlfriend and employer. The approach usually taken, explicitly or implicitly, is that such benefits and costs do not vary over time and districts, and that differences in crime must be explained by other factors. The effects of such costs and benefits will then be concealed in the estimated constant.

Some of the variables of Table 4.7 might possibly represent both psychic benefits and costs, tastes and norms. More comprehensive studies are needed in order to decide what kind of mechanisms are at work.

Many studies give weak arguments for choosing theoretical variables and empirical measures. Orsagh (1979) argues that the great diversity of variables in empirical criminology shows that no good theory exists, and that macrostudies of the usual kind has little interest. As an alternative to this non-constructive approach, I suggest that one should continue the theoretical discussion about determinants of crime, and make more empirical studies, in order to get a better foundation for choosing acceptable measures of theoretical constructs.

In this spirit in the next chapter we present two criminometric studies based on Norwegian data. When ideal methods are lacking, we find it useful to add more studies to those already existing, using slightly different procedures, and by necessity somewhat different measures of determinants of crime.

In Chapter 6 we finally circumvent the problem of finding acceptable measures of these determinants. We just assume that observational units may differ as far as individual norms, wants, and economic and other conditions are concerned, and that these differences

Table 4.7

Environmental, sosio-economic and demographic variables

Measures of SED-factors	Studies where used
Ethnic minorities immigrants, proportion of Male proportion of population population that is non-white	Ehrlich (1973); Mathur (1978), Forst (1976), Greenwood and Wadycki (1973), Chapman (1973), Swimmer (1974)
Proportion of population that is male, 15-24 years	Tittle (1974), Forst (1976) Carr-Hill & Stern (1973)
Proportion of population, 14-25 years	Hoenack, Kurdle & Sjøquist (1978)
Do., 10-25 years	Wolpin (1978)
Do., 18-20 years	Forst (1976)
Do., 14-17 years in school	Swimmer (1974)
Proportion of households that are not husband-wife households	Forst (1976)
No. of inhabitants	
Consumption of alcohol	Greenberg, Kessler & Logan (1979)
No. of alcoholics	
Consumption of drugs	
Proportion of drug abusers	
No. of divorces	
Density of population	Forst (1976), Swimmer (1974), Sjoquist (1973), Willis (1983), Greenwood and Wadycki (1973), Wilson and Boland (1978), Sjoquist (1973)
Migration	Forst (1976)
Temperature	Forst (1976)
Regional dummies	
Mean school years	Sjoquist (1973)
Population	Swimmer (1974), Mathur (1978)
Proportion of families who have lived in the same house for five years or more	Mathieson & Passell (1974)

influence both the number of crimes and the number of clear-ups. We lump all these determinants into what we call crime and clear-up tendencies, and then model the distribution of these tendencies across police districts and over time.

Chapter 5

CONVENTIONAL CRIMINOMETRIC STUDIES

The discussion of macro studies in Chapter 3, and the survey of such studies in Chapter 4, demonstrate the difficulties in designing valid empirical analyses of crime and crime prevention. I have argued that, when flawless analyses are not obtainable, the best alternative is to use several different approaches with the hope that the batch as a whole will give reliable information. In this vein I present below several criminometric studies of both conventional type (in this chapter) and of a more novel category (in Chapter 6), all based on Norwegian data. I start with a cross section study using data from 1974. This year is chosen because data on many interesting variables are available. The following section contains a simple pooled cross-section time series study where dummies are used for each police district.

5.1. A cross section study - 1974

5.1.1. The model

A crime supply function has been estimated, where the crime rate X is assumed to be a function of:

Y_{lag} = the average of the clear-up proportion lagged one year and the same proportion lagged two years,

UEM = the rate of unemployment,

$LOWIN$ = the proportion of income-earners with an annual net income below NOK 16.000,

ASS_N = total value of assets per inhabitant,

$SALE_N$ = total sales in wholesaling, retail trade, restaurants and hotels per inhabitant,

M_N = the number of men, 12-19 years old, per 1000 inhabitants,
$RC_{N,-1}$ = the number of male recent comers to a police district per 1000 inhabitants,
             lagged one year.
D_N = the number of divorced men in the population per 1000 inhabitants.

The reasons for including most of these variables have been discussed in previous chapters. Let me briefly present some reminders, and add a few remarks relevant for a criminometric study for Norway.

All the theoretical models discussed in section 2.2 show that crime decreases with an increase in the probability of punishment. All the empirical studies reviewed in Chapter 4 are consistent with these results. As punishment variable I have chosen the average of the clear-up proportion lagged one year and the clear-up proportion lagged two years. People probably have better information about clear-up proportions of previous years than that of the present year. The criticism of other studies that people cannot be deterred by the same year's clear-up ratio - because they do not know it - is avoided. If the probability of punishment has a deterrent effect, it must be the individual's assessment of this probability that is of importance for his behaviour. How these assessments come about is an intricate problem, but one thing is certain: they are not influenced by the official clear-up proportions of the current year, for the simple reason that these are not known until the year after. Individual assessments are probably based on various types of information gathered over several years: personal experience, hearsay, publicized clear-up proportions etc. As a proxy for all this information one has to use official clear-up proportions, implicitly assuming that there is a functional relationship between this proportion and other information that individual assessments are based on. Given that an official crime rate has to be used, the proportion for previous years seems to be more relevant than that for the current year. One could argue that individual assessments of the clear-up proportion are based mainly on informal information gathered the same year, and as this information presumably is reflected in the official clear-up proportion for the same year, the clear-up proportion should not be lagged. But introspection as well as some empirical studies suggest that our assessments are based on information gathered over several years. How far back one should go is difficult to decide. In this study I have used the clear-up proportions for the two previous years. Hopefully, the average of these proportions will catch the relevant information. An average measure is also recommendable because the very low number of crimes and clear-ups in some of the small police districts makes the clear-up proportions rather volatile.

Furthermore, the use of lagged clear-up proportions is a way of handling the difficult problem of identification. As explained in section 3.4 the possibility of identifying the crime supply function by excluding exogenous variables is at best meagre, and it is debatable how much is gained by using a simultaneous model like (3.1) - (3.3) if the crime supply function is the only object of scrutiny (as it is in this study). Using lagged clear-up proportions the problem of identification is formally solved. A high correlation between clear-up proportions of consecutive years may, however, make identification more formal than real. Anyway, I think the use of a lagged variable is preferable to the simultaneous analyses discussed in Chapter 4.

No severity of punishment variable is included. The reason is that punishment seems to be quite similar among all police districts. In part, this is because Norway is a rather homogeneous society, but the main explanation is that both the plaintiff (or the prosecution) and the defendant can appeal to the Supreme Court against the sentence. By this arrangement the Supreme Court secures similar sentences all over the country. The disadvantage of this circumstance is that the effect of variation in severity cannot be studied in cross section analyses. On the other hand, it is usually difficult to define variables that adequately represent the severity of punishment, and empirical deficiencies often caused by this problem are avoided in the present study.

In section 2.2 it is demonstrated that the effect on crime of the individual's exogenous income or wealth (i.e. income or wealth that does not depend on current legal or illegal "work") for all models depends on the attitude towards risk, see Table 2.3 for a summary. With the common assumption of decreasing absolute risk aversion income has a positive effect on crime. By at least two mechanisms, however, an individual's exogenous income or wealth may influence crime. The exogenous income or wealth of individuals constitute a part of the environment and as such form targets for crime: the higher the income of others, the more there is to gain from theft, robbery, burglary, embezzlement, etc. Furthermore, variation in income among individuals may influence norms by differential association or similar mechanisms. In empirical studies it seems almost impossible to find separate variables to represent these three mechanisms. This problem does not require income or wealth variables to be excluded, but if a single variable is used, there is no good theoretical basis for a priori expectations of the total effect on crime. In the present study exogenous income is represented by the value of assets per inhabitant (ASS_N). In evaluating the estimated effect of this variable on crime all three mechanisms must be kept in mind.

Similar mechanisms are relevant also for the individual's legal income. In section 2.2 it is shown that for all models studied the effect on crime of the individual's legal income depends on the attitude towards risk, and for most models also on the values of the income and substitution effects. Even if we assume decreasing absolute risk aversion, the effect remains indeterminate for two of the models. Furthermore, variation in legal income may represent variation in targets of crime. If, however, our variable of exogenous income or wealth adequately represents these targets, the effect of legal income will be cleansed of this component. Finally, an effect of low income on norms may be present. Here too, one cannot expect to obtain very conclusive results about these effects. The variation in results in the studies reviewed in Chapter 4 emphasizes this problem. In the hope of singling out just a portion of the effect of income I have included, somewhat arbitrarily, as a variable the proportion of personal tax payers with an annual net income below NOK 16.000. This amount is equal to about half of the average taxable income that year, and may possibly be considered as an income level below which people will develop crime prone norms. But according to most of the theoretical models poor people with decreasing absolute risk aversion will commit fewer crimes than others, and the total effect also of this variable is indeterminate.

Total sales in wholesaling, retail trade, restaurants and hotels are included to represent the amount of targets for crime, and thereby the gains to crime. For all the models of Chapter 2 the effect on crime of these gains depends on the attitude towards risk. For the common assumption of decreasing absolute risk aversion the effect is positive in all but the labour supply model with non-monetized attributes. If this environmental variable adequately represents gains to crime, the effects of our income variables will not include the gains to crime factor.

Unemployment is often considered to be a cause of crime because of a) lack of income, b) much free time that can be used in criminal activity, and c) animosity to conventional norms. To the extent that unemployment causes income to be low, the remarks on the effect of income variables above are relevant also here. No definite effect on crime can therefore be expected. More free time will increase the gains to crime in the sense that less legal income is foregone in using time to prepare and commit crimes. As already explained the effect on crime of changes in the gains to crime depends on the attitude towards risk, and also on the values of the substitution and income effects. Adding the mechanism of norm formation, it becomes evident that there is no simple a priori effect of unemployment on crime. The complexity is underscored by the review in Chapter 4, where the estimates of the effect of unemployment are found to be positive in some studies and negative in others. A special reason for expecting unemployment not to have a significant effect on crime in Norway is that the unemployment rate in 1974 was only about 3 per cent on average and with slight variation among police districts.

The knowledge that most crimes are committed by young men requires that one or more age variables should be included. Theory does not suggest exactly which age groups to include. Rather arbitrary, I have chosen the proportion of men from 12 to 19 years as an independent variable.

The proportion of the population that are recent comers to a district is included as a variable because these people are not well known by their neighbours and thereby less susceptible to informal social control. Thus the environment will produce lower costs of crime for these individual than for permanent residents. Moreover, the probability of formal sanctions may be lower because these people are not easily recognized in the neighbourhood.

Many offenders are divorced men, and the proportion of these might contribute to the explanation of crime. It is unclear, however, if it is divorce that causes crime, or if it is crime that causes divorce, or if there is a common cause to both. It will nevertheless be interesting to observe the correlation between crime and divorce, at least as a departure for further study, and the proportion of divorced men is therefore included.

Most of the variables are per capita measures in order to avoid some problems of heteroscedasity.

Obviously, a great number of determinants of crime are not included as specific explanatory variables, and are thus included in the error terms.

Incapacitation is of little relevance to the studies of crime in Norway. Not only does the Supreme Court secure rather similar sentences across jurisdictions, but a central Board of Prison coordinates the reductions in time served for all prisons in the country. At least in cross section studies differences in crime cannot be ascribed to differences in incapacitation.

In previous studies various mathematical specifications have been employed, without conclusive theoretical or empirical outcomes, cf section 4.7.5. Linear and loglinear specification have been used below.

5.1.2. Data and estimation

Data on the 53 police districts of Norway in 1974 used in the regressions below is given in Appendix A and Appendix C.

Table 5.1 shows the results of OSL regressions with both linear and loglinear specifications of the crime function[1]. Both ordinary and stepwise procedures have been employed. In the stepwise procedure the F test level of taking a variable into the equation is 0.05, and the level for expelling one that has previously been accepted is 0.10. To test multicollinearity, the tolerance level is set equal to 0.01. The statistically nonsignificant variables of the ordinary procedure have been rejected by these tests. The lagged average clear-up proportion, the total value of assets, total sales, and the proportion of divorced men in the population are found to be significant. The t-value of the former, however, is rather

---

[1]SPSSPC+ has been employed to do the regressions.

low in the ordinary linear regression.

The estimates of the four regressions, which are the elasticities of crime supply w.r.t. the corresponding variables, are found to be quite similar. The coefficient of the lagged average clear-up proportion must be considered as an underestimated value in absolute terms because of the possibility of simultaneous equation bias.

Table 5.1
Estimated elasticities of crime supply function 1974[a].

	Linear	Linear Stepwise	Log.	Log. Stepwise
Y_{lag}	-.128 (1.632)	-.188 (2.733)	-.169 (2.335)	-.186 (2.334)
UEM	-.051 (.578)		-.143 (1.274)	
LOWIN	-.120 (1.102)		.104 (.856)	
ASS_N	.150 (1.901)	.155 (2.489)	.201 (2.313)	.233 (3.311)
$SALE_N$	.396 (5.083)	.420 (5.877)	.387 (4.279)	.428 (5.248)
M_N	-.056 (.644)		.076 (.816)	
$RC_{N,-1}$	-.015 (.207)		-.026 (.311)	
D_N	.389 (3.984)	.452 (6.108)	.462 (4.649)	.401 (4.956)
R^2	.851	.836	.807	.792
F	31.47	61.38	22.95	44.65

[a] Numbers in parentheses are t-values.

The elasticity of crime w.r.t. total value of assets is positive and highly significant. Considering this variable as representing exogenous income or wealth, the outcome is consistent with the theoretical results of the theoretical models summarized in Table 2.3 in the cases of decreasing absolute risk aversion and of increasing absolute risk preference. Considering the value of assets as a measure of the gains to crime, the result is also consistent with the same theories in the same cases of attitude towards risk and also in the case of risk neutrality. If assets are more unevenly distributed in police districts with high assets than in those with low, the estimates are consistent also with the theory of differential association or similar theories.

The elasticity of crime w.r.t. sales is also found to be positive and highly significant. Considering sales as a measure of gains to crime, this outcome is consistent with the results of Table 2.3 in the same cases as for assets, cf previous paragraph.

The elasticity of crime w.r.t. divorce is also found to be positive and highly significant. It is interesting to note that Schuller (1986) obtained a similar result for Sweden. The question of causality is of course not solved by this result, but the important correlation between these variables is worth noticing.

As anticipated, unemployment is found not to have a significant effect on crime. The same conclusion is obtained for the proportion of low income earners. Many students and housewives are included in this group, and it was perhaps too optimistic to try to test the importance of unequal income distribution by this variable. The proportion of recent comers is also found not to be significant. The number of men that moved into each district in 1973 has been used as a measure of this variable. Perhaps one should have used the number of recent comers for a longer period of time. The reason why the proportion of young males is found not to be significant is probably that the variation in this proportion among police districts is very low.

Some regressions with alternate specifications of independent variables have been run. The subjective probabilities of punishment are probably depending on information for more than one year, and the clear-up proportion for both 1973 and 1972 have been employed in the same regression. The crime profile of young men at various ages being different, separate variables for men from 12 to 15 years (not punishable according to the criminal law), and from 16 to 19 years have been introduced. Finally, crime and alcohol consumption being highly correlated, a variable of alcohol consumption, inadequately measured by the number of places per inhabitant where alcoholic drinks may be legally bought, has been used. All these specifications have resulted in statistically nonsignificant estimates for the additional variables. The estimates of both clear-up proportions, however, have the right sign and add up to about the same value as the corresponding estimates of Table 5.1.

5.2. A panel study 1970-1978

5.2.1. The model

The weak aspects of cross section and time series studies can to some extent be avoided by employing panel models. In this section I present a panel study of crime using data from

Norwegian police districts during the period 1968-1978. A main problem of using such models is lack of data on various variables for all districts and years. In the present model a dummy variable for each police district is introduced as a summary of all the norm, taste, economic and other variables that permanently causes the crime rate to differ among police districts. The following equation is postulated:

$$X_{it} = a + bY_{it-2} + cY_{it-1} + d_1 D_{1t} +, \ldots +d_{53} D_{53t} + u_{it} \tag{5.1}$$

where

X_{it}	= crime rate
Y_{it-2}	= clear-up proportion, lagged two years
Y_{it-1}	= clear- up proportion, lagged one year
i	= 1,2,...,53 (police districts)
t	= 1970, 1971, ..., 1978
D_{it}	= a dummy variable (1 for police district i, and 0 elsewhere)
u_{it}	= a IIND error term.

I further posit that people assess the probability of punishment on the basis of clear-up ratios of the two previous years.

One explanation for the observed negative correlation between the crime rate and punishment is incapacitation: as long as people are in jail, they do not easily commit new crimes. As explained in Chapter 3 the effect of incapacitation can be estimated only if the intensity of criminal activity of people convicted to prison is known. Lacking such information a rough estimate can be made from data on the number of crimes prisoners are convicted for. Data specifying the number of crimes from 1 to 10, and over 10, is published from 1978 on. Multiplying the number of persons convicted by the corresponding number of crimes, and adding up over all groups, the total number of crimes committed by convicted people in 1978 is 22,056[2]. In addition comes the number of crimes committed by people where the number of crimes is not given. If the average number of crimes in this group of 1279 persons is the same as for those 8724 persons included in the groups just considered, i.e. 2.53 crimes per person, the total number of crimes committed by convicted offenders amounts to 25291. This amounts to 27,6 % of the total number of crimes that year. Furthermore, average sentence for those imprisoned was 173 days in 1978. Time served is as a rule 2/3 of the sentence, i.e. 115 days. Time served as an average for

---

[2]Published data does not include information about the exact number of crimes committed by the 101 persons imprisoned for having committed more than 10. I have assumed that the average number of crimes in this group is 20.

the total number of crimes is then only 27.6 % of 115 days, i.e. 32 days. Offenders at large are thus in prison only about 9 % of the year. Consequently, the crime rate cannot be significantly influenced by the small differences in incapacitation.

5.2.2. Estimation and results

Data for 53 police districts in Norway for the years 1968-1978 are used in estimating (5.1) by OLS. The data are given in Appendix A.

An OLS-regression gives the following estimate for police district No. i:

$$X = 28 - 0.0917Y_{t-2} - 0.0812Y_{t-1} + d_i \quad (i=1,2,...,52)$$
$$\quad (4) \quad (0.0251) \qquad (0.0251)$$

where adj $R^2 = 0.86$, the F-statistic $F = 54$ and the standard errors are given in brackets. (The standard errors of the d_is are all about 1.9). The estimates are significant at the 0.01 level.

The clear-up proportions have a rather small, but statistically significant impact upon the crime rate. By far the largest part of the differences in the crime rate is "explained" by the dummy-variables.

The estimated coefficients are transformed to elasticities by

$$e_j = (\partial X/\partial Y_{t-j})(Y_{t-j}/X) \quad j = 1,2.$$

Computed at the mean values of the variables these elasticities are given in Table 5.2, regression No. 1. In order to obtain an idea about the importance of the introduction of dummy variables, some other regressions have been made. In regression No. 2 only the dummy variables 20 to 52 have been included (the constant term in the regression function representing the other police districts). It is seen that the elasticities are appreciably higher for this regression than for the first one.

The results of similar regressions with fewer dummies are also included in Table 5.2. As expected, there is a clear tendency for the elasticities to increase as the number of dummy variables decrease.

By looking at the data it is easily observed that police districts with a high clear-up proportion have a low crime rate, and vice versa. Thus, the data reveals an important negative correlation between the two rates. This relationship is reflected by the high elasticities for regression No. 6. By introducing dummy variables, this spurious correlation is eliminated (or rather absorbed by these variables). As a result, the elasticities become

Table 5.2
Elasticities of the crime function w.r.t. the clear-up proportion

Regression no.	Dummy variable no.	Adj. R^2	Elasticities	
			e1	*e2*
1	1-52	0.86	-0.10	-0.09
2	20-52	0.75	-0.37	-0.35
3	1-35	0.79	-0.41	-0.36
4	1-20	0.65	-0.53	-0.57
5	1-10	0.56	-0.59	-0.62
6	none	0.30	-0.70	-0.72

rather small for regression No. 1, where dummies for all the police districts are used. Comparing these results with what is obtained in other studies, one should be careful not to accept high elasticities if sufficient measures have not been taken to eliminate the spurious negative correlation between the crime rate and the clear-up proportion. In some studies a part of this correlation is absorbed by various SED-variables. One might question whether these variables capture all the relevant properties of the various districts, or whether there is a rest that shows up in too high values of the estimated elasticities.

5.3. Conclusion

Both studies support the view that the clear-up proportion has a negative influence on crime. However, the estimated coefficients, do not suggest that crime can be drastically reduced by increasing the clear-up proportion. Roughly, an increase in the clear-up proportion of one per cent seems to reduce crime by about 0.2 - 0.3 per cent, and one cannot rely on more police to increase the clear-up proportion substantially. However, a more sophisticated analysis in the next chapter will show a stronger effect of clear-ups on crime.

Chapter 6

CRIMINOMETRIC ANALYSES USING EQUILIBRIUM MODELS, LATENT VARIABLES AND PANEL DATA

by

JØRGEN AASNESS, ERLING EIDE AND TERJE SKJERPEN[1]

6.1. Introduction

Most empirical studies are plagued by substantial underregistration of crime. Registration depends on the attitude of those who discover a crime, on the access to telephone, on insurance, on police routines, etc. If recording differs between police districts (in cross section studies) or over the years (in time series studies), a spurious negative correlation will appear between the crime rate and the proportion of crimes that are cleared up (see e.g. Blumstein et al., 1978). If, on the other hand, an increase in the number of policemen increases the number of crimes that are formally recorded, but not cleared up, there will be a spurious negative correlation between the number of policemen and clear-up proportion. Thus, underreporting and changes in recording will usually introduce a bias in favour of deterrence, but against the hypothesis that the police produces it (Cameron 1988), cf section 3.7. These spurious correlations impede the evaluation of criminometric studies, that most often confirm that crime increases with a decrease in the clear-up proportion, but that more police does not increase the clear-up proportion. This difficulty has inspired us to deal more explicitly with measurement errors. Especially, we introduce latent variables

---

[1]A shorter and less elaborated version of sections 6.1-6.5 has been published as Aasness, Eide and Skjerpen (1993). In the present version a minor mistake in the covariance matrix has been corrected, and the estimates are therefore slightly different from those of the previous version.

and employ the maximum likelihood method in estimating the structural relations of a simultaneous model.

Fisher and Nagin (1978) have discussed the serious problem of identification of models of crime. They are reluctant to accept the commonly used procedure in empirical crime studies of identifying models by excluding various socioeconomic variables from the equations. Using panel data we have succeeded in identifying our model by showing that the structural parameters are explicit functions of the theoretical 2. order moments of the logs of the crime and clear-up rates.

When designing the model, we have emphasized simplicity in order to focus on some basic theoretical and empirical issues. In particular, we have not included sociodemographic variables explicitly. We include, however, latent police districts effects which summarize the effects of socioeconomic variables on crimes and on clear-ups, and we model the distributions of these latent variables across police districts and over time. The strength of sentences is not included as a variable, because no perceptible difference in this factor seems to exist between police districts and over time in the period studied.

The chapter is organized as follows: In section 6.2 the criminometric model is derived by combining an equilibrium model of the latent number of crimes and clear-ups, based on behavioural relations of the offenders and the police, and measurement relations allowing for random and systematic measurement errors in the registered crimes and clear-ups. Furthermore, submodels and hypotheses are classified. Section 6.3 presents detailed and subtle identification results within this model class for panel data. Data and inference procedures are presented in section 6.4, and empirical results using Norwegian data in section 6.5. In section 6.6 twelve types of crime are analysed in a similar manner. The main conclusions are summarized in section 6.7.

6.2. Model framework and hypotheses

The criminometric model is designed to describe and explain crime and clear-up rates for I ($i=1,2,...I$) police districts in T ($t=1,2,...,T$) years. Section 6.2.1 presents the equilibrium model of crimes and clear-ups based on behavioural relations between the true latent variables. The crime and clear-up tendencies of the police districts are discussed in section 6.2.2. In section 6.2.3 we introduce measurement relations connecting the true latent variables with the observed crimes and clear-ups. The criminometric model in final form, derived from the submodels in 6.2.1, 6.2.2 and 6.2.3, is given in section 6.2.4, and in section 6.2.5 we define submodels and present hypotheses to be tested. Note that the equations below hold for all relevant i and t.

6.2.1 An equilibrium model of crimes and clear-ups

The equilibrium model consists of the following three equations:

$$P_{it} = Y_{it}/X_{it},$$ (6.1a)

$$X_{it} = P_{it}^{b}C_{it},$$ (6.1b)

$$Y_{it} = X_{it}^{r}U_{it}.$$ (6.1c)

X_{it} is the (true) *crime rate*, i.e. the number of crimes per 1000 inhabitants, in police district i in year t. Y_{it} is the *clear-up rate* defined as the number of clear-ups per 1000 inhabitants. P_{it} is the *clear-up proportion* defined in (6.1a), i.e. the number of clear-ups as a share of the number of crimes. (In the literature this concept (P_{it}) is sometimes denoted "clear-up rate", while we prefer to use this term to denote the concept symbolized by Y_{it}, treating crimes and clear-ups "symmetrically" throughout the analysis.)

The crime function (6.1b) says that the crime rate (X_{it}) is a simple power function of the clear-up proportion (P_{it}). It can be interpreted as a behavioural relation for an average offender with rational expectations on the probability of being caught. Furthermore, it can be derived from a utility maximizing model in the tradition of Becker (1968), keeping the severity of punishment constant. For convenience we will call the parameter b the *deterrence elasticity* and the variable C_{it} the *crime tendency* in police district i in year t. The crime tendency (C_{it}) summarizes the effect of the socioeconomic environment and other variables not explicitly modelled. The distribution of these latent crime tendencies across districts and over time will be modelled below.

The clear-up function (6.1c) says that the clear-up rate (Y_{it}) is a simple power function of the crime rate (X_{it}). It can be interpreted as a behavioural relation of the police. One may also interpret it as a combined relation of the behaviour of the police and the political authorities financing the police force. For convenience we will call the parameter r the *clear-up elasticity*, and the variable U_{it} the *clear-up tendency*.

We will below interpret, exploit, and/or test the following hypotheses on the deterrence elasticity (b) and the clear-up elasticity (r):

$$H_{b0}: b<0, \quad H_{r0}: r>0, \quad H_{r1}: r<1, \quad H_{d0}: d\equiv1+b(1-r)>0.$$ (6.2)

The theory of Becker (1968) implies H_{b0}, and most empirical studies reviewed in Chapter 4 support this hypothesis. The various weak aspects of the majority of these studies, however, require further testing of the deterrent effect of the probability of sanctions. Hypothesis H_{r0} seems reasonable because more crimes make it possible to get more cases cleared up. With more crimes, however, less police force would be available per case, thus H_{r1} seems plausible. This hypothesis, too, is (indirectly) supported by several empirical studies, where the probability of sanctions is found to be a decreasing function of the crime rate, see e.g. Vandaele (1978). Restriction H_{d0} secures that there will exist a meaningful and stable solution to our equilibrium model. (The significance of the sign of the "stability parameter" d is discussed below.) Assuming H_{r1}, the restriction H_{d0} is equivalent to $b > -1/(1-r)$, i.e. the deterrence elasticity must not, for a fixed value of r, be too negative. Furthermore, from H_{b0}, H_{r1}, and H_{d0} follows

H_{d1}: $0 < d < 1$.

The system of equations (6.1) has three endogenous variables (P_{it}, X_{it}, Y_{it}), and two exogenous variables (C_{it}, U_{it}), with the following solution:

$$P_{it} = C_{it}^{(r-1)/d} U_{it}^{1/d}, \tag{6.3a}$$

$$X_{it} = C_{it}^{1/d} U_{it}^{b/d}, \tag{6.3b}$$

$$Y_{it} = C_{it}^{r/d} U_{it}^{(1+b)/d}. \tag{6.3c}$$

Assuming (6.2), we obtain clear-cut sign results in five out of six cases: Increased crime tendency (C_{it}) decreases the clear-up proportion (P_{it}), increases the crime rate (X_{it}) and increases the clear-up rate (Y_{it}). Increased clear-up tendency (U_{it}) increases the clear-up proportion (P_{it}), and reduces the crime rate (X_{it}), whereas the sign effect on the clear-up rate depends on the magnitude of the deterrence effect:

$$El_{U_{it}} Y_{it} = (1+b)d \gtrless 0 \quad \text{iff} \quad b \gtrless -1. \tag{6.4}$$

Thus, if the deterrence elasticity is less than -1, an increased clear-up tendency (U_{it}) reduces the number of clear-ups (Y_{it}) due to the strong reduction in the number of crimes.

The question of stability of the equilibrium solution (6.3) can most easily be discussed by help of Fig. 6.1, where the crime rate is measured along the horizontal axis, and the clear-up proportion along the vertical one. (For convenience, the subscripts i and t are here dropped.) The crime curves illustrate relation (6.1b) when $b < 0$. The crime control curves are obtained by eliminating the clear-up rate through substitution of (6.1c) into (6.1a):

$$P_{it} = X_{it}^{r-1} U_{it} , \quad \text{or} \tag{6.1c'}$$

$$X_{it} = P_{it}^{\frac{1}{r-1}} U_{it}^{\frac{1}{1-r}} . \tag{6.1c''}$$

Relation (6.1c') can be interpreted as the crime control function of the society (including the police). The clear-up activity represented by (6.1c) has been transformed into a function determining the clear-up probability (which again, in interaction with the crime function, determines the equilibrium values of the model).

In Fig. 6.1 we assume that there exist positive equilibrium values P^* and and X^* of the clear-up proportions and crime rates, respectively, and that H_{b0} and H_{r1} are satisfied. In Fig. 6.1 (a) the crime curve is steeper than the crime control curve, which means, cf (6.1b) and (6.1c''), that $1/(r-1) < b$, or $1+b(1-r) > 0$, which is the same as restriction H_{d0}. Considering, according to the correspondence-principle of Samuelson (1945), our equilibrium to be the stationary solution to a corresponding dynamic model, where the society (including the police) determines the clear-up probability (cf (6.1c')), and the potential offenders thereafter determines the number of crimes (cf (6.1b)), the following mechanism is obtained: If we start out with a hypothetical crime rate $X1$, the society's crime control (cf (6.1c')) will result in a clear-up rate $P1$, a rate at which crime (cf (6.1b)) will be reduced to $X2$, which again will result in a higher clear-up rate $P2$, etc. The crime rate and the clear-up proportion will move towards the equilibrium solution. A similar move towards equilibrium will obtain if we start from a crime rate below its equilibrium value. Thus, restriction $d>0$ is sufficient for a stable equilibrium under the stated conditions. If $d<0$, we have the situation in Fig. 6.1 (b). Here, the society's crime control activity will produce, from a hypothetical crime rate $X3$, say, a clear-up proportion $P3$, that will result in a higher crime rate $X4$, which again will produce a lower clear-up proportion $P4$, etc. The crime rate will explode. Starting with any crime rate below X^*, the clear-up proportion will increase and the crime rate decrease. With our assumptions, we thus find that $d>0$ is also a necessary condition for the equilibrium solution to be stable. (If $d=0$, the two curves merge, and no single equilibrium solution is obtained.) It is straightforward to formally prove stability by analyzing an appropriate difference equation.

6.2.2. Distribution of crime and clear-up tendencies

The model determines an equilibrium for each police district in every year. By specifying

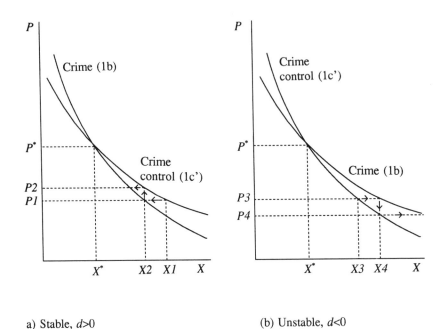

a) Stable, *d*>0   (b) Unstable, *d*<0

Fig. 6.1. Stability of equilibrium

a distribution on the crime and clear-up tendencies (C_{it}, U_{it}) across police districts, and how it varies over time, we obtain a corresponding distribution of crimes and clear-ups (X_{it}, Y_{it}) through the reduced form model (6.3). Consider the following decomposition:

$$\ln C_{it} = \omega_{0t} + \omega_{1i} + t\omega_{2i}, \tag{6.5a}$$
$$\ln U_{it} = \lambda_{0t} + \lambda_{1i} + t\lambda_{2i}, \tag{6.5b}$$

where ω_{0t} and λ_{0t} are deterministic (police district invariant) time trends, and the remaining ωs and λs are time invariant latent district effects. Stochastic specifications are given in (6.15) below. The assumptions that the covariance matrices, of ωs and λs respectively, are positive semidefinite can be stated as the following hypotheses:

$$H_{\omega}: \sigma_{\omega 1\omega 1} \geq 0,\ \sigma_{\omega 2\omega 2} \geq 0,\ \sigma^2_{\omega 1\omega 2} \leq \sigma_{\omega 1\omega 1}\sigma_{\omega 2\omega 2} \tag{6.6a}$$
$$H_{\lambda}: \sigma_{\lambda 1\lambda 1} \geq 0,\ \sigma_{\lambda 2\lambda 2} \geq 0,\ \sigma^2_{\lambda 1\lambda 2} \leq \sigma_{\lambda 1\lambda 1}\sigma_{\lambda 2\lambda 2}. \tag{6.6b}$$

These hypotheses will be discussed and tested below.

This structure allows for a restricted evolution over time in the distribution of the crime and clear-up tendencies across police districts. In particular, it follows that

$$\text{var } \ln C_{it} = \sigma_{\omega 1\omega 1} + 2t\sigma_{\omega 1\omega 2} + t^2\sigma_{\omega 2\omega 2}, \tag{6.7a}$$
$$\text{var } \ln U_{it} = \sigma_{\lambda 1\lambda 1} + 2t\sigma_{\lambda 1\lambda 2} + t^2\sigma_{\lambda 2\lambda 2}. \tag{6.7b}$$

Note that if $\ln C_{it}$ is assumed to be normally distributed, the coefficient of variation of the crime tendency, $\sqrt{\text{var} C_{it}}/EC_{it}$, will be a simple transformation of var $\ln C_{it}$, cf Aitchison and Brown (1957, p. 8). Thus, dropping the term ω_{2i} implies a constant coefficient of variation of the crime tendency C_{it}.

From (6.7) it follows that

$$\Delta\text{var } \ln C_{it} = 2\sigma_{\omega 1\omega 2} + (2t+1)\sigma_{\omega 2\omega 2}, \tag{6.8a}$$
$$\Delta\text{var } \ln U_{it} = 2\sigma_{\lambda 1\lambda 2} + (2t+1)\sigma_{\lambda 2\lambda 2}, \tag{6.8b}$$

where Δ denotes the first difference operator. From (6.8a) we see that the variance of the log of the crime tendency decreases if and only if $\sigma_{\omega 1\omega 2} < -\sigma_{\omega 2\omega 2}(2t+1)/2$. Thus, a necessary condition for this to happen, interpreting $\sigma_{\omega 2\omega 2}$ as a positive variance, is that the covariance between the two components ω_1 and ω_2 is negative.

It should be noted, however, that it is possible to give another interpretation of (6.7) and (6.8) above. We may drop (6.5) and (6.6) and start with specifying (6.7). Then we may interpret, say $\sigma_{\omega 2\omega 2}$, just as a parameter in a relation which describes how var $\ln C_{it}$ evolves over time. With such an interpretation it is meaningful to have a negative value of $\sigma_{\omega 2\omega 2}$, which implies a time trend towards decreasing spread in the log of the crime tendencies across police districts.

Observe further that our model allows for four different time trends in the logs of crime and clear-up tendencies: i) monotonically increasing, ii) monotonically decreasing, iii) first increasing and then decreasing, and iv) first decreasing and then increasing.

We consider the 2. order polynomial in (6.7a) to be a valid approximation only for a limited time period. In particular, we are interested to test the hypotheses that the derived variances of the crime and clear-up tendencies are positive for a set of time periods, i.e.

$$H_C: \text{var } C_{it} > 0, \ t=1,2,\dots,T, \tag{6.9a}$$
$$H_U: \text{var } U_{it} > 0, \ t=1,2,\dots,T. \tag{6.9b}$$

In our empirical test we shall interpret $t=1,2,\dots,T$ as the sample period. It may happen that our second order polynomial can make these variances negative for some years, not only outside the sample period, but also within it.

It may occur that H_{ω} is not fulfilled, while H_C is valid, a result which is connected with the interpretation above of (6.7). Both types of hypotheses will be tested in our empirical analyses.

6.2.3. Measurement relations

Let x_{it} and y_{it} be the logs of the *registered crime and clear-up rates*, respectively. These are related to the true rates by the following equations:

$$x_{it} = \ln X_{it} + e_t + \varepsilon_{it}, \tag{6.10a}$$
$$y_{it} = \ln Y_{it} + f_t + \varphi_{it}. \tag{6.10b}$$

Here, $\exp(e_t)$ and $\exp(f_t)$ represent systematic, multiplicative measurement errors in $\exp(x_{it})$ and $\exp(y_{it})$, respectively. The terms e_t and f_t are police district invariant variables. They may, however, change over time. They are both deterministic variables. The term e_t takes account of the problem of systematic underreporting (dark number) of crime. The variables ε_{it} and φ_{it} can be interpreted as random measurement errors. Stochastic specifications are given in (6.15).

The assumption that the covariance matrix of the measurement errors is positive definite, can be stated as the following hypothesis:

$$H_M: \sigma_{\varepsilon\varepsilon} > 0, \ \sigma_{\varphi\varphi} > 0, \ \sigma^2_{\varepsilon\varphi} < \sigma_{\varepsilon\varepsilon}\sigma_{\varphi\varphi} . \tag{6.11}$$

Note that the random measurement errors (ε_{it} and φ_{it}) are allowed to be correlated. We expect this correlation to be positive: If, in a police district, registration is particularly sloppy, some crimes that elsewhere normally would have resulted in separate files, are only informally recorded. As formal files, including eventual clear-ups, constitute the basis for the production of statistics, both the registered numbers of crimes and the registered number of clear-ups will be lower than in a similar police district with better registration procedures. This underregistration results in a positive correlation between the random measurement errors. The same will happen if some files disappear or are disposed of in the police departments, or forgotten when statistics are produced by the end of the year. We thus state the hypothesis

H_{MC}: $\sigma_{\varepsilon\varphi} > 0$. (6.12)

For convenience we define the following transformed variables:

$$\chi_{it} = \ln X_{it} + e_t,$$ (6.13a)
$$\psi_{it} = \ln Y_{it} + f_t,$$ (6.13b)
$$\pi_{it} = \psi_{it} - \chi_{it},$$ (6.13c)
$$a_t = \omega_{0t} + (1+b)e_t - bf_t,$$ (6.13d)
$$k_t = \lambda_{0t} - re_t + f_t.$$ (6.13e)

In (6.13a) we define the log of the *latent crime rate* (χ_{it}) as the sum of the log of the true crime rate (X_{it}) and the systematic measurement error (e_t). The log of the *latent clear-up rate* (ψ_{it}), and the log of the *latent clear-up proportion* (π_{it}) are defined in (6.13b) and (6.13c). The parameters a_t and k_t are introduced in order to simplify the criminometric model below. Note that a_t and k_t are composed of the deterministic time trends of (6.5) and (6.10). We do not try to identify and estimate these components separately.

6.2.4. The criminometric model in final form

From (6.1), (6.5), (6.10), and (6.13) we can now derive the following criminometric model:

$$x_{it} = \chi_{it} + \varepsilon_{it},$$ (6.14a)
$$y_{it} = \psi_{it} + \varphi_{it},$$ (6.14b)
$$\pi_{it} = \psi_{it} - \chi_{it},$$ (6.14c)
$$\chi_{it} = b\pi_{it} + a_t + \omega_{1i} + t\omega_{2i},$$ (6.14d)
$$\psi_{it} = r\chi_{it} + k_t + \lambda_{1i} + t\lambda_{2i}.$$ (6.14e)

We consider (ε_{it}, φ_{it}, ω_{1i}, ω_{2i}, λ_{1i}, λ_{2i}) as a vector of exogenous, random variables independently drawn from the same distribution, with the following first and second order moments:

$$E\varepsilon_{it} = E\varphi_{it} = E\omega_{1i} = E\omega_{2i} = E\lambda_{1i} = E\lambda_{2i} = 0,$$ (6.15a)

$$E\varepsilon_{it}^2 = \sigma_{\varepsilon\varepsilon}, \quad E\varphi_{it}^2 = \sigma_{\varphi\varphi}, \quad E\varepsilon_{it}\varphi_{it} = \sigma_{\varepsilon\varphi},$$ (6.15b)

$$E\omega_{1i}^2=\sigma_{\omega1\omega1}, \quad E\omega_{2i}^2=\sigma_{\omega2\omega2}, \quad E\omega_{1i}\omega_{2i}=\sigma_{\omega1\omega2}, \tag{6.15c}$$

$$E\lambda_{1i}^2=\sigma_{\lambda1\lambda1}, \quad E\lambda_{2i}^2=\sigma_{\lambda2\lambda2}, \quad E\lambda_{1i}\lambda_{2i}=\sigma_{\lambda1\lambda2}. \tag{6.15d}$$

All other covariances between the exogenous variables (ε,φ, ω, and λ) are assumed to be zero. Note that the assumptions of (6.15a) are innocent because of the constant terms defined in (6.5) and (6.10). The other assumptions are to some degree commented on above. In section 6.4 we will also exploit and discuss the assumption that the variables are multinormally distributed.

6.2.5 Hypotheses and model specifications

We have in (6.2), (6.6), (6.9), (6.11), and (6.12) formulated various interval hypoteses about the parameters of our model framework. These are restated in Table 6.1. On the basis of point hypotheses about some of the parameters we have in Table 6.2 classified various models within our model framework. The assumptions of the models correspond to some of the hypotheses we are interested in testing, especially hypotheses about the correlation of measurement errors, and about the distributions of latent police district effects. Each assumption is given a label, and each model will be denoted by the corresponding combination of labels. (See Aasness, Biørn, and Skjerpen (1993) for a similar framework.) On the basis of the model classification of Table 6.2 it is possible to specify 2x4x4=32 different models defined by different assumptions in the M-, W- and L-dimensions, where these dimensions refer to correlations of measurement errors (M), correlations of police district effects on crimes (W), and correlations of police district effects on clear-ups (L). All these specific models are estimated and/or tested in the empirical analysis. We could, of course, introduce other specifications, e.g. time trends in the police district invariant terms a_t and k_t, but this is not carried out in the present analysis.

6.3. Identification

Identification of most of the submodels are proven by showing that the structural parameters are explicit functions of the theoretical 2. order moments of the crime and clear-up rates, see Appendix B. The results of our investigation of identification are summarized in Table 6.3. Here Wi^* ($i=0,1,2,3$) denotes the same assumptions as Wi in Table 6.2, except that all parameters assumed to be free in Table 6.2 now are assumed not to be zero.

Table 6.1
Interval hypotheses

Name of hyp.	Hypothesis	Explanation	Eq. no.
H_{b0}	$b<0$	Negative deterrence elasticity	6.2
H_{r0}	$r>0$	Positive clear-up elasticity	
H_{r1}	$r<1$	Clear-ups increase proportionally less than crimes	6.2
H_{d0}	$d \equiv 1+b(1-r)>0$	Requirement of stable solution to crime model	6.2
H_{d1}	$0<d<1$	Derived from H_{b0}, H_{r1}, and H_{d0}.	
H_{ω}	$\sigma_{\omega 1\omega 1} \geq 0$, $\sigma_{\omega 2\omega 2} \geq 0$, $\sigma^2_{\omega 1\omega 2} \leq \sigma_{\omega 1\omega 1}\sigma_{\omega 2\omega 2}$	Positive semidefinite covariance matrices for district effects in crime	6.6a
H_{λ}	$\sigma_{\lambda 1\lambda 1} \geq 0$, $\sigma_{\lambda 2\lambda 2} \geq 0$, $\sigma^2_{\lambda 1\lambda 2} \leq \sigma_{\lambda 1\lambda 1}\sigma_{\lambda 2\lambda 2}$	Positive semidefinite covariance matrices for district effects in clear-ups	6.6b
H_C	$\text{var } C_{it}>0$, $t=1,2,\ldots,T$	Positive variances of crime tendencies for all years in the sample period	6.9a
H_U	$\text{var } U_{it}>0$, $t=1,2,\ldots,T$	Positive variances of clear-up tendencies for all years in sample period	6.9b
H_M	$\sigma_{\varepsilon\varepsilon}>0$, $\sigma_{\varphi\varphi}>0$, $\sigma^2_{\varepsilon\varphi}<\sigma_{\varepsilon\varepsilon}\sigma_{\varphi\varphi}$	Positive definite covariance matrix of measurement errors	6.11
H_{MC}	$\sigma_{\varepsilon\varphi}>0$	Positively correlated measurement errors	6.12

Criminometric analyses

Table 6.2
Classification of hypotheses and models[a]

Assumptions w.r.t. correlations of measurement errors

Label	Parameter restriction	Interpretation
	$\sigma_{\varepsilon\varphi}$	
M0	0	No correlation of measurement errors
M1	free	Measurement errors correlated

Assumptions w.r.t. correlations of police district effects on crimes

Label	$\sigma_{\omega1\omega1}$	$\sigma_{\omega2\omega2}$	$\sigma_{\omega1\omega2}$	Interpretation
W0	0	0	0	No district effect in crime
W1	free	0	0	Time invariant district effect in crime
W2	free	free	0	Trend in distribution of district effect in crime
W3	free	free	free	Time invariant and trend effects correlated

Assumptions w.r.t. correlations of police district effects on clear-ups

Label	$\sigma_{\lambda1\lambda1}$	$\sigma_{\lambda2\lambda2}$	$\sigma_{\lambda1\lambda2}$	Interpretation
L0	0	0	0	No district effect in clear-up
L1	free	0	0	Time invariant district effect in clear-up
L2	free	free	0	Trend in distribution of district effect in clear-up
L3	free	free	free	Time invariant and trend effects correlated

[a] A model is specified by a combination of 3 labels: e.g. model M0W1L1 is a model where there is no correlation of measurement errors, and no trends in the police district effects on crimes and clear-ups.

Table 6.3
Identification of submodels of W3L3[ab]

	W3*	W2*	W1*	W0*
L3*	Identified if assuming H_{d1} or #A=1	Identified	Identified	Not identified[c]
L2*	Identified	Identified if assuming H_{d1} or #A=1	Identified	Not identified[c]
L1*	Identified	Identified	Not identified[e]	Not identified[c]
L0*	Not identified[d]	Not identified[d]	Not identified[d]	Not identified

[a] See section 6.2.5 and Table 6.2 for definitions of models. The results hold for both M0 and M1.

[b] $\sigma_{\epsilon\epsilon}$, $\sigma_{\varphi\varphi}$, and $\sigma_{\epsilon\varphi}$ are identified for W3L3 (and for all submodels).

[c] b is identified.

[d] r is identified.

[e] If one of the 4 non-identified parameters is given a fixed value, the remaining ones are identified.

Lj^* is defined similarly, and we have, for instance, that W1*L0 corresponds to W1L0, the difference being that $\sigma_{\omega1\omega1}$ can be zero in the latter, but not in the former. Table 6.3 thus contains a complete set of submodels of W3L3.

A particular problem arises in models W3*L3* and W2*L2*. Here identification of r (or b) requires the solution of a second order equation in this parameter, and we will in general have two different roots, corresponding to two observationally equivalent structures. The model can nevertheless be identified if only one of the two solutions satisfy a priori restrictions on the set of parameter values. The simplest case is to assume H_{d1}, i.e. $0<d<1$, which can be derived from (6.2), since we have shown (Appendix B, Section B.10) that only one of the two solutions can satisfy this restriction.

If one is not willing to use H_{d1} as a maintained assumption, for example because one is interested in testing this hypothesis, or the hypothesis of $b<0$, there are still possibilities for discriminating between the two observationally equivalent structures, combining a priori and empirical information. We will give an example of this, which we will exploit in our empirical analysis below.

Let θ denote the vector of n=11 structural parameters in our model. Consider first the following set of parameters:

$$\Theta_1=\{\theta\in R^n\,|\,\sigma_{\epsilon\epsilon}\geq0,\ \sigma_{\varphi\varphi}\geq0,\ \sigma^2_{\epsilon\varphi}\leq\sigma_{\epsilon\epsilon}\sigma_{\varphi\varphi},\ \text{var}\ \ln C_{it}\geq0,\ \text{var}\ \ln U_{it}\geq0,\ t=1,2,...,T\},\qquad(6.16a)$$

i.e. the parameter values are meaningful with respect to our interpretation with measurement errors and variation in crime tendencies and clear-up tendencies across police districts. If, say, solution I belongs to Θ_1, while solution II does not, we can discriminate between them, i.e. solution I identifies the structure.

It may happen that both solutions belong to Θ_1. Then we may want to consider further restrictions, say

$$\Theta_2 = \{\theta \in R^n \,|\, r > 0,\ d > 0\}, \qquad\qquad (6.16b)$$

cf hypotheses H_{r0} and H_{d0} in section 6.2.1. It turns out that (6.16b) is all we need in our empirical analysis for total crime in section 6.5.

In section 6.6, analyzing various types of crime, we need further restrictions, and we apply

$$\Theta_3 = \{\theta \in R^n \,|\, b < 1,\ r < 2\}. \qquad\qquad (6.16c)$$

These restrictions are somewhat more arbitrary, but the idea is the following. One may imagine societies with a positive deterrence elasticity b and/or a clear-up elasticity larger than 1, i.e. where hypotheses H_{b0} and H_{r1} are not fulfilled. It seems incredible, however, if these parameters are very high. We have in (6.16c) chosen limits that are 1 higher than those on which H_{b0} and H_{r1} are based. We denote the corresponding hypotheses H_{b1} and H_{r2}. Restriction (6.16c) is exploited in our empirical analysis in section 6.6.

Let $\Sigma(\theta)$ denote the theoretical covariance matrix of the observed variables as a function of the unknown parameters θ of our model. Let

$$A = \{\theta \in R^n \,|\, \Sigma(\theta) = \Sigma\} \cap \Theta$$

for an arbitrary value of the covariance matrix Σ, where Θ is a set of parameters, say Θ_1, Θ_2, Θ_3, or a combination of these. If, for a given model, the number of elements in A is equal to one ($\#A = 1$), we consider the corresponding solution the only one that can be accepted, conditional on the choice of Θ. The number of elements in A can depend on Σ, and the question of identification of $W3^*L3^*$ and $W2^*L2^*$ thus involves empirical issues. In the empirical analysis below we argue that only one of the two solutions of $W3^*L3^*$ is relevant in our case.

It is demonstrated in Appendix B (Section B.9) that, Wi^*Lj^* is observationally equivalent to Wj^*Li^* for $i \neq j$ and $i,j = 0,1,2,3$. It is also shown, however, that assuming H_{d1} for one such model, the symmetric one is unstable, i.e. $d < 0$. That is, within the set of two symmetric models $\{W i^* L j^*, W j^* L i^*\}$ $(i \neq j, i,j=1,2,3)$, we can identify the correct model under assumption H_{d1}. Furthermore, the restrictions in (6.16) will in our empirical analysis turn out to be sufficient to determine which of two "symmetric" models is relevant or acceptable.

The parameters $\sigma_{\epsilon\epsilon}$, $\sigma_{\phi\phi}$, and $\sigma_{\epsilon\phi}$ are identified for W3L3 as a whole. Six of the submodels are completely identified. Identification of b is further obtained in the three first models of the last column of Table 6.3, whereas identification of the remaining parameters here requires one supplementary piece of information (e.g. fixing the value of one of them). Similarly, r is identified in the three first models of the last line, and here too one more piece of information is necessary in order to identify the remaining parameters.

6.4. Data and estimation

The model is estimated by use of data on the number of crimes and clear-ups for 53 police districts in Norway for the period 1970-78, (cf Central Bureau of Statistics, annual). Our main reasons for choosing this period is the absence of substantial changes in legal rules or registration practices. The effects on crime and crime registration of such changes being difficult to model, it is convenient to study a period where these problems are negligible or of minor importance. These data are transformed into crime rates and clear-up rates (Tables A3 and A5 of Appendix C) and further into logs of these rates (Tables A7 and A8 of Appendix C). Finally, the logs are used to calculate a covariance matrix of the log numbers of crime and clear-up rates for the nine years. This covariance matrix (see Appendix C) is all the data we use in our econometric analysis of total crime.

Let S be this sample covariance matrix of our observed variables, and

$$F = \ln|\Sigma(\theta)| + \text{tr}(S\Sigma(\theta)^{-1}) - \ln|S| - 2T, \tag{6.17}$$

where "tr" is the trace operator, i.e. the sum of the diagonal elements of the matrix.

Minimization of F w.r.t. θ is equivalent to maximization of the likelihood function when assuming that all the observed variables (i.e. the logs of x and y) are multinormally distributed. (All the first order moments are used to estimate the constant terms a_t and k_r.) We have used the computer program LISREL 7 by Jöreskog and Sörbom (1988) to perform the numerical analysis.

A standard measure of the goodness of fit of the entire model in LISREL is
GFI = $1 - \text{tr}[(\Sigma^{-1}S - I)^2]/\text{tr}[(\Sigma^{-1}S)^2]$,
where I is the identity matrix; GFI = 1 indicates perfect fit. Standard asymptotic t-values

and χ^2- statistics are utilized. We use a significance level of 0.01 as a standard in our test, but report also significance probabilities.

We will test a specific model 0 (the null hypothesis) against a more general model 1 (the maintained hypothesis) by a likelihood ratio test. Let F_0 and F_1 be the minimum of F under model 0 and model 1, respectively, and let s be the difference in the number of parameters of the two models. It can be shown that minus twice the logarithm of the likelihood ratio is equal to $I(F_0 - F_1)$, where I is the number of police districts. According to standard theory this statistic is approximately χ^2 distributed with s degrees of freedom. The χ^2 value for each model, given in Table 6.4, is defined as IF_0, which can be interpreted as the test statistic above when the alternative hypothesis is an exactly identified model, giving a perfect fit to the sample covariance matrix and accordingly $F_1=0$. The test statistic $I(F_0 - F_1)$ for an arbitrary pair of models may thus be computed by simply subtracting the corresponding pair of χ^2 values. The significance probability corresponding to the value of a test statistic, i.e. the probability of getting a χ^2 value greater than the value actually obtained given that the null hypothesis is true, is reported in Table 6.5.

LISREL 7 minimizes the function F without imposing any constraints on the admissible values of the parameter vector θ. Thus the LISREL estimate of a parameter which we interpret as a variance, may well turn out to be negative. This may be considered as a drawback of this computer program. However, if our model and its interpretation is correct, the LISREL estimates should turn out to have the expected signs, apart from sampling errors. Thus, if for a given model the estimates fulfill all the conditions in (6.16a), we will take this as a confirmation that the model has passed an important test. This in fact happened in our empirical analysis of both total crime and of the 12 different types of crime.

If one is unwilling to assume normality of the observed variables, the estimators derived from minimizing F above can be labelled quasi maximum likelihood estimators. These estimators will be consistent, but their efficiency and the properties of the test procedures are not so obvious. A large literature on the robustness of these types of estimators and test procedures for departure from normality prevails, see e.g. Jøreskog and Sørbom (1988) for an extensive list of references, with quite different results depending on the assumptions and methods used. A recent and growing literature shows, however, that the estimators and test statistics derived under normality assumptions within LISREL type of models retain their asymptotic properties for wide departures from normality, exploiting assumptions on independently distributed nonnormal latent variables, see e.g. Anderson and Amemiya (1988), Amemiya and Anderson (1990), Browne (1987), and Browne and Shapiro (1988).

The assumption of normality can be tested by use of the (moment coefficient of) skewness $m_3/\sqrt{m_2^3}$ and the (moment coefficient of) kurtosis m_4/m_2^2. In a normal distribution the skewness is equal to zero, and the kurtosis is equal to three. Given that the distribution is normal, the observed skewness and kurtosis are asymptotically independent, and can thus be used for two asymptotically independent tests of normality. Skewness and kurtosis for our samples have been calculated (by SPSS) for the crime and clear-up rates, and for their logs, and are included in Tables A3-A8 of Appendix C. In 98% of all samples of size 50 from a normal population we have that the absolute value of skewness is less than 0.787, and the value of kurtosis is within the interval [1.95, 4.88][2]. We find that normality is rejected for the crime rate (Table A3 of Appendix C) by the skewness test for all years, and by the kurtosis test for two years. As for the clear-up rate (Table A5 of Appendix C), normality is rejected by both tests for all years. The log of crime rates (Table A7 of Appendix C) passes the skewness test for all years, but the kurtosis test for none, whereas the log of clear-up rates (Table A8 of Appendix C) passes the skewness test in three years, and the kurtosis test also in three years. Obviously, a logarithmic specification of our model is to be preferred to a linear one. The values of the observed kurtosis are low, indicating platykurtic or "flat" distributions. This departure from normality is considered in the χ^2 tests below.

Another approach, based on an assumption of a multivariate elliptical distribution of the observed variables, shows that the likelihood ratio statistics derived under normality are still applicable, by rescaling the test statistics by a factor equal to the inverse of Mardia's coefficient of relative multivariate kurtosis, see Shapiro and Browne (1987). In the present data set of total crime this coefficient is 1.06. This supports our hypothesis that our procedure is robust against deviations from normality, and we do not consider it necessary here to study distributions in more detail.

6.5. Empirical results - total crime

6.5.1. Likelihood ratio tests

All 32 models classified in Table 6.2 have been fitted. Table 6.4 contains for all models the degrees of freedom (df), the goodness of fit (GFI), and the likelihood ratio χ^2 test statistic for each model against a model with no restriction on the covariance matrix.

First, we have studied the presence of correlation of measurement errors by testing M0

---

[2]The critical values of skewness and kurtosis can be found in Pearson (1965). A discussion of the present tests of normality is found in White and MacDonald (1980).

against M1. For all (16) possible combinations of maintained assumptions in the W- and L-dimensions M0 is rejected, even at a level of significance of 10^{-6}.

Table 6.5.1 presents significance probabilities for tests of each of the hypotheses in the W-dimension against a more general hypothesis of the same dimension. These tests are performed for each of the alternative maintained assumptions in the L-dimension. Table 6.5.2 contains similar tests of the L-dimension. From Tables 6.5.1 and 6.5.2 we conclude that the hypotheses of W0, L0, W1, and L1 are rejected. We have further found (not included in Table 6.5) that W0L0 is rejected against W1L1, W1L1 against W2L2, and W2L2 against W3L3. This leaves us with the general model M1W3L3 and the two non-rejected models M1W3L2 and M1W2L3. The choice between them can be made on the basis of parsimony, and of the acceptability of the estimated parameters. It will be argued below that M1W3L2 is the model to be preferred.

6.5.2. Evaluation of models not rejected by likelihood ratio tests

As identification of certain parameters in some of our models depends on the solution of a second order equation, there will in general exist two observationally equivalent structures, and correspondingly two global minima to the fit function in (6.17). Depending on the starting values, LISREL will find one or the other of these two solutions. The second one, which has the same F-value as the first, can be located by choosing appropriate starting values. This is done for the model M1W3L3, where we obtain the solutions I and II, the parameter estimates of which are given in Table 6.6. Both solutions satisfy restriction (6.16a), which then cannot distinguish between them.

The two solutions are further characterized in Fig. 6.2, where the minimum value of F is plotted for various given values of r. The two global minima of F are obtained for those values of r that correspond to the solutions I and II. As a check of our conclusions, the minimum value of F has been calculated for a series of values of r in the interval [-200, 200]. F is decreasing for values of r to the left of the lower solution. For values of r higher than 1.8, F is decreasing, but very slowly, and does not reach lower than 2.829 in the interval studied. Solution II violates restrictions H_{r0} and H_{d0}, cf (6.16b), whereas all the estimates in solution I seem sensible. Thus, we prefer solution I.

We observe that the estimates of M1W3L3^I and M1W3L3^{II} are almost identical with those of M1W3L2 and M1W2L3, respectively. Furthermore, from the estimates of b and r we calculate the value of the stability parameter d to be 0.83 in M1W3L2 and -5.01 in M1W2L3. Thus we prefer the former model to the latter, cf section 6.3. The final choice is then between M1W3L3^I and M1W3L2. Both models have rather similar estimates. The

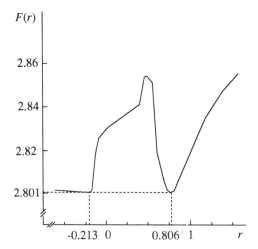

Fig. 6.2. *F*-values of M1W3L3 with two solutions

latter being more parsimonious, we consider this model to be the (slightly) preferred one. We focus on this model in sections 6.5.3 to 6.5.5, and discuss robustness of results across models in section 6.5.6.

6.5.3. The deterrence and clear-up elasticities

The estimate of the deterrence elasticity (b) is significantly negative in our preferred model, and close to -1. The estimate of the clear-up elasticity (r) is about 0.8 in the same model, and the confidence interval is clearly within the boudaries argued a priori, cf (6.2). These estimates of b and r imply that the estimate of the stability parameter d is 0.8, and the corresponding confidence interval is clearly within the boundaries (0,1), in agreement with our hypothesis H_{d1}.

6.5.4. Distribution of crime and clear-up tendencies

The estimates of the distribution parameters of the district effects on crime are also given in Table 6.6. All three are statistically significant. Straightforward calculation shows that

Table 6.4
Overview of fitted models

M1-models[a]

District effects on clear-ups		District effects on crime			
		W3	W2	W1	W0
L3	df	160	161	162	163[c]
	χ^2	291.25	291.87	304.69	509.72
	GFI	0.641	0.639	0.632	0.392
L2	df	161	162	163	164[c]
	χ^2	291.87	305.11	309.32	519.03
	GFI	0.639	0.631	0.628	0.386
L1	df	162	163	164[c]	165[c]
	χ^2	304.69	309.32	415.35	620.03
	GFI	0.632	0.628	0.508	0.329
L0	df	163[b]	164[b]	165[b]	166[bc]
	χ^2	509.72	519.03	620.03	1484.8
	GFI	0.392	0.386	0.329	0.185

M0-models[a]

District effects on clear-ups		District effects on crime			
		W3	W2	W1	W0
L3	df	161	162	163	164[c]
	χ^2	600.37	604.21	604.28	704.53
	GFI	0.467	0.460	0.460	0.428
L2	df	162	163	164	165[c]
	χ^2	604.21	622.64	622.65	717.73
	GFI	0.460	0.458	0.458	0.424
L1	df	163	164	165[c]	166[c]
	χ^2	604.28	622.65	742.98	815.16
	GFI	0.460	0.458	0.398	0.387
L0	df	164[b]	165[b]	166[b]	167[bc]
	χ^2	704.53	717.73	815.16	2055
	GFI	0.428	0.424	0.387	0.088

[a] See section 3 regarding the symmetry between WiLj and WjLi (i≠j; i=0,1,2,3).
[b] The model is estimated for a fixed value of b, any b would give the same χ^2.
[c] The model is estimated for a fixed value of r, any r would give the same χ^2.

Table 6.5

Significance probabilities in likelihood ratio tests[a]

	1. Tests of district effects on crimes			
Maintained	Null and alternative hypotheses			
assumptions	W0 against W1	W1 against W2	W2 against W3	W1 against W3
M1L3	0.000000	0.000451	0.442419	0.001581
M1L2	0.000000	0.049156	0.000273	0.000192
M1L1	0.000000	0.000000	0.028295	0.000000
M1L0	0.000000	0.000000	0.002206	0.000000

	2. Tests of district effects on clear-ups			
Maintained	Null and alternative hypotheses			
assumptions	L0 against L1	L1 against L2	L2 against L3	L1 against L3
M1W3	0.000000	0.000451	0.442419	0.001581
M1W2	0.000000	0.049156	0.000273	0.000192
M1W1	0.000000	0.000000	0.028295	0.000000
M1W0	0.000000	0.000000	0.002206	0.000000

[a] The equality of the significance probabilities between Tables 6.5.1 and 6.5.2 is due to the symmetry between the models $WiLj$ and $WjLi$, cf Table 6.4.

for our preferred model the variance of the log of the crime tendency, var $\ln C_{it} = \sigma_{\omega1\omega1} + t^2\sigma_{\omega2\omega2} + 2t\sigma_{\omega1\omega2}$, is estimated to be positive for all years, i.e. for $t=1,2,...,9$. As this estimate is not restricted to positive values by LISREL, we take the result as a confirmation that our model, and our interpretation of it, has passed an interesting test.

We note that $\sigma_{\omega1\omega2}$ is significantly negative. Furthermore, the estimates indicate a decrease in the variance of the log of the district effects over time. Denoting the first difference operator by Δ, we see in fact that Δvar $\ln C_{it} = (2t+1)\sigma_{\omega2\omega2} + 2\sigma_{\omega1\omega2}$ is negative for the whole period. The estimate of var $\ln C_{it}$ is, in this period, reduced from 0.250 to 0.171. The estimate of the variance of the log of the crime tendency is thus substantially reduced during the period.

Table 6.6
Estimates of non-rejected models[a][b]

Parameter	M1W3L3[I]	M1W3L2	M1W2L3	M1W3L3[II]
b	-0.824	-0.850	-5.107	-5.157
	(0.353)	(0.308)	(2.144)	(2.487)
r	0.810	0.804	-0.177	-0.213
	(0.094)	(0.082)	(0.426)	(0.519)
$\sigma_{\omega_1\omega_1}$	0.271	0.268	1.030	1.145
	(0.069)	(0.065)	(1.108)	(1.402)
$\sigma_{\omega_2\omega_2}$	0.0010	0.0010	0.0093	0.0109
	(0.0004)	(0.0003)	(0.0092)	(0.0125)
$\sigma_{\omega_1\omega_2}$	-0.0095	-0.0094	0[c]	-0.0194
	(0.0037)	(0.0035)		(0.0364)
$\sigma_{\lambda_1\lambda_1}$	0.043	0.040	0.371	0.398
	(0.015)	(0.013)	(0.323)	(0.407)
$\sigma_{\lambda_2\lambda_2}$	0.0004	0.0004	0.0013	0.0014
	(0.0002)	(0.0001)	(0.0012)	(0.0016)
$\sigma_{\lambda_1\lambda_2}$	-0.0007	0[c]	-0.0131	-0.0139
	(0.0010)		(0.0115)	(0.0145)
$\sigma_{\varepsilon\varepsilon}$	0.028	0.028	0.028	0.028
	(0.002)	(0.002)	(0.002)	(0.002)
$\sigma_{\varphi\varphi}$	0.066	0.066	0.066	0.066
	(0.005)	(0.005)	(0.005)	(0.005)
$\sigma_{\varepsilon\varphi}$	0.032	0.033	0.033	0.032
	(0.003)	(0.003)	(0.003)	(0.003)
d	0.843	0.833	-5.011	-5.255
	(0.044)	(0.045)	(1.609)	(1.725)

[a] See Table 6.2 for definitions of models. Solutions I and II correspond to the two solutions of a second order equation obtained in identifying the model.
[b] Standard errors in parentheses.
[c] A priori restriction.

The estimates of the distribution parameters of the district effects on clear-ups ($\sigma_{\lambda_1\lambda_1}$ and $\sigma_{\lambda_2\lambda_2}$) are positive, and significantly different from zero in our preferred model. The variance of the log of the clear-up tendency is increasing during the period from 0.040 to 0.072.

The distribution parameters $\sigma_{\omega_i\omega_i}$ and $\sigma_{\lambda_i\lambda_i}$ ($i=1,2$) are all positive, and interpreting these parameters as variances we find that our model has passed another interesting test.

6.5.5. Measurement errors

The estimates of the variances and the covariance of the errors of measurement are positive and highly significant. This confirms our hypothesis in section 2.3 of a positive $\sigma_{\varepsilon\varphi}$. Also note that the covariance matrix of the measurement errors (section 6.3) is positive definite.

6.5.6. Robustness of results

Table 6.7 shows the estimates of all models with two global maxima (solutions I and II). We observe that for all four solutions II the estimates of both r and d are negative. These models are thus rejected according to (6.16b).

Tables 6.8 and 6.9 contain the estimates of all identified M1- and M0-models, respectively (solutions II not included). The M0-models are strongly rejected against the corresponding M1-models, and we may thus expect that at least some of the estimators of the structural parameters are biased in the M0-models. But no clear-cut results emerge by comparing Tables 6.8 and 6.9. For example, the estimates of b and r are rather close to each other for M1W3L3 and M0W3L3. For the latter, however, the estimate of the variance of λ_2 is negative, thus modelling measurement errors correctly can be important for estimating the other parameters.

Just like in our preferred model, the estimate of b is found to be negative in all but 2 of the 16 estimated models in Tables 6.8 and 6.9. The two models in question, M1W2L1 and M1W3L1 have not significant estimates of b. They are strongly rejected by the likelihood ratio tests, and have some quite nonsensical estimates. Thus, we do not give them weight as evidence on b. We conclude that the estimated sign of b is robust across models, although the value varies substantially. This result suggests that misspecification in modelling may not hinder the sign of the deterrence elasticity to be correctly determined, but that a reliable estimate of its value requires thorough empirical analysis.

The estimate of r is, as expected, and just as in our preferred model, located in the interval [0,1] for all 11 models where the estimate is significant. The estimate is positive in 3 of the remaining models, and negative in two, i.e. in M0W1L2 and M1W2L3. Of these, model M0W1L2 is firmly rejected. According to Table 6.5, M1W2L3 is not rejected against M1W3L3. We nevertheless disregard the former model, because the estimated value of d is significantly negative, and because its symmetric counterpart M1W3L2 is perfectly

Table 6.7

Estimates of models with two global maxima[a][b]

Parameter	M1W3L3[I]	M1W3L3[II]	M1W2L2[I]	M1W2L2[II]	M0W3L3[I]	M0W3L3[II]	M0W2L2[I]	M0W2L2[II]
b	-0.824	-5.157	-0.890	-4.436	-.920	-4.892	-0.137	-6.312
	(0.353)	(2.487)	(0.541)	(2.356)	(0.296)	(1.591)	(1.028)	(1.060)
r	0.810	-0.213	0.775	-0.124	0.796	-0.087	0.715	-3.503
	(0.094)	(0.519)	(0.120)	(0.684)	(0.067)	(0.350)	(0.086)	(54.9)
$\sigma_{\omega1\omega1}$	0.271	1.145	0.221	0.725	0.271	0.455	0.375	0.434
	(0.069)	(1.402)	(0.079)	(1.010)	(0.063)	(0.559)	(0.240)	(0.301)
$\sigma_{\omega2\omega2}$	0.0010	0.0109	0.0007	0.0072	0.0014	-0.0066	0.0017	-0.0002
	(0.0004)	(0.0125)	(0.0004)	(0.0086)	(0.0003)	(0.0046)	(0.0011)	(0.002)
$\sigma_{\omega1\omega2}$	-0.0095	-0.0194	0[c]	0[c]	-0.0114	0.0649	0[c]	0[c]
	(0.0037)	(0.0364)			(0.0034)	(0.0422)		
$\sigma_{\lambda1\lambda1}$	0.043	0.398	0.037	0.279	0.0190	0.320	0.0354	20
	(0.0148)	(0.407)	(0.014)	(0.425)	(0.0137)	(0.249)	(0.0095)	(313)
$\sigma_{\lambda2\lambda2}$	0.0004	0.0014	0.0004	0.0008	-0.0003	0.0016	-0.0000	0.089
	(0.0002)	(0.0016)	(0.0001)	(0.0015)	(0.0002)	(0.0011)	(0.0002)	(1.392)
$\sigma_{\lambda1\lambda2}$	-0.0007	-0.0139	0[c]	0[c]	0.0027	-0.0134	0[c]	0[c]
	(0.0010)	(0.0145)			(0.0011)	(0.0094)		
$\sigma_{\varepsilon\varepsilon}$	0.028	0.028	0.028	0.028	0.028	0.028	0.027	0.027
	(0.002)	(0.002)	(0.002)	(0.002)	(0.002)	(0.002)	(0.002)	(0.002)
$\sigma_{\varphi\varphi}$	0.066	0.066	0.067	0.067	0.064	0.064	0.064	0.064
	(0.005)	(0.005)	(0.005)	(0.005)	(0.005)	(0.005)	(0.005)	(0.005)
$\sigma_{\varepsilon\varphi}$	0.032	0.032	0.033	0.033	0[c]	0[c]	0[c]	0[c]
	(0.003)	(0.003)	(0.003)	(0.003)				
d	0.843	-5.255	0.800	-3.986	0.812	-4.318	0.961	-27.4

[a] See Table 6.2 for definitions of models. Solutions I and II correspond to the two solutions of a second order equation obtained in identifying the model.

[b] Standard errors in parentheses.

[c] A priori restriction.

acceptable. Thus, none of the more interesting models have estimates of r that are outside the assumed interval.

Table 6.8
Estimates of M1-models[a][b]

Para-meter	M1W3L3	M1W3L2	M1W3L1	M1W2L3	M1W2L2	M1W2L1	M1W1L3	M1W1L2
b	-0.824	-0.850	1.764	-5.107	-0.890	230	-2.122	-1.677
	(0.353)	(0.308)	(2.517)	(2.144)	(0.541)	(8815)	(0.447)	(0.273)
r	0.810	0.804	0.529	-0.177	0.775	0.404	1.567	1.004
	(0.094)	(0.082)	(0.099)	(0.426)	(0.120)	(0.097)	(0.809)	(0.167)
$\sigma_{\omega1\omega1}$	0.271	0.268	1.142	1.030	0.221	4201	0.199	0.170
	(0.069)	(0.065)	(1.508)	(1.108)	(0.079)	(319619)	(0.063)	(0.036)
$\sigma_{\omega2\omega2}$	0.0010	0.0010	0.0056	0.0093	0.0007	27.0	0[c]	0[c]
	(0.0004)	(0.0003)	(0.0079)	(0.0092)	(0.0004)	(2055)		
$\sigma_{\omega1\omega2}$	-0.0095	-0.0094	-0.0308	0[c]	0[c]	0[c]	0[c]	0[c]
	(0.0037)	(0.0035)	(0.0446)					
$\sigma_{\lambda1\lambda1}$	0.043	0.040	0.044	0.371	0.037	0.060	0.367	0.079
	(0.0148)	(0.013)	(0.013)	(0.323)	(0.014)	(0.023)	(0.573)	(0.048)
$\sigma_{\lambda2\lambda2}$	0.0004	0.0004	0[c]	0.0013	0.0004	0[c]	0.0018	0.0005
	(0.0002)	(0.0001)		(0.0012)	(0.0001)		(0.0027)	(0.0002)
$\sigma_{\lambda1\lambda2}$	-0.0007	0[c]	0[c]	-0.0131	0[c]	0[c]	-0.0099	0[c]
	(0.0010)			(0.0115)			(0.0152)	
$\sigma_{\epsilon\epsilon}$	0.028	0.028	0.028	0.028	0.028	0.029	0.028	0.029
	(0.002)	(0.002)	(0.002)	(0.002)	(0.002)	(0.002)	(0.002)	(0.002)
$\sigma_{\varphi\varphi}$	0.066	0.066	0.070	0.066	0.067	0.071	0.070	0.071
	(0.005)	(0.005)	(0.005)	(0.005)	(0.005)	(0.005)	(0.005)	(0.005)
$\sigma_{\epsilon\varphi}$	0.032	0.033	0.034	0.033	0.033	0.035	0.034	0.035
	(0.003)	(0.003)	(0.003)	(0.003)	(0.003)	(0.003)	(0.003)	(0.003)
d	0.843	0.833	1.831	-5.011	0.800	138	2.203	1.007

[a] See Table 6.2 for definitions of models. Only solutions I are included; see Table 6 for solutions II.

[b] Standard errors in parentheses.

[c] A priori restriction.

Table 6.9
Estimates of M0-models[a][b]

Para-meter	M0W3L3	M0W3L2	M0W3L1	M0W2L3	M0W2L2	M0W2L1	M0W1L3	M0W1L2
b	-.920	-1.439	-1.427	-15.901	-0.138	-0.106	-14.153	-3.473
	(0.296)	(0.407)	(0.395)	(33.86)	(1.028)	(1.206)	(24.55)	(1.181)
r	0.796	0.937	0.929	0.305	0.715	0.711	0.299	-8.440
	(0.067)	(0.134)	(0.123)	(0.197)	(0.086)	(0.098)	(0.194)	(107.5)
$\sigma_{\omega 1 \omega 1}$	0.271	0.248	0.249	14.288	0.375	0.382	11.313	0.419
	(0.063)	(0.055)	(0.055)	(66.89)	(0.240)	(0.283)	(43.74)	(0.312)
$\sigma_{\omega 2 \omega 2}$	0.0014	0.0014	0.0014	0.009	0.0017	0.0017	0^c	0^c
	(0.0003)	(0.0005)	(0.0005)	(0.058)	(0.0011)	(0.0013)		
$\sigma_{\omega 1 \omega 2}$	-0.0114	-0.0116	-0.0120	0^c	0^c	0^c	0^c	0^c
	(0.0034)	(0.0044)	(0.0043)					
$\sigma_{\lambda 1 \lambda 1}$	0.0190	0.0565	0.0565	0.120	0.0354	0.0347	0.122	33.99
	(0.0137)	(0.0271)	(0.0255)	(0.072)	(0.0095)	(0.0086)	(0.073)	(798)
$\sigma_{\lambda 2 \lambda 2}$	-0.0003	0.0000	0^c	0.0007	-0.0000	0^c	0.0007	0.151
	(0.0002)	(0.0001)		(0.0003)	(0.0002)		(0.0003)	(3.552)
$\sigma_{\lambda 1 \lambda 2}$	0.0027	0^c	0^c	-0.006	0^c	0^c	-0.006	0^c
	(0.0011)			(0.003)			(0.003)	
$\sigma_{\varepsilon \varepsilon}$	0.028	0.027	0.027	0.027	0.027	0.027	0.027	0.027
	(0.002)	(0.002)	(0.002)	(0.002)	(0.002)	(0.002)	(0.002)	(0.002)
$\sigma_{\varphi \varphi}$	0.064	0.063	0.063	0.063	0.064	0.064	0.063	0.064
	(0.005)	(0.005)	(0.005)	(0.005)	(0.005)	(0.006)	(0.005)	(0.005)
$\sigma_{\varepsilon \varphi}$	0^c	0^c	0^c	0^c	0^c	0^c	0^c	0^c

[a] See Table 6.2 for definitions of models. Only solutions I are included; see Table 6 for solutions II.
[b] Standard errors in parentheses.
[c] A priori restriction.

For all models the variance of the log of the crime tendency (var $\ln C_{it}$) is found to be positive in all years. We note that $\sigma_{\omega 1 \omega 2}$ is significantly negative for the fitted models where this parameter is not zero a priori (i.e. for the W3-models). Furthermore, the estimates indicate a decrease in the variance of the district effects over time for most models.

The estimates of the variances of the district effects on clear-ups ($\sigma_{\lambda 1 \lambda 1}$ and $\sigma_{\lambda 2 \lambda 2}$) are positive in all models, but one. Here, in M0W3L3, the estimate of $\sigma_{\lambda 2 \lambda 2}$ is negative, but not significant.

The estimates of the variances and the covariance of the errors of measurement are very robust with respect to model specifications.

6.5.7. Estimate of M0W1L1

As shown in Table 6.3, model W1L1 cannot be identified without further restrictions. In Table 6.10 we present the results when a constant value of r is introduced as such a restriction. The table illustrates the effect of choosing various values of this parameter. We see that an increase in r causes a strong decrease in the estimate of b. The estimates of the measurement errors do not depend on the value of r. Observe that the χ^2-value, as expected, is independent of r.

Table 6.10[a]
Estimate of M0W1L1 with r constant

r	0.5	0.6	0.7	0.82	0.85	0.90
b	4.284	1.017	-0.241	-1.004	-1.135	-1.319
	(3.919)	(0.966)	(0.438)	(0.285)	(0.271)	(0.258)
$\sigma_{\omega 1 \omega 1}$	2.502	0.623	0.284	0.184	0.174	0.165
	(3.073)	(0.351)	(0.098)	(0.046)	(0.042)	(0.038)
$\sigma_{\lambda 1 \lambda 1}$	0.043	0.034	0.033	0.040	0.043	0.049
	(0.010)	(0.009)	(0.009)	(0.010)	(0.011)	(0.012)
$\sigma_{\varepsilon \varepsilon}$	0.041	0.041	0.041	0.041	0.041	0.041
	(0.003)	(0.003)	(0.003)	(0.003)	(0.003)	(0.003)
$\sigma_{\varphi \varphi}$	0.073	0.073	0.073	0.073	0.073	0.073
	(0.005)	(0.005)	(0.005)	(0.005)	(0.005)	(0.005)
χ^2	742.98	742.98	742.98	742.98	742.98	742.98
GFI	0.398	0.398	0.398	0.398	0.398	0.398

[a] Standard errors in parentheses.

6.6. Empirical results - various types of crime

6.6.1. Overview of procedure

Our model framework has been applied to 12 different types of crime. In section 6.6.2 we present estimates of the general model W3L3 (solution I) for each of the 12 specific types of crime. In section 6.6.3 we test for each type of crime the various models within our framework. In particular, we give an empirical investigation of properties related to problems of identification. The estimates for each type of crime of models not rejected by various criteria are given in section 6.6.4. It will be seen that the estimates of most of these models are not very different from those of our general model W3L3 (solution I), which is one reason for presenting the results of the latter model first. We find, however, that for some types of crime there are models more parsimonious than W3L3 that turn out to perform well, whereas some of the rejected models give unreasonable or meaningless results. These results underscores the importance of using a model framework with various models specifications, instead of sticking to one particular specification. In summing-up in section 6.7 we notice how some results are rather common to all types of crime, whereas others differ.

Unpublished data from Statistics Norway, which we have used in this study, contains a rather detailed categorization of crime. In order not to have too few observations in some police districts we have chosen to study only those types of offence numbering more than 500 for the whole country in at least some of the years. The following types of crime, which account for more than 95 percent of the total number of crimes, meet this requirement (the numbers being those used to categorize the types of crime in the official crime statistics):

13 Public disorder (incl. burglary).

18 Forgery.

19 Sexual offence.

21 Offence against the personal liberty.

22 Offence of violence against the person.

23 Slander and libel.

24 Embezzlement.

26 Fraud and breach of trust.

28 Offence inflicting damage to property.

40 Aggravated larcenies.

41 Simple larcenies.

43 Theft of motor vehicles.

Our general model has been applied to the 12 different types of crime with data for the period 1972-78. At variance with the study of total crime, data on specific types of crime are not available for the years 1970 and 1971. The covariance matrices of the logs of the crime and clear-up rates for each type of crime are included in Appendix D, together with the data used to calculate these matrices. Because of the log specification, zero values are treated as missing values. Missing values are then handled by listwise deletion: if data from a police district is missing in one or more years, this district is excluded from the calculation of the covariance matrix of the observed variables.

6.6.2. Estimates of the general model W3L3

The estimates of our most general model W3L3 are given in Table 6.11. These are the estimates of solution I, cf section 6.3 and 6.5.2. Our analysis which discriminates between solutions I and II is presented in section 6.6.3, and estimates for both solutions are given in section 6.6.4.

The deterrence and clear-up elasticities
According to our discussion of rational behaviour in previous chapters we hypothesize that the deterrence elasticity b is negative also for each specific type of offence, even for so-called "expressive crimes", such as sexual abuses, where a precise calculation of costs and benefits hardly is the rule. We find it natural to test whether a lower probability of detection will increase crime also in this case.

The deterrence elasticity (b) is found to be negative for seven of the 12 types of crime, and significantly so in four cases. None of the positive estimates are statistically significant. Thus, we find that H_{b0}, cf Table 6.1, is not rejected against the alternative hypothesis $b>0$, whereas the latter is rejected against the former in a majority of cases. We conclude that our results give rather strong support to H_{b0}. As one would expect, some of the estimates are higher than the corresponding one obtained for all crimes taken together, and some are lower.

We further expect the clear-up elasticity r to be positive, although one might imagine that the police in certain situations has to use such an amount of their resources on recording an increase in crime that the *number* of those cleared up will decrease.

The estimate of the clear-up elasticity (r) is positive in all cases, and significantly so in 11 of them. Our hypothesis H_{r0} is not rejected against the alternative hypothesis $r<0$, whereas the latter is rejected against the former. We thus conclude that H_{r0} is strongly supported.

In contrast to our expectation in the case of total crime we do not exclude $r>1$ for some types of crime. For a single type of crime the number of clear-ups might increase proportionally more than the number of crimes because the police becomes more efficient in clearing up certain crimes when they are "trained" in solving many cases of a similar type. Within some police districts resources might also be reallocated in order to solve specific types of crime that attract public interest, thus producing a proportionally larger increase in clear-ups than in crimes.

For six types of crime the clear-up elasticity is higher than 1. In most of these cases, however, the estimate of r is less than about one standard error higher than 1. This means that H_{r1} is not rejected against the alternative hypothesis $r>1$, whereas the latter also is not rejected against the former.

Hypothesis H_{d0} of a positive value of the stability parameter d implies that the system of equations have a stable solution. The stability parameter is found to be positive for all types of crime.

Distribution of crime and clear-up tendencies
Hypotheses H_ω and H_λ implies that we interpret the σ parameters of these hypotheses as variances and covariances. The estimates of the distribution parameters of the district effects on crime ($\sigma_{\omega1\omega1}$, $\sigma_{\omega2\omega2}$, and $\sigma_{\omega1\omega2}$) and on clear-ups ($\sigma_{\lambda1\lambda1}$, $\sigma_{\lambda2\lambda2}$, and $\sigma_{\lambda1\lambda2}$) are statistically significant at the 0.05 level according to the t-test in 10, 5, 3, 4, 3, and 2 cases, respectively. In all these cases, but one, the sign of the estimates of the variances is in accordance with the hypotheses. The condition $\sigma^2_{\omega1\omega2}\leq\sigma_{\omega1\omega1}\sigma_{\omega2\omega2}$ in H_ω is fulfilled for all types of crime, except forgery, sexual offence, slander and label, and offence against personal liberty. The analogous condition in H_λ is fulfilled for all types of crime, except forgery, embezzlement and fraud.

Hypotheses H_C and H_U state that the variances of the log of the crime and clear-up tendencies are positive. These variances, as well as those in the previous paragraph, are not restricted to positive values by LISREL, cf section 6.4. Straightforward calculation, using these estimates whether they are significant or not, shows that the variance of the log of the crime tendency, var $\ln C_{it} = \sigma_{\omega1\omega1} + t^2\sigma_{\omega2\omega2} + 2t\sigma_{\omega1\omega2}$, is positive for all years, i.e. for t=1,2,...,7, for all types of crime, see Table 6.12. The same holds true for the variance of the log of the clear-up tendency var $\ln U_{it}$, except for an insignificant negative estimate in the first year in the case of embezzlement. Thus, we consider hypotheses H_C and H_U not to be rejected in any of the cases. We take this result as a confirmation that our model framework, and our interpretation of it, has passed another interesting test (in addition to the analogous one for the total number of crimes).

The variance of the log of the crime tendency is decreasing during the period studied for all types of crime, except public disorder, embezzlement, fraud, and slander and libel. In the former three cases there is first a decrease and then an increase, whereas in the latter case there is a steady increase. As a whole there is a general tendency for police districts to become less different as far as log of the crime tendencies are concerned. This is in a relative sense, since the variance of the log of the crime tendency corresponds to the coefficient of variation of the crime tendency, cf comments to (6.7) in section 6.2.2.

The variance of the log of the clear-up tendencies develops less uniformly across types of crime. It is

a) increasing for offence against personal liberty, violence against the person, embezzlement, aggravated larcenies, simple larcenies, and thefts of motor vehicles,

b) decreasing for public disorder, slander and libel, and fraud,

c) decreasing and then increasing for sexual abuses and offence inflicting damage to property, and

d) increasing and then decreasing for forgery.

Measurement errors

The estimates of the variances and the covariance of the errors of measurement are all positive and highly significant. We find that hypotheses H_M and H_{MC} are not rejected in any of the cases. Hypothesis H_M states that the covariance matrix of the measurement errors is positive definite. Hypothesis H_{MC} is explained as a result of sloppy registration procedures: for some of the crimes committed the registration of both crimes and clear-ups are lost in the administrative process.

Summing up on the W3L3 model.

We may thus conclude that solution I of the W3L3 model performs more or less equally well for specific types of crime as for total crime. The estimates have in a large majority of cases the expected signs. The only exceptions are the positive (non-significant) estimates of the deterrence elasticity b for public disorder, slander and libel, forgery, embezzlement, and fraud. (In the next section it will be seen that more parsimonious models give negative estimates of b for the latter three types of crime.)

The change in the variance of the log of the crime tendencies demonstrates a reduction in the relative differences in crime between police districts. The variance of the log of the clear-up tendencies develops differently across types of crime. For nine of the 12 types, however, the variance is higher at the end of the period than at the beginning.

Table 6.11
Estimates of the general model (W3L3[1])[a] for various types of crime[b]

Para-meter	All offence	Public disorder	Forgery	Sexual offence	Offence against personal liberty	Violence against the person	Slander and libel
		13	18	19	21	22	23
b	-0.824	0.040	0.048	-0.397	-3.748	-1.060	0.883
	(0.353)	(0.435)	(0.660)	(0.241)	(1.718)	(0.593)	(0.485)
r	0.806	0.670	1.018	0.870	1.466	1.072	0.714
	(0.094)	(0.122)	(0.098)	(0.199)	(0.379)	(0.067)	(0.244)
$\sigma_{\omega_1\omega_1}$	0.2707	0.5256	0.2469	0.1939	1.1520	0.2861	0.1515
	(0.0693)	(0.2015)	(0.1015)	(0.0839)	(1.0205)	(0.0751)	(0.1235)
$\sigma_{\omega_2\omega_2}$	0.0010	0.0075	-0.0016	-0.0002	0.0011	0.0016	-0.0014
	(0.0004)	(0.0034)	(0.0020)	(0.0019)	(0.0127)	(0.0011)	(0.0038)
$\sigma_{\omega_1\omega_2}$	-0.0095	-0.0386	-0.0051	-0.0038	-0.0755	-0.0113	0.0240
	(0.0037)	(0.0196)	(0.0123)	(0.0109)	(0.1031)	(0.0073)	(0.0216)
$\sigma_{\lambda_1\lambda_1}$	0.0430	0.2387	0.0024	0.1682	0.0953	0.0213	0.2909
	(0.0148)	(0.0901)	(0.0132)	(0.0633)	(0.1310)	(0.0081)	(0.1324)
$\sigma_{\lambda_2\lambda_2}$	0.0004	0.0038	-0.0010	0.0055	0.0013	0.0008	0 0039
	(0.0002)	(0.0028)	(0.0005)	(0.0023)	(0.0018)	(0.0003)	(0.0022)
$\sigma_{\lambda_1\lambda_2}$	-0.0007	-0.0282	0.0047	-0.0219	0.0032	-0.0021	-0.0260
	(0.0010)	(0.0149)	(0.0021)	(0.0104)	(0.0076)	(0.0014)	(0.0159)
$\sigma_{\varepsilon\varepsilon}$	0.028	0.138	0.363	0.198	0.188	0.079	0.177
	(0.002)	(0.013)	(0.027)	(0.021)	(0.024)	(0.007)	(0.022)
$\sigma_{\phi\phi}$	0.066	0.349	0.344	0.345	0.251	0.117	0.290
	(0.005)	(0.033)	(0.035)	(0.036)	(0.032)	(0.010)	(0.037)
$\sigma_{\varepsilon\phi}$	0.033	0.118	0.267	0.206	0.151	0.085	0.121
	(0.003)	(0.016)	(0.029)	(0.024)	(0.024)	(0.008)	(0.023)
d	0.840	1.013	0.999	0.952	2.747	1.076	1.253
χ^2	291.87	155.27	152.36	138.21	179.22	240.17	123.04
GFI	0.639	0.676	0.699	0.682	0.549	0.594	0.649
P	0.000	0.000	0.000	0.002	0.000	0.000	0.024
NO.[c]	53	39	38	38	25	53	26

(Cont.)

Table 6.11 (cont.)
Estimates of the general model (W3L3[l])[a] for various types of crime[b]

Para-meter	All offence	Embezzle-ment	Fraud	Offence inflicting damage to property	Aggravated larcenies	Simple larcenies	Thefts of motor vehicles
		24	26	28	40	41	43
b	-0.824	0.055	0.200	-0.502	-2.437	-1.072	-2.679
	(0.353)	(0.629)	(0.758)	(0.930)	(0.566)	(0.193)	(0.472)
r	0.806	0.902	0.962	0.901	1.420	1.132	1.608
	(0.094)	(0.070)	(0.046)	(0.442)	(0.419)	(0.257)	(0.934)
$\sigma_{\omega1\omega1}$	0.2707	0.3121	0.5249	0.3426	0.7338	0.3362	0.7264
	(0.0693)	(0.1269)	(0.141)	(0.1041)	(0.3530)	(0.0945)	(0.2054)
$\sigma_{\omega2\omega2}$	0.0010	0.0102	0.0075	0.0067	0.0048	0.0037	0.0019
	(0.0004)	(0.0049)	(0.0030)	(0.0026)	(0.0051)	(0.0016)	(0.0038)
$\sigma_{\omega1\omega2}$	-0.0095	-0.0355	-0.0349	-0.0350	-0.0463	-0.0300	-0.0233
	(0.0037)	(0.0214)	(0.0172)	(0.0135)	(0.0388)	(0.0111)	(0.0229)
$\sigma_{\lambda1\lambda1}$	0.0430	-0.0113	0.0223	0.1413	0.3665	0.2891	0.7138
	(0.0148)	(0.0116)	(0.0152)	(0.0782)	(0.3960)	(0.1667)	(1.3772)
$\sigma_{\lambda2\lambda2}$	0.0004	0.0001	-0.0006	0.0036	0.0012	0.0032	0.0041
	(0.0002)	(0.0007)	(0.0004)	(0.0020)	(0.0015)	(0.0020)	(0.0078)
$\sigma_{\lambda1\lambda2}$	-0.0007	0.0038	0.0006	-0.0155	-0.0006	-0.0087	-0.0094
	(0.0010)	(0.0025)	(0.0023)	(0.0096)	(0.0057)	(0.0088)	(0.0216)
$\sigma_{\varepsilon\varepsilon}$	0.028	0.232	0.194	0.096	0.054	0.049	0.070
	(0.002)	(0.026)	(0.018)	(0.009)	(0.005)	(0.004)	(0.006)
$\sigma_{\phi\phi}$	0.066	0.272	0.291	0.163	0.198	0.122	0.134
	(0.005)	(0.030)	(0.027)	(0.009)	(0.017)	(0.011)	(0.012)
$\sigma_{\varepsilon\phi}$	0.032	0.215	0.210	0.087	0.071	0.044	0.074
	(0.003)	(0.026)	(0.021)	(0.010)	(0.008)	(0.006)	(0.006)
d	0.840	0.995	0.992	0.960	2.022	1.142	2.629
χ^2	291.25	141.49	184.22	172.42	181.24	166.43	155.06
GFI	0.641	0.641	0.674	0.684	0.670	0.724	0.682
P	0.000	0.001	0.000	0.000	0.000	0.000	0.000
NO.[c]	53	33	47	51	53	52	51

[a] See Table 6.2 for definition of the model.

[b] Standard errors in parentheses.

[c] Number of police districts after listwise deletion of missing values.

Table 6.12
Development of crime tendencies (var $\ln C_{it}$) and clear-up tendencies (var $\ln U_{it}$), various types of crime, model W3L3[1]

t	Public disorder 13	Forgery 18	Sexual abuses 19	Offence against personal liberty 21	Violence against the person 22	Slander and libel 23	Embezzlement 24	Fraud 26	Offence inflict. damage to prop. 28	Aggr. larc. 40	Simple larc. 41	Thefts of motor veh. 43
CRIME												
1	0.456	0.235	0.178	1.002	0.265	0.198	0.251	0.463	0.279	0.646	0.310	0.428
2	0.401	0.220	0.162	0.861	0.247	0.242	0.211	0.416	0.230	0.568	0.261	0.387
3	0.361	0.202	0.145	0.719	0.233	0.282	0.192	0.384	0.193	0.500	0.220	0.350
4	0.336	0.181	0.128	0.575	0.222	0.321	0.192	0.367	0.170	0.441	0.186	0.317
5	0.326	0.157	0.111	0.431	0.214	0.356	0.214	0.365	0.160	0.392	0.159	0.287
6	0.332	0.129	0.093	0.285	0.209	0.388	0.255	0.378	0.164	0.352	0.140	0.262
T. 7	0.351	0.098	0.074	0.139	0.207	0.418	0.318	0.406	0.181	0.323	0.128	0.240
CLEAR UP												
1	0.186	0.006	0.130	0.103	0.021	0.243	-0.004	0.023	0.114	0.367	0.275	0.699
2	0.141	0.012	0.103	0.113	0.016	0.203	0.004	0.022	0.094	0.369	0.267	0.692
3	0.104	0.017	0.086	0.126	0.016	0.170	0.013	0.021	0.081	0.374	0.266	0.694
4	0.074	0.019	0.081	0.142	0.018	0.146	0.021	0.019	0.075	0.382	0.271	0.704
5	0.052	0.019	0.087	0.160	0.021	0.129	0.030	0.015	0.077	0.392	0.282	0.722
6	0.038	0.017	0.104	0.181	0.027	0.120	0.039	0.010	0.086	0.404	0.300	0.748
T. 7	0.031	0.013	0.132	0.204	0.033	0.119	0.049	0.004	0.102	0.414	0.324	0.782

6.6.3. Tests of model specifications

In order to test various model specifications we present in Table 6.13 the χ^2-values for various models and in Table 6.14 the corresponding significance probabilities. Our model framework consists now of a hierarchy of models with W3L3 on the top and W1L1 at the bottom. We have dropped all models with either M0, L0 or W0 in our analysis of different types of crimes in order to save time and space, cf Tables 6.2-6.4. Testing of models within this framework by likelihood ratio tests can be performed in various ways. The simplest procedure is to test each model against the general model W3L3. The significance probabilities corresponding to these tests are presented in the first five columns in Table 6.14. Models rejected by these tests, at a significance level of 0.01 and 0.05, are marked in Table 6.15 by $R_{0.01}$ and $R_{0.05}$, respectively.

Another procedure is to start at the top and test each model against the one immediately higher in the hierarchy, and if a model is rejected, then all models below in the hierarchy are also rejected. Significance probabilities corresponding to such tests can also be found in Table 6.14. The test results in Table 6.15 will in our case be the same for both procedures. Other procedures, and other levels of significance, can be applied based on the information in Table 6.13, but in the following we stick to the test results presented in Table 6.15. In order to limit our analysis we will give no further consideration of models rejected at a significance level of 0.05.

Since our class of models is not fully identified without restrictions in the parameter space, we also reject models which do not satisfy the restrictions in (6.16), see section 6.3. It turns out that restrictions (6.16a) on the distribution of measurement errors, crime tendencies, and clear-up tendencies, are not binding for any of the models not rejected by the likelihood ratio test. The models with point estimates outside the interval hypotheses in (6.16b) and (6.16c) are marked in Table 6.15 with the names of the hypotheses they contradict, cf Table 6.1.

Observe first that for each type of crime, one of the solutions of W3L3 is rejected by at least one of our criteria, whereas the other is not. This is a remarkable result, since we could well imagine that both solutions were rejected, or none of them. Thus, in our situation, the potential identification problem does not seem to be empirically relevant. The solution that is not rejected is denoted solution I, the other solution II. The parameter estimates of both solutions are presented in Tables 6.17-6.27. It is seen that the estimates of solution II almost without exceptions are imprecise and rather unreasonable. Our choice of restrictions has clearly separated the appropriate solutions from the non-appropriate ones.

Considering now the less general models in Table 6.15 we find that quite a few of them satisfy all our criteria. The estimates of these non-rejected models are given in Tables

Table 6.13
χ^2-values for various types of models and types of crime

Types of crime	Models/Degrees of freedom					
	W3L3 94	W3L2 W2L3 95	W3L1 W1L3 96	W2L2 96	W2L1 W1L2 97	W1L1 98
Public disorder, 13	155.27	160.10	161.92	171.58	174.13	183.21
Forgery, 18	152.36	155.46	155.64	155.60	155.80	159.09
Sexual offence, 19	138.21	138.67	140.73	149.66	155.16	156.25
Offence against personal liberty, 21	179.22	179.41	181.73	180.60	184.13	186.60
Offence against the person, 22	240.17	243.11	243.23	247.90	248.21	265.32
Slander and libel, 23	123.04	124.45	125.21	128.90	129.00	131.60
Embezzlement, 24	141.49	143.06	148.68	147.88	152.05	159.71
Fraud, 26	184.22	184.29	187.59	190.94	194.51	200.49
Damage to property, 28	172.42	182.77	185.50	206.00	208.34	231.00
Aggravated larcenies, 40	181.24	181.25	185.74	187.01	187.11	211.70
Simple larcenies, 41	166.43	168.47	179.02	190.28	190.39	240.93
Thefts of motor vehicles, 43	155.06	156.03	156.51[a]	157.34	157.63[a]	190.45

[a] The χ^2-value for these models refers to LISREL solutions at a maximum of 300 permitted iterations of the optimization procedure. Convergence has not been obtained.

Table 6.14
Significance probabilities[a]

Models/degrees of freedom (DF)

Types of crime	W3L2/W2L3 vs W3L3, DF=1	W3L1/W1L3 vs W3L3, DF=2	W2L2 vs W3L3, DF=2	W2L1/W1L2 vs W3L3, DF=3	W1L1 vs W3L3, DF=4	W3L1/W1L3 vs W3L2/W2L3, DF=1	W2L2 vs W3L2/W2L3, DF=1	W2L1/W1L2 vs W3L2/W2L3, DF=2	W1L1 vs W3L2/W2L3, DF=3	W2L1/W1L2 vs W3L1/W1L3, DF=1	W1L1 vs W3L1/W1L3, DF=2	W2L1/W1L2 vs W2L2, DF=1	W1L1 vs W2L2, DF=2	W1L1 vs W2L1/W1L2, DF=1
Public disorder, 13	0.028	0.036	0.000	0.000	0.000	0.177	0.001	0.001	0.000	0.000	0.000	0.110	0.003	0.003
Forgery, 18	0.078	0.194	0.198	0.329	0.151	0.671	0.708	0.844	0.304	0.689	0.178	0.654	0.175	0.070
Sexual offence, 19	0.498	0.284	0.003	0.001	0.001	0.151	0.001	0.000	0.001	0.000	0.000	0.019	0.037	0.296
Off., pers. liberty, 21	0.663	0.285	0.502	0.179	0.117	0.128	0.275	0.094	0.066	0.121	0.088	0.060	0.050	0.116
Off. against person, 22	0.086	0.217	0.021	0.045	0.000	0.729	0.029	0.078	0.000	0.026	0.000	0.578	0.000	0.000
Slander and libel, 23	0.235	0.338	0.053	0.114	0.073	0.383	0.035	0.103	0.067	0.052	0.041	0.752	0.259	0.107
Embezzlement, 24	0.210	0.027	0.041	0.014	0.001	0.018	0.028	0.011	0.001	0.066	0.004	0.041	0.003	0.006
Fraud, 26	0.791	0.185	0.035	0.016	0.003	0.069	0.010	0.006	0.001	0.008	0.001	0.059	0.008	0.014
Damage to property, 28	0.001	0.001	0.000	0.000	0.000	0.098	0.000	0.000	0.000	0.000	0.000	0.126	0.000	0.000
Aggr. larcenies, 40	0.920	0.105	0.056	0.118	0.000	0.034	0.016	0.053	0.000	0.241	0.000	0.752	0.000	0.000
Simple larcenies, 41	0.153	0.002	0.000	0.000	0.000	0.001	0.000	0.000	0.000	0.001	0.000	0.740	0.000	0.000
Thefts, motor veh., 43	0.325	0.484	0.320	0.463	0.000	0.488	0.252	0.449	0.000	0.290	0.000	0.590	0.000	0.000

[a] The significance probabilities are relevant only for nested models. The numbers in col. 6 may e.g. be used to test W3L1 against W3L2, but not against W2L3.

6.17-6.27, and the variances of the crime and clear-up tendencies are given in Table 6.16. In these tables we find the estimates demonstrating our observation above that the non-rejected models satisfy (6.16).

In order not to burden our presentation we have not included the estimates of the rejected models. Our inspection of these have shown, however, that almost all of them perform badly as far as precision and plausibility of estimates are concerned. Thus, our rejection criteria (6.16) seem to perform quite well. We have further observed that the estimates of these models to a large extent resemble those of W3L3^{II}.

The models that meet all our criteria will on the other hand have estimates rather similar to those of W3L3^{I}. For each type of crime parsimony of parameters may guide our choice of model within the group of these reasonable ones.

6.6.4. Estimates for various types of crime.

In this section we present estimates of the models that satisfy restrictions (6.16).

Public disorder
Most offence within the category of "offence against public order and peace" (here called "public disorder") are burglaries. Table 6.15 shows that all submodels are rejected against W3L3 by likelihood ratio tests, and that W3L3^{II} is rejected by H$_{r2}$. The estimates of the two W3L3 solutions are given in Table 6.17. One observes that several of the estimates of W3L3^{II} are unreasonable and do not satisfy (16). The estimates of W3L3^{I} are mostly statistically significant with expected signs. An exception is the estimate of the deterrence elasticity, which is positive and not statistically significant. There is a decline in the variance of the log of the crime tendency (see Table 6.12), suggesting a reduction in the relative differences between police districts for this type of crime. The variance of the log of the clear-up tendency is also decreasing during the period.

Looking at the number of crimes in the various police districts (Table 13.2 in Appendix D) one is surprised to observe how few instances of public disorder are registered in the capital compared to other police districts. One might suspect that in Oslo, and perhaps in other districts, burglaries are not recorded as public disorder. Apparently, there are special problems of recording for this type of crime.

Table 6.15
Rejection of models by various criteria

	W3L3^{I}	W3L3^{II}	W3L2	W2L3	W3L1	W1L3	W2L2^{I}	W2L2^{II}	W2L1	W1L2	W1L1
Public disorder, 13	H_{r2}	H_{d0}, H_{r2}, H_{b1}	$R_{0.05}$	$R_{0.05}$	$R_{0.05}$	$R_{0.05}$	$R_{0.01}$	$R_{0.01}$	$R_{0.01}$	$R_{0.01}$	$R_{0.01}$
Forgery, 18	H_{d0}, H_{r2}, H_{b1}	H_{r0}, H_{b1}	H_{r0}, H_{b1}	H_{r0}, H_{b1}	H_{r0}, H_{b1}	H_{r0}, H_{b1}	H_{r0}, H_{b1}	H_{r0}, H_{b1}	H_{r0}, H_{b1}	H_{r0}, H_{b1}	H_{r0}, H_{b1}
Sexual offence, 19	H_{d0}, H_{r0}	H_{d0}, H_{r0}	H_{d0}, H_{r0}	H_{d0}, H_{r0}	H_{d0}, H_{r0}	H_{b1}	$R_{0.01}$	$R_{0.01}$	$R_{0.01}$	$R_{0.01}$	$R_{0.01}$
Off. pers. liberty, 21	H_{b1}	H_{b1}	H_{b1}	H_{b1}	H_{b1}	H_{b1}	H_{r2}	H_{b1}	H_{r2}	H_{r2}	H_{r2}
Off. against person, 22	H_{b1}	H_{b1}	H_{b1}	H_{b1}	H_{b1}	H_{b1}	$R_{0.05}$	H_{d0}, H_{r2}, H_{b1}	$R_{0.05}$	H_{r2}	$R_{0.01}$
Slander and libel, 23	H_{r2}	H_{r2}	H_{r2}	H_{r2}	H_{r2}	H_{b1}	$R_{0.05}$	H_{d0}, H_{r2}, H_{b1}	$R_{0.05}$	H_{r2}	
Embezzlement, 24	H_{r2}	H_{r2}	H_{d0}, H_{r0}	H_{d0}, H_{r0}	$R_{0.05}$	$R_{0.05}$	$R_{0.05}$	$R_{0.05}$	$R_{0.05}$	$R_{0.05}$	$R_{0.01}$
Fraud, 26	H_{r2}	H_{r2}	H_{r2}	H_{r2}	H_{r2}	H_{r2}, H_{b1}	$R_{0.05}$	$R_{0.05}$	$R_{0.05}$	$R_{0.05}$	$R_{0.01}$
Damage to property, 28	H_{d0}, H_{r0}	H_{d0}, H_{r0}	H_{b1}	$R_{0.01}$	$R_{0.01}$	$R_{0.01}$	$R_{0.01}$	$R_{0.01}$	$R_{0.01}$	$R_{0.01}$	$R_{0.01}$
Aggr. larcenies, 40	H_{b1}	H_{b1}	H_{b1}	H_{b1}	H_{b1}	$R_{0.01}$	$R_{0.01}$	H_{b1}	H_{b1}	$R_{0.01}$	$R_{0.01}$
Simple larcenies, 41	H_{b1}	H_{b1}	H_{r0}, H_{b1}	H_{r0}, H_{b1}	$R_{0.01}$	$R_{0.01}$	$R_{0.01}$	$R_{0.01}$	$R_{0.01}$	$R_{0.01}$	$R_{0.01}$
Thefts, motor veh. 43	H_{b1}	H_{b1}	H_{b1}	H_{b1}	$*)$	$*)$	H_{b1}	H_{b1}	$*)$	$*)$	$R_{0.01}$

[a] $R_{0.01}$: Rejected against W3L3 by a likelihood ratio test at a significance level of 0.01.
$R_{0.05}$: Rejected against W3L3 by a likelihood ratio test at a significance level of 0.05.
H_{d0}: Estimates do not satisfy H_{d0}: $d>0$. H_{r0}: Estimates do not satisfy H_{r0}: $r>0$. H_{r2}: Estimates do not satisfy H_{r2}: $r<2$. H_{b1}: Estimates do not satisfy H_{b1}: $b<1$.
*): No ordinary optimal solution has been found by LISREL7 within a maximum of 300 permitted iterations of the optimization procedure.

Table 6.16

Development of crime tendencies (var $\ln C_{it}$) and clear-up tendencies (var $\ln U_{it}$), various types of crime, non-rejected models

t	Forgery, 18				Sexual offence, 19		Offence against personal liberty, 21			Violence against the person, 22		Slander and libel, 23			
	W3L2	W3L1	W2L2[I]	W2L1	W2L3	W1L3	W3L2	W3L1	W1L2	W2L3	W1L3	W2L3	W2L2[II]	W2L1	W1L3
C r i m e t e n d. 1	0.24	0.24	0.24	0.22	0.143	0.13	1.00	1.89	0.396	0.338	0.24	0.42	0.21	0.21	0.30
2	0.23	0.22	0.23	0.21	0.139	"	0.86	1.53	"	0.239	"	0.25	0.22	0.22	"
3	0.20	0.21	0.22	0.20	0.132	"	0.72	1.21	"	0.240	"	0.26	0.24	0.24	"
4	0.19	0.18	0.21	0.18	0.121	"	0.56	0.91	"	0.242	"	0.27	0.26	0.26	"
5	0.16	0.16	0.19	0.16	0.108	"	0.43	0.64	"	0.245	"	0.29	0.28	0.28	"
6	0.13	0.13	0.16	0.13	0.092	"	0.28	0.40	"	0.248	"	0.31	0.31	0.31	"
7	0.10	0.10	0.17	0.10	0.072	"	0.14	0.19	"	0.252	"	0.34	0.34	0.35	"
C l e a r - u p t e n d. 1	0.023	0.02	0.013	0.02	0.142	0.141	0.11	0.27	0.038	0.020	0.020	0.22	0.120	0.12	0.23
2	0.022	"	0.014	"	0.112	0.113	0.12	"	0.037	0.018	0.018	0.19	0.119	"	0.19
3	0.021	"	0.016	"	0.093	0.095	0.13	"	0.034	0.018	0.018	0.15	0.117	"	0.16
4	0.020	"	0.019	"	0.086	0.089	0.14	"	0.029	0.019	0.019	0.13	0.114	"	0.14
5	0.019	"	0.023	"	0.090	0.093	0.16	"	0.023	0.022	0.023	0.11	0.110	"	0.12
6	0.018	"	0.027	"	0.105	0.108	0.18	"	0.014	0.028	0.028	0.10	0.105	"	0.11
7	0.016	"	0.032	"	0.131	0.135	0.20	"	0.004	0.034	0.034	0.10	0.100	"	0.11

(Cont.)

Table 6.16 (cont.)
Development of crime tendencies (var $\ln C_{it}$) and clear-up tendencies (var $\ln U_{it}$), various types of crime, non-rejected models.

t	Embezzlement, 24	Fraud and breach of trust, 26		Aggravated larcenies, 40					Simple larcenies, 41	Theft of motor vehicles, 43	
	W3L2	W3L2	W3L1	W3L2	W3L1	W1L3	W2L2^I	W1L2	W3L2	W3L2	W2L2^I
Crime tend. 1	0.24	0.45	0.46	0.64	0.47	0.39	0.424	0.38	0.31	0.41	0.303
2	0.20	0.41	0.41	0.56	0.43	"	0.421	"	0.26	0.38	0.300
3	0.18	0.38	0.37	0.49	0.39	"	0.417	"	0.22	0.34	0.295
4	0.18	0.36	0.35	0.44	0.37	"	0.410	"	0.19	0.31	0.288
5	0.20	0.36	0.35	0.39	0.35	"	0.402	"	0.17	0.28	0.279
6	0.24	0.37	0.36	0.35	0.34	"	0.392	"	0.14	0.26	0.268
7	0.30	0.39	0.39	0.32	0.34	"	0.380	"	0.13	0.24	0.255
Clear-up tend. 1	0.004	0.029	0.02	0.35	0.14	0.179	0.258	0.14	0.27	0.53	0.258
2	0.007	0.027	"	0.35	"	0.180	0.261	0.15	0.27	0.54	0.263
3	0.013	0.023	"	0.36	"	0.183	0.268	0.15	0.27	0.56	0.271
4	0.021	0.019	"	0.36	"	0.187	0.277	0.16	0.28	0.58	0.282
5	0.030	0.013	"	0.37	"	0.194	0.288	0.16	0.30	0.61	0.297
6	0.043	0.005	"	0.39	"	0.202	0.302	0.17	0.32	0.64	0.314
7	0.057	0.004	"	0.40	"	0.213	0.319	0.18	0.36	0.68	0.335

Forgery

In the case of forgery, the estimates of the five models which satisfy the likelihood ratio test, H_{d0}, and H_{r0} are given in Table 6.18. The estimates of these models are rather similar to each other. The clear-up elasticity r is found to be slightly higher than 1 for all these models. The only notable difference between our general model and the other models is that b is positive in the former and negative in the remaining ones (none of them significant). Our desire for parsimony of parameters points at W2L1 as a good model for forgery. In the case of forgery, too, we note a decrease in the variance of the log of the crime tendency during the period, indicating a shrinking difference in relative terms between police districts in this respect. The clear-up tendency is constant by definition.

Sexual offence

In the case of sexual offence we have three models that are not rejected by the likelihood ratio test, and that also satisfy our restrictions (6.16). Their estimates are almost identical, see Table 6.19. With few exceptions the estimates are statistically significant and of expected sign. Thus, we find our model framework to be rather successful for what is often considered to be an expressive crime.

The standard errors of the estimates are as a whole slightly smaller for W2L3 than for the other two models. Only the estimate of $\sigma_{\omega 2\omega 2}$ is not statistically significant. The estimate of the deterrence elasticity is negative and that of the clear-up elasticity is positive, and less than 1. The variance of both the crime and clear-up tendencies are decreasing during the period studied, indicating a shrinking relative difference between police districts in both respects. In the more parsimonious model W1L3 the estimate of b is of the same size as in W2L3, but slightly less precise.

Offence against the personal liberty

Table 6.20 shows that the four non-rejected models for offence against personal liberty divide into two groups: the estimates of W3L3[I], W3L2, and W3L1 are very similar to each other, whereas those of W2L3 are more alike those of the rejected W3L3[II]. In the first group the estimate of the clear-up elasticity is greater than 1, and in the other group smaller than 1. In the first group the estimates of the deterrence elasticity is negative and (for two of the models) statistically significant, whereas they in the second group are positive and non-significant. In the former group the variances of both the crime and the clear-up tendencies are decreasing during the period, indicating also for this type of crime a growing similarity in relative terms between police districts.

Table 6.17
Public disorder (13), estimates of non-rejected
models [ab]

Parameter	W3L3[I]	W3L3[II]
b	0.040 (0.435)	-3.026 (1.112)
r	0.670 (0.122)	26.267 (277.4)
$\sigma_{\omega 1 \omega 1}$	0.5256 (0.2015)	2.1856 (1.7758)
$\sigma_{\omega 2 \omega 2}$	0.0075 (0.0034)	-0.035 (0.0362)
$\sigma_{\omega 1 \omega 2}$	-0.0386 (0.0196)	-0.258 (0.2301)
$\sigma_{\lambda 1 \lambda 1}$	0.2387 (0.0901)	335.54 (7272.5)
$\sigma_{\lambda 2 \lambda 2}$	0.0038 (0.0028)	4.776 (103.5)
$\sigma_{\lambda 1 \lambda 2}$	-0.0282 (0.0149)	-24.12 (534.2)
$\sigma_{\varepsilon \varepsilon}$	0.138 (0.013)	0.138 (0.013)
$\sigma_{\phi \phi}$	0.349 (0.033)	0.349 (0.033)
$\sigma_{\varepsilon \phi}$	0.118 (0.016)	0.118 (0.016)
d	1.013	77.9
χ^2	155.27	155.27
GFI	0.676	0.676
P	0.000	0.000

[a] See Table 6.2 for definition of models. Solutions I and II
correspond to the two solutions of a second order equation
obtained in identifying the model.
[b] Standard errors in parentheses.

Table 6.18
Forgery (18), estimates of non-rejected models[a][b]

Para-meter	W3L3[I]	W3L3[II]	W3L2	W3L1	W2L2[I]	W2L1
b	0.048	56.2	-0.440	-0.359	-0.899	-0.454
	(0.660)	(309)	(2.983)	(1.557)	(3.912)	(1.65)
r	1.018	21.9	1.056	1.048	1.106	1.058
	(0.098)	(289)	(0.322)	(0.165)	(0.430)	(0.177)
$\sigma_{\omega 1 \omega 1}$	0.2469	-7.48	0.2503	0.2493	0.2339	0.2184
	(0.1015)	(90)	(0.1346)	(0.1106)	(0.1916)	(0.0704)
$\sigma_{\omega 2 \omega 2}$	-0.0016	-3.20	-0.0017	-0.0017	-0.0026	-0.0024
	(0.0020)	(35)	(0.0022)	(0.0021)	(0.0026)	(0.0013)
$\sigma_{\omega 1 \omega 2}$	-0.0051	14.7	-0.0048	0.0049	0[c]	0[c]
	(0.0123)	(162)	(0.0129)	(0.0126)		
$\sigma_{\lambda 1 \lambda 1}$	0.0024	108	0.0227	0.0198	0.0245	0.0200
	(0.0132)	(2989)	(0.0111)	(0.0073)	(0.0208)	(0.0077)
$\sigma_{\lambda 2 \lambda 2}$	-0.0010	-0.70	-0.0001	0[c]	-0.0002	0[c]
	(0.0005)	(19)	(0.0003)		(0.0004)	
$\sigma_{\lambda 1 \lambda 2}$	0.0047	-2.21	0[c]	0[c]	0[c]	0[c]
	(0.0021)	(61)				
$\sigma_{\varepsilon \varepsilon}$	0.263	0.263	0.264	0.263	0.267	0.267
	(0.027)	(0.027)	(0.027)	(0.027)	(0.026)	(0.026)
$\sigma_{\phi \phi}$	0.344	0.344	0.341	0.341	0.346	0.346
	(0.035)	(0.035)	(0.034)	(0.034)	(0.033)	(0.033)
$\sigma_{\varepsilon \phi}$	0.267	0.266	0.266	0.266	0.267	0.271
	(0.029))	(0.027)	(0.029)	(0.029)	(0.028)	(0.028)
d	0.999	-1175	1.025	1.017	1.095	1.026
χ^2	152.36	152.36	155.46	155.64	155.60	155.80
GFI	0.699	0.699	0.684	0.683	0.684	0.683
P	0.000	0.000	0.000	0.000	0.000	0.000

[a] See Table 6.2 for definition of models. Solutions I and II correspond to the two solutions of a second order equation obtained in identifying the model.

[b] Standard errors in parentheses.

[c] A priori restriction.

Table 6.19

Sexual offence (19), estimates of non-rejected models[ab]

Para-meter	W3L3[I]	W3L3[II]	W2L3	W1L3
b	-0.397 (0.241)	-7.71 (11.8)	-0.495 (0.214)	-0.419 (0.266)
r	0.870 (0.199)	-1.521 (1.529)	0.933 (0.200)	0.947 (0.248)
$\sigma_{\omega1\omega1}$	0.1939 (0.0839	10.00 (34.2)	0.1449 (0.0411)	0.1265 (0.0376)
$\sigma_{\omega2\omega2}$	-0.0002 (0.0019)	0.3287 (1.0270)	-0.0015 (0.0010)	0[c]
$\sigma_{\omega1\omega2}$	-0.0038 (0.0109)	-1.3034 (4.1200)	0[c]	0[c]
$\sigma_{\lambda1\lambda1}$	0.1682 (0.0633)	1.2324 (1.7219)	0.1828 (0.0681)	0.1807 (0.0709)
$\sigma_{\lambda2\lambda2}$	0.0055 (0.0023)	-0.0014 (0.0017)	0.0056 (0.0023)	0.0055 (0.0024)
$\sigma_{\lambda1\lambda2}$	-0.0219 (0.0104)	-0.0495 (0.1046)	-0.0233 (0.0107)	-0.0225 (0.0109)
$\sigma_{\varepsilon\varepsilon}$	0.198 (0.021)	0.198 (0.021)	0.202 (0.020)	0.195 (0.019)
$\sigma_{\phi\phi}$	0.345 (0.036)	0.345 (0.036)	0.354 (0.035)	0.345 (0.033)
$\sigma_{\varepsilon\phi}$	0.206 (0.024)	0.206 (0.024)	0.212 (0.024)	0.204 (0.022)
d	0.952	-18.44	0.967	0.978
χ^2	138.21	138.21	138.67	140.73
GFI	0.682	0.682	0.687	0.686
P	0.002	0.002	0.002	0.002

[a] See Table 6.2 for definition of models. Solutions I and II correspond to the two solutions of a second order equation obtained in identifying the model.

[b] Standard errors in parentheses.

[c] A priori restriction.

Table 6.20

Offence against the personal liberty (21), estimates of non-rejected models[ab]

Parameter	W3L3[I]	W3L3[II]	W3L2	W3L1	W1L2
b	-3.748	2.146	-3.806	-5.117	0.755
	(1.718)	(1.744)	(1.829)	(2.770)	(1.026)
r	1.466	0.733	1.479	1.744	0.822
	(0.379)	(0.122)	(0.408)	(0.672)	(0.110)
$\sigma_{\omega1\omega1}$	1.1520	0.4388	1.1429	2.2712	0.3958
	(1.0205)	(0.3045)	(1.0394)	(2.5280)	(0.1809)
$\sigma_{\omega2\omega2}$	0.0011	0.0060	-0.0005	0.0145	0[c]
	(0.0127)	(0.0098)	(0.0122)	(0.0316)	
$\sigma_{\omega1\omega2}$	-0.0755	0.0149	-0.0699	-0.1993	0[c]
	(0.1031)	(0.0366)	(0.0992)	(0.2775)	
$\sigma_{\lambda1\lambda1}$	0.0953	0.0820	0.1144	0.2695	0.0374
	(0.1310)	(0.0478)	(0.1494)	(0.3695)	(0.0182)
$\sigma_{\lambda2\lambda2}$	0.0013	0.0001	0.0018	0[c]	-0.0009
	(0.0018)	(0.0009)	(0.0018)		(0.0005)
$\sigma_{\lambda1\lambda2}$	0.0032	-0.0054	0[c]	0[c]	0[c]
	(0.0076)	(0.0059)			
$\sigma_{\varepsilon\varepsilon}$	0.188	0.188	0.186	0.196	0.203
	(0.024)	(0.024)	(0.023)	(0.024)	(0.024)
$\sigma_{\phi\phi}$	0.251	0.251	0.252	0.251	0.274
	(0.032)	(0.032)	(0.032)	(0.032)	(0.033)
$\sigma_{\varepsilon\phi}$	0.151	0.151	0.150	0.156	0.168
	(0.024)	(0.024)	(0.024)	(0.024)	(0.025)
d	2.75	1.57	2.82	2.81	1.134
χ^2	179.22	179.22	179.41	181.73	184.65
GFI	0.549	0.549	0.549	0.537	0.539
P	0.000	0.000	0.000	0.000	0.000

[a] See Table 6.2 for definition of models. Solutions I and II correspond to the two solutions of a second order equation obtained in identifying the model.

[b] Standard errors in parentheses.

[c] A priori restriction.

Offence of violence against the person

Table 6.21 contains the estimates of two models, in addition to W3L3, applied to the offence of violence against the person. The estimates of the parameters for W3L3^I, W2L3, and W1L3 are very similar. Parsimony of parameters and slightly more precise estimates are arguments for choosing W1L3. All, but one of the estimates are here statistically significant, and of the expected sign. We find a strong deterrent effect of the probability of clear-up. The variance of the log of the crime tendency is constant by definition, and the variance of the log of the clear-up tendency is increasing. In the W3L3^I-model the variance of the log of the crime tendency is decreasing, indicating gradually more similar police district also with respect to this type of crime.

Slander and libel

None of the models applied to slander and label seem to be appropriate, cf. Table 6.22. The five non-rejected models have positive, but not statistically significant estimates of b, and reasonable positive estimates of *r*. The most parsimonious model, W2L1, seems to be just as good as the other four. A reason for the rather inconclusive results for this type of crime might be that the offender has some interest in the slander being known, although not that it should be cleared up by the police.

Embezzlement

In the case of embezzlement only two models satisfy our restrictions (6.16), cf Table 6.23. The estimates are not very different from each other. We note, though, that W3L2 is the more parsimonious one, and has a negative, but non-significant estimate of *b*. Both have first a decreasing, and then an increasing variance of the log of the crime tendency, whereas the variance of the log of the clear-up tendency is increasing for both. This indicates growing differences in relative terms between police districts in both respects in the late seventies.

Fraud

Three models satisfy our restrictions (6.16) in the case of fraud, see Table 6.24. None of them have statistically significant estimates of *b*. The one for W3L1 is negative, those for the two others are positive. The variance of the log of the crime tendency is mainly decreasing for all three, with a slight increase at the end of the period. The variance of the log of the clear-up tendency is strongly decreasing. In both respects, then, the differences in relative terms between police districts are reduced.

Table 6.21

Offence of violence against the person (22), estimates of non-rejected models[a,b]

Parameter	W3L3[I]	W3L3[II]	W2L3	W1L3
b	-1.060	14.00	-1.459	-1.591
	(0.593)	(13.05)	(0.644)	(0.569)
r	1.072	0.057	1.103	1.101
	(0.067)	(0.528)	(0.071)	(0.067)
$\sigma_{\omega1\omega1}$	0.2861	4.1629	0.2375	0.2436
	(0.0751)	(7.3936)	(0.0629)	(0.0587)
$\sigma_{\omega2\omega2}$	0.0016	0.1654	0.0003	0[c]
	(0.0011)	(0.3103)	(0.0009)	
$\sigma_{\omega1\omega2}$	-0.0113	-0.4121	0[c]	0[c]
	(0.0073)	(0.7991)		
$\sigma_{\lambda1\lambda1}$	0.0213	0.2545	0.0234	0.0237
	(0.0081)	(0.2730)	(0.0084)	(0.0084)
$\sigma_{\lambda2\lambda2}$	0.0008	0.0014	0.0009	0.0009
	(0.0003)	(0.0021)	(0.0003)	(0.0003)
$\sigma_{\lambda1\lambda2}$	-0.0021	-0.0101	-0.0023	-0.0023
	(0.0014)	(0.0130)	(0.0014)	(0.0013)
$\sigma_{\varepsilon\varepsilon}$	0.079	0.079	0.082	0.082
	(0.007)	(0.007)	(0.007)	(0.007)
$\sigma_{\phi\phi}$	0.117	0.117	0.122	0.124
	(0.010)	(0.010)	(0.010)	(0.010)
$\sigma_{\varepsilon\phi}$	0.085	0.085	0.084	0.089
	(0.008)	(0.008)	(0.008)	(0.008)
d	1.076	14.2	1.150	1.161
χ^2	240.17	240.17	243.11	243.23
GFI	0.594	0.594	0.601	0.600
P	0.000	0.000	0.000	0.000

[a] See Table 6.2 for definition of models. Solutions I and II correspond to the two solutions of a second order equation obtained in identifying the model.

[b] Standard errors in parentheses.

[c] A priori restriction.

Table 6.22

Slander and libel (23), estimates of non-rejected models[a,b]

Para-meter	W3L3[I]	W3L3[II]	W2L3	W1L3	W2L2[I]	W2L1
b	0.883	-3.493	0.610	0.705	0.201	0.327
	(0.485)	(2.972)	(0.508)	(0.533)	(0.776)	(0.983)
r	0.714	2.132	0.824	0.783	1.026	0.966
	(0.244)	(0.621)	(0.274)	(0.285)	(0.348)	(0.432)
$\sigma_{\omega1\omega1}$	0.1515	3.5493	0.2405	0.2956	0.2121	0.2111
	(0.1235)	(5.4861)	(0.0964)	(0.1149)	(0.0801)	(0.0788)
$\sigma_{\omega2\omega2}$	-0.0014	0.0480	0.0020	0[c]	0.0027	0.0028
	(0.0038)	(0.0861)	(0.0024)		(0.0021)	(0.0024)
$\sigma_{\omega1\omega2}$	0.0240	-0.3172	0[c]	0[c]	0[c]	0[c]
	(0.0216)	(0.5577)				
$\sigma_{\lambda1\lambda1}$	0.2909	0.1942	0.2661	0.2826	0.1204	0.1194
	(0.1324)	(0.2890)	(0.1236)	(0.1326)	(0.0478)	(0.0546)
$\sigma_{\lambda2\lambda2}$	0.0039	-0.0018	0.0035	-0.0041	-0.0004	0[c]
	(0.0022)	(0.0044)	(0.0027)	(0.0028)	(0.0013)	
$\sigma_{\lambda1\lambda2}$	-0.0260	0.0307	-0.0239	-0.0268	0[c]	0[c]
	(0.0159)	(0.0253)	(0.0158)	(0.0163)		
$\sigma_{\varepsilon\varepsilon}$	0.177	0.177	0.172	0.175	0.174	0.174
	(0.022)	(0.022)	(0.021)	(0.021)	(0.021)	(0.021)
$\sigma_{\phi\phi}$	0.290	0.290	0.290	0.290	0.315	0.313
	(0.037)	(0.037)	(0.037)	(0.037)	(0.038)	(0.038)
$\sigma_{\varepsilon\phi}$	0.121	0.121	0.120	0.122	0.127	0.127
	(0.023)	(0.023)	(0.022)	(0.023)	(0.023)	(0.023)
d	1.253	4.951	1.107	1.153	0.995	1.011
χ^2	123.04	123.04	124.45	125.21	128.89	129.00
GFI	0.649	0.649	0.641	0.643	0.640	0.639
P	0.024	0.024	0.023	0.024	0.014	0.017

[a] See Table 6.2 for definition of models. Solutions I and II correspond to the two solutions of a second order equation obtained in identifying the model.

[b] Standard errors in parentheses.

[c] A priori restriction.

Offence inflicting damage to property
Only W3L3^I satisfy our restrictions in the case of offence inflicting damage to property. For this solution the estimate of b is negative (see Table 6.11), but non-significant. The other estimates have also expected signs, and most of them are statistically significant. The variance of the log of the crime tendency is decreasing, whereas that of the clear-up tendency is first decreasing, and then increasing.

Aggravated larcenies
In the case of aggravated larcenies six models satisfy (6.16). Precision of estimates and parsimony of parameters are arguments for choosing either W3L2 or W1L2 instead of W3L3^I, cf Table 6.25. The high negative estimates of the deterrence elasticity indicate that the clear-up probability has a substantial influence on this type of crime. The variance of the log of the crime tendency is decreasing and that of the clear-up tendency increasing for the models allowing for changes in these tendencies. Police districts become less different with respect to aggravated larcenies, and more different with respect to clearing up such crimes, both in relative terms.

Simple larcenies
Two of the models applied to simple larcenies, W3L3^I and W3L2 are not rejected. Table 6.26 shows that their estimates are rather similar, and that those of the latter are statistically significant, and somewhat more precise than those of the former. The estimates are generally almost equal to those of crime at large. This is not surprising considered the large proportion of total crime that consists of simple larcenies. In both models the variance of the log of the crime tendency is decreasing, and that of the clear-up tendency increasing. Both tendencies are typical for most crimes: police districts become less different in crime tendencies and more different in clear-up tendencies, still in relative terms.

Thefts of motor vehicles
Our study of thefts of motor vehicles has not been totally successful, as we for some models have not been able to obtain optimal solutions by using LISREL. The three estimated and non-rejected models of Table 6.27 exhibit rather similar results. Precision and significance of the estimates are arguments for choosing W2L2^I. Also for this type of crime the clear-up proportion is found to have a strong negative influence on crime. Here, too, we find a growing similarity in crime between police districts, whereas there is a growing dissimilarity in clear-up.

Table 6.23

Embezzlement (24), estimates of non-rejected models[ab]

Parameter	W3L3[I]	W3L3[II]	W3L2
b	0.055 (0.629)	-10.21 (7.284)	-0.223 (0.768)
r	0.902 (0.070)	19.1 (205)	0.926 (0.098)
$\sigma_{\omega 1 \omega 1}$	0.3121 (0.1269)	-1.1829 (2.0581)	0.2986 (0.1197)
$\sigma_{\omega 2 \omega 2}$	0.0102 (0.0049)	0.0106 (0.0802)	0.0096 (0.0046)
$\sigma_{\omega 1 \omega 2}$	-0.0355 (0.0214)	0.3963 (0.6160)	-0.0336 (0.0203)
$\sigma_{\lambda 1 \lambda 1}$	-0.0113 (0.0116)	102 (2302)	0.0029 (0.0074)
$\sigma_{\lambda 2 \lambda 2}$	0.0001 (0.0007)	3.34 (75)	0.0011 (0.0005)
$\sigma_{\lambda 1 \lambda 2}$	0.0038 (0.0025)	-11.6 (262)	0[c]
$\sigma_{\varepsilon \varepsilon}$	0.232 (0.026)	0.232 (0.026)	0.233 (0.026)
$\sigma_{\phi \phi}$	0.272 (0.030)	0.272 (0.030)	0.269 (0.030)
$\sigma_{\varepsilon \phi}$	0.215 (0.026)	0.215 (0.026)	0.216 (0.026)
d	0.995	186	0.983
χ^2	141.49	141.49	143.06
GFI	0.641	0.641	0.642
P	0.001	0.001	0.001

[a] See Table 6.2 for definition of models. Solutions I and II correspond to the two solutions of a second order equation obtained in identifying the model.

[b] Standard errors in parentheses.

[c] A priori restriction.

Table 6.24

Fraud (26), estimates of non-rejected models[ab]

Parameter	W3L3[I]	W3L3[II]	W3L2	W3L1
b	0.200 (0.758)	−26.23 (31.4)	0.239 (0.793)	−0.795 (2.162)
r	0.962 (0.046)	6.00 (18.9)	0.961 (0.047)	1.005 (0.112)
$\sigma_{\omega1\omega1}$	0.5249 (0.141)	15.34 (38)	0.5256 (0.1418)	0.5218 (0.1468)
$\sigma_{\omega2\omega2}$	0.0075 (0.0030)	−0.3790 (0.9281)	0.0076 (0.0031)	0.0076 (0.0036)
$\sigma_{\omega1\omega2}$	−0.0349 (0.0172)	0.4284 (1.8335)	−0.0348 (0.0172)	−0.0365 (0.0195)
$\sigma_{\lambda1\lambda1}$	0.0223 (0.0152)	13.10 (99)	0.0260 (0.0073)	0.0194 (0.0069)
$\sigma_{\lambda2\lambda2}$	−0.0006 (0.0004)	0.1884 (1.4249)	−0.0004 (0.0002)	0[c]
$\sigma_{\lambda1\lambda2}$	0.0006 (0.0023)	−0.9707 (6.579)	0[c]	0[c]
$\sigma_{\varepsilon\varepsilon}$	0.194 (0.018)	0.194 (0.018)	0.194 (0.018)	0.193 (0.018)
$\sigma_{\phi\phi}$	0.291 (0.027)	0.291 (0.027)	0.290 (0.021)	0.286 (0.026)
$\sigma_{\varepsilon\phi}$	0.210 (0.021)	0.210 (0.021)	0.210 (0.027)	0.208 (0.021)
d	0.992	132	0.991	1.004
χ^2	184.22	184.22	184.29	187.59
GFI	0.674	0.674	0.673	0.668
P	0.000	0.000	0.000	0.000

[a] See Table 6.2 for definition of models. Solutions I and II correspond to the two solutions of a second order equation obtained in identifying the model.

[b] Standard errors in parentheses.

[c] A priori restriction.

Table 6.25

Aggravated larcenies (40), estimates of non-rejected models[ab]

Para-meter	W3L3[I]	W3L3[II]	W3L2	W3L1	W1L3	W2L2[I]	W1L2
b	-2.437	2.384	-2.408	-1.909	-2.121	-2.363	-2.007
	(0.566)	(2.380)	(0.497)	(0.563)	(1.007)	(1.158)	(0.797)
r	1.420	0.590	1.397	1.065	1.163	1.285	1.102
	(0.419)	(0.095)	(0.353)	(0.190)	(0.491)	(0.773)	(0.337)
$\sigma_{\omega1\omega1}$	0.7338	2.083	0.7194	0.5153	0.3910	0.4248	0.3798
	(0.353)	(2.0056)	(0.321)	(0.161)	(0.1345)	(0.233)	(0.1054)
$\sigma_{\omega2\omega2}$	0.0048	0.0070	0.0047	0.0038	0[c]	-0.0009	0[c]
	(0.005)	(0.0070)	(0.005)	(0.0031)		(0.004)	
$\sigma_{\omega1\omega2}$	-0.0463	-0.0032	-0.0448	-0.0258	0[c]	0[c]	0[c]
	(0.039)	(0.0294)	(0.036)	(0.019)			
$\sigma_{\lambda1\lambda1}$	0.3665	0.1235	0.3433	0.1381	0.1799	0.2562	0.1446
	(0.396)	(0.0404)	(0.314)	(0.094)	(0.2819)	(0.569)	(0.1696)
$\sigma_{\lambda2\lambda2}$	0.0012	0.0008	0.0011	0[c]	0.0009	0.0013	0.0008
	(0.002)	(0.0007)	(0.001)		(0.0010)	(0.002)	(0.0006)
$\sigma_{\lambda1\lambda2}$	-0.0006	-0.0078	0[c]	0[c]	-0.0010	0[c]	0[c]
	(0.006)	(0.0048)			(0.0025)		
$\sigma_{\varepsilon\varepsilon}$	0.054	0.054	0.054	0.054	0.056	0.056	0.056
	(0.005)	(0.005)	(0.005)	(0.005)	(0.005)	(0.005)	(0.005)
$\sigma_{\phi\phi}$	0.198	0.198	0.198	0.198	0.206	0.208	0.206
	(0.017)	(0.017)	(0.017)	(0.017)	(0.017)	(0.017)	(0.017)
$\sigma_{\varepsilon\phi}$	0.071	0.071	0.071	0.070	0.075	0.076	0.075
	(0.008)	(0.008)	(0.008)	(0.008)	(0.008)	(0.008)	(0.008)
d	2.022	1.977	1.956	1.124	1.346	1.673	1.205
χ^2	181.24	181.24	181.25	185.74	185.74	187.01	187.11
GFI	0.670	0.670	0.670	0.671	0.671	0.657	0.656
P	0.00	0.000	0.00	0.000	0.000	0.071	0.000

[a] See Table 6.2 for definition of models. Solutions I and II correspond to the two solutions of a second order equation obtained in identifying the model.

[b] Standard errors in parentheses.

[c] A priori restriction.

Table 6.26
Simple larcenies (41), estimates of non-rejected models[a][b]

Parameter	W3L3^{I}	W3L3^{II}	W3L2
b	-1.072	7.583	-0.998
	(0.193)	(14.79)	(0.150)
r	1.132	0.067	1.025
	(0.257)	(0.168)	(0.167)
$\sigma_{\omega 1 \omega 1}$	0.3362	16.62	0.3544
	(0.0945)	(56.19)	(0.087)
$\sigma_{\omega 2 \omega 2}$	0.0037	0.1850	0.0036
	(0.0016)	(0.6307)	(0.0014)
$\sigma_{\omega 1 \omega 2}$	-0.0300	-0.5025	-0.0285
	(0.0111)	(1.6548)	(0.0102)
$\sigma_{\lambda 1 \lambda 1}$	0.2891	0.3188	0.2063
	(0.1667)	(0.1182)	(0.0864)
$\sigma_{\lambda 2 \lambda 2}$	0.0032	0.0032	0.0022
	(0.0020)	(0.0016)	(0.0011)
$\sigma_{\lambda 1 \lambda 2}$	-0.0087	-0.0261	0[c]
	(0.0088)	(0.0112)	
$\sigma_{\varepsilon\varepsilon}$	0.049	0.049	0.049
	(0.004)	(0.004)	(0.004)
$\sigma_{\phi\phi}$	0.122	0.122	0.122
	(0.011)	(0.011)	(0.011)
$\sigma_{\varepsilon\phi}$	0.044	0.044	0.043
	(0.006)	(0.006)	(0.006)
d	1.142	8.07	1.025
χ^2	166.43	166.43	168.47
GFI	0.724	0.724	0.722
P	0.000	0.000	0.000

[a] See Table 6.2 for definition of models. Solutions I and II correspond to the two solutions of a second order equation obtained in identifying the model.

[b] Standard errors in parentheses.

[c] A priori restriction.

Table 6.27

Thefts of motor vehicles (43), estimates of non-rejected models[ab]

Parameter	W3L3[II]	W3L3[II]	W3L2	W2L2[I]
b	-2.679	1.645	-2.620	-2.480
	(0.472)	(2.527)	(0.392)	(0.532)
r	1.608	0.627	1.490	1.222
	(0.934)	(0.066)	(0.625)	(0.509)
$\sigma_{\omega1\omega1}$	0.7264	1.9321	0.4524	0.3035
	(0.2054)	(2.2664)	(0.1849)	(0.0997)
$\sigma_{\omega2\omega2}$	0.0019	0.0110	0.0016	-0.0010
	(0.0038)	(0.0135)	(0.0034)	(0.0020)
$\sigma_{\omega1\omega2}$	-0.0233	-0.0255	-0.0021	0[c]
	(0.0229)	(0.0379)	(0.0201)	
$\sigma_{\lambda1\lambda1}$	0.7138	0.0659	0.5309	0.2563
	(1.3772)	(0.0234)	(0.7758)	(0.4246)
$\sigma_{\lambda2\lambda2}$	0.0041	0.0003	0.0030	0.0016
	(0.0078)	(0.0005)	(0.0043)	(0.0023)
$\sigma_{\lambda1\lambda2}$	-0.0094	-0.0032	0[c]	0[c]
	(0.0216)	(0.0030)		
$\sigma_{\varepsilon\varepsilon}$	0.070	0.070	0.071	0.072
	(0.006)	(0.006)	(0.006)	(0.006)
$\sigma_{\phi\phi}$	0.134	0.134	0.134	0.139
	(0.012)	(0.012)	(0.012)	(0.012)
$\sigma_{\varepsilon\phi}$	0.074	0.074	0.074	0.077
	(0.006)	(0.006)	(0.008)	(0.008)
d	2.629	1.614	2.284	1.551
χ^2	155.06	155.06	156.03	157.34
GFI	0.682	0.682	0.683	0.684
P	0.000	0.000	0.000	0.000

[a] See Table 6.2 for definition of models. Solutions I and II correspond to the two solutions of a second order equation obtained in identifying the model.

[b] Standard errors in parentheses.

[c] A priori restriction.

6.7. Summing up

A new criminometric model is derived from a theory of criminal and police behaviour, and measurement relations with random and systematic measurement errors. The effects of the socioeconomic environment, called crime and clear-up tendencies, are summarized by the latent district effects in the crime and clear-up functions. The distribution of these latent variables across police districts and over time is modelled,

The model has been successfully applied on panel data on the number of crimes and clear-ups for the 53 police districts in Norway for 1970-78, confirming the hypothesis that our approach is fruitful.

The model is not identified if the latent district effects are constant over time, but these submodels are strongly rejected empirically, both for total crime and for 9 out of 12 types of crime. In the general model there will be two observationally equivalent structures, and correspondingly two global maxima in the likelihood function, due to the two solutions of a 2. order equation. However, by reasonable a priori restrictions on the parameter space, only one of the two solutions come out as empirically relevant. It is remarkable that this result was obtained both for total crime and for each of the 12 types of crime.

In our analysis of total crime we find the deterrence elasticity to be significantly negative and close to -1 in our preferred model. The estimate of this elasticity varies considerably between submodels, and illustrates the importance of our systematic approach to classifying, estimating, testing, and evaluating submodels.

Applying our most general model (W3L3) to 12 different types of crime, we find the deterrence elasticity to be negative in seven cases, four of which significantly so. The five positive estimates are mostly rather small and are all statistically non-significant. In three of the five cases the estimates of the deterrence elasticity changes from being positive to being (non-significant) negative when going to more parsimonious models. Only in the cases of public disorder, and slander and label the deterrence elasticity is found to be positive for all non-rejected models. The clear-up probability has a rather strong negative effect on crime for "simple" economic crimes, such as larcenies and thefts of motor vehicles, whereas more "sophisticated" forms, such as fraud, embezzlement and forgery, are less affected.

The estimate of the clear-up elasticity is for total crime expected to be positive, but less than 1. Presumably, an increase in crime will cet. par. result in a proportionally less increase in clear-ups. In our preferred model it is found to be 0.8. Also for various types of crime we expect a positive estimate, but not necessarily less than 1. Reallocation of police resources within a district might produce a proportionally higher number of clear-ups than of crimes when a specific type of crime is increasing. The estimates are in accordance with this expectation. They are all positive, and for some types of crimes and models they are greater than 1, although not much so.

The variance of the log of the crime tendency for total crime is decreasing for all models (in which a change is allowed) during the period. Except for embezzlement, and slander and label this variance is for all models lower at the end of the period than at the beginning, demonstrating a growing similarity, in relative (log) terms, among police districts for most types of crime.

The estimates of the variance of the log of the clear-up tendency is increasing for total crime and for half of the specific types of crime. In the remaining cases the development of this tendency is less uniform. For nine of the 12 types of crime, however, our most general model gives a higher variance at the end of the period than at the beginning, indicating a growing dissimilarity among police districts as far as clear-up tendencies is concerned. The more parsimonious models give, with a couple of exceptions, the same result.

The estimates of the variances and covariance of the errors of measurement are all significantly positive and very robust with respect to model specifications.

Chapter 7

CONCLUSIONS

In order to judge the relevance of regarding crime as rational behaviour, various competing theories of crime have been integrated into a theoretical framework of norm-guided rational choice. Discussing a large number of explanations of crime, referring to mental, physical, developmental, economic, social, and cultural causes, I have found that at the centre of each theory there is an acting individual. The behaviour of this individual has been analyzed with reference to his preferences (norms and wants), to his abilities, and to benefits and costs of both legal and illegal activities. Cognitive limitations and expressive behaviour have not been regarded as decisive objections to the assumption that people are rational. This assumption makes it possible to find the effects on crime of changes in benefits and costs, including changes in formal sanctions. A survey of expected utility models of crime shows that an increase in the probability of punishment has a clear negative effect on crime, whereas the effects of increased severity of punishment and of various benefits and (other) costs of legal and illegal activities depend on the attitude towards risk and other factors. This discussion concludes that studies of crime based on the assumption of rational behaviour are warranted.

More demanding is the question of whether aggregated data can be satisfactorily used in such studies. Certain authors find the many weak elements of common empirical macro studies to be so overwhelming that they advice against using them. Some of the critical points have little weight, whereas others represent serious objections. The answer to the question is two-fold: One has to survey as many empirical studies as possible in order to see if they produce similar results. If they do, one may have some confidence in the results even if each and every study has weak elements. The second and more constructive path is to face each problem, and try to carry out studies where some of the problems are solved or avoided.

In order to present a rather comprehensive guide to empirical studies of crime I have discussed some general questions like identification of models, measurement errors, measures of theoretical concepts, estimation methods, etc. The survey of empirical macro studies has been carried out from the viewpoint of assessing to which extent these studies have resulted in conclusions about the impact on crime of variables representing norms, wants, abilities, and benefits and costs of crime (including sanctions). Various types of crime have been reviewed.

Almost all correlation and cross section regression studies show a negative association between punishment variables and crime. In a large number of studies the elasticities of crime with respect to variables of probability and severity of punishment are found to lie between 0 and -2, with median values around -0.5. With few exceptions time series studies, studies based on individual data, studies of substitution of crime, etc. produce similar results.

Discussing whether this observation is a result of general deterrence, norm formation or other mechanisms, it was concluded that the results in the studies reviewed most likely come from the former. However, other mechanisms may in some instances contribute to the negative effect of sanctions on crime. Certainly, norms are important in decisions on whether to behave illegally or not, but apparently they are not crucial for assessing the aggregate variation in crime between districts and over (not very long periods of) time.

The various studies produce conflicting results regarding the impact on crime of various benefits and (other) costs of crime. As a whole it seems that measures chosen to represent the opportunities of legal and illegal activities are not appropriate. One reason might be that average or median income for an observational unit measures both legal end illegal income opportunities, whereas (other) proxies representing what can be gained from criminal activity are poor measures of the real gains to crime. The impact on crime of income differentials is ambiguous. The estimated effects of unemployment, a proxy for lack of legal income opportunities, are also not consistent across the studies reviewed. Insurance schemes and unemployed parents' surveying of delinquent sons may explain why unemployment does not produce more crime on an aggregate level.

In most studies various socio-economic and/or demographic variables have been included. Unfortunately, the reasons for including many of these variables often are not thoroughly discussed. Some variables, like race and age, may represent norms, wants, and abilities of people, but also the benefits and costs of legal and illegal acts. This multitude of possible mechanisms may be especially relevant for race. In studies where the proportion of non-whites in the population is included, this variable almost without exception has a positive effect on crime, but to what extent this is due to racially dependent constitutional characteristics, to acquired abilities, or to differences in income opportunities is still unsettled. It will also be recalled that IQ and race are correlated, and that the empirical results may reflect variation in IQ, whatever that measure measures.

In the three studies where the proportion of youth is included, and where the estimates are statistically significant, a positive effect on crime seems to occur. Considering that most crimes are committed by young people, one would have expected even stronger results. To what extent crime among young people is a consequence of preferences and abilities, or of their meagre legal income opportunities is an open question. Young people are perhaps not different, just poorer.

In several studies the population density is found to have a positive effect on crime. This variable may reflect various phenomena, such as differences in social control, psychic diseases, etc. The studies reviewed are hardly suitable for a discussion of which of these mechanisms have been at work.

A few empirical studies based on special theories of crime have been reviewed in brief to see if they shed additional light on the development of crime. The routine activity theory and the theory of situational opportunity both emphasize that the probability of clear-up decreases by the fact that there are more unguarded targets. Both theories fit well as special theories within our framework of norm-guided rational behaviour, concentrating on the reduction in the sanction costs of crime. Empirical studies corroborate these theories. Victimization studies also support the hypothesis of general deterrence.

The survey of empirical studies shows great diversity in the empirical measures used to represent various determinants of crime. This diversity cannot exclusively - not even mainly - be explained by a corresponding diversity in problems that have been discussed and in hypotheses that have been tested. The reason is to some extent lack of good theory, but first and foremost lack of data. Instead of abandoning empirical macro studies because of these difficulties I have suggested that one should continue the theoretical discussion about determinants of crime in order to obtain a better foundation for choosing acceptable measures of theoretical constructs, and to carry out more empirical studies to see to what extent conclusions depend on the choice of measures.

In this spirit two somewhat traditional criminometric studies based on data from Norwegian police districts are included. A cross section study corroborates the preventive effect of the clear-up probability. High values of assets and of sales of goods have a positive impact on crime, indicating that the more there is to steal, the more crime there is. A high positive effect of divorce on crime is difficult to interpret. Does divorce cause crime, does crime cause divorce, or do we have other factors causing both? At variance with the studies reviewed it is argued in a times series study that one should use *lagged* clear-up proportions because people do not know the clear-up proportion at the time when crimes are committed. Using lagged variables the study corroborates the hypothesis of the general deterrence of sanctions.

In a final chapter we present an equilibrium model of crimes and clear-ups containing measurement relations allowing for random and systematic errors of measurement. We have faced two of the more serious problems of criminometric studies: lack of identification and measurement errors. Using a panel model we are able by a rather intricate analysis to identify our model without recurring to the common, criticized procedures. Measurement errors are handled by introducing latent variables corresponding to the registered crime and clear-up rates. Finally, we circumvent the problem of finding acceptable measures of many of the determinants of crime. The rather inconclusive results obtained from the survey of empirical macro studies suggest that one should try to estimate the impact on crime of sanction variables without relying on explanatory variables of debatable merit. Therefore, we do not employ such variables, but assume that observational units may differ as far as individual norms, wants, and economic and other conditions are concerned, and that these differences influence both the number of crimes and the number of clear-ups. We lump all these determinants into what we call crime and clear-up tendencies, and then model the distribution of these tendencies across police districts and over time. We find that the probability of clear-up has a significant negative effect on both total crime and on most of the specific types of crime studied. We further conclude that the relative differences in crime tendencies between Norwegian police districts have been reduced in the period studied.

REFERENCES

Aasness, J., E. Biørn and T. Skjerpen (1993): Engel functions, panel data and latent variables. *Econometrica, 61,* 6 (Nov.), 1395-1422.

Aasness, J., E. Eide and T. Skjerpen (1993): Criminometrics, latent variables and panel data. In K. Haagen et al. (eds.): *Statistical modelling and latent variables.* Amsterdam, North-Holland.

Allingham, M.G. & A. Sandmo (1972): Income tax evasion: A theoretical analysis. *J. Publ. Econ.,* 323-38.

Amemiya, Y. and T. W. Anderson (1990): Asymptotic Chi-square tests for a large class of factor analysis models, *Ann. Stat., 18,* 1453-63.

Andenæs, J. (1974a): *Punishment and deterrence.* Ann Arbor, Univ. of Michigan Pr.

"   (1975): General prevention revisited: Research and policy implications. *J. Cr. Law & Cr., 66,* 3, 338-65.

"   (1977): Nyere forskning om almenprevensjon - status og kommentar. *Nord.T. Krim., 65,* 1-2, 61-101.

"   (1989, 3. utg.): *Alminnelig strafferett.* Oslo, Universitetsforlaget.

Anderson, R.W. (1976): *The economics of crime.* London, Macmillan.

Anderson, T.W. and Y. Amemiya (1988): The asymptotic normal distribution of estimators in factor analysis under general conditions, *The Annals of Statistics, 14,* 759-71.

Antunes, G. & A.L. Hunt (1973): The deterrent impact of criminal sanctions: some implications for criminal justice policy. *J. Urban Law, 51,* 2, 145-61.

Arrow, K.J. (1971): *Essays in the theory of risk bearing.* Amsterdam.

Athens, L. H. (1980): *Violent criminal acts and actors - A symbolic interactionist study.* Boston, Routledge and Kegan Paul.

Avio, K. L. (1973): An economic analysis of criminal corrections: The Canadian case. *Can. J. Econ.,* 6, 164-178.

"   (1979): Capital punishment in Canada: a time-series analysis of the deterrent hypothesis. *Can. J. Econ.,* 647-76.

"   & C.S. Clark (1976): Property crime in Canada: an econometric study. *Ontario Council Economic Research Studies,* Ontario, Canada.

"   (1978): The supply of property offences in Ontario: evidence on the deterrent effect of punishment. *Can. J. Econ., XI,* 1 (Febr.), 1-19.

Axelrod, R. (1984): *The evolution of cooperation.* New York, Basic Books.

Ayllon, T. and N. Azrin (1965): The measurement and reinforcement of behavior of psychotics. *J. of the Experimental Analysis of Behavior, 8,* 5 (nov.), 357-83.

Azzi, C. & R. Ehrenberg (1975): Household allocation of time and church attendance. *J.*

Pol. Econ., 82, 1 (Jan./Febr.), 27-56.

Bailey, W.C. (1978): The deterrent effect of arrest and conviction on crime rates in Indian states and territories. *Ann. Intern. de Crim., 17*, 1 et 2, 21-50.

Bailey, W. C., J. D. Martin and L. N. Gray (1974): Crime and deterrence: A correlation study. *J. Res. Cr. Delinq., 11*, 2, 124-143.

Bailey, W. C. and R. W. Smith (1972): Punishment: Its severity and certainty. *J. Cr. Law, Cr. Police Sc., 63*, 4, 530-9.

Bean, F. and R. Cushing (1971): Criminal homicide, punishment and deterrence. *Soc. Sc. Q., 52*, 2, 277-89.

Beccaria, C. ([1764]): On crime and punishment. In: S.E. Grupp ed. (1971, 117-137): *Theories of punishment.* Indiana Univ. Pr., Bloomington.

Becker, G. S. (1962): Irrational Behavior and economic theory. *J. Pol. Econ., LXX*, 1 (Febr.), 1-13.

" (1968): Crime and punishment: an economic approach. *J. Pol. Econ., 76*, 2 (March/April), 169-217.

" (1973): A theory of marriage: Part I and Part II. *J. Pol. Econ., 81*, 4 (July/Aug.), 813-46 and *82*, 2 (March/April), 11-26.

Becker, G. S. & W. M. Landes (eds.) (1974): *Essays in the economics of crime and punishment.* N. Y., Columbia Univ. Pr.

Becker, G.S. & G.J. Stigler (1974): Law enforcement, malfeasance and compensation of enforcers. *J. Legal Stud., 3*, 1, 1-18.

Bentham, J. (1843): Principles of penal law. In: *1 Works*, 399.

" (1962): Principles of penal law. In: Brownind (ed.): *The work of Jeremy Bentham 1748-1832.* N.Y., Russel & Russel.

Bentham, J. (1864): *Theory of legislation.* London, Trüber & Co. (Tanslated from the french).

Beyleveld, D. (1980): *A bibliography on general deterrence research.* Westmead, Saxon House.

Bigelow, G. (1973): *The Public Interest*, 32 (Summer), 119-120.

Block, M.K. & J.M. Heineke (1973): *The criminal choice and trading ethics.* Mimeo.

" (1974/75): Factor allocation under uncertainty: an extension, *Southern Ec. J., 41*, 526-30.

Block, M.K. & J.M. Heineke (1975): A labor theoretic analysis of the criminal choice.*J. Legal St., 4*, 3 (June), 314-25.

Block, M.K. & R.C. Lind (1975a): Crime and punishment reconsidered. *J. Legal St., 4*, 1 (Jan), 241-7.

" (1975b): An economic analysis of crimes punishable by imprisonment. *J. Legal St.,*

4, (June), 479-92.

Blumstein, A., J. Cohen & D. Nagin, eds. (1978): *Deterrence and incapacitation; estimating the effects of criminal sanctions on crime rates.* National Academy of Sciences, Washington, D.C.

Blumstein, A. and D. Nagin (1977): The deterrent effect of legal sanctions on draft evasion. *Stanford Law Rev., 29*, Jan., 241-76.

Bowers, W.J. & G.L. Pierce (1975): The illusion of deterrence in Isach Ehrlich's research on capital punishment. *Yale Law J., 85*, 2, 187-208.

Brennan, G. (1990): Comment: What might rationality fail to do. In: Cook and Levy eds., 47-59

Brier, S. S. & S. E. Fienberg (1980): Recent econometric modeling of crime and punishment support for the deterrence hypothesis. *Eval. Rev., 4*, 2 (Apr.), 147-91. Sage Publ.

Brown, D. W. (1978): Arrest rates and crime rates: when does a tipping effect occur? *Soc. Forces, 57*, 2 (Dec.), 671-82.

Brown, M.K. & M.O. Reynolds (1973): Crime and "punishment": risk implications. *J. Econ. Th., 6*, 508-14.

Browne, M. W. (1987): Robustness of statistical inference in factor analysis and related models, *Biometrica, 74*, 375-84.

Browne, M. W. and A. Shapiro (1988): Robustness of normal theory methods in the analysis of linear latent models, *Br. J. Math. Stat. Psychol.*, 41, 193-208.

Buck, A. J. & S. Hakim and U. Spiegel (1985): The natural rate of crime by type of community. *Rev. Soc. Econ., 43*, 245-59.

Cameron, S. (1987): Substitution between offence categories in the supply of property crimes: Some new evidence. *Int. J. Soc. Econ., 14*, 11, 48-60.

"   (1988): The economics of crime deterrence: A survey of theory and evidence. *Kyklos, 41*, 2, 301-23.

Carr-Hill, R.A. & N.H. Stern (1973): An econometric model of the supply and control of recorded offences in England and Wales. *J. Publ. Econ. 2*, 289-318.

"   (1979): *Crime, the police and criminal statistics.* London, Academic Pr.

Central Bureau of Statistics (annual): Criminal Statistics. *Norges Offisielle Statistikk,* Oslo.

Chapman, J. I. (1976): An economic model of crime and police: Some empirical results. *J. Res. in Cr. and Delinq.*, (Jan.), 48-63.

Chew, S. H. (1983): A generalization of the quasilinear mean with applications to the measurement of income inequality and decision theory resolving the Allais Paradox. *Econometrica, 51*, (July), 1065-92.

Chiricos, T.G. & G.P. Waldo (1970): Punishment and crime: an examination of some empirical evidence. *Soc. Prob., 18,* 200-17.

Christie, N. (1968): Hidden delinquency: Some scandinavian experience. *3rd National Conference on research and teaching in criminology, University of Cambridge, Institute of Criminology, Cambridge.*

Clarke, R. (1985): *Applied microeconomic problems.* Deddington.

Cloninger, D. O. (1992): Capital punishment and deterrence: a portfolio approach. *Appl. Econ., 24,* 635-45.

Cloninger, D. O. & L. C. Sartorius (1979): Crime rates, clearance rates and enforcement effort: The case of Houston, Texas. *Amer J. Econ. Soc.,* 4 (Oct.), 389-402.

Clotfelter, C.T. (1977a): Urban crime and household protective measures. *Rev. Econ. Stat.,* (Nov.), 499-503.

" (1977b): Public services, private substitutes, and the demand for protection against crime, *Amer. Econ. Rev.,* (Dec.), 867-77.

" (1983): Tax evasion and tax rates: an analysis of individual returns. *Rev. Econ. Stat., LXV,,* 3 (Aug.), 363-73.

Cloward, R. A. and L. E. Ohlin (1961): *Delinquency and opportunity.* Illinois, Free Press of Glencoe.

Cohen, A. K. (1966): *Deviance and control.* Englewood Cliffs, New Jersey, Prentice-Hall.

Cohen, J. (1978): The incapacitative effect of imprisonment: A critical review of the literature. In: Blumstein et al.

Cohen, J. (1984): The legal control of drunken driving: a comment on methodological concerns in assessing deterrent effectiveness. *J. Crim. Just., 12,* 2 (March-Apr.), 149-54.

Cohen, L. E., M. Felson and K.C. Land (1980): Property crime rates in the United States: A macrodynamic analysis 1947-1977; with ex ante forecasts for the mid-1980s. *Amer. J. Soc., 86,* 1, 90-118.

Cohen, L. E. & M. Felson (1979): Social change and crime rate trends: a routine activity approach. *Amer. J. Soc. Rev., 44,*(Aug.), 588-608.

Coleman, J.S. (1973): *The mathematics of collective action.* Chicago, Aldine.

Cook, K. S. and M. Levy (1990): *The limits of rationality.* Chicago and London, Univ. of Chicago Pr.

Cook, P.J. (1977): Punishment and crime: a critique of current findings concerning the preventive effects of punisment. *Law and Contemp. Pr. 41* 1 (Winter), 165-204.

Cook, P.J. (1979): The clearance rate as a measure of criminal justice system effectiveness, *J. Publ. Econ., 11.*

Cornish, D.B. and R.V. Clarke, eds. (1986): *The reasoning criminal.* New York, Berlin, Heidelberg, Tokyo, Springer-Verlag.

Dalgard, O. S. and E. Kringlen (1976): Norwegian twin study of criminality. *Br. J. Cr., 16*, 213-232.

Danziger, S. & D. Wheeler (1975): The economics of crime: punishment or income distribution. *Rev. Soc. Econ.*, 113-31.

Davis, M. L. (1988): Time and punishment: An intertemporal model of crime. *J. Polit. Econ. 96*, 2 (April), pp. 383-90.

Dijkstra, T. K. (1991): Pyrrho's lemma, or have it your way. Paper presented to the *Econometric Society European Meeting,* Cambridge, 2-6 Sept.

Dobash, R. E. and R. P. Dobash (1984): The nature and antecedents of violent events. *Br. J. Cr., 24*, 3, 269-88.

Dodge, R. W. et al. (1976): Crime in the United States: A report on the National Crime Survey. In: W. G. Skogan, ed.: *Sample Surveys of the victims of crime.* Cambridge, Mass., Ballinger, 1-26.

Downes, D. (1966): *The delinquent solution.* London, Routledge and Kegan Paul.

Durkheim, E. (1966): *The division of labour in society.* Illinois, Free Press of Glencoe.

Ehrlich, I. (1972): The deterrent effect of criminal law enforcement. *J. Legal Stud., 1*, 2 (June), 259-76.

"   (1973): Participation in illegitimate activities: a theoretical and empirical investigation. *J. Pol. Econ., 81* (May/June), 521-65.

"   (1975 a): Deterrence: evidence and inference. *Yale Law J., 85*, 2, 209-27.

"   (1975 b): The deterrent effect of capital punishment: a question of life and death. *Am. Econ. Rev., 63*, 3 397-417.

"   (1977): Capital punishment and deterrence: some further thoughts and additional evidence. *J. Pol. Econ., 85*, 4 (Aug.), 741-88.

"   (1982): The market for offenses and the public enforcement of laws - An equilibrium analysis. *Br. J. Soc. Psych., 21*, 2, 107-20.

"   & G. D. Brower (1987): On the issue of causality in the economic model of crime and the law enforcement: some theoretical considerations and experimental evidence. *Am. Econ. Rev., 77*, 2 (May), 99-110.

"   & J. C. Gibbons (1977): On the measurement of the deterrent effect of capital punishment and the theory of deterrence. *J. Legal Stud., 6*, 35-50.

"   in cooperation with R. Mark (1977): Fear of deterrence. *J. Legal Stud., 6*, 293-316.

Eide, E. (1987): Punishment works - but do not waste money on the police. Paper presented to the *Econometric Society European Meeting,* Copenhagen, Aug.

Ellickson, R. C. (1991): *Order without law, How neighbours settle disputes.* Cambridge, Massachusetts and London, Harvard Univ. Pr.

Elster, J. (1983): *Sour grapes.* Cambridge, Cambridge Univ. Pr.

"   (1989a): Social norms and economic theory. *J. Econ. Persp., 3,* 4, 99-117.

"   (1989b): *The Cement of society.* Cambridge, New York, Port Chester, Melborne, Sidney, Cambridge Univ. Pr.

"   (1990): When rationality fails. In: Cook and Levy, eds., 19-51.

Erickson, M. L. and L. T. Empey (1963): Court records, undetected delinquency and decision-making. *J. Crim. Law, Criminol. & Police Sc., 54,* 456-69.

Eysenck, H. J. (1957): *The dynamics of anziety and hysteria.* London, Routledge and Kegan Paul.

Fair, R.C. (1978): A theory of extramarital affairs. *J. Pol. Econ., 86, 3,* 1 (Febr.), 45-62.

Fishburn, P. C. (1987): Reconsiderations in the foundations of decision under uncertainty. *Econ. J., 97,* 825-841.

"   (1987): Nonlinear preference and utility theory. Brighton, Wheatsheaf Books.

Fisher, F.M. (1966): *The identification problem in econometrics.* New York, McGraw-Hill.

Fisher, F. M. and D, Nagin (1978): On the feasibility of identifying the crime function in a simultaneous model of crime rates and sanction levels. In: Blumstein et al., eds.

Fleisher, B.M. (1966): *The economics of delinquency.* Chicago, Quadrangle.

Forst, B. (1976): Participation in illegitimate activities: further empirical findings. *Policy Anal., 2,* 3, 477-92.

Forst, B (1977): The deterrent effect of capital punishment: a cross-state analysis of the 1960's. *Minnesota Law Rev.,* 5, 743-67.

Furlong, W. J. (1987): A general equilibrium model of crime commission and prevention. *J. Public Econ., 34,* 1, 87-103.

Furlong, W. J. and S. L. Mehay (1981): Urban law enforcement in Canada: an empirical analysis. *Can. J. Econ., XIV,* 1 (Febr.), 44-57.

Føllesdal, D. (1982): The status of rationality assumptions in interpretion and in the explanation of action. *Dialectica, 36,* 301-316.

Gibbons, T. (1982): The utility of economic analysis of crime. *Int. Rev. Law Econ., 2,* 173-91.

Gibbs, J.P. (1975): *Crime, punishment and deterrence.* New York, Elsevier.

Gordon, R. A. (1975): Crime and cognition: An evolutionary perspective, *Proceedings of the II International Symposium on Criminology.* San Paulo, Brazil. International Center for Biological and Medico-forensic Criminology.

Gravelle, H. and R. Rees (1981): *Microeconomics.* London and New York, Longman.

Gray, L. N. & J. D. Martin (1969): Punishment and deterrence: Another analysis of Gibbs' data. *Soc. Sc. Q.,* 50, (Sept.), 389-95.

Greenberg, D.F., R.C. Kessler & C.H. Logan (1979): A panel model of crime rates and arrest rates. *Am. Soc. Rev.,* 843-50.

Greenwood, M.J. & W.J. Wadycki (1973): Crime rates and public expenditures for police protection: their interaction. *Rev. Soc. Econ., 31,* 2, 138-51.

"   (1975): Crime rates and public expenditures for police protection: a reply. *Rev. Soc. Econ., 33,* 1, 81-5.

Grogger, J. (1990): The deterrent effet of capital punishment: An analysis of daily homicide counts. *J. of the American Statistical Association, 85,* 410, 295-303.

Harris, J.R. (1970): On the economics of law and order. *J. Pol. Econ., 78,* 1 (Jan./Febr.), 165-74.

Heineke, J.M. (1975): A note on modelling the criminal choice problem. *J. Econ. Th., 10,* 113-6.

"   (1978): *Economic models of criminal behaviour.* Amsterdam, North-Holland.

Hindelang, M. J. (1976): *Criminal victimization in eight american cities: a descriptive analysis of common theft and assault.* Cambridge, Mass., Balinger.

Hindelang, M. J. and Gottfredson (1976): The victim's decision not to invoke the criminal justice process. In: W. F. McDonald ed.: *Criminal justice and the victim.* Beverly Hills, Calif., Sage Publ., 57-78

Hoenack, S.A., R.T. Kurdle & D. Sjøquist (1978): The deterrent effect of capital punishment: a question of identification: *Pol. Anal., 4,* 491-527.

Hoenack, S.A. & W.C. Weiler (1980): A structural model of murder behavior. *Am. Econ. Rev., 70,* 3 (June), 327-41.

Holtman, A. G. and L. Yap (1978): Does punishment pay? *Publ. Fin., 33,* 1-2, 90-7.

Johnston, J. (1984, 3rd. ed.): *Econometric Methods.* Auckland, McGraw-Hill, International Book company.

Jöreskog, K. G. and D. Sörbom (1988): *LISREL 7: A guide to the program and applications,* SPSS Inc., Chicago.

Kahneman, D. and A. Tversky (1979): Prospect theory: an analysis of decision under risk. *Econometrica, 47,* (March), 263-91.

Karmarkar, U. S. (1978): Subjectively weighted utility: a descriptive extension of the expected utility model. *Organizational Behaviour and Human Performance, 21,* (Febr.), 61-72.

Klein, L. R., B. Forst and V. Filatov (1978): The deterrent effect of capital punishment: An assessment of the estimates. In: Blumstein et al., eds.

Klepper, S. & D. Nagin (1989): The anatomy of tax evasion. *J. Law, Econ. Org., 5,* 1 (Spring), 1-24.

"   (1989b): The criminal deterrence literature: implications for research on taxpayer compliance. In: J. T. Scholz et al. eds.: *Paying taxes: an agenda for compliance research.* Philadelphia, Univ. of Philadelphia Pr.

Kloeck, T. (1987): The deterrent effect of capital punishment; a countable data approach. Report 8716/A, Econometric Institute, Univ. of Rotterdam.

Kolm, S.-C. (1973): A note on optimum tax evasion. *J. Publ. Econ., 2*, 265-70.

Køberer, W. von (1982): Læsst sich Generalprævention messen? *Monatsschr. Krim. Strafrechtsreform, 65*, 4, 200-19.

Landes, W. M. (1978): An economic study of U.S. aircraft hijacking, 1961-1976, *J. Law and Econ., 21*, 1-31.

Layson, S. (1983): Homicide and deterrence: another view of the Canadian time-series evidence. *Can. J. Econ., 16*, 1 (Febr.), 52-73.

"   (1985): Homicide and deterrence: a reexamination of the United States time-series evidence. *Southern J. Econ., 52*, 1 (July), 68-89.

Lattimore, P. K. (1992): The influence of probability on risky choice: A parametric examination. *J. Econ. Beh. Org., 17*, 377-400.

Leamer, E. E. (1982): Sets of posterior means with bounded variance priors. *Econometrica, 50*, 3 (May), 725-36.

"   (1983): Let's take the con out of econometrics. *Am. Econ. Rev., 73*, 1 (March), 1-43.

"   (1985): Sensitivity analyses would help. *Am. Acon. Rev., 75*, 3 (June), 308-13.

Lejeune, R. (1977): Managenment of a mugging. *Urb. Life, 6*, 2 (July), 123-48.

Logan, C.H. (1971): On punishment and crime (Chiricos and Waldo, 1970): Some methodological commentary. 3 *Soc. Probl.*, 280-4.

"   (1972a): Evaluation research in crime and delinquency: a reappraisal. *J. Cr. Law, Cr. and Police Sc.*, (Sept.), 378-87.

"   (1972b): General deterrent effects of imprisonment. *Soc. Forces, 51*, 1, 64-73.

"   (1975): Arrest rates and deterrence. *Soc. Sc. Quart., 56*, 3, 376-89.

"   (1982): Problems in ratio correlation: the case of deterrence research. *Social Forces, 60*, 3 (March), 791-810.

Long, J. Scott (1983): *Coviariance structure models: an introduction to LISREL.* Sage University Paper series on Quantitative applications in the social sciences, series no. 34. Beverly Hills and London: Sage Publ.

Machina, M. J. (1982): "Expected utility" analysis without the independence axiom. *Econometrica, 50*, (March), 277-323.

"   (1987): Choice under uncertainty: Problems solved and unsolved. *J. Econ. Persp., 1*, 1 (Summer), 121-54.

Manski, C.F. (1978): Prospects for inference on deterrence through empirical analysis of individual criminal behavior. In: *Heineke*, ed.

Mathieson, D. & P. Passell (1976): Homicide and robbery in New York city: an econometric model. *J. Legal Stud., 5*, 83-98.

Mathur, V.K. (1978): Economics of crime: an investigation of the deterrent hypothesis for urban areas. *Rev. Econ. Stat., 60*, 3 (Aug.), 459-66.

McPheters, L. R. (1978): Econometric analysis of factors influencing crime on the campus. *J. Crim. Just., 6*, 47-52.

Mehey S. (1977): Interjurisdictional spillovers of urban police services. *South. Ec. J, 43*, 1352-9.

Merton, R. K. (1957, rev. ed.): New York, Free Press.

Myers, S. L. jr. (1980): Why are crimes underreported? What is the crime rate; Does it really matter? *Soc. Sc. Q., 61*, 1 (June), 23-43.

"   (1982): Crime in urban areas: new evidence and results. *J. Urban Econ., 11*, 148-58.

Myers, S. L. jr. (1983): Estimating the economic model of crime: employment versus punishment effects, *Q. J. Econ.*, (Febr.).

Nagin, D. (1978): General deterrence: A review of the empirical evidence. In: *Blumstein et al.*, eds.

Nettler, G. (1978): *Explaining crime*, 2d ed. New York, McGraw-Hill.

Orsagh, T. (1973): Crime, sanctions and scientific explanation. *J. Cr. Law and Cr., 64*, 3, 354-61.

"   (1979): Empirical criminology: Interpreting results derived from aggregate data. *J. Res. in Cr. and Delinq., 16*, 2, 294-306.

Passell, P. (1975): The deterrent effect of the death penalty: a statistical test. *Stanford Law Rev., 28, 1, 61-80.*

Passell, P. & J.B. Taylor (1977): The deterrent effect of capital punishment: another view. *Am. Econ. Rev., 67*, 3 (June), 445-51.

Pearson, E. S. (1965): Tables of percentage points of $\sqrt{b_1}$ and b_2 in normal sampels; rounding off. *Biometrika, 52*, 282-85.

Peck, J. (1976): The deterrent effect of capital punishment: A comment. *Yale Law J. 86*, 354-67.

Phillips, L. & H.L. Votey (1972): An economic analysis of the deterrent effect of law enforcement on criminal activities. *J. Cr. Law, Cr., and Police Sc. 63*, 3, 336-42.

"   (1975): Crime control in California, *J. Legal Stud., 4*, 2 (June).

"   (1981): *The economics of crime control*. Beverly Hills, London, Sage Publications.

Pogue, T. F. (1975): Effects of police expenditure on crime rates: some evidence. *Publ. Fin. Q., 3*, 1 (Jan), 14-44.

Prisching, M. von (1982): Sozioøkonomische Bedingungen der Kriminalität - Über empirische Divergenzen und theoretische Kontroversen. *Monatss. Krim.*

Strafrechtsr., 65, 3, 163-76.

Pyle, D. J. (1983): *The economics of crime and law enforcement.* London, Macmillan.

" (1984): Combating crime: do the police give value for money? *Public Money, 4,* 1 (June), 27-30.

Pålsson, A.-M. (1980): Ekonometriska studier av allmænprevention. In: *Rapport 2, Brottførebyggande rådet.*

" (1975): The Scandinavian myth: the effectiveness of drinking-and-driving legislation in Sweden and Norway. *J. Legal Stud.,* 4, 2, 285-310.

Rowe, A. R. and C. R. Tittle (1977): Life cycle changes and criminal propensity. *The sociological Quarterly, 18,* 223-36.

Rawls, J. (1992): *A theory of justice.* Oxford, Oxford U. Pr.

Samuelson, P. A. (1945): *Foundations of economic analysis.* Cambridge, Mass. Sandelin, B. and G. Skogh, (1986): Property crimes and the police: An Emperical analysis of svedish data, *Scand. J. Econ., 88,* 3, 547-61.

" (1985): Polisinsatser och brottslighet, *Ekonomisk Debatt, 6.*

Sandelin, B. and G. Skogh (1986): Property crimes and the police: An empirical analysis of Swedish data. *Scand. J. Econ., 88,* 3, 547-61

Schmidt, P. and A.D. Witte (1984): *An economic analysis of crime and justice: Theory, methods and applications.* Orlando, Academic Pr..

Schuller, Bernd-Joachim (1986): Ekonomi och kriminalitet: En empirisk undersøkning av brottsligheten i Sverige. *Economiska studier utgivna av Nationalekonomiska institutionen vid Gøteborgs Universitet, 17.*

Sellin, T. (1938): Culture, conflict and crime. *Soc. Sci. Res. Counc. Bull. 44.* New York.

Sesnowitz, M. L. & J. L. Hexter (1982): Economic determinants of theft: Som empirical results. *Publ. Fin. Q., 10,* 4 (Oct.), 489-98.

Shapiro, A. and M. W. Browne (1987): Analysis of covariance structures under elliptical distributions, *J. Am. Stat. Ass., 82,* 1092-97.

Shinnar, R. & S. Shinnar (1975): The effects of the criminal justice system on the control of crime: a quantitative approach. *Law and Soc. Rev., 9,* 4, 581-611.

Simon, H. (1955): A behavioral model of rational choice, *Quart J. of Econ., 69,* 99-118.

" (1957): *Models of man.* New York, Wiley and Sons.

" (1978): Rationality as process and as product of thought. *Am. Econ. Rev., 68,* 2 (May), 1-16.

Sims, C. A. (1980): Macroeconomics and reality. *Econometrica, 48,* 1 (Jan.), 1-48.

Singh, B. (1973): Making honesty the best policy. *J. Publ. Econ., 2,* (July), 257-263.

Sjoquist, D. (1973): Property crime and economic behavior: some empirical results. *Am. Econ. Rev., 63,* 3, 439-46.

Skogan, W. (1974): The validity of official crime statistics. *Soc. Sc. Q., 55*, (June), 25-38.

Skogh, G. (1973): A note on Becker's "Crime and punishment: an economic approach". *Swed. J. Econ.*, 305-311.

" & C. Stuart (1982): An economic analysis of crime rates, punishment, and the social consequences of crime, *Publ. Choice, 38*, 171-9.

Slemrod, J. (1985): An empirical test of tax evasion. *Rev. Econ. Stat., LXVII*, 232-8.

Sparks, R., H. Genn and D. Dodd (1977): *Surveying victims.* Chichester, Wiley.

Stewart, M. B. and K. F. Wallis (1981, 2nd. ed.): *Introductory econometrics.* Oxford, Basil Blackwell.

Stigler, G.S. (1970): The optimum enforcement of laws. *J. Pol. Econ., 78,* 3 (May/June), 526-36.

Stigler, G.S. & G. S. Becker (1977): De gustibus non est disputandum. *Am. Econ. Rev., 67,* 2 (March), 76-90.

Sutherland, E. H. and D. R. Cressey (1966): *Principles of criminology.* New York, Lippincott.

Swimmer, E.R. (1974): Measurement of the effectiveness of urban law enforcement - A simultaneous approach. *Southern Econ. J., 40,* (April), 618-30.

Taylor, M. (1987)[1976]: *The possibility of cooperation.* Cambridge and New York, Cambidge. Univ. Pr.

Thaler, R. (1977): An econometric analysis of property crime, *J. Publ. Econ., 8,* 323-38.

Tittle, R. (1969): Crime rates and social forces. *Sos. Probl.,* 16, 4, 409-23.

Tittle, C. R. and C.H. Logan (1973): Sanctions and deviance: Evidence and remaining questions. *Law and Society Rev,,* (Spring), 371-92.

" and A.R. Rowe (1974): Certainty of arrest and crime rates: a further test of the deterrence hypothesis. *Social Forces,* 4, 455-62.

Trasler, G. (1962): *The explanation of criminality.* London, Routledge and Kegan Paul.

Trumbull, W.N. (1989): Estimations of the economic model of crime using aggregate and individual data. *Southern Econ. J.,* 2 (Oct.), 423-39.

Tversky, A., P. Slovic and D. Kahneman (1990): The causes of preference reversal. *Am. Ec. Rev., 80,* 1 (March), 204-17

US Department of Justice (1974): *Sourcebook of criminal justice statistics - 1974.* Washington D.C., Government Printing Office.

Vandaele, W. (1978): Participation in illegitimate activities: Ehrlich revisited. In: *Blumstein et al.,* 270-335.

Viscusi, W. K. (1986): The risks and rewards of criminal activity: a comprehensive test of criminal deterrence. *J. of Labour Econ.,* 3, 317-39.

Votey, H.L. (1979): The control of drunken driving accidents in Norway: an uncertainty-cross section - time series analysis. Prosjektrapport, *Transportøkonomisk institutt, Oslo.*

Votey, H.L. & L. Phillips (1972): Police effectiveness and the production function for law enforcement. *J. Legal St., 1*, 423-36.

"   (1981): *The economics of crime control.* London, Sage Publ.

"   (1973): Social goals and appropriate policy for corrections: an economic appraisal. *J. Cr. Just., 1*, 219-40.

Wadycki, W. J. & S. Balkin (1979): Participation in illegitimate activities - Forst's model revisited. *J. Beh. Econ., 8*, 2 (Winter), 151-63.

Wahlroos, B. (1981): On finnish property criminality: An empirical analysis of the post war era using an Ehrlich model. *Scand. J. Econ., 83*, 4, 553-62.

White, H. and G. M. MacDonald (1980): Some large-sample tests for nonnormality in the linear regression model, *J. Amer. Stat. Ass., 75*, 16-28.

Willis, K. G. (1983): Spatial variations in crime in England and Wales: testing an economic model. *Reg. Stud., 17*, 4, 261-72.

Willcock, H.D. & S. Stokes (1968): Deterrents and incentives to crime among youth aged 15-21 years.

Wilson, J. Q. & B. Boland (1978): The effect of the police on crime. *Law & Soc. Rev., 12*, 3 (Spring), 367-90.

Wilson J. C. and R. J. Herrnstein (1986): *Crime and human nature.* N.Y., Simon & Schuster.

Withers, G. (1984): Crime, punishment and deterrence in Australia: An empirical investigation. *Econ. Record, 60*, (June), 176-85.

Witte, A.D. (1980): Estimating the economic model of crime with individual data. *Quart J. Econ.*, (Febr.), 57-84.

Witte, A. D. and D. F. Woodbury (1985): The effect of tax laws and tax administration on tax compliance: the case of the U.S. individual income tax. *Nat. Tax J. XXXVIII*, 1-13.

Wolpin, K.I. (1978a): An economic analysis of crime and punishment in England and Wales, 1894-1967. *J. Pol. Econ., 5*, 815-40.

"   (1978b): Capital punishment and homicide in England: a summary of results. *Amer. Ec. Rev., Papers and Proceedings, 68*, 2 (May), 422-7.

"   (1980): A time series-cross section analysis of international variation in crime and punishment. *Rev. Econ. Stat.*, (Aug.).

Zimring, F.E. & G.J. Hawkins (1973): *Deterrence.* Chicago, Chicago Univ. Pr.

Zipin P. M. et al. (1973): Crime rates and public expenditure for policy protection: a comment. *Rev. Soc. Econ., 31*, 222-5.

APPENDIX A: DATA - SOCIODEMOGRAPHIC VARIABLES

Pol. distr.	No	UNEM	LOWI	ASS	SALE	M1	M2	RC	ALK	DIV	POL	N
Oslo	1	531	63641	1329615	4376763	7809	10997	11434	1069	1183	1308	468.49
Halden	2	172	5175	57038	48855	776	1047	794	96	34	52	35.07
Sarpsborg	3	257	10275	136623	126206	1732	2291	2300	175	117	85	75.67
Fredrikstad	4	219	7709	74580	121458	1425	1993	1946	134	92	83	64.74
Moss	5	100	6615	80362	89145	1260	1657	1709	103	89	64	51.40
Follo	6	33	6265	70984	149760	1807	2073	2636	107	108	57	66.16
Romerike	7	121	18394	174401	269191	3860	4796	5847	345	203	144	165.11
Kongsvinger	8	207	8392	65287	80670	1203	1661	1103	222	36	46	54.08
Hamar	9	197	11166	91945	164639	1859	2563	1834	197	63	67	78.28
Østerdal	10	134	8894	64310	68017	1115	1571	943	152	42	53	49.25
Gudbrandsd.	11	321	12639	114995	116849	1629	2272	1556	135	45	64	68.52
Vest-Oppl.	12	284	17544	161468	166285	2540	3494	2207	343	86	88	108.36
Ringerike	13	82	10163	171164	118524	1410	2149	1510	226	56	67	65.65
Asker & B.	14	85	10850	163406	307727	2990	3952	5125	138	213	132	114.70
Drammen	15	67	12651	161762	293110	2127	2858	3098	244	149	128	100.15
Kongsberg	16	62	5448	81715	55084	900	1192	1118	114	33	45	39.48
N.-Jarlsb.	17	21	6289	74140	54563	1198	1608	1843	115	82	64	49.58
Tønsberg	18	47	7843	143049	121366	1377	1865	1894	170	108	68	56.94
Sandefjord	19	54	5039	93211	62003	896	1149	738	96	64	43	37.03
Larvik	20	28	4788	61631	73060	873	1254	1094	84	53	51	37.03
Skien	21	104	6981	69000	116779	1197	1745	1167	100	81	57	54.89
Telemark	22	189	7745	152535	87112	1230	1818	1281	68	68	70	53.99
Notodden	23	104	4474	58240	33069	586	847	514	45	19	37	25.65
Rjukan	24	59	1530	28295	9040	125	242	90	16	6	19	7.82
Kragerø	25	72	2219	19863	16052	344	435	259	22	21	20	14.91
Arendal	26	210	11548	109711	109641	1856	2360	2156	121	77	99	76.52
Kristians.	27	66	10948	135394	218837	2201	2840	2281	100	86	116	85.55
Vest-Agder	28	108	8283	99893	55592	1202	1680	1230	32	37	65	50.83
Rogaland	29	80	11383	121210	174469	2317	3028	2003	28	77	75	85.68
Stavanger	30	142	15217	180247	372176	2933	3888	2510	151	165	166	116.35
Haugesund	31	244	11065	132649	127726	1994	2598	1476	60	89	84	77.52
Hardanger	32	61	4384	61808	27453	694	952	646	38	9	32	27.09
Hordaland	33	314	20753	148307	102441	3952	5177	3139	42	75	104	141.04
Bergen	34	304	26573	255000	795597	4972	6490	2597	401	335	376	214.60
Sogn	35	105	7463	89183	36811	1021	1329	953	79	12	41	39.91
Fjordane	36	131	11582	68833	88525	1722	2253	1284	48	20	50	62.19
Sunnmøre	37	283	16192	133735	280391	3130	4302	2180	69	76	108	114.57
Romsdal	38	205	8007	62015	92312	1400	1891	1321	17	43	46	52.16
Nordmøre	39	347	10773	92398	86895	1615	2192	1257	86	47	66	62.65
Ut-Trønd.	40	405	18593	111393	78303	2642	3553	2125	147	61	97	103.46
Trondheim	41	532	16224	123027	609754	2885	4014	3134	266	238	223	136.01
Inn-Trønd.	42	435	13199	70919	112517	2194	2981	1910	115	62	70	85.08
Namdal	43	186	6392	38825	41440	930	1268	722	55	29	41	36.08
Helgeland	44	540	13111	122953	92343	2181	2747	1489	96	73	100	80.10
Bodø	45	375	9918	62268	122218	1708	2260	1744	55	79	83	66.33
Narvik	46	284	5732	21350	49615	976	1304	776	87	37	56	35.36
Lof. & Ves.	47	306	10453	41414	111739	1571	2234	1240	47	48	61	60.78
Senja	48	251	7659	38040	102714	1210	1646	1132	52	22	54	47.54
Troms	49	527	9777	89933	281337	2492	3183	2360	143	113	97	94.34
Vest-Finnm.	50	249	7299	32798	66291	1137	1465	1128	16	46	70	42.49
Vardø	51	137	2034	8053	31494	261	340	338	0	11	28	10.51
Vadsø	52	164	2876	10958	13635	411	483	451	9	20	34	15.05
Sør-Var.	53	55	1592	17867	15155	252	402	302	23	23	35	10.79

Definitions

UNEM:	No. of unemployed, 1974.
LOWI:	No. of income earners with an annual net income below NOK 16.000, 1974.
ASS:	Total taxable value of assets (in 1000 NOK), 1974.
SALES:	Total sales in wholesaling, retail trade, and restaurants and hotels (in 1000 NOK), 1974.
M1:	No. of men, 12–15 years, 1974.
M2:	No. of men, 16-19 years, 1974.
RC:	No. of recent comers to a police district in 1973.
ALK:	No. of places where alcoholic drinks may be bought, 1974.
DIV:	No. of men divorced in 1974.
POL:	No. of policemen, 1974.
N:	Population (in 10), 1974.

Sources: Data on all variables except POL has been provided by the Norwegian Social Science Data Services (NSD, Kommunedatabanken).[1] Data on POL has been provided by the Ministry of Justice.

----

[1]NSD is not responsible for the use of the data or of the interpretation of the results.

APPENDIX B: IDENTIFICATION

B.1. Introduction

Identification is proved by showing that the structural parameters are explicit functions of the theoretical 2. order moments of the crime and clear-up rates. It turns out to be suitable to first deduce differences of the 2. order moments, and general 2. order differences of the 2. order moments of the crime and clear-up rates. Identification of $\sigma_{\varepsilon\varepsilon}$, $\sigma_{\varphi\varphi}$, and $\sigma_{\varepsilon\varphi}$ is proved for our most general model under investigation (M1W3L3), and for all its submodels. Then, identification of r, b and the remaining variances and covariances is considered for various submodels. For two of these there exist two observationally equivalent structures. They may still be identified if one is willing to make restrictions in the parameter space as discussed in section 3, and empirically analyzed in section 5. It is further proved that full identification is not obtainable for some of the submodels. The 1. order moments are used to identify a_t and k_t, whereas our assumption of normality excludes the possibility of obtaining supplementary information from moments of higher order than two.

B.2. Derivation of 2. order moments

Omitting subscript i for all variables we have for all t

(B1) $x_t = \chi_t + \varepsilon_t$,

(B2) $y_t = \psi_t + \phi_t$,

(B3) $\chi_t = a_t + b\pi_t + \omega_1 + t\omega_2$,

(B4) $\pi_t = \psi_t - \chi_t$,

(B5) $\psi_t = k_t + r\chi_t + \lambda_1 + t\lambda_2.$

Defining $\tilde{\chi}_t = \chi_t - E\chi_t$, etc., we obtain

(B1′) $\tilde{x}_t = \tilde{\chi}_t + \varepsilon_t$,

(B2′) $\tilde{y}_t = \tilde{\psi}_t + \phi_t$,

(B3′) $\tilde{\chi}_t = b\tilde{\pi}_t + \omega_1 + t\omega_2$,

(B4′) $\tilde{\pi}_t = \Psi_t - \tilde{\chi}_t$,

(B5′) $\Psi_t = r\tilde{\chi}_t + \lambda_1 + t\lambda_2$.

Substitution of (B4') and (B5') into (B3') gives

(B3∗) $d\tilde{\chi}_t = \omega_1 + t\omega_2 + b(\lambda_1 + t\lambda_2)$,

where $d = 1 + b(1-r)$ as defined in (2d).
Assuming $d \neq 0$, we have

(B3″) $\tilde{\chi}_t = \dfrac{1}{d}(\omega_1 + t\omega_2) + \dfrac{b}{d}(\lambda_1 + t\lambda_2)$,

which substituted into (B5') gives

(B5″) $\Psi_t = \dfrac{r}{d}(\omega_1 + t\omega_2) + \dfrac{1+b}{d}(\lambda_1 + t\lambda_2)$.

Substitution of (B3'') into (B1'), and (B5'') into (B2') gives

(B1″) $\tilde{x}_t = \dfrac{1}{d}(\omega_1 + t\omega_2) + \dfrac{b}{d}(\lambda_1 + t\lambda_2) + e_t$,

and

(B2″) $\tilde{y}_t = \dfrac{r}{d}(\omega_1 + t\omega_2) + \dfrac{1+b}{d}(\lambda_1 + t\lambda_2) + \phi_t$.

For convenience we define

$$K = \left(\frac{1}{d}\right)^2.$$

Note that it follows from (2d) that $K > 0$.
   From (B1'') and (B2'') we obtain, with the stochastic specifications assumed in 2.3, the

following second order moments for $t,s=1,2,...,T$:

(B6) $cov(x_t,x_s) = K[\sigma_{\omega_1\omega_1}+(t+s)\sigma_{\omega_1\omega_2}+ts\sigma_{\omega_2\omega_2}+b^2\sigma_{\lambda_1\lambda_1}+b^2(t+s)\sigma_{\lambda_1\lambda_2}+b^2ts\sigma_{\lambda_2\lambda_2}]+\delta_{ts}\sigma_{\epsilon\epsilon}$,

(B7) $cov(y_t,y_s) = K[r^2\sigma_{\omega_1\omega_1}+r^2(t+s)\sigma_{\omega_1\omega_2}+r^2ts\sigma_{\omega_2\omega_2}$

$$+(1+b)^2\sigma_{\lambda_1\lambda_1}+(1+b)^2(t+s)\sigma_{\lambda_1\lambda_2}+(1+b)^2ts\sigma_{\lambda_2\lambda_2}] + \delta_{ts}\sigma_{\phi\phi} ,$$

(B8) $cov(x_t,y_s) = K[r\sigma_{\omega_1\omega_1}+r(t+s)\sigma_{\omega_1\omega_2}+rts\sigma_{\omega_2\omega_2}$

$$+ (1+b)b\sigma_{\lambda_1\lambda_1}+(1+b)b(t+s)\sigma_{\lambda_1\lambda_2}+(1+b)bts\sigma_{\lambda_2\lambda_2}] + \delta_{ts}\sigma_{\epsilon\phi} ,$$

where δ_{ts} are Kronecker deltas.

B.3. Differences of 2. order moments

We define, for all possible combinations of i, j, t, and s, the differences of 2. order moments

(B9) $\Delta_{ij}cov(x_t,x_s) = cov(x_t,x_s)-cov(x_{t-i},x_{s-j})$,

and similarly for $cov(y_t,y_s)$ and $cov(x_t,y_s)$. With these definitions we obtain from (B6)-(B8):

(B10) $\Delta_{ij}cov(x_t,x_s) = K[(i+j)\sigma_{\omega_1\omega_2}+(is+jt-ij)\sigma_{\omega_2\omega_2}+b^2[(i+j)\sigma_{\lambda_1\lambda_2}+(is+jt-ij)\sigma_{\lambda_2\lambda_2}]]$

$$+ (\delta_{ts}-\delta_{t-i,s-j})\sigma_{\epsilon\epsilon},$$

(B11) $\Delta_{ij}cov(y_t,y_s)=K[r^2[(i+j)\sigma_{\omega_1\omega_2}+(is+jt-ij)\sigma_{\omega_2\omega_2}]+(1+b)^2[(i+j)\sigma_{\lambda_1\lambda_2}+(is+jt-ij)\sigma_{\lambda_2\lambda_2}]]$

$$+ (\delta_{ts}-\delta_{t-i,s-j})\sigma_{\phi\phi},$$

(B12) $\Delta_{ij}cov(x_t,y_s)=K[r[(i+j)\sigma_{\omega_1\omega_2}+(is+jt-ij)\sigma_{\omega_2\omega_2}]+(1+b)b[(i+j)\sigma_{\lambda_1\lambda_2}+(is+jt-ij)\sigma_{\lambda_2\lambda_2}]]$

$$+ (\delta_{ts}-\delta_{t-i,s-j})\sigma_{\epsilon\phi}.$$

For notational convenience we define, by the first equation in each of the following expressions

(B13) $D_{xx} = \Delta_{1,-1}cov(x_t,x_t) = K[\sigma_{\omega_2\omega_2}+b^2\sigma_{\lambda_2\lambda_2}] + \sigma_{\varepsilon\varepsilon}$,

(B14) $D_{yy} = \Delta_{1,-1}cov(y_t,y_t) = K[r^2\sigma_{\omega_2\omega_2}+(1+b)^2\sigma_{\lambda_2\lambda_2}] + \sigma_{\varphi\varphi}$,

(B15) $D_{xy} = \Delta_{1,-1}cov(x_t,y_t) = K[r\sigma_{\omega_2\omega_2}+(1+b)b\sigma_{\lambda_2\lambda_2}] + \sigma_{\varepsilon\varphi}$,

(B16) $E_{xx} = \Delta_{11}cov(x_t,x_s) = K[2\sigma_{\omega_1\omega_2}+(s+t-1)\sigma_{\omega_2\omega_2}+b^2[2\sigma_{\lambda_1\lambda_2}+(s+t-1)\sigma_{\lambda_2\lambda_2}]]$,

(B17) $E_{yy} = \Delta_{11}cov(y_t,y_s) = K[r^2[2\sigma_{\omega_1\omega_2}+(s+t-1)\sigma_{\omega_2\omega_2}]+(1+b)^2[2\sigma_{\lambda_1\lambda_2}+(s+t-1)\sigma_{\lambda_2\lambda_2}]]$,

(B18) $E_{xy} = \Delta_{11}cov(x_t,y_s) = K[r[2\sigma_{\omega_1\omega_2}+(s+t-1)\sigma_{\omega_2\omega_2}]+(1+b)b[2\sigma_{\lambda_1\lambda_2}+(s+t-1)\sigma_{\lambda_2\lambda_2}]]$.

B.4. General 2. order differences of 2. order moments

We define, for all possible combinations of k, l, m, n, i, j, t, and s, the following general 2. order differences of 2. order moments:

(B19) $\Delta_{klmn}\Delta_{ij}cov(x_t,x_s) = cov(x_t,x_s)-cov(x_{t-i},x_{s-j}) - [cov(x_{t-k},x_{s-l})-cov(x_{t-k-m},x_{s-l-n})]$,

and similarly for $cov(y_t,y_s)$ and $cov(x_t,y_s)$. From (B10)-(B12) we then obtain

(B20) $\Delta_{klmn}\Delta_{ij}cov(x_t,x_s) = K[K_1(\sigma_{\omega_1\omega_2}+b^2\sigma_{\lambda_1\lambda_2})+K_2(\sigma_{\omega_2\omega_2}+b^2\sigma_{\lambda_2\lambda_2})]+M\sigma_{\varepsilon\varepsilon}$,

(B21) $\Delta_{klmn}\Delta_{ij}cov(y_t,y_s) = K[K_1(r^2\sigma_{\omega_1\omega_2}+(1+b)^2\sigma_{\lambda_1\lambda_2})+K_2(r^2\sigma_{\omega_2\omega_2}+(1+b)^2\sigma_{\lambda_2\lambda_2})]+M\sigma_{\varphi\varphi}$,

(B22) $\Delta_{klmn}\Delta_{ij}cov(x_t,y_s) = K[K_1(r\sigma_{\omega_1\omega_2}+(1+b)b\sigma_{\lambda_1\lambda_2})+K_2(r\sigma_{\omega_2\omega_2}+(1+b)b\sigma_{\lambda_2\lambda_2})]+M\sigma_{\varepsilon\varphi}$,

where

$K_1 = i+j-m-n$,
$K_2 = (i-m)s+(j-n)t-ij+ml+kn+mn$,

$$M = \delta_{t,s} - \delta_{t-i,s-j} - \delta_{t-k,s-l} + \delta_{t-k-m,s-l-n}.$$

Note that M can take the following values: -2, -1, 0, 1, 2. For the purpose of generating some of the identification results we define

(B23) $F = \{(t,s,i,j,k,l,m,n)| K_1=0, K_2\neq0\}$,
(B24) $G = \{(t,s,i,j,k,l,m,n)| K_1\neq0, K_2=0\}$.

These sets are non-empty: all elements satisfying $i=m$, $j=n$, *and* $il+kj\neq0$ constitute a subset of F; an example of an element in G is $t=4$, $s=3$, $i=2$, $j=-1$, $k=l=m=n=1$. From (B20)-(B23) it then follows:

(B25) $F_{xx} = \dfrac{\Delta_{klmn}\Delta_{ij}cov(x_t,x_s)}{K_2} = K(\sigma_{\omega_2\omega_2}+b^2\sigma_{\lambda_2\lambda_2})$,

(B26) $F_{yy} = \dfrac{\Delta_{klmn}\Delta_{ij}cov(y_t,y_s)}{K_2} = K[r^2\sigma_{\omega_2\omega_2}+(1+b)^2\sigma_{\lambda_2\lambda_2}]$,

(B27) $F_{xy} = \dfrac{\Delta_{klmn}\Delta_{ij}cov(x_t,y_s)}{K_2} = K[r\sigma_{\omega_2\omega_2}+(1+b)b\sigma_{\lambda_2\lambda_2}]$,

where the Fs are defined by the first equation in these formulas.
Similarly, it follows from (B20)-(B22) and (B24):

(B28) $G_{xx} = \dfrac{\Delta_{klmn}\Delta_{ij}cov(x_t,x_s)}{K_1} = K[\sigma_{\omega_1\omega_2}+b^2\sigma_{\lambda_1\lambda_2}]$,

(B29) $G_{yy} = \dfrac{\Delta_{klmn}\Delta_{ij}cov(y_t,y_s)}{K_1} = K[r^2\sigma_{\omega_1\omega_2}+(1+b)^2\sigma_{\lambda_1\lambda_2}]$,

(B30) $G_{xy} = \dfrac{\Delta_{klmn}\Delta_{ij}cov(x_t,y_s)}{K_1} = K[r\sigma_{\omega_1\omega_2}+(1+b)b\sigma_{\lambda_1\lambda_2}]$.

We note that the Ds, Es, Fs, and Gs are observables. Viewed as sample statistics these expressions will depend on k, l, m, n, i, j, t, and s, (the Ds and Es only on t and s), but viewed as population parameters they will, according to our model, be independent of these values. (In fact, any weighted average of any possible set of $\Delta_{klmn}\Delta_{ij}cov(x_t,x_s)/K_2$ will be a consistent estimate of the population parameter F_{xx}, and similarly for F_{yy} and F_{xy}, and for all the Ds, Es, and Gs.) The equations defining the Ds, Es, Fs, and Gs can be used for various tests. In this appendix they are used only to study identification.

B.5. Identification of $\sigma_{\varepsilon\varepsilon}$, $\sigma_{\varphi\varphi}$, and $\sigma_{\varepsilon\varphi}$ for all models

From (B25)-(B27) and (B13)-(B15) we obtain

(B31) $\sigma_{\varepsilon\varepsilon} = D_{xx} - F_{xx}$,

(B32) $\sigma_{\varphi\varphi} = D_{yy} - F_{yy}$,

(B33) $\sigma_{\varepsilon\varphi} = D_{xy} - F_{xy}$,

which identify the variances and covariances of the errors of measurement for M1W3L3 and for all its submodels. Note that the parameter $\sigma_{\varepsilon\varphi}$ is not involved in the identification of $\sigma_{\varepsilon\varepsilon}$ and $\sigma_{\varphi\varphi}$, and neither in the identification of the other parameters below. Our identification results are thus equally valid for M0W3L3, where $\sigma_{\varepsilon\varphi}=0$, and for M1W3L3, where this covariance is not restricted.

B.6. Identification of r and b

Relationship between b and r
From (B7) and (B8) we obtain, for $t \neq s$

(B37) $cov(y_t,y_s)-rcov(x_t,y_s) = K(1+b)d[\sigma_{\lambda_1\lambda_1}+(t+s)\sigma_{\lambda_1\lambda_2}+ts\sigma_{\lambda_2\lambda_2}]$.

From (B8) and (B6) we obtain, also for $t \neq s$

(B38) $cov(x_t,y_s)-rcov(x_t,x_s) = Kbd[\sigma_{\lambda_1\lambda_1}+(t+s)\sigma_{\lambda_1\lambda_2}+ts\sigma_{\lambda_2\lambda_2}]$.

Assuming $\sigma_{\lambda1\lambda1}\neq0$, (which for $t\neq s$ secures that the square bracket in (B38) is not zero), we divide (B37) by (B38) to obtain

(B39) $\quad b = \dfrac{cov(x_t,y_s)-rcov(x_t,x_s)}{cov(y_t,y_s)-cov(x_t,y_s)+r(cov(x_t,x_s)-cov(x_t,y_s))},$

which identifies b in all models where r already has been identified, with the exception of the four submodels in W3L0 (when $\sigma_{\lambda1\lambda1}=0$, and the denominator in (B39) also is zero). In section B.7 below it is demonstrated that b is not identifiable in W3L0.

Solving (B39) with respect to r gives, if the denominator is different from zero,

(B40) $\quad r = \dfrac{(1+b)cov(x_t,y_s)-bcov(y_t,y_s)}{(1+b)cov(x_t,x_s)-bcov(x_t,y_s)},$

which identifies r if b already has been identified. In model W0L3 the denominator (and also the numerator) is zero, and (B40) cannot be used to identify r in this case (including four submodels). It can be demonstrated, analogously to the proof in section B.7 of the non-identifiabilify of b in W3L0, that r cannot be identified in W0L3.

We will now first identify r in those models where this is easily done by help of Fs and Gs. Equation (B39) can in these cases be used to identify b. Similarly, we will identify b in some of the remaining models, and use (B40) to identify r. Finally, identification of these two parameters in two of the models will be obtained by a more comprehensive analysis. The number of the equations used to identify each parameter in the various models are given in Table B1. The first four rows of this table show the results for the four submodels of W3*L3, the next four those of W2*L3, etc.

*W3*L2**

For model W3*L2* identification of r is obtained by dividing (B30) by (B29), which gives

(B41) $\quad r = \dfrac{G_{xy}}{G_{xx}}.$

Table B1

Overview of equations used to identify the parameters in the different models[a,c]

Model	Parameter							
	r	b	$\sigma_{\omega1\omega2}$	$\sigma_{\omega2\omega2}$	$\sigma_{\omega1\omega1}$	$\sigma_{\lambda1\lambda2}$	$\sigma_{\lambda2\lambda2}$	$\sigma_{\lambda1\lambda1}$
W3*L3*[b]	B56	B39	B28/B29	B25/B26	B6/B8	B28/B29	B25/B26	B6/B8
W3*L2*	B41	B39	B28/B29	B25/B26	B6/B8	0	B25/B26	B6/B8
W3*L1*	B42	B39	B28/B29	B25/B26	B6/B8	0	0	B6/B8
W3*L0*	B42	NI	NI[d]	NI[d]	NI[d]	0	0	0
W2*L3*	B40	B47	0	B25/B26	B6/B8	B28/B29	B25/B26	B6/B8
W2*L2*[b]	B61	B39	0	B25/B26	B6/B8	0	B25/B26	B6/B8
W2*L1*	B42	B39	0	B25/B26	B6/B8	0	0	B6/B8
W2*L0*	B42	NI	0	NI[d]	NI[d]	0	0	0
W1*L3*	B40	B48	0	0	B6/B8	B28/B29	B25/B26	B6/B8
W1*L2*	B40	B48	0	0	B6/B8	0	B25/B26	B6/B8
W1*L1*	NI[d]	NI[e]	0	0	NI[f]	0	0	NI[f]
W1*L0*	B46	NI	0	0	NI[d]	0	0	0
W0*L3*	NI	B48	0	0	0	NI[e]	NI[e]	NI[e]
W0*L2*	NI	B48	0	0	0	0	NI[e]	NI[e]
W0*L1*	NI	B49	0	0	0	0	0	NI[e]
W0*L0*	NI	NI	0	0	0	0	0	0

[a] The numbers refer to the equations used for identification. NI=not identifiable.

[b] Identified assuming $0<d<1$ or $\#A=1$, cf section 3.

[c] The parameters $\sigma_{\epsilon\epsilon}$, $\sigma_{\varphi\varphi}$, and $\sigma_{\epsilon\varphi}$ are identified by (B31), (B32), and (B33), respectively.

[d] Identified if b is given a fixed value.

[e] Identified if r is given a fixed value.

[f] Identified if either b or r is given a fixed value.

*W3*LI*, W3*L0*, W2*LI*, and W2*L0**

For these models identification of r is obtained by dividing (B27) by (B25), which gives

(B42) $\quad r = \dfrac{F_{xy}}{F_{xx}}.$

*WI*LI*, WI*L0*, WI*LI*, and WI*L0**

For model W1L1 (including the four above mentioned submodels) the differences of the 2. order moments, (B10)-(B12), and the differences of these differences, (B20)-(B22) are zero, and one is left with the simple covariances for identification. (B6)-(B8) are now simplified to

(B43) $\quad cov(x_t,x_s) = K[\sigma_{\omega_1\omega_1} + b^2\sigma_{\lambda_1\lambda_1}] + \delta_{ts}\sigma_{\varepsilon\varepsilon}$,

(B44) $\quad cov(y_t,y_s) = K[r^2\sigma_{\omega_1\omega_1} + (1+b)^2\sigma_{\lambda_1\lambda_1}] + \delta_{ts}\sigma_{\phi\phi}$,

(B45) $\quad cov(x_t,y_s) = K[r\sigma_{\omega_1\omega_1} + (1+b)b\sigma_{\lambda_1\lambda_1}] + \delta_{ts}\sigma_{\varepsilon\phi}$.

For submodel W1*L1*, for which $\sigma_{\omega1\omega1} \neq 0$ and $\sigma_{\lambda1\lambda1} \neq 0$, we thus, for $t \neq s$, have only three equations, independent of time, in the four parameters b, r, $\sigma_{\omega1\omega1}$, and $\sigma_{\lambda1\lambda1}$. They cannot all be identified without further information. If, for instance, r is given a fixed value, the remaining parameters are easily identified, cf section 5.7.

For submodel W1*L0* identification is obtained by dividing, for $t \neq s$, (B45) by (B43), which in this case, when $\sigma_{\lambda1\lambda1}=0$, gives

(B46) $\quad r = \dfrac{cov(x_t,y_s)}{cov(x_t,x_s)}.$

For submodel W0*L0*, r cannot be identified even if b is given a fixed value, and vice versa.

*W2*L3**

Identification of b in model W2*L3* is obtained by dividing (B28) by (B30) which gives

(B47) $b = \dfrac{G_{xx}}{G_{xy}-G_{xx}}.$

W1*L3*, W1*L2*, W0*L3*, and W0*L2*

Identification of b in these four models is obtained by dividing (B25) by (B27), which gives, after some ordering

(B48) $b = \dfrac{F_{xx}}{F_{xy}-F_{xx}}.$

W0*L1*

Identification of b in W0*L1* is obtained by dividing (B43) by (B45), which gives

(B49) $b = \dfrac{cov(x_t,x_s)}{cov(x_t,y_s)-cov(x_t,x_s)}.$

W3*L3*

Multiplying (B25) by r, and subtracting (B27) from the resulting equation gives

(B50) $F_{xx}r-F_{xy} = K[rb^2-(1+b)b]\sigma_{\lambda_2\lambda_2} = -Kbd\sigma_{\lambda_2\lambda_2}.$

Multiplying (B27) by r, and subtracting the resulting equation from (B26) gives

(B51) $F_{yy}-F_{xy}r = K[(1+b)^2-r(1+b)b]\sigma_{\lambda_2\lambda_2} = K(1+b)d\sigma_{\lambda_2\lambda_2}.$

Assuming $\sigma_{\lambda_2\lambda_2} \neq 0$ and $b \neq -1$ (identification when $b = -1$ is demonstrated below), we divide (B50) by (B51) to obtain

(B52) $\dfrac{F_{xx}r-F_{xy}}{F_{yy}-F_{xy}r} = -\dfrac{b}{(1+b)}.$

Multiplying, for $i=j=1$, (B16) by r and subtracting (B18) from the resulting equation gives:

(B53) $rE_{xx}-E_{xy} = -Kbd[2\sigma_{\lambda_1\lambda_2}+(t+s-1)\sigma_{\lambda_2\lambda_2}]$.

Multiplying, also here for $i=j=1$, (B16) by r, and subtracting the resulting equation from (B17) gives

(B54) $E_{yy}-rE_{xy} = K(1+b)d[2\sigma_{\lambda_1\lambda_2}+(t+s-1)\sigma_{\lambda_2\lambda_2}]$.

Observing that, for at least some t and s, $2\sigma_{\lambda_1\lambda_2}+(t+s-1)\sigma_{\lambda_2\lambda_2} \neq 0$, we divide (B53) by (B54) to obtain

(B55) $\dfrac{rE_{xx}-E_{xy}}{E_{yy}-rE_{xy}} = -\dfrac{b}{1+b}$.

From equations (B52) and (B55) then follows

(B56) $r^2[F_{xy}E_{xx}-F_{xx}E_{xy}] + r[F_{xx}E_{yy}-F_{yy}E_{xx}] + [F_{yy}E_{xy}-F_{xy}E_{yy}] = 0$.

This equation cannot be used to identify r if the first two square brackets are zero. Inserting from equations (B16)-(B18) and (B25)-(B27) into (B56) gives

(B57) $r^2[2K^2bd\sigma_{\lambda_2\lambda_2}\sigma_{\omega_1\omega_2}]+r[2K^2(r^2b^2-(1+b)^2)\sigma_{\lambda_2\lambda_2}\sigma_{\omega_1\omega_2}]+[2K^2r(1+b)d\sigma_{\lambda_2\lambda_2}\sigma_{\omega_1\omega_2}]=0$,

where the three square brackets are equal to those of (B56), respectively. Equation (B57) shows that all three square brackets in (B56) are equal to zero except for W3*L2* and W3*L3*. Identification of b and r in the former model is already proved. For the latter model, (B56) is a second order equation in r that in general has two different solutions. This problem of two roots is discussed in Sections 3 and B.10, where additional assumptions are introduced in order to choose between the two. If r is identified by this procedure, identification of b follows from (B39).

W2*L2*

Observing that we in model W2*L2* have $\sigma_{\omega_1\omega_2} = \sigma_{\lambda_1\lambda_2} = 0$, multiplication of (B6) by r and subtraction of (B8) from the resulting equation gives, for $t \neq s$

(B58) $rcov(x_t x_s) - cov(x_t y_s) = -Kbd(\sigma_{\lambda_1 \lambda_1} + ts\sigma_{\lambda_2 \lambda_2}).$

Multiplying (B8) by r and subtracting the resulting equation from (B7) gives

(B59) $cov(y_t y_s) - rcov(x_t y_s) = K(1+b)d(\sigma_{\lambda_1 \lambda_1} + ts\sigma_{\lambda_2 \lambda_2}).$

Dividing the former by the latter gives

(B60) $\dfrac{rcov(x_t x_s) - cov(x_t y_s)}{cov(y_t y_s) - rcov(x_t y_s)} = -\dfrac{b}{1+b}.$

From (B52) (which is valid also for the present model) and (B60) follows

(B61) $r^2[F_{xy}cov(x_t x_s) - F_{xx}cov(x_t y_s)]$

$+ \ r[F_{xx}cov(y_t y_s) - F_{yy}cov((x_t x_s)]$

$+ \ [F_{yy}cov(x_t y_s) - F_{xy}cov(y_t y_s)] = 0.$

Here, too, identification of r is not possible if the square brackets are equal to zero. Inserting (B6)-(B8) (for $t \neq s$, and $\sigma_{\omega 1 \omega 2} = \sigma_{\lambda 1 \lambda 2} = 0$) and (B25)-(B27) into (B61) gives

(B62) $r^2[-K^2bd(\sigma_{\lambda_1 \lambda_1}\sigma_{\omega_2 \omega_2} - \sigma_{\lambda_2 \lambda_2}\sigma_{\omega_1 \omega_1})]$

$+ \ r[K^2(b^2r^2 - (1+b)^2)(\sigma_{\lambda_1 \lambda_1}\sigma_{\omega_2 \omega_2} - \sigma_{\lambda_2 \lambda_2}\sigma_{\omega_1 \omega_1})]$

$+ \ [K^2r(1+b)d(\sigma_{\lambda_1 \lambda_1}\sigma_{\omega_2 \omega_2} - \sigma_{\omega_1 \omega_1}\sigma_{\lambda_2 \lambda_2})] = 0.$

The three brackets in (B62), corresponding to those of (B61), are in general not zero, and equation (B61) can be used to identify r and b by the same procedure as for W3*L3*.

Identification of r when b = -1

Discussing identification of W3*L3* and W2*L2* we used the assumption $b \neq -1$. When $b = -1$, it follows from (B40) that

(B63) $\quad r = \dfrac{cov(y_t, y_s)}{cov(x_t, y_s)},$

which identifies r. Identification of the remaining parameters does not depend on the value of b, cf section B.8.

B.7. Proof of non-identifiability of b in W3L0

If $\sigma_{\lambda 1 \lambda 1} = 0$, which then gives model W3L0, full identification of all parameters are not possible. Additional information, for instance a fixed value of one of the parameters, is needed to obtain complete identification.

Rewriting (B6)-(B8)

(B69) $\quad cov(x_t, x_s) - \delta_{ts}\sigma_{\varepsilon\varepsilon} = K[\sigma_{\omega_1\omega_1} + (t+s)\sigma_{\omega_1\omega_2} + ts\sigma_{\omega_2\omega_2}],$

(B70) $\quad cov(y_t, y_s) - \delta_{ts}\sigma_{\phi\phi} = Kr^2[\sigma_{\omega_1\omega_1} + (t+s)\sigma_{\omega_1\omega_2} + ts\sigma_{\omega_2\omega_2}],$

(B71) $\quad cov(x_t, y_s) - \delta_{ts}\sigma_{\varepsilon\phi} = Kr[\sigma_{\omega_1\omega_1} + (t+s)\sigma_{\omega_1\omega_2} + ts\sigma_{\omega_2\omega_2}],$

we remark that $\sigma_{\varepsilon\varepsilon}$, $\sigma_{\phi\phi}$, $\sigma_{\varepsilon\phi}$, and r are already identified in W3*L0*, W2*L0*, and W1*L0*, cf Table B1. (In submodel W0*L0* r cannot be identified, and the proof below is irrelevant.)

Assume that $\hat{b}$, $\hat{\sigma}_{\omega1\omega1}$, $\hat{\sigma}_{\omega2\omega2}$, and $\hat{\sigma}_{\omega1\omega2}$ satisfy (B69)-(B71) for given values of $\sigma_{\varepsilon\varepsilon}$, $\sigma_{\phi\phi}$, $\sigma_{\varepsilon\phi}$, and r. Then it can be shown that the same must be true for

$$b^* = \frac{\sqrt{h}(1+\hat{b}-\hat{b}r)-1}{1-r}, \quad \sigma^*_{\omega_1\omega_1} = h\hat{\sigma}_{\omega_1\omega_1}, \quad \sigma^*_{\omega_1\omega_2} = h\hat{\sigma}_{\omega_1\omega_2}, \quad \sigma^*_{\omega_2\omega_2} = h\hat{\sigma}_{\omega_2\omega_2},$$

where h is a positive scalar. For the above assertion to hold we must have $hK(b^*,r) = K(\hat{b},r)$, where

$$K(b^*,r) = \left[\frac{1}{1+b^*-rb^*}\right]^2, \quad \text{and} \quad K(\hat{b},r) = \left[\frac{1}{1+\hat{b}-r\hat{b}}\right]^2$$

Inserting for b^* we obtain

$$hK(b^*,r) = h\left[\frac{1}{1+b^*-rb^*}\right]^2 = \left[\frac{\sqrt{h}}{1+\dfrac{\sqrt{h}(1+\hat{b}-\hat{b}r)-1}{1-r}-r\left(\dfrac{\sqrt{h}(1+\hat{b}-\hat{b}r)-1}{1-r}\right)}\right]^2 =$$

$$\left[\frac{\sqrt{h}}{1+\dfrac{(1-r)[\sqrt{h}(1+\hat{b}-\hat{b}r)-1]}{1-r}}\right]^2 = \left[\frac{1}{1+\hat{b}-\hat{b}r}\right]^2 = K(\hat{b},r)$$

This means that b, $\sigma_{\omega1\omega1}$, $\sigma_{\omega2\omega2}$, and $\sigma_{\omega1\omega2}$ cannot be identified. If, for instance, b is given a fixed value, the three remaining parameters can be obtained from (B69)-(B71).

A similar proof, not given in this paper, will show that r is not identifiable in W0L3.

B.8. Identification of $\sigma_{\omega1\omega1}$, $\sigma_{\lambda1\lambda1}$, $\sigma_{\omega2\omega2}$, $\sigma_{\lambda2\lambda2}$, $\sigma_{\omega1\omega2}$, and $\sigma_{\lambda1\lambda2}$

For the submodels where b and r have been identified, the parameters $\sigma_{\omega2\omega2}$ and $\sigma_{\lambda2\lambda2}$ are identified by (B25) and (B26), which are two linear equations in these parameters. Thereafter we identify the parameters $\sigma_{\omega1\omega2}$ and $\sigma_{\lambda1\lambda2}$ by (B28) and (B29), and finally we determine $\sigma_{\omega1\omega1}$ and $\sigma_{\lambda1\lambda1}$ from (B6) and (B8).

B.9. Observational equivalence between Wi^*Lj^* and Wj^*Li^*

The demonstration of identification above needs a qualification. The models Wi^*Lj^* and Wj^*Li^* for $i \neq j$ and $i,j=0,1,2,3$ can be shown to be pairwise observationally equivalent. Here we restrict ourselves to prove this proposition for the most general pair of models, i.e. $W2^*L3^*$ and $W3^*L2^*$. The proof for other pairs is analogous, but somewhat simpler.

Let b', r', d', $\sigma_{\omega1\omega1}'$, $\sigma_{\omega2\omega2}'$, $\sigma_{\lambda1\lambda1}'$, $\sigma_{\lambda2\lambda2}'$, $\sigma_{\varepsilon\varepsilon}'$, $\sigma_{\varphi\varphi}'$, and $\sigma_{\varepsilon\varphi}'$ be the values of b, r, d, $\sigma_{\omega1\omega1}$, $\sigma_{\omega2\omega2}$, $\sigma_{\lambda1\lambda1}$, $\sigma_{\lambda2\lambda2}$, $\sigma_{\varepsilon\varepsilon}$, $\sigma_{\varphi\varphi}$, and $\sigma_{\varepsilon\varphi}$, respectively, in W3L2, and b'', r'', d'', $\sigma_{\omega1\omega1}''$, $\sigma_{\omega2\omega2}''$, $\sigma_{\lambda1\lambda1}''$, $\sigma_{\lambda2\lambda2}''$, $\sigma_{\varepsilon\varepsilon}''$, $\sigma_{\varphi\varphi}''$, and $\sigma_{\varepsilon\varphi}''$ the values of the same parameters in W2L3. For W3L2 to be observationally equivalent to W2L3 they have to imply the same theoretical moments of the observable variables. This means that the following identities must hold for all possible combinations of t and s (cf (B6)-(B8)):

(B72) $\left[K(b',r')[\sigma'_{\omega_1\omega_1}+b'^2\sigma'_{\lambda_1\lambda_1}] - K(b'',r'')[\sigma''_{\omega_1\omega_1}+b''^2\sigma''_{\lambda_1\lambda_1}]\right]$

$+ \left[K(b',r')\sigma'_{\omega_1\omega_2} - K(b'',r'')b''^2\sigma''_{\lambda_1\lambda_2}\right](t+s)$

$+ \left[K(b',r')[\sigma'_{\omega_2\omega_2}+b'^2\sigma'_{\lambda_2\lambda_2} - K(b'',r'')[\sigma''_{\omega_2\omega_2}+b''^2\sigma''_{\lambda_2\lambda_2}]\right]ts + \delta_{ts}[\sigma'_{\varepsilon\varepsilon}-\sigma''_{\varepsilon\varepsilon}] = 0,$

(B73) $\left[K(b',r')[r'^2\sigma'_{\omega_1\omega_1}+(1+b')^2\sigma'_{\lambda_1\lambda_1}] - K(b'',r'')[r''^2\sigma''_{\omega_1\omega_1}+(1+b'')^2\sigma''_{\lambda_1\lambda_1}]\right]$

$+ \left[K(b',r')r'^2\sigma'_{\omega_1\omega_2} - K(b'',r'')(1+b'')^2\sigma''_{\lambda_1\lambda_2}\right](t+s)$

$+ \left[K(b',r')[r'^2\sigma'_{\omega_2\omega_2}+(1+b')^2\sigma'_{\lambda_2\lambda_2}] - K(b'',r'')[r''^2\sigma''_{\omega_2\omega_2}+(1+b'')^2\sigma''_{\lambda_2\lambda_2}]\right]ts$

$+ \delta_{ts}[\sigma'_{\varphi\varphi}-\sigma''_{\varphi\varphi}] = 0 ,$

(B74) $\left[K(b',r')[r'\sigma'_{\omega_1\omega_1}+(1+b')b'\sigma'_{\lambda_1\lambda_1}] - K(b'',r'')[r''\sigma''_{\omega_1\omega_1}+(1+b'')b''\sigma''_{\lambda_1\lambda_1}]\right]$

$+ \left[K(b',r')r'\sigma'_{\omega_1\omega_2} - K(b'',r'')(1+b'')b''\sigma''_{\lambda_1\lambda_2}\right](t+s)$

$+ \left[K(b',r')[r'\sigma'_{\omega_2\omega_2}+(1+b')b'\sigma'_{\lambda_2\lambda_2}] - K(b'',r'')[r''\sigma''_{\omega_2\omega_2}+(1+b'')b''\sigma''_{\lambda_2\lambda_2}]\right]ts$

$+ \delta_{ts}[\sigma'_{\varepsilon\varphi}-\sigma''_{\varepsilon\varphi}] = 0.$

For (B72)-(B74) to hold as identities the following relations must apply:

(B75) $K(b',r')[\sigma'_{\omega_1\omega_1}+b'^2\sigma'_{\lambda_1\lambda_1}] = K(b'',r'')[\sigma''_{\omega_1\omega_1}+b''^2\sigma''_{\lambda_1\lambda_1}] ,$

(B76) $K(b',r')\sigma'_{\omega_1\omega_2} = K(b'',r'')b''^2\sigma''_{\lambda_1\lambda_2} .$

(B77) $K(b',r')[\sigma'_{\omega_2\omega_2}+b'^2\sigma'_{\lambda_2\lambda_2}] = K(b'',r'')[\sigma''_{\omega_2\omega_2}+b''^2\sigma''_{\lambda_2\lambda_2}] ,$

(B78) $\sigma'_{\varepsilon\varepsilon} = \sigma''_{\varepsilon\varepsilon} ,$

(B79) $K(b',r')[r'^2\sigma'_{\omega_1\omega_1}+(1+b')^2\sigma'_{\lambda_1\lambda_1}] = K(b'',r'')[r''^2\sigma''_{\omega_1\omega_1}+(1+b'')^2\sigma''_{\lambda_1\lambda_1}] ,$

(B80) $K(b',r')r'^2\sigma'_{\omega_1\omega_2} = K(b'',r'')(1+b'')^2\sigma''_{\lambda_1\lambda_2}$,

(B81) $K(b',r')[r'^2\sigma'_{\omega_2\omega_2}+(1+b')^2\sigma'_{\lambda_2\lambda_2}] = K(b'',r'')[r''^2\sigma''_{\omega_2\omega_2}+(1+b'')^2\sigma''_{\lambda_2\lambda_2}]$,

(B82) $\sigma'_{\varphi\varphi} = \sigma''_{\varphi\varphi}$,

(B83) $K(b',r')[r'\sigma'_{\omega_1\omega_1}+(1+b')b'\sigma'_{\lambda_1\lambda_1}] = K(b'',r'')[r''\sigma''_{\omega_1\omega_1}+(1+b'')b''\sigma''_{\lambda_1\lambda_1}]$,

(B84) $K(b'r')r'\sigma'_{\omega_1\omega_2} = K(b'',r'')(1+b'')b''\sigma''_{\lambda_1\lambda_2}$,

(B85) $K(b',r')[r'\sigma'_{\omega_2\omega_2}+(1+b')b'\sigma'_{\lambda_2\lambda_2}] = K(b'',r'')[r''\sigma''_{\omega_2\omega_2}+(1+b'')b''\sigma''_{\lambda_2\lambda_2}]$,

(B86) $\sigma'_{\varepsilon\varphi} = \sigma''_{\varepsilon\varphi}$.

From (B75)-(B86) it is now possible to solve for

$\sigma''_{\varepsilon\varepsilon}$, $\sigma''_{\varphi\varphi}$, $\sigma''_{\varepsilon\varphi}$, b'' , r'' , $\sigma''_{\omega_1\omega_1}$, $\sigma''_{\omega_2\omega_2}$, $\sigma''_{\lambda_1\lambda_1}$, $\sigma''_{\lambda_1\lambda_2}$, and $\sigma''_{\lambda_2\lambda_2}$ as functions of
$\sigma'_{\varepsilon\varepsilon}$, $\sigma'_{\varphi\varphi}$, $\sigma'_{\varepsilon\varphi}$, b' , r' , $\sigma'_{\omega_1\omega_1}$, $\sigma'_{\omega_1\omega_2}$, $\sigma'_{\omega_2\omega_2}$, $\sigma'_{\lambda_1\lambda_1}$, and $\sigma'_{\lambda_2\lambda_2}$.

From (B78), (B82), and (B86) we have

(I) $\sigma''_{\varepsilon\varepsilon} = \sigma'_{\varepsilon\varepsilon}$, $\sigma''_{\varphi\varphi} = \sigma'_{\varphi\varphi}$, $\sigma''_{\varepsilon\varphi} = \sigma'_{\varepsilon\varphi}$,

Dividing (B84) by (B76) we obtain

(II) $b'' = \dfrac{1}{r'-1}$.

Multiplying (B75) by r', and subtracting the resulting equation from (B83) we have

(B87) $K'(b',r')[(1+b')b'-r'b'^2]\sigma'_{\lambda_1\lambda_1} = K(b'',r'')[r''-\dfrac{1+b''}{b''}]\sigma''_{\omega_1\omega_1}$.

Multiplying (B83) by r', and subtracting the resulting equation from (B79) we have

(B88) $K'(b',r')[(1+b')^2-r'(1+b')b']\sigma'_{\lambda_1\lambda_1} = K(b'',r'')[r''^2-r''\dfrac{1+b''}{b''}]\sigma''_{\omega_1\omega_1}$.

Dividing (B88) by (B87), assuming $\sigma_{\omega1\omega1}$ and $\sigma_{\lambda1\lambda1} \neq 0$, and thus excluding the pair of models $(W1^*L0^*, W0^*L1^*)$ from the proof, we obtain

(III) $r'' = \dfrac{(1+b')^2-r'(1+b')b'}{(1+b')b'-r'b'^2} = \dfrac{1+b'}{b'}$.

From (B76) we obtain

(IV) $\sigma''_{\lambda_1\lambda_2} = \dfrac{K(b',r')}{K[b''(r'),r''(b')]b''(r')^2}\sigma'_{\omega_1\omega_2} = \dfrac{1}{b'^2}\sigma'_{\omega_1\omega_2}$.

From (B87) we obtain

(V) $\sigma''_{\omega_1\omega_1} = \dfrac{K(b',r')}{K[b''(r'),r''(b')]}\dfrac{(1+b')b'-r'b'^2}{r''(b')-\dfrac{1+b''(r')}{b''(r')}}\sigma'_{\lambda_1\lambda_1} = \dfrac{1}{(1-r')^2}\sigma'_{\lambda_1\lambda_1}$.

From (B85) and (V) we obtain

(VI) $\sigma''_{\lambda_1\lambda_1} = \dfrac{K(b',r')}{K[b''(r'),r''(b')](b''(r'))^2}[\sigma'_{\omega_1\omega_1}+b'^2\sigma'_{\lambda_1\lambda_1}] - \dfrac{\sigma''_{\omega_1\omega_1}(b',r',\sigma'_{\lambda_1\lambda_1})}{(b''(r'))^2} = \dfrac{1}{b'^2}\sigma'_{\omega_1\omega_1}$.

Multiplication of (B77) by r', and subtraction of the resulting equation from (B85) gives

(B89) $K'(b',r')[(1+b')b'-r'b'^2]\sigma'_{\lambda_2\lambda_2} = K(b'',r'')[r''-\dfrac{1+b''}{b''}]\sigma''_{\omega_2\omega_2}$,

from which we obtain

(VII) $\sigma''_{\omega_2\omega_2} = \dfrac{K(b',r')}{K[b''(r'),r''(b')]} \dfrac{(1+b')b'-r'b'^2}{r''(b')-\dfrac{1+b''(r')}{b''(r')}}\sigma'_{\lambda_2\lambda_2} = \dfrac{1}{(1-r')^2}\sigma'_{\lambda_2\lambda_2}$.

From (B77) and (VII) we, finally, obtain

(VIII) $\sigma''_{\lambda_2\lambda_2} = \dfrac{K(b',r')}{K[b''(r'),r''(b')]} \dfrac{1}{(b''(r'))^2}[\sigma'_{\omega_2\omega_2}+b'^2\sigma'_{\lambda_2\lambda_2}] - \dfrac{\sigma''_{\omega_2\omega_2}(b',r',\sigma'_{\lambda_1\lambda_1})}{(b''(r'))^2}$

$= \dfrac{1}{b'^2}\sigma'_{\omega_2\omega_2}$.

Thus we have proved that given an arbitrary set of parameters in W2*L3* we can find a corresponding set of parameters in W3*L2* which makes the models observationally equivalent.

From II and III we obtain the following relation between the stability parameters d' and d'' (cf (2d)) in W3L2 and W2L3, respectively:

(IX) $d'' = 1+b''(1-r'') = 1+\dfrac{1}{(r'-1)b'} = \dfrac{d'}{d'-1}$, or

(IX') $d' = \dfrac{d''}{d''-1}$.

Note that (IX) implies that if $0<d''<1$, then $d'<0$, and vice versa. Thus assuming (2e), i.e. $0<d<1$, only one of the symmetric models is relevant. That is, within the set of two symmetric models $\{Wi^*Lj^*, Wj^*Li^*\}$ we can identify the correct model under assumption (2e).

B.10. Observational equivalence between $WiLi^{I}$ and $WiLi^{II}$, $i=2,3$.

A pairwise observational equivalence analogous to that between Wi^*Lj^* and Wj^*Li^* exists between the two solutions of model WiLi, i=2,3, i.e. between WiLi^I and WiLi^{II}. Here we restrict ourselves to demonstrate that the parameters of W3L3^{II} are functions of those of W3L3^I. The proof for the two solutions of W2L2 is analogous, but somewhat simpler. Observational equivalence between the two solutions of W3L3 requires that identities analogous to (B72)-(B74) hold. Let b^I, r^I, etc. denote the values of the parameters in W3L3^I, and b^{II}, r^{II} those in W3L3^{II}. For all possible combinations of t and s we must now have

(B92) $\left[K(b^I,r^I)[\sigma^I_{\omega_1\omega_1} + b^{I2}\sigma^I_{\lambda_1\lambda_1}] - K(b^{II},r^{II})[\sigma^{II}_{\omega_1\omega_1} + b^{II2}\sigma^{II}_{\lambda_1\lambda_1}] \right]$

$+ \left[K(b^I,r^I)[\sigma^I_{\omega_1\omega_2} + b^{I2}\sigma^I_{\lambda_1\lambda_2}] - K(b^{II},r^{II})[\sigma^{II}_{\omega_1\omega_2} + b^{II2}\sigma^{II}_{\lambda_1\lambda_2}] \right](t+s)$

$+ \left[K(b^I,r^I)[\sigma^I_{\omega_2\omega_2} + b^{I2}\sigma^I_{\lambda_2\lambda_2}] - K(b^{II},r^{II})[\sigma^{II}_{\omega_2\omega_2} + b^{II2}\sigma^{II}_{\lambda_2\lambda_2}] \right]ts + \delta_{ts}[\sigma^I_{\varepsilon\varepsilon} - \sigma^{II}_{\varepsilon\varepsilon}] = 0,$

(B93) $\left[K(b^I,r^I)[r^{I2}\sigma^I_{\omega_1\omega_1} + (1+b^I)^2\sigma^I_{\lambda_1\lambda_1}] - K(b^{II},r^{II})[r^{II2}\sigma^{II}_{\omega_1\omega_1} + (1+b^{II})^2\sigma^{II}_{\lambda_1\lambda_1}] \right]$

$+ \left[K(b^I,r^I)[r^{I2}\sigma^I_{\omega_1\omega_2} + (1+b^I)^2\sigma^I_{\lambda_1\lambda_2}] - K(b^{II},r^{II})[r^{II2}\sigma^{II}_{\omega_1\omega_2} + (1+b^{II})^2\sigma^{II}_{\lambda_1\lambda_2}] \right](t+s)$

$+ \left[K(b^I,r^I)[r^{I2}\sigma^I_{\omega_2\omega_2} + (1+b^I)^2\sigma^I_{\lambda_2\lambda_2}] - K(b^{II},r^{II})[r^{II2}\sigma^{II}_{\omega_2\omega_2} + (1+b^{II})^2\sigma^{II}_{\lambda_2\lambda_2}] \right]ts$

$+ \delta_{ts}[\sigma^I_{\varphi\varphi} - \sigma^{II}_{\varphi\varphi}] = 0,$

(B94) $\left[K(b^I,r^I)[r^I\sigma^I_{\omega_1\omega_1} + (1+b^I)b^I\sigma^I_{\lambda_1\lambda_1}] - K(b^{II},r^{II})[r^{II}\sigma^{II}_{\omega_1\omega_1} + (1+b^{II})b^{II}\sigma^{II}_{\lambda_1\lambda_1}] \right]$

$+ \left[K(b^I,r^I)[r^I\sigma^I_{\omega_1\omega_2} + (1+b^I)b^I\sigma^I_{\lambda_1\lambda_2}] - K(b^{II},r^{II})[r^{II}\sigma^{II}_{\omega_1\omega_2} + (1+b^{II})b^{II}\sigma^{II}_{\lambda_1\lambda_2}] \right](t+s)$

$+ \left[K(b^I,r^I)[r^I\sigma^I_{\omega_2\omega_2} + (1+b^I)b^I\sigma^I_{\lambda_2\lambda_2}] - K(b^{II},r^{II})[r^{II}\sigma^{II}_{\omega_2\omega_2} + (1+b^{II})b^{II}\sigma^{II}_{\lambda_2\lambda_2}] \right]ts$

$+ \delta_{ts}[\sigma^I_{\varepsilon\varphi} - \sigma^{II}_{\varepsilon\varphi}] = 0.$

For (B92)-(B94) to hold as identities relations analogous to (B75)-(B86) must apply. In three of these relations, those corresponding to (B76), (B80), and (B84), some additional terms have to be included. The three enlarged relations are:

(B95) $K(b^I, r^I)[\sigma^I_{\omega_1\omega_2} + b^{I2}\sigma^I_{\lambda_1\lambda_2}] = K(b^{II}, r^{II})[\sigma^{II}_{\omega_1\omega_2} + b^{II2}\sigma^{II}_{\lambda_1\lambda_2}]$,

(B96) $K(b^I, r^I)[r^{I2}\sigma^I_{\omega_1\omega_2} + (1+b^I)^2\sigma^I_{\lambda_1\lambda_2}] = K(b^{II}, r^{II})[r^{II2}\sigma^{II}_{\omega_1\omega_2} + (1+b^{II})^2\sigma^{II}_{\lambda_1\lambda_2}]$,

(B97) $K(b^I, r^I)[r^I\sigma^I_{\omega_1\omega_2} + (1+b^I)b^I\sigma^I_{\lambda_1\lambda_2}] = K(b^{II}, r^{II})[r^{II}\sigma^{II}_{\omega_1\omega_2} + (1+b^{II})b^{II}\sigma^{II}_{\lambda_1\lambda_2}]$.

In the remaining equations it suffices to substitute the model notations ^{I} and ^{II} for the apostrophes used to designate the two models in (B75)-(B86). It can now easily be shown that when substituting solutions analogous to (I)-(VII), i.e.

(Ia) $\sigma^{II}_{\varepsilon\varepsilon} = \sigma^I_{\varepsilon\varepsilon}$, $\sigma^{II}_{\varphi\varphi} = \sigma^I_{\varphi\varphi}$, $\sigma^{II}_{\varepsilon\varphi} = \sigma^I_{\varepsilon\varphi}$.

(IIa) $b^{II} = \dfrac{1}{r^I - 1}$.

(IIIa) $r^{II} = \dfrac{1+b^I}{b^I} 0629$.

(IVa) $\sigma^{II}_{\lambda_1\lambda_2} = \dfrac{1}{b^{I2}}\sigma^I_{\omega_1\omega_2}$.

(Va) $\sigma^{II}_{\omega_1\omega_1} = \dfrac{1}{(1-r^I)^2}\sigma^I_{\lambda_1\lambda_1}$.

(VIa) $\sigma^{II}_{\lambda_1\lambda_1} = \dfrac{1}{b^{I2}}\sigma^I_{\omega_1\omega_1}$.

(VIIa) $\sigma^{II}_{\omega_2\omega_2} = \dfrac{1}{(1-r^I)^2}\sigma^I_{\lambda_2\lambda_2}$.

(VIIIa) $\sigma^{II}_{\lambda_2\lambda_2} = \dfrac{1}{b^{I2}}\sigma^I_{\omega_2\omega_2}$.

and in addition

(Xa) $\sigma^{II}_{\omega_1\omega_2} = \dfrac{1}{(1-r^I)^2}\sigma^I_{\lambda_1\lambda_2}$,

into these relations, in each of them the left hand side turns out to be equal to the right hand side. The two solutions are thus observationally equivalent.

From (IIa) and (IIIa) we obtain, analogous to (IX) and (IX')

(IXa) $\quad d^{II} = \dfrac{d^{I}}{d^{I}-1}$

(IXa') $\quad d^{I} = \dfrac{d^{II}}{d^{II}-1}$.

Note that (IXa) implies that if $0<d^{II}<1$, then $d^{I}<0$, and vice versa. Thus assuming (2e), i.e. $0<d<1$, only one of the two solutions is relevant, which means that the model is identified. This is empirically illustrated in Table 6.

APPENDIX C: DATA - TOTAL CRIME

Data on the number of crimes in Table A2 is found in Central Bureau of Statistics (annual): *Crime Statistics*. Data on the number of clear-ups are unpublished statistics from the Central Bureau of Statistics.

A crime is registered by the police for statistical purposes in the year when the investigation is closed. Accordingly, the statistics give information on investigated cases and not about crimes committed in the statistical year. The average period of investigation has for the country as a whole and for all crimes taken together increased from 4 months in 1970-1972 to 4.9 months in the period 1980-1982. Cases shelved for observation are considered closed, but if such cases are subsequently cleared up, a new statistical report is submitted. If this happens the same year, the first report is not included in the statistics, but if it happens in a subsequent year, the crime is registered as a separate crime and clear-up that year.

The only legal change of some importance to the number of crimes during the studied period, was the decriminalizing of "naskeri" (petty larceny of less than about 50 kr.) by the end of 1972. Until then this crime was included in the group of petty larceny, which accounted for about 30 per cent of total crimes. The number of crimes in this group did not decline from 1972 to 1973, probably because few incidents of "naskeri" were recorded in 1972.

Table A.1
Covariance matrix of logs of crime rates

Crimes	Crimes								
	1970	1971	1972	1973	1974	1975	1976	1977	1978
1970	.4019								
1971	.3614	.3695							
1972	.3693	.3673	.3947						
1973	.3714	.3718	.3912	.4187					
1974	.3411	.3367	.3476	.3645	.3660				
1975	.3390	.3402	.3524	.3689	.3505	.3836			
1976	.3107	.3149	.3209	.3390	.3311	.3551	.3475		
1977	.3001	.3070	.3143	.3324	.3151	.3351	.3240	.3331	
1978	.2942	.2894	.2990	.3074	.2973	.3162	.2956	.3017	.3449

Table A.2
Covariance matrix of logs of crime and clear-up rates

Clear-ups	Crimes								
	1970	1971	1972	1973	1974	1975	1976	1977	1978
1970	.2931	.2590	.2524	.2444	.2302	.2217	.2093	.1957	.1859
1971	.2525	.2622	.2430	.2441	.2144	.2143	.2010	.1918	.1727
1972	.2577	.2670	.2834	.2684	.2386	.2283	.2123	.2053	.1897
1973	.2506	.2713	.2762	.2962	.2458	.2526	.2344	.2242	.1931
1974	.2204	.2334	.2388	.2445	.2533	.2334	.2231	.1993	.1734
1975	.2117	.2205	.2313	.2374	.2222	.2539	.2321	.2056	.1827
1976	.2147	.2286	.2376	.2428	.2366	.2586	.2658	.2250	.1788
1977	.1882	.2062	.2135	.2231	.1911	.2075	.2085	.2231	.1758
1978	.1980	.1998	.2069	.1978	.1883	.1879	.1775	.1803	.2110

Table A.3
Covariance matrix of logs of clear-up rates

Clear-ups	Clear-ups								
	1970	1971	1972	1973	1974	1975	1976	1977	1978
1970	.2746								
1971	.2279	.2522							
1972	.2165	.2219	.2754						
1973	.1996	.2181	.2350	.2864					
1974	.1796	.1850	.2117	.2210	.2512				
1975	.1642	.1634	.1819	.1997	.1920	.2380			
1976	.1766	.1706	.1969	.2074	.2031	.2060	.2837		
1977	.1499	.1591	.1712	.1903	.1566	.1638	.1830	.2284	
1978	.1672	.1554	.1872	.1605	.1440	.1387	.1582	.1529	.2244

Table A2
Number of crimes, police districts, 1970-78

Police district	No	1970	1971	1972	1973	1974	1975	1976	1977	1978	Mean	St.dev.
Oslo	1	21395	23550	23559	26966	28648	31616	26411	29299	32836	27142.22	1210.51
Halden	2	378	521	512	503	551	632	528	546	625	532.89	23.38
Sarpsborg	3	1066	1143	1291	1386	1879	1760	1658	1516	1901	1511.11	97.41
Fredrikstad	4	1090	1513	1836	2036	1234	2335	2238	1818	1580	1742.22	134.28
Moss	5	514	620	636	667	808	966	1123	1288	1535	906.33	109.28
Follo	6	904	1129	1245	1233	1230	1382	1236	1327	1293	1219.89	43.36
Romerike	7	1933	2177	2333	3017	3687	3420	3523	3758	4015	3095.89	241.01
Kongsvinger	8	346	480	413	343	484	383	598	682	599	480.89	38.41
Hamar	9	304	686	660	938	811	1077	1063	1071	1009	846.56	81.75
Østerdal	10	412	510	565	571	723	489	563	569	537	548.78	26.21
Gudbrandsd.	11	369	392	549	566	468	629	691	622	617	544.78	35.18
Vest-Oppl.	12	768	1240	1073	1244	1607	1729	1680	1162	1365	1318.67	98.39
Ringerike	13	748	1144	1294	1544	1951	1783	1798	1564	1583	1489.89	117.53
Asker & B.	14	3271	2688	4315	5609	4066	4725	3581	3440	3715	3934.44	272.22
Drammen	15	1821	2019	2215	2719	2652	3154	2879	3285	3628	2708.00	189.71
Kongsberg	16	541	559	588	659	636	806	674	639	711	645.89	25.55
N.-Jarlsb.	17	650	692	770	902	1230	849	929	1058	1243	924.78	67.78
Tønsberg	18	962	1329	1759	1920	1506	2220	1918	1876	2516	1778.44	146.19
Sandefjord	19	522	710	869	815	985	1081	1151	952	1286	930.11	73.17
Larvik	20	432	400	531	576	801	1183	1175	860	988	771.78	95.39
Skien	21	606	1048	1149	1081	1533	1407	1448	1596	1547	1268.33	102.03
Telemark	22	628	1172	1073	1088	1170	1986	2157	1863	2100	1470.78	175.01
Notodden	23	240	335	373	376	473	426	490	550	400	407.00	28.82
Rjukan	24	88	100	114	111	102	142	133	159	114	118.11	7.06
Kragerø	25	154	211	199	297	224	194	158	217	226	208.89	13.28
Arendal	26	775	682	1024	890	1069	1261	1203	1131	1729	1084.89	97.01
Kristians.	27	2293	2814	2511	2689	2652	3420	2969	2486	3964	2866.44	164.87
Vest-Agder	28	190	259	184	217	338	356	395	435	426	311.11	31.57
Rogaland	29	812	954	891	1249	1101	1070	1251	1217	1397	1104.67	60.40
Stavanger	30	2023	2429	2370	2327	2426	2522	2529	2182	2703	2390.11	62.84
Haugesund	31	813	851	872	743	769	1137	1262	1590	2042	1119.89	139.88
Hardanger	32	357	374	420	227	317	354	272	178	211	301.11	26.11
Hordaland	33	1421	1575	1037	903	1189	1334	1301	1278	1523	1284.56	68.37
Bergen	34	4721	4462	6668	6986	7921	7065	6684	6263	7371	6460.11	364.40
Sogn	35	78	69	67	86	180	166	168	130	254	133.11	20.14
Fjordane	36	170	196	183	161	125	168	144	194	645	220.67	50.52
Sunnmøre	37	807	941	957	1235	1156	825	1077	876	731	956.11	53.18
Romsdal	38	265	456	441	425	483	486	490	497	481	447.11	22.78
Nordmøre	39	471	479	678	665	473	476	431	566	391	514.44	31.55
Ut-Trønd.	40	494	596	749	670	778	943	958	1108	1062	817.56	66.79
Trondheim	41	3862	4093	4205	3707	3898	3349	3260	3235	4097	3745.11	119.01
Inn-Trønd.	42	371	703	704	690	764	881	1032	1086	976	800.78	69.32
Namdal	43	178	234	237	220	228	280	270	230	235	234.67	9.16
Helgeland	44	871	822	910	737	777	758	848	912	920	839.44	21.98
Bodø	45	815	932	1140	1005	1231	1141	878	917	1077	1015.11	44.08
Narvik	46	451	463	486	532	512	524	462	476	460	485.11	9.52
Lof. & Ves.	47	325	323	488	503	547	491	527	546	603	483.67	30.52
Senja	48	418	399	486	516	445	480	505	479	683	490.11	25.79
Troms	49	1088	1311	1608	1574	1785	1411	1808	1189	2368	1571.33	122.27
Vest-Finnm.	50	396	357	258	372	396	598	694	652	478	466.78	46.87
Vardø	51	151	191	163	231	166	187	194	140	108	170.11	11.22
Vadsø	52	89	102	100	109	140	187	218	139	94	130.89	14.17
Sør-Var.	53	233	163	152	156	258	234	292	237	253	219.78	15.85
Mean		1228	1389	1508	1641	1728	1858	1734	1737	1986	1645.44	78.45
St.dev		2971	3238	3307	3777	3995	4361	3649	4018	4527	3760.33	174.17
Kurtosis		42.68	44.20	39.63	40.55	41.47	43.69	42.04	44.63	43.43	42.48	.56
Skewness		6.28	6.42	6.00	6.09	6.18	6.37	6.21	6.46	6.35	6.26	.05

Table A3
Crime rates, police districts, 1970-78

Police district	No	1970	1971	1972	1973	1974	1975	1976	1977	1978	Mean	St. dev.
Oslo	1	43.90	48.90	49.54	57.06	61.15	67.94	57.04	63.35	71.32	57.80	2.87
Halden	2	11.02	15.21	14.77	14.48	15.71	18.03	15.08	15.59	17.85	15.30	.64
Sarpsborg	3	14.77	15.56	17.35	18.51	24.83	23.10	21.76	19.79	24.57	20.03	1.18
Fredrikstad	4	17.35	23.84	28.67	31.42	19.06	36.05	34.64	28.23	24.62	27.10	2.04
Moss	5	10.44	12.34	12.49	13.04	15.72	18.59	21.32	24.11	28.41	17.38	1.93
Follo	6	15.75	18.50	19.77	19.12	18.59	20.50	17.81	18.71	17.86	18.51	.42
Romerike	7	12.86	14.04	14.74	18.61	22.33	20.42	20.75	21.94	23.21	18.77	1.23
Kongsvinger	8	6.53	9.07	7.74	6.38	8.95	7.04	10.88	12.34	10.77	8.86	.67
Hamar	9	4.01	8.91	8.51	12.04	10.36	13.73	13.48	13.57	12.73	10.82	1.02
Østerdal	10	8.27	10.35	11.50	11.62	14.68	9.88	11.35	11.38	10.63	11.07	.54
Gudbrandsd.	11	5.50	5.86	8.15	8.31	6.83	9.16	10.02	8.99	8.89	7.97	.49
Vest-Oppl.	12	7.33	11.74	10.06	11.57	14.83	15.88	15.38	10.62	12.44	12.21	.88
Ringerike	13	11.72	17.83	19.98	23.67	29.72	26.95	27.04	23.36	23.54	22.65	1.72
Asker & B.	14	31.30	24.82	38.73	49.35	35.45	40.88	30.92	29.74	32.07	34.81	2.29
Drammen	15	19.25	20.95	22.68	27.54	26.48	30.92	27.96	31.67	34.89	26.93	1.63
Kongsberg	16	14.28	14.60	15.11	16.80	16.11	20.20	16.77	15.72	17.40	16.33	.56
N.-Jarlsb.	17	14.06	14.72	16.04	18.42	24.81	16.97	18.49	20.92	24.46	18.77	1.23
Tønsberg	18	17.25	23.64	31.04	33.74	26.45	38.89	33.45	32.45	43.37	31.14	2.47
Sandefjord	19	14.79	19.86	23.99	22.24	26.60	29.14	30.88	25.39	33.98	25.21	1.84
Larvik	20	11.97	10.99	14.48	15.67	21.63	31.67	31.31	22.93	26.22	20.76	2.49
Skien	21	11.19	19.28	20.93	19.67	27.93	25.33	25.83	28.33	27.31	22.87	1.77
Telemark	22	11.68	21.82	19.84	20.12	21.67	36.81	39.78	33.87	37.73	27.04	3.16
Notodden	23	9.26	13.03	14.55	14.64	18.44	16.53	18.95	21.15	15.31	15.76	1.11
Rjukan	24	10.31	11.96	14.06	13.99	13.05	18.23	17.33	20.81	14.85	14.95	1.03
Kragerø	25	10.56	14.39	13.48	20.03	15.02	12.93	10.52	14.36	14.92	14.02	.89
Arendal	26	10.61	9.25	13.72	11.77	13.97	16.21	15.27	14.21	21.48	14.05	1.12
Kristians.	27	28.37	34.31	30.07	31.83	31.00	39.64	34.05	28.19	44.51	33.55	1.70
Vest-Agder	28	3.85	5.25	3.69	4.32	6.65	6.93	7.62	8.34	8.08	6.08	.58
Rogaland	29	10.27	11.78	10.77	14.80	12.85	12.23	14.07	13.47	15.19	12.83	.54
Stavanger	30	18.11	21.65	20.90	20.27	20.85	21.37	21.12	18.03	22.06	20.48	.46
Haugesund	31	10.77	11.27	11.42	9.67	9.92	14.54	15.96	19.95	25.37	14.32	1.68
Hardanger	32	12.95	13.69	15.39	8.39	11.70	13.14	10.07	6.61	7.86	11.09	.94
Hordaland	33	6.24	6.75	7.52	6.50	8.43	9.26	8.91	8.61	10.11	8.04	.42
Bergen	34	40.79	39.36	31.46	32.69	36.91	33.01	31.29	29.44	34.79	34.42	1.22
Sogn	35	1.94	1.71	1.65	2.14	4.51	4.18	4.24	3.28	6.41	3.34	.51
Fjordane	36	2.79	3.24	2.99	2.61	2.01	2.67	2.27	3.03	10.02	3.51	.78
Sunnmøre	37	7.29	8.48	8.52	10.86	10.09	7.14	9.29	7.52	6.24	8.38	.47
Romsdal	38	5.29	9.00	8.61	8.21	9.26	9.21	9.19	9.26	8.93	8.55	.40
Nordmøre	39	7.53	7.72	10.90	10.69	7.55	7.59	6.87	8.96	6.23	8.23	.51
Ut-Trønd.	40	4.76	5.74	7.22	6.47	7.52	9.12	9.26	10.67	10.22	7.89	.64
Trondheim	41	30.11	31.44	31.90	27.60	28.66	24.47	23.66	23.34	29.62	27.87	1.04
Inn-Trønd.	42	4.54	8.58	8.49	8.25	8.98	10.22	11.88	12.45	11.12	9.39	.75
Namdal	43	4.89	6.49	6.57	6.10	6.32	7.76	7.50	6.38	6.49	6.50	.26
Helgeland	44	10.75	10.24	11.38	9.19	9.70	9.47	10.56	11.37	11.50	10.46	.27
Bodø	45	12.57	14.35	17.48	15.29	18.56	17.08	13.05	13.59	15.91	15.32	.66
Narvik	46	12.58	13.09	13.71	15.07	14.48	14.88	13.18	13.68	13.29	13.77	.27
Lof. & Ves.	47	5.29	5.35	8.11	8.30	9.00	8.06	8.70	9.06	10.02	7.99	.51
Senja	48	8.89	8.55	10.37	10.94	9.36	10.05	10.57	10.03	14.31	10.34	.53
Tromsø	49	12.15	14.55	17.66	16.94	18.92	14.78	18.77	12.32	24.42	16.72	1.21
Vest-Finnm.	50	9.73	8.76	6.30	8.89	9.32	13.90	16.12	15.16	11.13	11.03	1.04
Vardø	51	14.68	18.32	15.62	22.37	15.80	17.97	18.93	13.59	10.54	16.42	1.08
Vadsø	52	6.01	6.96	6.77	7.30	9.30	12.35	14.37	9.21	6.25	8.72	.92
Sør-Var.	53	22.05	15.55	14.29	14.64	23.90	21.55	26.81	21.70	23.50	20.44	1.42
Mean		12.66	14.60	15.50	16.42	17.21	18.77	18.35	17.56	19.53	16.73	.73
St. dev.		8.67	8.97	9.30	10.68	10.30	11.91	10.36	10.20	12.36	10.31	.42
Kurtosis		4.17	3.88	2.71	4.09	5.05	4.34	2.41	6.45	4.69	4.20	.40
Skewness		1.91	1.71	1.45	1.74	1.69	1.69	1.28	1.86	1.74	1.67	.07

Table A4
Number of clear-ups, police districts, 1970-78

Police district	No	1970	1971	1972	1973	1974	1975	1976	1977	1978	Mean	St.dev.
Oslo	1	4870	5085	4942	5627	5088	5131	4540	4455	5597	5037.22	126.59
Halden	2	233	264	231	244	267	253	209	214	211	236.22	7.00
Sarpsborg	3	367	382	477	447	837	538	608	543	759	550.89	50.58
Fredrikstad	4	466	620	728	882	459	1142	895	746	607	727.22	69.44
Moss	5	238	257	228	250	273	255	368	409	400	297.56	22.93
Follo	6	247	344	266	313	265	276	325	366	297	299.89	12.60
Romerike	7	836	757	602	892	1274	862	969	977	877	894.00	57.27
Kongsvinger	8	267	310	225	122	179	101	266	284	292	227.33	24.01
Hamar	9	212	370	312	422	374	451	545	480	464	403.33	31.26
Østerdal	10	213	165	198	167	198	148	206	238	196	192.11	8.70
Gudbrandsd.	11	102	88	144	127	122	166	271	199	130	149.89	17.64
Vest-Oppl.	12	321	655	451	454	689	721	698	341	375	522.78	52.19
Ringerike	13	304	356	453	575	705	619	682	421	451	507.33	45.06
Asker & B.	14	603	619	555	791	636	957	684	662	689	688.44	37.85
Drammen	15	754	682	680	766	626	669	777	831	764	727.67	20.71
Kongsberg	16	166	193	169	153	144	222	238	159	205	183.22	10.31
N.-Jarlsb.	17	192	276	354	251	344	223	301	276	343	284.44	17.80
Tønsberg	18	307	331	455	456	263	442	435	430	424	393.67	22.89
Sandefjord	19	239	305	341	318	357	336	487	425	452	362.22	24.63
Larvik	20	158	117	202	145	213	362	327	146	160	203.33	26.91
Skien	21	196	259	358	476	497	371	443	368	322	365.56	30.95
Telemark	22	189	336	240	446	301	317	545	409	373	350.67	33.00
Notodden	23	72	119	144	104	198	138	97	210	93	130.56	14.87
Rjukan	24	38	37	26	40	44	80	35	92	17	45.44	7.71
Kragerø	25	58	86	68	124	64	46	32	79	57	68.22	8.31
Arendal	26	354	352	454	328	447	455	533	504	641	452.00	31.43
Kristians.	27	784	1000	883	887	879	959	884	959	1055	921.11	25.24
Vest-Agder	28	103	124	93	93	91	212	110	162	174	129.11	13.65
Rogaland	29	489	590	550	681	506	593	603	535	625	574.67	19.07
Stavanger	30	804	1107	1006	789	911	809	978	787	856	894.11	35.92
Haugesund	31	417	468	470	446	304	309	333	426	395	396.44	20.64
Hardanger	32	248	192	225	111	165	166	144	63	129	160.33	17.94
Hordaland	33	629	487	369	378	422	498	624	583	708	522.00	37.86
Bergen	34	1591	1233	2185	1834	2196	1609	1594	1322	1715	1697.67	104.92
Sogn	35	48	46	33	42	88	62	45	32	48	49.33	5.34
Fjordane	36	90	114	80	91	62	95	46	103	243	102.67	17.76
Sunnmøre	37	438	462	523	696	585	360	574	439	382	495.44	34.06
Romsdal	38	127	262	257	216	246	233	211	227	180	217.67	13.30
Nordmøre	39	260	302	425	380	232	205	233	353	218	289.78	24.93
Ut-Trønd.	40	232	307	343	220	294	362	423	533	531	360.56	36.27
Trondheim	41	1384	1577	1120	793	840	899	721	628	694	961.78	103.65
Inn-Trønd.	42	233	363	441	447	505	536	612	664	511	479.11	40.57
Namdal	43	102	159	122	124	117	132	132	117	116	124.56	4.97
Helgeland	44	489	393	477	336	328	316	424	328	401	388.00	20.70
Bodø	45	472	504	592	516	673	607	307	433	505	512.11	33.58
Narvik	46	221	239	190	215	203	183	163	168	173	195.00	8.23
Lof. & Ves.	47	177	164	239	257	257	249	263	262	280	238.67	12.67
Senja	48	194	176	215	213	180	217	225	254	299	219.22	12.02
Troms	49	502	564	587	519	546	513	598	441	631	544.56	18.15
Vest-Finnm.	50	247	278	97	125	114	182	240	272	135	187.78	22.75
Vardø	51	65	102	71	133	92	61	80	66	38	78.67	8.64
Vadsø	52	50	54	37	78	85	95	151	56	30	70.67	11.66
Sør-Var.	53	138	70	54	65	71	82	107	101	114	89.11	8.63
Mean		425	466	471	483	488	487	497	464	498	475.44	7.55
St. dev.		694	717	717	788	741	723	643	619	778	713.33	18.58
Kurtosis		33.49	34.29	30.19	36.25	29.60	33.77	30.91	34.30	36.89	33.30	.86
Skewness		5.38	5.43	5.09	5.63	5.02	5.36	5.03	5.38	5.68	5.33	.08

Table A5
Clear-up rates, police districts, 1970-78

Police district	No	1970	1971	1972	1973	1974	1975	1976	1977	1978	Mean	St. dev.
Oslo	1	9.99	10.56	10.39	11.91	10.86	11.03	9.81	9.63	12.16	10.70	.28
Halden	2	6.79	7.71	6.66	7.02	7.61	7.22	5.97	6.11	6.03	6.79	.21
Sarpsborg	3	5.08	5.20	6.41	5.97	11.06	7.06	7.98	7.09	9.81	7.30	.64
Fredrikstad	4	7.42	9.77	11.37	13.61	7.09	17.63	13.85	11.58	9.46	11.31	1.06
Moss	5	4.83	5.12	4.48	4.89	5.31	4.91	6.99	7.66	7.40	5.73	.39
Follo	6	4.30	5.64	4.22	4.85	4.01	4.09	4.68	5.16	4.10	4.56	.18
Romerike	7	5.56	4.88	3.80	5.50	7.72	5.15	5.71	5.70	5.07	5.45	.32
Kongsvinger	8	5.04	5.86	4.22	2.27	3.31	1.86	4.84	5.14	5.25	4.20	.44
Hamar	9	2.80	4.81	4.02	5.42	4.78	5.75	6.91	6.08	5.85	5.16	.38
Østerdal	10	4.28	3.35	4.03	3.40	4.02	2.99	4.15	4.76	3.88	3.87	.17
Gudbrandsd.	11	1.52	1.32	2.14	1.86	1.78	2.42	3.93	2.88	1.87	2.19	.25
Vest-Oppl.	12	3.06	6.20	4.23	4.22	6.36	6.62	6.39	3.12	3.42	4.85	.48
Ringerike	13	4.76	5.55	6.99	8.81	10.74	9.36	10.26	6.29	6.71	7.72	.67
Asker & B.	14	5.77	5.72	4.98	6.96	5.55	8.28	5.91	5.72	5.95	6.09	.30
Drammen	15	7.97	7.08	6.96	7.76	6.25	6.56	7.55	8.01	7.35	7.28	.19
Kongsberg	16	4.38	5.04	4.34	3.90	3.65	5.56	5.92	3.91	5.02	4.64	.25
N.-Jarlsb.	17	4.15	5.87	7.37	5.13	6.94	4.46	5.99	5.46	6.75	5.79	.35
Tønsberg	18	5.50	5.89	8.03	8.01	4.62	7.74	7.59	7.44	7.31	6.90	.39
Sandefjord	19	6.77	8.53	9.41	8.68	9.64	9.06	13.07	11.33	11.94	9.83	.61
Larvik	20	4.38	3.21	5.51	3.94	5.75	9.69	8.71	3.89	4.25	5.48	.71
Skien	21	3.62	4.76	6.52	8.66	9.05	6.68	7.90	6.53	5.68	6.60	.56
Telemark	22	3.52	6.26	4.44	8.25	5.57	5.88	10.05	7.44	6.70	6.45	.62
Notodden	23	2.78	4.63	5.62	4.05	7.72	5.35	3.75	8.08	3.56	5.06	.58
Rjukan	24	4.45	4.43	3.21	5.04	5.63	10.27	4.56	12.04	2.21	5.76	1.02
Kragerø	25	3.98	4.77	4.61	8.36	4.29	3.07	2.13	5.23	3.76	4.59	.56
Arendal	26	4.85	4.77	6.08	4.34	5.84	5.85	6.77	6.33	7.96	5.87	.35
Kristians.	27	9.70	12.19	10.57	10.50	10.27	11.12	10.14	10.87	11.85	10.80	.25
Vest-Agder	28	2.09	2.51	1.87	1.85	1.79	4.13	2.12	3.11	3.30	2.53	.26
Rogaland	29	6.18	7.29	6.65	8.07	5.91	6.78	6.78	5.92	6.80	6.71	.22
Stavanger	30	7.20	9.87	8.87	6.87	7.83	6.86	8.17	6.50	6.99	7.68	.35
Haugesund	31	5.52	6.20	6.16	5.80	3.92	3.95	4.21	5.35	4.91	5.11	.29
Hardanger	32	9.00	7.03	8.24	4.10	6.09	6.16	5.33	2.34	4.81	5.90	.65
Hordaland	33	2.76	2.09	2.68	2.72	2.99	3.46	4.27	3.93	4.70	3.29	.27
Bergen	34	3.75	10.88	10.31	8.58	10.23	7.52	7.46	6.21	8.09	9.23	.72
Sogn	35	1.19	1.14	.81	1.05	2.20	1.56	1.14	.81	1.21	1.23	.13
Fjordane	36	1.48	1.88	1.31	1.48	1.00	1.51	.73	1.61	3.77	1.64	.27
Sunnmøre	37	3.96	4.16	4.66	6.12	5.11	3.12	4.95	3.77	3.26	4.34	.30
Romsdal	38	2.54	5.17	5.02	4.17	4.72	4.42	3.96	4.23	3.34	4.17	.26
Nordmøre	39	4.16	4.87	6.83	6.11	3.70	3.27	3.71	5.59	3.47	4.63	.40
Ut-Trønd.	40	2.24	2.96	3.31	2.12	2.84	3.50	4.09	5.13	5.11	3.48	.35
Trondheim	41	10.79	12.11	8.50	5.90	6.18	6.57	5.23	4.53	5.02	7.20	.84
Inn-Trønd.	42	2.85	4.43	5.32	5.34	5.94	6.22	7.05	7.61	5.82	5.62	.44
Namdal	43	2.80	4.41	3.38	3.44	3.24	3.66	3.67	3.25	3.20	3.45	.14
Helgeland	44	6.04	4.90	5.97	4.19	4.09	3.95	5.28	4.09	5.01	4.83	.25
Bodø	45	7.28	7.76	9.08	7.85	10.15	9.09	4.56	6.42	7.46	7.74	.52
Narvik	46	6.16	6.76	5.36	6.09	5.74	5.20	4.65	4.83	5.00	5.53	.22
Lof. & Ves.	47	2.88	2.72	3.97	4.24	4.23	4.09	4.34	4.35	4.65	3.94	.21
Senja	48	4.13	3.77	4.59	4.52	3.79	4.54	4.71	5.32	6.26	4.62	.25
Troms	49	5.61	6.26	6.45	5.59	5.79	5.37	6.21	4.57	6.51	5.82	.19
Vest-Finnm.	50	6.07	6.82	2.37	2.99	2.68	4.23	5.57	6.32	3.14	4.47	.55
Vardø	51	6.32	9.78	6.80	12.88	8.76	5.86	7.81	6.41	3.71	7.59	.83
Vadsø	52	3.38	3.68	2.50	5.22	5.65	6.27	9.95	3.71	1.99	4.71	.76
Sør-Var.	53	13.06	6.68	5.08	6.10	6.58	7.55	9.82	9.25	10.59	8.30	.81
Mean		5.22	5.78	5.60	5.79	5.78	5.93	6.17	5.82	5.65	5.75	.09
St.dev.		2.71	2.55	2.45	2.76	2.53	2.85	2.69	2.40	2.53	2.61	.05
Kurtosis		1.79	.41	-.21	.75	-.37	4.27	.73	.73	.62	1.10	.42
Skewness		1.91	1.71	1.41	1.74	1.69	1.69	1.28	1.86	1.74	1.67	.07

Table A6
Clear-up proportions, police districts, 1970-78

Police district	No	1970	1971	1972	1973	1974	1975	1976	1977	1978	Mean	St. dev
Oslo	1	.23	.22	.21	.21	.18	.16	.17	.15	.17	.19	.01
Halden	2	.62	.51	.45	.49	.48	.40	.40	.39	.34	.45	.03
Sarpsborg	3	.34	.33	.37	.32	.45	.31	.37	.36	.40	.36	.01
Fredrikstad	4	.43	.41	.40	.43	.37	.49	.40	.41	.38	.41	.01
Moss	5	.46	.41	.36	.37	.34	.26	.33	.32	.26	.35	.02
Follo	6	.27	.30	.21	.25	.22	.20	.26	.28	.23	.25	.01
Romerike	7	.43	.35	.26	.30	.35	.25	.28	.26	.22	.30	.02
Kongsvinger	8	.77	.65	.54	.36	.37	.26	.44	.42	.49	.48	.05
Hamar	9	.70	.54	.47	.45	.46	.42	.51	.45	.46	.50	.03
Østerdal	10	.52	.32	.35	.29	.27	.30	.37	.42	.36	.36	.02
Gudbrandsd.	11	.28	.22	.26	.22	.26	.26	.39	.32	.21	.27	.02
Vest-Oppl.	12	.42	.53	.42	.36	.43	.42	.42	.29	.27	.40	.02
Ringerike	13	.41	.31	.35	.37	.36	.35	.38	.27	.28	.34	.01
Asker & B.	14	.18	.23	.13	.14	.16	.20	.19	.19	.19	.18	.01
Drammen	15	.41	.34	.31	.28	.24	.21	.27	.25	.21	.28	.02
Kongsberg	16	.31	.35	.29	.23	.23	.28	.35	.25	.29	.28	.01
N.-Jarlsb.	17	.30	.40	.46	.28	.28	.26	.32	.26	.28	.32	.02
Tønsberg	18	.32	.25	.26	.24	.17	.20	.23	.23	.17	.23	.01
Sandefjord	19	.46	.43	.39	.39	.36	.31	.42	.45	.35	.40	.02
Larvik	20	.37	.29	.38	.25	.27	.31	.28	.17	.16	.27	.02
Skien	21	.32	.25	.31	.44	.32	.26	.31	.23	.21	.30	.02
Telemark	22	.30	.29	.22	.41	.26	.16	.25	.22	.18	.25	.02
Notodden	23	.30	.36	.39	.28	.42	.32	.20	.38	.23	.32	.02
Rjukan	24	.43	.37	.23	.36	.43	.56	.26	.58	.15	.38	.05
Kragerø	25	.38	.41	.34	.42	.29	.24	.20	.36	.25	.32	.02
Arendal	26	.46	.52	.44	.37	.42	.36	.44	.45	.37	.42	.02
Kristians.	27	.34	.36	.35	.33	.33	.28	.30	.39	.27	.33	.01
Vest-Agder	28	.54	.48	.51	.43	.27	.60	.28	.37	.41	.43	.04
Rogaland	29	.60	.62	.62	.55	.46	.55	.48	.44	.45	.53	.02
Stavanger	30	.40	.46	.42	.34	.38	.32	.39	.36	.32	.38	.01
Haugesund	31	.51	.55	.54	.60	.40	.27	.26	.27	.19	.40	.05
Hardanger	32	.69	.51	.54	.49	.52	.47	.53	.35	.61	.52	.03
Hordaland	33	.44	.31	.36	.42	.35	.37	.48	.46	.46	.41	.02
Bergen	34	.34	.28	.33	.26	.28	.23	.24	.21	.23	.27	.01
Sogn	35	.62	.67	.49	.49	.49	.37	.27	.25	.19	.43	.05
Fjordane	36	.53	.58	.44	.57	.50	.57	.32	.53	.38	.49	.03
Sunnmøre	37	.54	.49	.55	.56	.51	.44	.53	.50	.52	.52	.01
Romsdal	38	.48	.57	.58	.51	.51	.48	.43	.46	.37	.49	.02
Nordmøre	39	.55	.63	.63	.57	.49	.43	.54	.62	.56	.56	.02
Ut-Trønd.	40	.47	.52	.46	.33	.38	.38	.44	.48	.50	.44	.02
Trondheim	41	.36	.39	.27	.21	.22	.27	.22	.19	.17	.25	.02
Inn-Trønd.	42	.63	.52	.63	.65	.66	.61	.59	.61	.52	.60	.02
Namdal	43	.57	.68	.51	.56	.51	.47	.49	.51	.49	.53	.02
Helgeland	44	.56	.48	.52	.46	.42	.42	.50	.36	.44	.46	.02
Bodø	45	.58	.54	.52	.51	.55	.53	.35	.47	.47	.50	.02
Narvik	46	.49	.52	.39	.40	.40	.35	.35	.35	.38	.40	.02
Lof. & Ves.	47	.54	.51	.49	.51	.47	.51	.50	.48	.46	.50	.01
Senja	48	.46	.44	.44	.41	.40	.45	.45	.53	.44	.45	.01
Tromsø	49	.46	.43	.37	.33	.31	.36	.33	.37	.27	.36	.02
Vest-Finnm.	50	.62	.78	.38	.34	.29	.30	.35	.42	.28	.42	.05
Vardø	51	.43	.53	.44	.58	.55	.33	.41	.47	.35	.45	.03
Vadsø	52	.56	.53	.37	.72	.61	.51	.69	.40	.32	.52	.04
Sør-Var.	53	.59	.43	.36	.42	.28	.35	.37	.43	.45	.41	.03
Mean		.46	.44	.40	.40	.38	.36	.37	.37	.33	.39	.01
St.dev.		.13	.13	.12	.13	.12	.12	.11	.12	.12	.12	.00
Kurtosis		-.41	-.43	-.41	-.37	-.52	-.70	-.03	-.63	-.97	-.50	.09
Skewness		1.91	1.71	1.45	1.74	1.69	1.69	1.28	1.86	1.74	1.67	.07

Table A7
Log of crime rates, police districts, 1970-78

Police district	No	X70	X71	X72	X73	X74	X75	X76	X77	X78	Mean	St. dev.
Oslo	1	3.78	3.89	3.90	4.04	4.11	4.22	4.04	4.15	4.27	4.05	.05
Halden	2	2.40	2.72	2.69	2.67	2.75	2.89	2.71	2.75	2.88	2.72	.04
Sarpsborg	3	2.69	2.74	2.85	2.92	3.21	3.14	3.08	2.99	3.20	2.98	.06
Fredrikstad	4	2.85	3.17	3.36	3.45	2.95	3.58	3.55	3.34	3.20	3.27	.08
Moss	5	2.35	2.51	2.52	2.57	2.75	2.92	3.06	3.18	3.35	2.80	.11
Follo	6	2.76	2.92	2.98	2.95	2.92	3.02	2.88	2.93	2.88	2.92	.02
Romerike	7	2.55	2.64	2.69	2.92	3.11	3.02	3.03	3.09	3.14	2.91	.07
Kongsvinger	8	1.88	2.20	2.05	1.85	2.19	1.95	2.39	2.51	2.38	2.16	.08
Hamar	9	1.39	2.19	2.14	2.49	2.34	2.62	2.60	2.61	2.54	2.32	.12
Østerdal	10	2.11	2.34	2.44	2.45	2.69	2.29	2.43	2.43	2.36	2.39	.05
Gudbrandsd.	11	1.70	1.77	2.10	2.12	1.92	2.21	2.30	2.20	2.18	2.06	.07
Vest-Oppl.	12	1.99	2.46	2.31	2.45	2.70	2.77	2.73	2.36	2.52	2.48	.08
Ringerike	13	2.46	2.88	2.99	3.16	3.39	3.29	3.30	3.15	3.16	3.09	.09
Asker & B.	14	3.44	3.21	3.66	3.90	3.57	3.71	3.43	3.39	3.47	3.53	.06
Drammen	15	2.96	3.04	3.12	3.32	3.28	3.43	3.33	3.46	3.55	3.28	.06
Kongsberg	16	2.66	2.68	2.72	2.82	2.78	3.01	2.82	2.75	2.86	2.79	.03
N.-Jarlsb.	17	2.64	2.69	2.78	2.91	3.21	2.83	2.92	3.04	3.20	2.91	.06
Tønsberg	18	2.85	3.16	3.44	3.52	3.28	3.66	3.51	3.48	3.77	3.41	.09
Sandefjord	19	2.69	2.99	3.18	3.10	3.28	3.37	3.43	3.23	3.53	3.20	.08
Larvik	20	2.48	2.40	2.67	2.75	3.07	3.46	3.44	3.13	3.27	2.96	.13
Skien	21	2.42	2.96	3.04	2.98	3.33	3.23	3.25	3.34	3.31	3.10	.09
Telemark	22	2.46	3.08	2.99	3.00	3.08	3.61	3.68	3.52	3.63	3.23	.13
Notodden	23	2.23	2.57	2.68	2.68	2.91	2.81	2.94	3.05	2.73	2.73	.08
Rjukan	24	2.33	2.48	2.64	2.64	2.57	2.90	2.85	3.04	2.70	2.68	.07
Kragerø	25	2.36	2.67	2.60	3.00	2.71	2.56	2.35	2.66	2.70	2.62	.06
Arendal	26	2.36	2.22	2.62	2.47	2.64	2.79	2.73	2.65	3.07	2.62	.08
Kristians.	27	3.35	3.54	3.40	3.46	3.43	3.68	3.53	3.34	3.80	3.50	.05
Vest-Agder	28	1.35	1.66	1.31	1.46	1.89	1.94	2.03	2.12	2.09	1.76	.10
Rogaland	29	2.33	2.47	2.38	2.69	2.55	2.50	2.64	2.60	2.72	2.54	.04
Stavanger	30	2.90	3.08	3.04	3.01	3.04	3.06	3.05	2.89	3.09	3.02	.02
Haugesund	31	2.38	2.42	2.44	2.27	2.29	2.68	2.77	2.99	3.23	2.61	.11
Hardanger	32	2.56	2.62	2.73	2.13	2.46	2.58	2.31	1.89	2.06	2.37	.09
Hordaland	33	1.83	1.91	2.02	1.87	2.13	2.23	2.19	2.15	2.31	2.07	.05
Bergen	34	3.71	3.67	3.45	3.49	3.61	3.50	3.44	3.38	3.55	3.53	.03
Sogn	35	.66	.54	.50	.76	1.51	1.43	1.44	1.19	1.86	1.10	.16
Fjordane	36	1.03	1.18	1.10	.96	.70	.98	.82	1.11	2.30	1.13	.15
Sunnmøre	37	1.99	2.14	2.14	2.39	2.31	1.97	2.23	2.02	1.83	2.11	.06
Romsdal	38	1.67	2.20	2.15	2.11	2.23	2.22	2.22	2.23	2.19	2.13	.06
Nordmøre	39	2.02	2.04	2.39	2.37	2.02	2.03	1.93	2.19	1.83	2.09	.06
Ut-Trønd.	40	1.56	1.75	1.98	1.87	2.02	2.21	2.23	2.37	2.32	2.03	.09
Trondheim	41	3.40	3.45	3.46	3.32	3.36	3.20	3.15	3.39	3.32	3.32	.04
Inn-Trønd.	42	1.51	2.15	2.14	2.11	2.19	2.32	2.47	2.52	2.41	2.20	.09
Namdal	43	1.59	1.87	1.88	1.81	1.84	2.05	2.01	1.85	1.87	1.86	.04
Helgeland	44	2.37	2.33	2.43	2.22	2.27	2.25	2.36	2.43	2.44	2.34	.03
Bodø	45	2.53	2.66	2.86	2.73	2.92	2.84	2.57	2.61	2.77	2.72	.04
Narvik	46	2.53	2.57	2.62	2.71	2.67	2.70	2.58	2.62	2.59	2.62	.02
Lof. & Ves.	47	1.67	1.68	2.09	2.12	2.20	2.09	2.16	2.20	2.30	2.06	.07
Senja	48	2.18	2.15	2.34	2.39	2.24	2.31	2.36	2.31	2.66	2.33	.05
Troms	49	2.50	2.68	2.87	2.83	2.94	2.69	2.93	2.51	3.20	2.79	.07
Vest-Finnm.	50	2.28	2.17	1.84	2.18	2.23	2.63	2.78	2.72	2.41	2.36	.10
Vardø	51	2.69	2.91	2.75	3.11	2.76	2.89	2.94	2.61	2.36	2.78	.07
Vadsø	52	1.79	1.94	1.91	1.99	2.23	2.51	2.67	2.22	1.83	2.12	.10
Sør-Var.	53	3.09	2.74	2.66	2.68	3.17	3.07	3.29	3.08	3.16	2.99	.07
Mean		2.34	2.51	2.57	2.61	2.68	2.75	2.75	2.71	2.80	2.64	.05
St. dev.		.63	.61	.63	.65	.60	.62	.59	.58	.59	.61	.01
Kurtosis		.44	1.40	1.58	.85	1.11	.40	1.19	.79	- .64	.93	.14
Skewness		- .11	- .47	- .67	- .42	- .48	- .23	- .55	- .41	.17	.39	.06

Table A8
Log of clear-up rates, police districts, 1970-78

Police district	No	Y70	Y71	Y72	Y73	Y74	Y75	Y76	Y77	Y78	Mean	St. dev.
Oslo	1	2.30	2.36	2.34	2.48	2.39	2.40	2.28	2.27	2.50	2.37	.03
Halden	2	1.92	2.04	1.90	1.95	2.03	1.98	1.79	1.81	1.80	1.91	.03
Sarpsborg	3	1.63	1.65	1.86	1.79	2.40	1.95	2.08	1.96	2.28	1.96	.08
Fredrikstad	4	2.00	2.28	2.43	2.61	1.96	2.87	2.63	2.45	2.25	2.39	.09
Moss	5	1.58	1.63	1.50	1.59	1.67	1.59	1.94	2.04	2.00	1.73	.07
Follo	6	1.46	1.73	1.44	1.58	1.39	1.41	1.54	1.64	1.41	1.51	.04
Romerike	7	1.72	1.59	1.34	1.71	2.04	1.64	1.74	1.74	1.62	1.68	.06
Kongsvinger	8	1.62	1.77	1.44	.82	1.20	.62	1.58	1.64	1.66	1.37	.13
Hamar	9	1.03	1.57	1.39	1.69	1.56	1.75	1.93	1.81	1.77	1.61	.08
Østerdal	10	1.45	1.21	1.39	1.22	1.39	1.10	1.42	1.56	1.36	1.35	.05
Gudbrandsd.	11	.42	.27	.76	.62	.58	.88	1.37	1.06	.63	.73	.10
Vest-Oppl.	12	1.12	1.82	1.44	1.44	1.85	1.89	1.85	1.14	1.23	1.53	.10
Ringerike	13	1.56	1.71	1.95	2.18	2.37	2.24	2.33	1.84	1.90	2.01	.09
Asker & B.	14	1.75	1.74	1.61	1.94	1.71	2.11	1.78	1.74	1.78	1.80	.05
Drammen	15	2.08	1.96	1.94	2.05	1.83	1.88	2.02	2.08	1.99	1.98	.03
Kongsberg	16	1.48	1.62	1.47	1.36	1.29	1.72	1.78	1.36	1.61	1.52	.05
N.-Jarlsb.	17	1.42	1.77	2.00	1.63	1.94	1.49	1.79	1.70	1.91	1.74	.06
Tønsberg	18	1.71	1.77	2.08	2.08	1.53	2.05	2.03	2.01	1.99	1.92	.06
Sandefjord	19	1.91	2.14	2.24	2.16	2.27	2.20	2.57	2.43	2.48	2.27	.06
Larvik	20	1.48	1.17	1.71	1.37	1.75	2.27	2.16	1.36	1.45	1.63	.12
Skien	21	1.29	1.56	1.88	2.16	2.20	1.90	2.07	1.88	1.74	1.85	.09
Telemark	22	1.26	1.83	1.49	2.11	1.72	1.77	2.31	2.01	1.90	1.82	.10
Notodden	23	1.02	1.53	1.73	1.40	2.04	1.68	1.32	2.09	1.27	1.56	.11
Rjukan	24	1.49	1.49	1.17	1.62	1.73	2.33	1.52	2.49	.80	1.62	.16
Kragerø	25	1.38	1.77	1.53	2.12	1.46	1.12	.76	1.65	1.33	1.46	.12
Arendal	26	1.58	1.56	1.81	1.47	1.76	1.77	1.91	1.85	2.07	1.75	.06
Kristians.	27	2.27	2.50	2.36	2.35	2.33	2.41	2.32	2.39	2.47	2.38	.02
Vest-Agder	28	.74	.92	.62	.62	.58	1.42	.75	1.13	1.19	.89	.09
Rogaland	29	1.82	1.99	1.89	2.09	1.78	1.91	1.91	1.78	1.92	1.90	.03
Stavanger	30	1.97	2.29	2.18	1.93	2.06	1.92	2.10	1.87	1.94	2.03	.04
Haugesund	31	1.71	1.82	1.82	1.76	1.37	1.37	1.44	1.68	1.59	1.62	.06
Hardanger	32	2.20	1.95	2.11	1.41	1.81	1.82	1.67	.85	1.57	1.71	.13
Hordaland	33	1.02	.74	.98	1.00	1.10	1.24	1.45	1.37	1.55	1.16	.08
Bergen	34	2.62	2.39	2.33	2.15	2.33	2.02	2.01	1.83	2.09	2.20	.08
Sogn	35	.18	.13	-.21	.04	.79	.45	.13	-.21	.19	.17	.10
Fjordane	36	.39	.63	.27	.39	-.00	.41	-.32	.48	1.33	.40	.14
Sunnmøre	37	1.38	1.43	1.54	1.81	1.63	1.14	1.60	1.33	1.18	1.45	.07
Romsdal	38	.93	1.64	1.61	1.43	1.55	1.49	1.38	1.44	1.21	1.41	.07
Nordmøre	39	1.42	1.58	1.92	1.81	1.31	1.18	1.31	1.72	1.25	1.50	.08
Ut-Trønd.	40	.80	1.08	1.20	.75	1.04	1.25	1.41	1.64	1.63	1.20	.10
Trondheim	41	2.38	2.49	2.14	1.78	1.82	1.88	1.65	1.51	1.61	1.92	.11
Inn-Trønd.	42	1.05	1.49	1.67	1.68	1.78	1.83	1.95	2.03	1.76	1.69	.09
Namdal	43	1.03	1.48	1.22	1.23	1.18	1.30	1.30	1.18	1.16	1.23	.04
Helgeland	44	1.80	1.59	1.79	1.43	1.41	1.37	1.66	1.41	1.61	1.56	.05
Bodø	45	1.99	2.05	2.21	2.06	2.32	2.21	1.52	1.86	2.01	2.02	.07
Narvik	46	1.82	1.91	1.68	1.81	1.75	1.65	1.54	1.57	1.61	1.70	.04
Lof. & Ves.	47	1.06	1.00	1.38	1.44	1.44	1.41	1.47	1.47	1.54	1.36	.06
Senja	48	1.42	1.33	1.52	1.51	1.33	1.51	1.55	1.67	1.83	1.52	.05
Troms	49	1.72	1.83	1.86	1.72	1.76	1.68	1.83	1.52	1.87	1.76	.04
Vest-Finnm.	50	1.80	1.92	.86	1.09	.99	1.44	1.72	1.84	1.15	1.42	.13
Vardø	51	1.84	2.28	1.92	2.56	2.17	1.77	2.05	1.86	1.31	1.97	.11
Vadsø	52	1.22	1.30	.92	1.65	1.73	1.84	2.30	1.31	.69	1.44	.15
Sør-Var.	53	2.57	1.90	1.62	1.81	1.88	2.02	2.28	2.22	2.36	2.08	.10
Mean		1.52	1.65	1.61	1.63	1.65	1.67	1.71	1.67	1.63	1.64	.02
St. dev.		.63	.61	.63	.65	.60	.62	.59	.58	.59	.61	.01
Kurtosis		.25	1.39	2.05	.82	1.29	.70	4.10	3.93	.79	1.70	.47
Skewness		- .30	- .91	-1.12	- .76	- .88	- .44	-1.49	-1.30	- .53	-.01	.33

APPENDIX D: DATA - VARIOUS TYPES OF CRIME

This appendix contains the data used in the empirical analyses of section 6.6. The data on the total number of crimes and clear-ups for each police district in the period 1972-78 have been provided by the Norwegian Social Science Data Services (NSD). As for the various types of crime, data have been obtained from unpublished material at Statistics Norway.

For convenience, the tables for the various types of crime have been numbered according to the numbers given by Statistics Norway to these various types of crime:

13 Offence against public order and peace.
18 Forgery.
19 Sexual offence.
21 Offence against the personal liberty.
22 Offence of violence against the person.
23 Slander and libel.
24 Embezzlement.
26 Fraud and breach of trust.
28 Offence inflicting damage to property.
40 Aggravated larcenies.
41 Simple larcenies.
43 Theft of motor vehicles.

For each type of crime the following tables are included for the 53 police districts of Norway in the period 1972-78:

1. Covariance matrix of the logs of the crime and clear-ups rates.
2. Crime rates (number of crimes per population).
3. Clear-up rates (number of clear-ups per population).

Table 13.1

Covariance matrix of logs of crime and clear-up rates of offences against public order and peace

	CRIMES							CLEAR-UPS						
	1972	1973	1974	1975	1976	1977	1978	1972	1973	1974	1975	1976	1977	1978
C 1972	.9201													
R 1973	.4483	.7483												
I 1974	.2827	.3697	.7912											
M 1975	.3116	.3323	.3717	.8589										
E 1976	.2977	.3127	.3480	.3654	.6138									
S 1977	.2953	.2974	.3319	.3171	.3758	.6827								
1978	.3026	.2307	.3016	.2773	.3249	.3117	.7668							
C 1972	.5617	.2814	.1496	.2425	.2315	.2118	.2548	1.0778						
L 1973	.3994	.4415	.2711	.3003	.2914	.2801	.1932	.4274	.6891					
E 1974	.2260	.1760	.1840	.1758	.2075	.1549	.1164	.2402	.2716	.6883				
A 1975	.2172	.1929	.1889	.2664	.3309	.2420	.1526	.1855	.1968	.2193	.4811			
R 1976	.2085	.1985	.2231	.2883	.4577	.2738	.2630	.2426	.2580	.2332	.3421	.8437		
U 1977	.2228	.2470	.2235	.2171	.2712	.3437	.1989	.2478	.2563	.2152	.1929	.1830	.5699	
P 1978	.3149	.1983	.1810	.1832	.1977	.2105	.3036	.2828	.2194	.1691	.0977	.2000	.2121	.6113

Table 13.2
Crime rates of offence against public order and peace, police districts, 1972-78

Police district	No	1972	1973	1974	1975	1976	1977	1978
Oslo	1	.07	.12	.11	.17	.18	.14	.14
Halden	2	.26	.37	.31	.40	.37	.51	.97
Sarpsborg	3	1.33	1.10	.66	.60	.28	.23	.48
Fredrikstad	4	3.87	3.92	.73	2.02	2.94	1.21	1.01
Moss	5	.04	.22	.10	.02	.17	.19	.48
Follo	6	1.62	.64	.36	1.13	1.01	.56	.73
Romerike	7	.71	.64	.84	.64	.57	.62	.50
Kongsvinger	8	.24	.52	.41	.33	.45	.38	.49
Hamar	9	.45	.53	.65	.87	.52	.76	.56
Østerdal	10	1.04	.81	.30	.38	.60	.46	.59
Gudbrandsd.	11	.37	.23	.36	.45	.49	.27	.48
Vest-Oppl.	12	.39	.33	.47	.55	.67	.28	.59
Ringerike	13	1.25	1.07	2.09	1.63	2.21	1.49	1.59
Asker & B.	14	.66	1.22	.61	.49	.47	.53	.48
Drammen	15	1.99	1.70	1.60	1.41	.98	1.71	1.66
Kongsberg	16	.85	1.25	.91	1.10	.82	.71	.78
N.-Jarlsb.	17	1.00	1.27	.99	.70	.66	1.05	1.42
Tønsberg	18	2.59	2.57	1.41	2.45	1.97	2.27	2.67
Sandefjord	19	2.46	1.45	2.81	1.89	1.77	1.47	2.25
Larvik	20	1.09	1.61	1.81	1.74	2.61	1.89	1.88
Skien	21	.66	.84	1.77	1.42	1.82	1.95	1.32
Telemark	22	1.09	1.70	1.20	1.35	1.33	1.16	1.38
Notodden	23	.66	1.28	1.33	1.05	1.59	1.77	.73
Rjukan	24	.37	1.26	.64	.90	.39	.65	.26
Kragerø	25	1.02	1.75	1.27	1.40	.93	.66	.53
Arendal	26	1.31	1.10	1.07	1.27	1.08	1.22	1.08
Kristians.	27	1.01	.80	.78	1.10	1.18	1.00	1.54
Vest-Agder	28	.26	.24	.47	.47	.83	.88	.97
Rogaland	29	.63	.81	1.03	.45	.70	1.17	1.00
Stavanger	30	1.87	2.11	1.41	1.75	1.32	1.30	1.33
Haugesund	31	.42	.29	.61	1.13	.39	.84	1.74
Hardanger	32	1.65	.67	.52	.78	.37	.48	.56
Hordaland	33	.41	.36	.66	.88	1.16	.75	.78
Bergen	34	2.02	2.02	1.64	1.64	1.92	2.08	2.10
Sogn	35	.15	.15	.08	.05		.03	.03
Fjordane	36	.16	.06	.05	.13	.13	.19	.30
Sunnmøre	37	.69	.93	.65	.50	.67	.58	.52
Romsdal	38	.43	.77	.50	.44	.79	.88	.67
Nordmøre	39	.93	.88	.38	.41	.56	.44	.56
Ut-Trønd.	40	.79	.68	.69	.83	.91	.76	.49
Trondheim	41	.54	.58	.59	.31	.10	.34	.42
Inn-Trønd.	42	.59	.23	.26	.45	.93	1.30	.66
Namdal	43	.19	.19	.11	.19	.19	.22	.06
Helgeland	44	.55	.21	.30	.51	.51	.54	.69
Bodø	45	1.06	.65	1.15	1.09	1.28	.73	1.00
Narvik	46	1.10	.85	.59	.94	.48	.60	.58
Lof. & Ves.	47	.38	.31	.35	.28	.28	.30	.25
Senja	48	.49	.83	.44	.50	.88	.92	.63
Troms	49	1.42	1.52	1.82	.94	1.55	.75	1.56
Vest-Finnm.	50	.07	.91	1.88	2.14	1.02	.56	.37
Vardø	51	1.25	1.65	.67	1.06	.49	1.16	.20
Vadsø	52	.14	.20	.60	.66	1.38	.86	.20
Sør-Var.	53	1.32	1.50	2.87	2.49	2.57	2.56	1.58

Table 13.3
Clear-up rates of offence against public order and peace, police districts, 1972-78

Police district	No	1972	1973	1974	1975	1976	1977	1978
Oslo	1	.03	.04	.04	.06	.05	.07	.05
Halden	2	.12	.06	.17	.14	.23	.11	.20
Sarpsborg	3	.34	.16	.13	.08	.14	.07	.19
Fredrikstad	4	1.26	1.65	.31	.79	.87	.33	.12
Moss	5	.02	.14	.04		.02	.17	.11
Follo	6	.41	.12	.11	.27	.32	.13	.17
Romerike	7	.16	.13	.13	.17	.14	.23	.08
Kongsvinger	8	.09	.09	.06	.02	.09	.18	.16
Hamar	9	.15	.14	.22	.22	.28	.33	.16
Østerdal	10	.14	.10	.08	.12	.16	.12	.26
Gudbrandsd.	11	.07	.01	.06	.22	.23	.04	.03
Vest-Oppl.	12	.07	.08	.23	.23	.26	.04	.19
Ringerike	13	.26	.49	.93	.24	.86	.36	.59
Asker & B.	14	.01	.06	.15	.10	.10	.15	.12
Drammen	15	.35	.38	.16	.13	.22	.36	.29
Kongsberg	16	.31	.25	.05	.18	.27	.22	.17
N.-Jarlsb.	17	.21	.37	.12	.12	.20	.22	.59
Tønsberg	18	.28	.54	.14	.23	.37	.42	.41
Sandefjord	19	.33	.05	.32	.24	.32	.56	.58
Larvik	20	.22	.14	.03	.27	.91	.08	.37
Skien	21	.16	.11	.05	.14	.18	.23	.04
Telemark	22	.20	.48	.17	.17	.28	.31	.18
Notodden	23	.23	.16	.55	.39	.31	.42	.08
Rjukan	24	.12	.13		.39	.39	.26	
Kragerø	25	.14	.34		.07	.07		.26
Arendal	26	.47	.22	.43	.26	.37	.26	.15
Kristians.	27	.30	.08	.11	.28	.23	.27	.35
Vest-Agder	28	.02	.04	.06	.27	.25	.15	.19
Rogaland	29	.15	.17	.18	.13	.19	.30	.20
Stavanger	30	.34	.30	.16	.31	.21	.32	.26
Haugesund	31	.20	.16	.10	.10	.11	.16	.22
Hardanger	32	1.21	.33	.30	.30	.11	.15	.34
Hordaland	33	.05	.14	.22	.28	.33	.15	.15
Bergen	34	.41	.46	.29	.27	.22	.22	.36
Sogn	35	.05		.03			.03	.03
Fjordane	36	.02		.02	.05	.02	.08	.05
Sunnmøre	37	.12	.40	.14	.12	.19	.15	.15
Romsdal	38	.06	.27	.19	.21	.28	.20	.09
Nordmøre	39	.45	.29	.13	.16	.26	.21	.22
Ut-Trønd.	40	.34	.16	.14	.19	.19	.30	.12
Trondheim	41	.08	.07	.04	.04	.01	.11	.09
Inn-Trønd.	42	.40	.16	.21	.21	.39	.87	.30
Namdal	43		.08		.08	.14	.08	.03
Helgeland	44	.24	.07	.07	.09	.20	.07	.15
Bodø	45	.20	.14	.56	.21	.19	.15	.27
Narvik	46	.06	.25	.11	.09	.11	.06	.14
Lof. & Ves.	47	.15	.18	.10	.08	.12	.03	.03
Senja	48	.11	.15	.11	.29	.19	.36	.17
Troms	49	.24	.32	.30	.19	.37	.13	.18
Vest-Finnm.	50	.02	.22	.16	.26	.33	.16	.07
Vardø	51	.10	.19	.19	.29	.10	.29	.10
Vadsø	52		.07	.20	.46	.99	.46	.13
Sør-Var.	53	.09	.47	.09	.64	.46	.37	.28

Table 18.1

Covariance matrix of logs of crime and clear-up rates of forgery

				C R I M E S							C L E A R - U P S			
	1972	1973	1974	1975	1976	1977	1978	1972	1973	1974	1975	1976	1977	1978
C 1972	.4649													
R 1973	.1444	.7114												
I 1974	.2373	.3232	.5455											
M 1975	.1661	.2822	.2935	.5477										
E 1976	.1748	.1743	.1816	.1479	.6444									
S 1977	.0695	.1986	.1526	.1479	.0827	.3051								
1978	.1934	.2290	.2120	.1612	.1013	.1541	.4911							
C 1972	.3905	.1472	.2385	.1520	.1651	.0823	.2226	.5147						
L 1973	.1217	.5943	.3507	.3364	.1942	.1956	.1977	.1405	.7004					
E 1974	.2881	.3139	.5446	.3014	.2496	.1692	.1874	.2832	.3384	.7412				
A 1975	.1535	.2694	.2598	.5319	.1436	.1508	.1508	.1579	.3291	.2611	.6151			
R 1976	.1400	.1512	.1715	.1436	.4060	.0919	.1023	.1556	.2275	.2481	.1697	.6496		
U 1977	.0544	.1887	.1683	.1683	.0803	.1890	.1532	.0997	.2549	.1893	.1783	.1464	.4050	
P 1978	.2067	.1897	.2290	.1415	.0694	.1482	.4304	.2455	.1689	.2173	.1440	.0915	.1721	.4878

Table 18.2
Crime rates of forgery, police districts, 1972-78

Police district	No	1972	1973	1974	1975	1976	1977	1978
Oslo	1	.19	.52	.31	.28	.28	.21	.25
Halden	2	.09	.14	.26	.20	.20	.26	.06
Sarpsborg	3	.32	.19	.37	.21	.25	.14	.56
Fredrikstad	4	.25	.39	.46	.88	.56	.30	.30
Moss	5	.04	.10	.04	.29	.17	.09	.15
Follo	6	.13	.12	.11	.10	.09	.16	.26
Romerike	7	.10	.15	.12	.13	.14	.19	.13
Kongsvinger	8	.17	.15	.07	.04	.18	.13	.20
Hamar	9	.14	.26	.17	.23	.44	.18	.24
Østerdal	10	.16	.16	.20	.14	.18	.12	.18
Gudbrandsd.	11	.07	.03	.03	.04	.32	.04	.03
Vest-Oppl.	12	.06	.08	.12	.17	.33	.10	.11
Ringerike	13	.15	.51	.35	.44	.26	.27	.12
Asker & B.	14	.16	.42	.17	.22	.41	.18	.24
Drammen	15	.18	.32	.21	.17	.71	.29	.23
Kongsberg	16	.05	.10	.18	.10	.10		.07
N.-Jarlsb.	17	.08	.14	.18	.28	.10	.18	.26
Tønsberg	18	.02	.23	.12	.09	.12	.19	.17
Sandefjord	19	.11	.03	.08	.16	.24	.16	.18
Larvik	20	.14	.05	.14	.05	.16	.11	.08
Skien	21	.05	.29	.18	.07	.12	.21	.19
Telemark	22	.11	.24	.06	.13	.11	.24	.52
Notodden	23	.04	.08	.04	.08	.12	.04	.08
Rjukan	24	.12		.26			.13	.13
Kragerø	25			.07		.07	.07	
Arendal	26	.13	.09	.10	.17	.18	.16	.25
Kristians.	27	.40	.18	.16	.19	.26	.12	.22
Vest-Agder	28	.08	.06	.06	.12	.02	.10	.09
Rogaland	29	.12	.06	.19	.18	.19	.22	.17
Stavanger	30	.19	.04	.22	.06	.16	.12	.29
Haugesund	31	.09	.03	.08	.04	.01	.14	.04
Hardanger	32	.11	.15		.11	.04	.04	.04
Hordaland	33	.07	.04	.05	.06	.18	.11	.06
Bergen	34	.19	.12	.22	.18	.25	.16	.21
Sogn	35	.02	.05	.10				
Fjordane	36	.02	.02	.02		.02	.08	.09
Sunnmøre	37	.05	.05	.10	.08	.09	.11	.06
Romsdal	38	.08	.19	.06	.25	.17	.35	.17
Nordmøre	39	.06	.06	.05		.11	.13	.06
Ut-Trønd.	40	.05	.10	.09	.11	.05	.13	.17
Trondheim	41	.08	.10	.12	.08	.09	.06	.03
Inn-Trønd.	42	.24	.12	.21	.14	.24	.23	.35
Namdal	43	.08	.08	.03	.11	.11	.11	.06
Helgeland	44	.14	.14	.11	.11	.20	.12	.25
Bodø	45	.29	.23	.21	.46	.15	.19	.16
Narvik	46	.11	.11	.06	.03	.14	.20	.14
Lof. & Ves.	47	.07	.13	.07	.03	.23	.13	.15
Senja	48	.09	.02	.04	.08	.13	.13	.13
Troms	49	.10	.13	.11	.13	.12	.10	.17
Vest-Finnm.	50		.02	.07	.05	.07	.05	
Vardø	51	.10			.10	.29	.29	
Vadsø	52	.14			.46	.20	.13	.07
Sør-Var.	53	.28			.18	.09	.55	.09

Table 18.3
Clear-up rates of forgery, police districts, 1972-78

Police district	No	1972	1973	1974	1975	1976	1977	1978
Oslo	1	.12	.44	.23	.15	.14	.15	.15
Halden	2	.03	.14	.26	.14	.17	.20	.06
Sarpsborg	3	.16	.09	.26	.13	.18	.08	.53
Fredrikstad	4	.22	.34	.39	.79	.48	.22	.28
Moss	5	.02	.08	.02	.25	.09	.06	.09
Follo	6	.08	.09	.11	.06	.07	.14	.22
Romerike	7	.08	.10	.08	.09	.10	.16	.09
Kongsvinger	8	.15	.11	.06	.04	.18	.09	.20
Hamar	9	.13	.21	.11	.17	.37	.13	.13
Østerdal	10	.10	.12	.12	.08	.12	.10	.12
Gudbrandsd.	11	.06	.03	.03	.04	.25	.04	.03
Vest-Oppl.	12	.05	.07	.09	.14	.29	.06	.07
Ringerike	13	.14	.48	.34	.29	.23	.19	.12
Asker & B.	14	.12	.30	.11	.17	.31	.11	.16
Drammen	15	.06	.25	.15	.13	.28	.19	.14
Kongsberg	16	.03	.08	.10	.05	.05		.07
N.-Jarlsb.	17	.06	.10	.16	.22	.08	.18	.22
Tønsberg	18	.02	.18	.05	.07	.12	.19	.14
Sandefjord	19	.08	.03	.08	.16	.21	.11	.13
Larvik	20	.14	.05	.08	.03	.16	.11	
Skien	21	.05	.24	.15	.05	.09	.11	.11
Telemark	22	.09	.17	.02	.13	.11	.16	.36
Notodden	23	.04	.04			.04	.04	.08
Rjukan	24	.12		.26				
Kragerø	25					.07	.07	
Arendal	26	.11	.04	.05	.08	.03	.06	.15
Kristians.	27	.38	.14	.11	.13	.17	.11	.15
Vest-Agder	28	.08	.06	.02	.12	.02	.08	.09
Rogaland	29	.12	.06	.19	.16	.18	.21	.15
Stavanger	30	.12	.02	.15	.04	.10	.06	.28
Haugesund	31	.04	.03	.08	.03	.01	.10	
Hardanger	32	.11	.15		.11	.04	.04	.04
Hordaland	33	.05	.04	.01	.04	.16	.10	.05
Bergen	34	.14	.07	.13	.12	.19	.08	.13
Sogn	35	.02	.05	.10				
Fjordane	36	.02	.02	.02			.06	.03
Sunnmøre	37	.04	.04	.09	.06	.09	.10	.05
Romsdal	38	.08	.12	.04	.23	.13	.34	.11
Nordmøre	39	.05	.05	.02		.10	.13	.06
Ut-Trønd.	40	.02	.07	.05	.07	.03	.09	.15
Trondheim	41	.05	.07	.10	.05	.03	.04	.02
Inn-Trønd.	42	.22	.12	.21	.12	.22	.21	.35
Namdal	43	.03	.03	.03	.08	.08	.03	.03
Helgeland	44	.10	.09	.11	.09	.17	.12	.21
Bodø	45	.25	.20	.21	.40	.09	.16	.15
Narvik	46	.11	.03	.06	.03	.06	.09	.14
Lof. & Ves.	47	.05	.12	.07	.02	.20	.10	.10
Senja	48	.06	.02	.04	.04	.10	.13	.10
Troms	49	.07	.11	.04	.10	.07	.06	.13
Vest-Finnm.	50			.05		.02	.02	
Vardø	51	.10			.10	.20	.29	
Vadsø	52	.07			.33	.20	.13	
Sør-Var.	53				.18	.09	.55	.09

Table 19.1

Covariance matrix of logs of crime and clear-up rates of sexual offences

		C R I M E S							C L E A R - U P S						
		1972	1973	1974	1975	1976	1977	1978	1972	1973	1974	1975	1976	1977	1978
C	1972	.3291													
R	1973	.1997	.4127												
I	1974	.2294	.2848	.4493											
M	1975	.1240	.1705	.1552	.3848										
E	1976	.1381	.2047	.1413	.1261	.5052									
S	1977	.1812	.2090	.1871	.1673	.0972	.3093								
	1978	.0714	.1420	.1016	.1837	.0466	.0968	.4308							
C	1972	.2549	.0552	.1622	.0827	.0623	.1115	.0634	.4862						
L	1973	.1201	.3580	.1832	.1577	.1484	.1345	.1489	.0910	.4464					
E	1974	.1175	.2214	.3958	.1483	.0556	.1373	.0739	.1876	.2123	.5313				
A	1975	.0369	.1342	.0984	.3214	.0216	.1291	.2577	.0725	.1943	.1906	.5454			
R	1976	.0736	.1442	.1091	.1068	.2689	.0700	.0184	.0826	.1727	.1098	.1021	.5547		
U	1977	.1604	.1979	.2687	.1244	.0808	.2439	.0543	.1331	.1898	.2920	.1640	.2085	.4570	
P	1978	.0074	.0347	.0415	.0780	.0001	.0556	.2661	.0875	.0804	.1418	.2119	.0001	.1437	.4776

Table 19.2
Crime rates of sexual offence, police districts, 1972-78

Police district	No	1972	1973	1974	1975	1976	1977	1978
Oslo	1	.37	.37	.42	.35	.43	.34	.37
Halden	2	.12	.17	.20	.26	.06	.26	.26
Sarpsborg	3	.22	.32	.26	.32	.28	.12	.25
Fredrikstad	4	.14	.05	.19	.22	.14	.12	.08
Moss	5	.16	.12	.23	.12	.15	.06	.15
Follo	6	.17	.33	.11	.15	.19	.17	.18
Romerike	7	.15	.20	.16	.11	.11	.21	.11
Kongsvinger	8	.13	.11	.17	.07	.07	.11	.02
Hamar	9	.18	.15	.06	.18	.18	.10	.14
Østerdal	10	.16	.08	.12	.04	.14	.12	.12
Gudbrandsd.	11	.06	.10	.04		.01	.09	.06
Vest-Oppl.	12	.16	.11	.12	.07	.06	.11	.17
Ringerike	13	.09	.21	.14	.14	.18	.10	.13
Asker & B.	14	.36	.28	.22	.24	.23	.20	.11
Drammen	15	.32	.20	.20	.22	.15	.16	.13
Kongsberg	16	.15	.18	.10	.10	.07	.10	.07
N.-Jarlsb.	17	.21	.18	.18	.06	.06	.18	.08
Tønsberg	18	.18	.18	.11	.05	.14	.14	.16
Sandefjord	19	.58	.19	.19	.30	.51	.32	.42
Larvik	20	.19	.11	.19	.19	.19	.08	.08
Skien	21	.35	.20	.11	.05	.23	.14	.14
Telemark	22	.20	.37	.07	.26	.22	.20	.34
Notodden	23	.20	.19	.08	.08	.19	.31	.19
Rjukan	24		.25	.13		.13		.13
Kragerø	25		.07	.07				
Arendal	26	.31	.08	.18	.13	.10	.10	.20
Kristians.	27	.31	.30	.53	.43	.22	.29	.21
Vest-Agder	28	.08	.08	.10	.18	.04	.17	.11
Rogaland	29	.07	.19	.09	.15	.28	.12	.20
Stavanger	30	.40	.32	.37	.36	.33	.32	.34
Haugesund	31	.14	.07	.09	.13	.11	.20	.06
Hardanger	32	.22		.18	.30	.07	.04	
Hordaland	33	.17	.14	.10	.30	.13	.15	.15
Bergen	34	.61	.49	.64	.49	.42	.52	.43
Sogn	35	.05	.05	.10	.05			
Fjordane	36	.05	.03	.05	.14	.06	.05	.47
Sunnmøre	37	.17	.14	.26	.16	.20	.18	.16
Romsdal	38	.37	.14	.17	.13	.32	.17	.04
Nordmøre	39	.23	.13	.30	.16	.11	.38	.19
Ut-Trønd.	40	.30	.06	.12	.16	.13	.16	.23
Trondheim	41	.24	.34	.20	.21	.20	.22	.32
Inn-Trønd.	42	.34	.23	.08	.13	.16	.19	.15
Namdal	43	.11	.06	.06	.11	.11	.08	.11
Helgeland	44	.26	.27	.22	.10	.21	.17	.31
Bodø	45	.46	.30	.39	.60	.07	.31	.53
Narvik	46	.28	.23	.34	.11	.26	.09	.14
Lof. & Ves.	47	.33	.18	.15	.13	.10	.30	.25
Senja	48	.15	.13	.11	.13	.17	.17	.21
Troms	49	.31	.19	.28	.07	.15	.10	.11
Vest-Finnm.	50	.15	.12	.07	.19	.21	.23	.12
Vardø	51	.29	.77	.86	.19	.29	.29	.20
Vadsø	52	.14	.20	.60	.33	1.19		.13
Sør-Var.	53	.19	.19	.19	.28	.18		.37

Table 19.3
Clear-up rates of sexual offence, police districts, 1972-78

Police district	No	1972	1973	1974	1975	1976	1977	1978
Oslo	1	.12	.11	.11	.07	.10	.11	.09
Halden	2	.06	.06	.17	.26	.06	.20	.17
Sarpsborg	3	.09	.12	.20	.16	.13	.07	.12
Fredrikstad	4	.12	.05	.11	.09	.06	.06	.05
Moss	5	.08	.08	.10	.04	.06	.06	.04
Follo	6	.02	.14	.03	.09	.09	.13	.08
Romerike	7	.05	.07	.08	.03	.05	.09	.08
Kongsvinger	8	.11	.06	.06		.07	.11	
Hamar	9	.14	.13	.06	.08	.10	.08	.04
Østerdal	10	.06	.02	.04	.02	.04	.06	.06
Gudbrandsd.	11	.04	.01	.03			.07	.03
Vest-Oppl.	12	.07	.04	.06	.03	.02	.02	.12
Ringerike	13	.02	.15	.11	.11	.12	.09	.09
Asker & B.	14	.07	.04	.03	.05	.05	.03	.02
Drammen	15	.14	.09	.12	.07	.04	.05	.06
Kongsberg	16	.08	.05	.08	.03	.05		.05
N.-Jarlsb.	17	.15	.10	.12	.04	.02	.06	.04
Tønsberg	18		.09	.05	.02	.02	.05	.07
Sandefjord	19	.19	.11	.03	.08	.24	.08	.03
Larvik	20	.05		.08	.13	.05	.05	
Skien	21	.13	.13	.07		.05	.09	.05
Telemark	22	.13	.24	.04	.11	.04	.02	.11
Notodden	23	.08	.16			.15	.23	.08
Rjukan	24		.13	.13		.13		.13
Kragerø	25		.07	.07				
Arendal	26	.21	.04	.08	.09	.05	.04	.11
Kristians.	27	.14	.21	.30	.28	.13	.19	.06
Vest-Agder	28	.02	.08	.04	.12		.04	.06
Rogaland	29	.07	.13	.07	.14	.21	.03	.03
Stavanger	30	.12	.10	.15	.16	.11	.16	.12
Haugesund	31	.04	.04	.04	.04	.05	.05	.01
Hardanger	32	.15		.15	.26			
Hordaland	33	.11	.06	.05	.22	.10	.07	.10
Bergen	34	.20	.17	.27	.16	.14	.20	.20
Sogn	35	.05	.05	.10	.05			
Fjordane	36	.05	.03	.05	.10	.03	.02	.30
Sunnmøre	37	.12	.05	.17	.05	.10	.10	.07
Romsdal	38	.27	.06	.13	.02	.17	.09	.04
Nordmøre	39	.14	.10	.18	.08	.10	.32	.18
Ut-Trønd.	40	.27	.03	.11	.14	.07	.10	.18
Trondheim	41	.07	.15	.09	.07	.08	.06	.12
Inn-Trønd.	42	.27	.23	.06	.08	.13	.11	.13
Namdal	43	.11	.06	.03	.06	.11	.08	.11
Helgeland	44	.20	.14	.09	.06	.10	.14	.16
Bodø	45	.26	.15	.21	.40	.03	.13	.22
Narvik	46	.20	.11	.20	.09	.20	.06	.03
Lof. & Ves.	47	.28	.10	.08	.10	.07	.18	.18
Senja	48		.08	.04	.04	.08	.08	.08
Troms	49	.12	.05	.05	.02	.06	.06	.08
Vest-Finnm.	50	.07	.02	.05	.09	.09	.07	.05
Vardø	51	.19	.29	.76	.10	.20	.29	.10
Vadsø	52	.07	.13	.47	.07	1.12		.07
Sør-Var.	53	.09	.19	.19	.09	.18		.19

Table 21.1

Covariance matrix of logs of crime and clear-up rates of offence against the personal liberty

		CRIMES							CLEAR-UPS					
		1972	1973	1974	1975	1976	1977	1978	1972	1973	1974	1975	1976	1977	1978
C	1972	.7165													
R	1973	.2484	.5721												
I	1974	.4518	.2894	.6275											
M	1975	.3400	.2321	.2669	.4500										
E	1976	.2861	.1887	.2632	.2905	.4040									
S	1977	.4311	.2116	.3208	.3940	.3960	.6909								
	1978	.5126	.2022	.3329	.3097	.2505	.4382	.6536							
C	1972	.5864	.1999	.4203	.2552	.1712	.2425	.3712	.7032						
L	1973	.2186	.3691	.3022	.2078	.1580	.2009	.1340	.2132	.6557					
E	1974	.4424	.2981	.4680	.2758	.2666	.3541	.3399	.4462	.3813	.5875				
A	1975	.3525	.2215	.3017	.3844	.2644	.3837	.2812	.3033	.2866	.3936	.5041			
R	1976	.3325	.2125	.2979	.3015	.3237	.4043	.2128	.2380	.2480	.2992	.3214	.5630		
U	1977	.2576	.1238	.1745	.3105	.2578	.4858	.3052	.1677	.1359	.2477	.2969	.2865	.6008	
P	1978	.5277	.1924	.3859	.2593	.2210	.3041	.4827	.4956	.1360	.3342	.2110	.2347	.2182	.5440

Table 21.2
Crime rates of offence against the personal liberty, police districts, 1972-78

Police district	No	1972	1973	1974	1975	1976	1977	1978
Oslo	1	.28	.30	.35	.32	.44	.40	.49
Halden	2	.03	.06	.26	.17	.06		.20
Sarpsborg	3	.24	.23	.25	.21	.17	.23	.21
Fredrikstad	4	.23	.08	.11	.31	.20	.19	.19
Moss	5	.12	.10	.19	.04	.06	.04	.15
Follo	6	.14	.16	.15	.07	.16	.13	.12
Romerike	7	.13	.21	.15	.12	.18	.14	.16
Kongsvinger	8		.06		.06	.04	.05	.02
Hamar	9	.04	.08	.06	.15	.08	.09	.10
Østerdal	10	.12	.04	.12	.06	.10	.16	.06
Gudbrandsd.	11	.03	.04	.01	.03		.01	
Vest-Oppl.	12	.07	.02	.06	.09	.09	.10	.07
Ringerike	13	.06	.14	.09	.23	.12	.03	.04
Asker & B.	14	.10	.18	.11	.15	.13	.22	.11
Drammen	15	.05	.11	.04	.10	.11	.22	.13
Kongsberg	16	.10	.08	.10	.08	.10	.15	.10
N.-Jarlsb.	17	.08	.02	.04	.04	.06	.06	
Tønsberg	18	.12	.11	.09	.11	.09	.07	.16
Sandefjord	19	.14	.05	.11	.13	.11	.24	.29
Larvik	20		.05	.05	.05	.03		.16
Skien	21	.05	.07	.07	.16	.11	.16	.12
Telemark	22	.07	.15	.09	.09	.15	.16	.16
Notodden	23	.12	.12	.19	.16	.12	.08	.04
Rjukan	24	.12	.25	.38	.13		.13	.13
Kragerø	25							
Arendal	26	.13	.07	.08	.14	.11	.09	.17
Kristians.	27	.20	.32	.26	.24	.15	.29	.45
Vest-Agder	28	.04	.04	.06	.12	.14	.08	.06
Rogaland	29		.04	.13	.14	.09	.10	.10
Stavanger	30	.09	.08	.08	.12	.17	.14	.07
Haugesund	31	.03	.07	.04	.05	.04	.04	.07
Hardanger	32			.18	.04			
Hordaland	33	.09	.04	.05	.07	.10	.05	.05
Bergen	34	.37	.27	.34	.39	.31	.29	.41
Sogn	35			.08	.13	.03		
Fjordane	36		.02	.02	.03	.03	.02	.09
Sunnmøre	37	.06	.05	.07	.03	.09	.13	.12
Romsdal	38	.02	.14	.08	.06	.09	.07	.09
Nordmøre	39	.08	.19	.08	.10	.05	.05	.03
Ut-Trønd.	40	.01	.02	.03	.20	.06	.09	.05
Trondheim	41	.04	.05	.03	.03	.03	.01	.08
Inn-Trønd.	42	.01	.12	.06	.06	.10	.03	.01
Namdal	43		.03	.11	.08	.17	.06	.06
Helgeland	44	.05	.05	.02	.06	.09	.05	.04
Bodø	45	.03	.18	.02	.07	.07	.12	.16
Narvik	46	.08	.06	.11	.06	.11	.03	.12
Lof. & Ves.	47	.07	.07	.05	.10	.17	.18	.15
Senja	48	.04	.06	.04	.06	.10	.04	.02
Troms	49	.08	.11	.06	.15	.12	.16	.22
Vest-Finnm.	50	.02	.02	.12	.05	.26	.12	.23
Vardø	51	.29	.10	.19		.20	.19	
Vadsø	52		.13	.07	.33	.33	.46	.07
Sør-Var.	53	.28	.09	.37		.09	.09	.28

Table 21.3

Clear-up rates of offence against the personal liberty, police districts, 1972-78

Police district	No	1972	1973	1974	1975	1976	1977	1978
Oslo	1	.07	.13	.16	.13	.11	.10	.16
Halden	2	.03		.06	.14			.11
Sarpsborg	3	.12	.09	.13	.14	.07	.09	.12
Fredrikstad	4	.12		.05	.19	.05	.08	.09
Moss	5	.10	.08	.08	.04	.06	.02	.09
Follo	6	.03	.08	.06	.04	.09	.03	.08
Romerike	7	.08	.15	.09	.08	.09	.08	.09
Kongsvinger	8		.04				.04	
Hamar	9	.03	.08	.04	.10	.06	.06	.04
Østerdal	10	.08	.04	.06	.04	.04	.06	.06
Gudbrandsd.	11	.01	.03					
Vest-Oppl.	12	.03		.03	.06	.04	.06	.02
Ringerike	13	.03	.09	.06	.15	.08		.01
Asker & B.	14	.03	.11	.07	.08	.07	.10	.03
Drammen	15	.02	.04	.01	.03	.06	.13	.04
Kongsberg	16	.05	.03	.03		.02	.10	.02
N.-Jarlsb.	17	.06	.02	.04	.02	.04	.02	
Tønsberg	18	.09	.05	.05	.07	.03	.05	.10
Sandefjord	19	.08	.05	.11	.13	.05	.19	.08
Larvik	20		.03		.05			.05
Skien	21	.02	.04	.02	.07	.05	.09	.07
Telemark	22	.02	.15	.06	.07	.07	.11	.07
Notodden	23		.04	.08	.08	.08	.08	.04
Rjukan	24		.25					.13
Kragerø	25							
Arendal	26	.08	.04	.03	.08	.05	.04	.10
Kristians.	27	.08	.21	.14	.09	.11	.15	.21
Vest-Agder	28	.02	.02	.04	.04	.06	.08	.06
Rogaland	29		.04	.06	.06	.03	.06	.03
Stavanger	30	.04	.05	.04	.08	.10	.09	.05
Haugesund	31	.01	.05	.04	.04	.01	.03	.01
Hardanger	32			.18	.04			
Hordaland	33		.01		.02	.01	.01	.03
Bergen	34	.28	.14	.21	.18	.16	.16	.25
Sogn	35			.05	.05	.03		
Fjordane	36			.02	.03		.02	.03
Sunnmøre	37	.04	.04	.05	.03	.06	.09	.08
Romsdal	38	.02	.08	.08	.04	.02	.06	.04
Nordmøre	39	.06	.18	.06	.08	.05	.05	.03
Ut-Trønd.	40	.01	.01		.14	.01	.05	.04
Trondheim	41	.02	.01	.01	.01	.01	.01	.06
Inn-Trønd.	42	.01	.10	.02	.03	.06	.02	.01
Namdal	43		.03	.06	.03	.14	.03	
Helgeland	44	.01	.04		.06	.04	.02	.04
Bodø	45	.02	.11		.06	.06	.04	.07
Narvik	46			.03	.03	.03		.06
Lof. & Ves.	47	.02	.03	.03	.07	.07	.07	.02
Senja	48	04			.06	.04	.02	.02
Troms	49		.03		.02	.07	.04	.05
Vest-Finnm.	50	.02				.07		.07
Vardø	51			.10		.20		
Vadsø	52		.13	.07	.26	.33	.27	.07
Sør-Var.	53	.19	.09	.28				.19

Table 22.1

Covariance matrix of logs of crime and clear-up rates of offence of violence against the person

| | | CRIMES | | | | | | | CLEAR-UPS | | | | | |
	1972	1973	1974	1975	1976	1977	1978	1972	1973	1974	1975	1976	1977	1978
C 1972	.3079													
R 1973	.2347	.2758												
I 1974	.2187	.2145	.2664											
M 1975	.2022	.1863	.2158	.2543										
E 1976	.2312	.2077	.2885	.2890	.4912									
S 1977	.1741	.1551	.1766	.2057	.2831	.2342								
1978	.1545	.1524	.1587	.1871	.1782	.1429	.2198							
C 1972	.3157	.2316	.2172	.1963	.2131	.1657	.1647	.3708						
L 1973	.2314	.2738	.2044	.1722	.2047	.1505	.1507	.2411	.2985					
E 1974	.2309	.2194	.2695	.2073	.2940	.1753	.1538	.2442	.2304	.3165				
A 1975	.2083	.1873	.2104	.2254	.2577	.1847	.1639	.2199	.1878	.2314	.2402			
R 1976	.2567	.2354	.3207	.2981	.5412	.2929	.1748	.2500	.2423	.3376	.2833	.6371		
U 1977	.1800	.1749	.1716	.1927	.2771	.2299	.1430	.1778	.1895	.1873	.1892	.3060	.2712	
P 1978	.1737	.1660	.1511	.1687	.1797	.1519	.2085	.1931	.1796	.1725	.1630	.1877	.1789	.2705

Table 22.2
Crime rates of offence of violence against the person, police districts, 1972-78

Police district	No	1972	1973	1974	1975	1976	1977	1978
Oslo	1	1.66	1.52	1.85	1.98	2.05	2.18	2.23
Halden	2	.63	.63	.43	.37	.26	.51	.86
Sarpsborg	3	.94	.95	1.03	1.06	.98	.95	1.03
Fredrikstad	4	.66	.62	.45	.74	.74	.75	.56
Moss	5	.57	.39	.93	.56	.55	.62	.78
Follo	6	.35	.59	.60	.50	.42	.54	.48
Romerike	7	.39	.46	.56	.59	.54	.64	.56
Kongsvinger	8	.15	.39	.37	.46	.44	.52	.70
Hamar	9	.36	.40	.66	.64	.62	.61	.79
Østerdal	10	.65	.43	.39	.46	.50	.80	.55
Gudbrandsd.	11	.46	.47	.51	.48	.52	.46	.53
Vest-Oppl.	12	.56	.48	.55	.56	.56	.53	.36
Ringerike	13	.60	.90	.75	.83	.81	.91	.92
Asker & B.	14	.64	.88	.91	.61	.85	.87	.61
Drammen	15	.70	.76	.61	.81	.66	.83	.85
Kongsberg	16	.41	.31	.53	.80	.65	.81	.83
N.-Jarlsb.	17	.42	.20	.40	.32	.56	.36	.30
Tønsberg	18	.49	.44	.35	.39	.35	.52	.78
Sandefjord	19	.99	1.04	1.35	.92	1.58	1.12	1.40
Larvik	20	.27	.49	.84	.43	.61	.45	.53
Skien	21	.67	.80	.78	.85	1.09	.71	.97
Telemark	22	.33	.67	.63	.63	.68	.91	.56
Notodden	23	.78	.86	.70	.97	.50	.54	1.03
Rjukan	24	1.36	1.01	1.15	1.41	.91	.92	.91
Kragerø	25	.68	.54	.54	.60	.13	.40	.59
Arendal	26	.29	.57	.71	.46	.50	.29	.86
Kristians.	27	1.32	1.30	1.40	1.29	1.15	1.11	1.40
Vest-Agder	28	.34	.32	.37	.21	.23	.38	.21
Rogaland	29	.51	.60	.53	.71	.83	.73	.70
Stavanger	30	1.31	1.40	1.36	1.11	1.29	1.12	1.15
Haugesund	31	.42	.29	.25	.40	.34	.60	.55
Hardanger	32	.48	.48	.92	.67	.85	.45	.41
Hordaland	33	.60	.48	.52	.51	.47	.54	.40
Bergen	34	1.83	1.72	1.75	1.52	1.36	1.55	1.73
Sogn	35	.15	.20	.38	.71	.53	.50	.91
Fjordane	36	.21	.36	.18	.27	.05	.28	.73
Sunnmøre	37	.58	.92	.78	.46	.47	.49	.62
Romsdal	38	.62	.79	.71	.78	.71	.69	.50
Nordmøre	39	.74	.98	.56	.53	.65	.65	.65
Ut-Trønd.	40	.57	.46	.57	.80	.93	.82	.78
Trondheim	41	1.22	.96	.81	.63	.27	.25	1.34
Inn-Trønd.	42	.70	.85	.71	.78	.67	.76	.70
Namdal	43	.50	.31	.47	.47	.64	.61	.55
Helgeland	44	.73	1.00	.99	.84	.87	.84	.75
Bodø	45	.84	1.03	.90	.90	1.04	.74	1.05
Narvik	46	.93	.93	1.33	1.14	1.11	1.24	1.13
Lof. & Ves.	47	.75	.83	.84	.72	.74	.83	.88
Senja	48	.75	.95	.99	.80	.88	.90	.69
Troms	49	1.09	.86	1.40	1.09	1.18	.80	1.41
Vest-Finnm.	50	.71	1.00	1.01	1.77	1.67	1.21	1.54
Vardø	51	1.53	2.42	1.62	1.54	2.15	1.55	.98
Vadsø	52	.88	.60	.86	1.25	2.24	1.33	1.26
Sør-Var.	53	1.41	.94	2.22	2.76	3.12	2.93	2.23

Appendix D

Table 22.3
Clear-up rates of offence of violence against the person, police districts, 1972-78

Police district	No	1972	1973	1974	1975	1976	1977	1978
Oslo	1	.79	.81	.91	.86	.84	.86	.84
Halden	2	.63	.52	.37	.34	.20	.40	.80
Sarpsborg	3	.58	.52	.66	.56	.47	.40	.56
Fredrikstad	4	.47	.45	.29	.51	.53	.48	.36
Moss	5	.49	.35	.62	.42	.36	.45	.57
Follo	6	.11	.37	.38	.39	.27	.37	.33
Romerike	7	.23	.25	.40	.39	.35	.43	.38
Kongsvinger	8	.07	.26	.18	.20	.27	.27	.34
Hamar	9	.27	.28	.46	.43	.38	.41	.43
Østerdal	10	.31	.28	.22	.24	.20	.42	.42
Gudbrandsd.	11	.21	.32	.23	.22	.33	.30	.20
Vest-Oppl.	12	.38	.27	.39	.35	.35	.30	.20
Ringerike	13	.42	.61	.50	.47	.54	.55	.58
Asker & B.	14	.36	.52	.54	.45	.41	.54	.33
Drammen	15	.45	.50	.27	.38	.41	.48	.35
Kongsberg	16	.23	.20	.30	.48	.30	.47	.34
N.-Jarlsb.	17	.33	.16	.32	.22	.42	.16	.22
Tønsberg	18	.41	.39	.32	.32	.23	.47	.62
Sandefjord	19	.80	.93	1.30	.70	1.45	.83	1.11
Larvik	20	.19	.30	.51	.37	.45	.21	.13
Skien	21	.33	.53	.51	.54	.61	.30	.62
Telemark	22	.20	.44	.43	.32	.41	.49	.40
Notodden	23	.51	.55	.58	.66	.23	.35	.61
Rjukan	24	.86	.76	.77	.90	.78	.52	.26
Kragerø	25	.61	.20	.20	.40	.07	.13	.26
Arendal	26	.19	.33	.35	.26	.37	.20	.52
Kristians.	27	.91	.97	1.08	.97	.83	.86	1.06
Vest-Agder	28	.24	.24	.26	.19	.17	.23	.15
Rogaland	29	.35	.44	.37	.61	.65	.55	.49
Stavanger	30	.99	.98	1.07	.79	.94	.75	.81
Haugesund	31	.29	.18	.13	.22	.18	.31	.31
Hardanger	32	.29	.33	.92	.56	.52	.26	.22
Hordaland	33	.21	.24	.30	.27	.28	.32	.24
Bergen	34	1.23	1.19	1.26	1.00	.89	1.05	1.16
Sogn	35	.12	.12	.18	.25	.25	.23	.33
Fjordane	36	.16	.32	.16	.25	.02	.20	.37
Sunnmøre	37	.39	.69	.61	.30	.35	.38	.38
Romsdal	38	.43	.70	.56	.68	.54	.37	.32
Nordmøre	39	.51	.74	.40	.38	.57	.47	.51
Ut-Trønd.	40	.37	.29	.42	.51	.61	.56	.65
Trondheim	41	.89	.65	.52	.40	.18	.15	.66
Inn-Trønd.	42	.46	.67	.49	.50	.48	.60	.46
Namdal	43	.36	.25	.44	.36	.36	.36	.36
Helgeland	44	.60	.81	.74	.64	.72	.60	.46
Bodø	45	.61	.70	.62	.60	.71	.47	.69
Narvik	46	.65	.59	1.10	.65	.57	.43	.72
Lof. & Ves.	47	.35	.48	.44	.43	.53	.56	.52
Senja	48	.53	.55	.69	.65	.73	.54	.34
Troms	49	.67	.56	.79	.68	.73	.36	.65
Vest-Finnm.	50	.37	.72	.66	.98	1.00	.70	.84
Vardø	51	1.15	1.84	.86	.86	1.37	1.26	.68
Vadsø	52	.61	.40	.66	.92	1.91	.73	.47
Sør-Var.	53	1.03	.56	1.39	1.75	2.48	1.83	1.58

Table 23.1

Covariance matrix of logs of crime and clear-up rates of slander and libel

	CRIMES							CLEAR-UPS						
	1972	1973	1974	1975	1976	1977	1978	1972	1973	1974	1975	1976	1977	1978
C 1972	.5860													
R 1973	.2619	.5529												
I 1974	.2458	.1457	.5357											
M 1975	.2509	.2731	.2568	.3830										
E 1976	.2315	.2469	.2434	.3009	.5459									
S 1977	.2777	.2396	.2529	.3167	.3678	.5397								
1978	.2131	.2178	.2056	.2142	.2292	.3113	.5702							
C 1972	.3921	.3309	.3138	.2762	.2580	.2150	.1814	.7857						
L 1973	.3414	.3954	.3196	.3266	.2516	.2317	.2269	.5758	.6102					
E 1974	.2339	.1498	.3977	.0976	.2132	.1953	.1639	.4032	.3984	.6911				
A 1975	.2362	.2418	.2037	.4133	.1715	.2282	.1540	.4273	.4829	.2293	.6629			
R 1976	.2770	.3501	.2477	.2758	.3583	.3615	.2254	.3669	.5733	.3350	.4182	.6067		
U 1977	.3086	.2727	.3435	.3771	.3173	.4632	.3177	.3197	.4310	.2677	.3625	.4379	.5574	
P 1978	.3314	.2822	.3051	.1804	.3004	.4378	.4198	.3292	.3958	.3975	.2242	.4251	.4546	.7582

Table 23.2
Crime rates of slander and libel, police districts, 1972-78

Police district	No	1972	1973	1974	1975	1976	1977	1978
Oslo	1	.16	.09	.15	.17	.21	.17	.22
Halden	2	.03					.06	.06
Sarpsborg	3	.22	.24	.12	.22	.12	.22	.22
Fredrikstad	4	.31	.08	.14	.12	.09	.19	.05
Moss	5	.10	.16	.08	.10	.08	.09	.09
Follo	6	.05	.08	.12	.04	.01	.07	.07
Romerike	7	.09	.07	.12	.09	.14	.10	.07
Kongsvinger	8	.09	.24	.18	.07	.20	.29	.07
Hamar	9	.21	.12	.13	.17	.20	.15	.08
Østerdal	10	.28	.14	.32	.24	.16	.10	.20
Gudbrandsd.	11	.24	.03	.12	.09	.13	.06	.04
Vest-Oppl.	12	.14	.21	.19	.13	.16	.12	.15
Ringerike	13	.12	.15	.05	.20	.09	.10	.12
Asker & B.	14	.04	.06	.07	.07	.07	.07	.08
Drammen	15	.16	.20	.18	.07	.12	.04	.08
Kongsberg	16		.05	.03	.13	.32	.20	
N.-Jarlsb.	17	.12	.04	.08	.08		.08	.08
Tønsberg	18	.07	.04	.04		.02		.02
Sandefjord	19		.08	.14	.13	.08	.16	.08
Larvik	20		.03	.08	.16	.19	.03	.03
Skien	21	.16	.20	.13	.22	.16	.16	.23
Telemark	22	.15	.07	.07	.07	.06	.18	.13
Notodden	23	.04	.12	.16	.12	.04	.04	.11
Rjukan	24	.12		.13		.13		.13
Kragerø	25	.14		.27		.20	.13	.13
Arendal	26	.09	.09	.07	.06	.08	.01	.16
Kristians.	27	.30	.26	.11	.15	.17	.19	.25
Vest-Agder	28	.08	.12	.02	.04	.17	.15	.11
Rogaland	29	.19	.08	.11	.08	.09	.14	.03
Stavanger	30	.05	.06	.11	.06	.08	.03	.07
Haugesund	31	.03	.03	.04	.06	.08	.06	.04
Hardanger	32	.11	.11	.07		.07	.04	.04
Hordaland	33	.20	.10	.11	.17	.16	.13	.13
Bergen	34	.33	.23	.34	.25	.23	.28	.24
Sogn	35	.02	.10	.45	.10			.08
Fjordane	36	.10	.06	.10	.11	.05	.11	.36
Sunnmøre	37	.23	.16	.18	.16	.19	.15	.20
Romsdal	38	.14	.04	.19	.02	.08	.09	.13
Nordmøre	39	.29	.11	.05	.13	.03	.05	
Ut-Trønd.	40	.10	.22	.24	.23	.30	.17	.20
Trondheim	41	.20	.11	.08	.09	.04	.02	.04
Inn-Trønd.	42	.17	.13	.18	.17	.14	.11	.10
Namdal	43	.25	.19	.19	.42	.19	.17	.17
Helgeland	44	.29	.21	.21	.22	.20	.17	.23
Bodø	45	.35	.21	.21	.16	.19	.27	.31
Narvik	46	.28	.51	.31	.06	.14	.14	.12
Lof. & Ves.	47	.37	.50	.38	.48	.64	.48	.60
Senja	48	.38	.21	.29	.15	.27	.21	.31
Troms	49	.30	.25	.18	.15	.25	.21	.35
Vest-Finnm.	50	.15	.05	.26	.35	.30	.23	.19
Vardø	51	.57	.68	.67	.19	.20	.19	.10
Vadsø	52	.68	.13		.13	.26	.13	.33
Sør-Var.	53	.09	.09	.37	.18	.18	.09	

Table 23.3
Clear-up rates of slander and libel, police districts, 1972-78

Police district	No	1972	1973	1974	1975	1976	1977	1978
Oslo	1	.03	.01	.04	.02	.01	.03	.04
Halden	2						.03	
Sarpsborg	3	.03	.05	.01	.03		.01	.05
Fredrikstad	4	.22	.06	.08	.09		.11	.05
Moss	5	.04	.08	.06		.08	.04	
Follo	6		.02	.05	.04		.01	.01
Romerike	7	.04	.04	.02	.02	.05	.05	.01
Kongsvinger	8		.07	.07		.04	.02	
Hamar	9	.10	.04	.05	.04	.04	.03	.03
Østerdal	10		.06	.02	.06	.06		
Gudbrandsd.	11	.04	.03	.01	.01	.03		
Vest-Oppl.	12	.05	.06	.06	.01	.03	.05	.08
Ringerike	13	.03	.02	.02	.05	.02	.04	.01
Asker & B.	14	.01	.02	.03	.04	.05	.03	.05
Drammen	15	.04	.04	.06	.02	.03		.01
Kongsberg	16		.03	.03	.10	.10	.10	
N.-Jarlsb.	17	.04		.06	.04		.04	.06
Tønsberg	18	.04		.04		.02		.02
Sandefjord	19		.05	.11	.11	.08	.11	.08
Larvik	20				.05	.03		
Skien	21	.05	.13	.04	.11	.04	.07	.05
Telemark	22	.02	.04	.02	.04	.04	.05	.05
Notodden	23	.04	.04	.04	.04		.04	.04
Rjukan	24	.12		.13				
Kragerø	25	.14		.13		.07	.13	.13
Arendal	26	.05	.04	.03	.03	.03	.01	.04
Kristians.	27	.18	.17	.05	.07	.10	.09	.11
Vest-Agder	28	.04	.02	.02	.02	.06	.02	.06
Rogaland	29	.02	.04	.01	.05	.06	.07	
Stavanger	30	.03	.05	.07	.03	.04	.02	.01
Haugesund	31	.01	.01	.03	.04	.03		.02
Hardanger	32	.07	.11	.07		.07		.04
Hordaland	33	.03	.05	.04	.07	.12	.08	.06
Bergen	34	.21	.16	.25	.17	.13	.16	.18
Sogn	35		.10	.28	.08			
Fjordane	36	.03	.03	.03	.05	.02	.05	.06
Sunnmøre	37	.18	.10	.10	.06	.09	.05	.07
Romsdal	38	.08	.02	.19	.02	.02	.04	.11
Nordmøre	39	.14	.06	.05	.03		.03	
Ut-Trønd.	40	.02		.04	.01	.03	.03	.04
Trondheim	41	.14	.07	.04	.06	.01	.02	.02
Inn-Trønd.	42	.11	.12	.16	.13	.08	.03	.05
Namdal	43	.22	.19	.06	.39	.17	.14	.08
Helgeland	44	.15	.04	.04	.07	.07	.06	.04
Bodø	45	.29	.15	.08	.04	.07	.12	.19
Narvik	46	.08	.08	.08		.03	.03	.12
Lof. & Ves.	47	.22	.31	.18	.23	.35	.30	.27
Senja	48	.09	.13	.25	.04	.15	.10	.19
Troms	49	.03	.08	.05	.02	.11	.09	.18
Vest-Finnm.	50	.05	.02	.05	.05	.02	.12	.07
Vardø	51	.29	.10	.19		.10		.10
Vadsø	52		.13		.13	.07	.07	.20
Sør-Var.	53			.28	.18	.18		

Table 24.1
Covariance matrix of logs of crime and clear-up rates of embezzlement

	CRIMES							CLEAR-UPS						
	1972	1973	1974	1975	1976	1977	1978	1972	1973	1974	1975	1976	1977	1978
C 1972	.6134													
R 1973	.2484	.6550												
I 1974	.2687	.1753	.5332											
M 1975	.1001	.1501	.0541	.4445										
E 1976	.1728	.1181	.1813	.1047	.4944									
S 1977	.1370	.1510	.1470	.1592	.3088	.6736								
1978	.2827	.1540	.1498	.2248	.2831	.2912	.5141							
C 1972	.6019	.1974	.2346	.0949	.1651	.1151	.2305	.4716						
L 1973	.2389	.3282	.1921	.1335	.1096	.1825	.1486	.1961	.6454					
E 1974	.2817	.1740	.4517	.0389	.1816	.1372	.1775	.2529	.2079	.5742				
A 1975	.0742	.1416	.0608	.2915	.0804	.1722	.2230	.0725	.1549	.0543	.4562			
R 1976	.2010	.0979	.1879	.0809	.3994	.2782	.2766	.2022	.1125	.2125	.0944	.5243		
U 1977	.1457	.1421	.0689	.1490	.2327	.3882	.2753	.1190	.1953	.0892	.1917	.2525	.5431	
P 1978	.2088	.1485	.1175	.2090	.2459	.2309	.5046	.1964	.1737	.1424	.2412	.2827	.2474	.5225

Table 24.2
Crime rates of embezzlement, police districts, 1972-78

Police district	No	1972	1973	1974	1975	1976	1977	1978
Oslo	1	.45	.50	.47	.35	.34	.29	.40
Halden	2	.14	.06	.31	.03	.11	.14	.06
Sarpsborg	3	.24	.31	.15	.18	.30	.20	.16
Fredrikstad	4	.05	.19	.12	.31	.17	.17	.17
Moss	5	.08	.06	.08	.10	.17	.09	.20
Follo	6	.14	.20	.17	.19	.04	.04	.10
Romerike	7	.16	.40	.96	.16	.12	.10	.12
Kongsvinger	8	.15		.07	.07	.11	.14	.18
Hamar	9	.09	.19	.33	.18	.20	.10	.18
Østerdal	10	.06	.10	.08	.14	.10	.08	.12
Gudbrandsd.	11	.10	.10	.23	.17	.06	.04	.13
Vest-Oppl.	12	.19	.41	.27	.18	.21	.27	.08
Ringerike	13	.26	.12	.21	.14	.08	.06	.12
Asker & B.	14	.10	.29	.16	.14	.13	.12	.06
Drammen	15	.28	.36	.36	.20	.16	.25	.32
Kongsberg	16	.10	.18	.20	.18	.05	.17	.10
N.-Jarlsb.	17	.15	.08	.08	.04	.06	.02	.04
Tønsberg	18	.05	.28	.11	.12	.16	.07	.12
Sandefjord	19	.17	.22	.70	.19	.24	.19	.16
Larvik	20	.03	.11	.24	.19	.27	.13	.05
Skien	21	.16	.27	.26	.16	.23	.16	.30
Telemark	22	.11	.22	.20	.09	.13	.11	.16
Notodden	23	.20	.08	.19	.08	.04	.04	.04
Rjukan	24	.12	.13			.13		
Kragerø	25	.07	.20	.07	.13	.13	.07	.07
Arendal	26	.17	.15	.14	.19	.14	.16	.24
Kristians.	27	.25	.19	.18	.15	.17	.22	.13
Vest-Agder	28		.04	.14	.08	.08	.04	.06
Rogaland	29	.01	.09	.11	.08	.03	.04	.01
Stavanger	30	.10	.13	.08	.15	.17	.10	.13
Haugesund	31	.07	.04	.06	.08	.05	.01	.06
Hardanger	32	.07	.11	.33	.04	.04	.04	.07
Hordaland	33	.09	.02	.04	.09	.06	.04	.05
Bergen	34	.37	.29	.22	.21	.24	.27	.27
Sogn	35	.02	.07	.13	.03		.03	.03
Fjordane	36	.05	.02		.02	.05	.08	.09
Sunnmøre	37	.13	.26	.28	.10	.14	.20	.09
Romsdal	38	.02	.14	.06	.32	.06	.15	.19
Nordmøre	39	.16	.16	.10	.08	.02	.02	.03
Ut-Trønd.	40	.04	.09	.10	.06	.14	.09	.07
Trondheim	41	.34	.21	.18	.30	.09	.06	.12
Inn-Trønd.	42	.18	.42	.13	.08	.10	.09	.08
Namdal	43	.14	.08	.03	.11	.14		
Helgeland	44	.16	.19	.07	.20	.10	.22	.04
Bodø	45	.25	.21	.27	.28	.16	.13	.27
Narvik	46	.28	.17	.25	.17	.14		.09
Lof. & Ves.	47	.20	.26	.23	.16	.30	.15	.17
Senja	48	.21	.13	.17	.08	.17	.02	.04
Troms	49	.31	.46	.47	.22	.22	.17	.10
Vest-Finnm.	50		.02	.07	.14	.23	.40	.16
Vardø	51	.29	.68	.38	.29	.49	.29	.10
Vadsø	52	.07	.13	.07	.07	.33	.13	
Sør-Var.	53	.19		.09	.18	.28	.09	.19

Table 24.3
Clear-up rates of embezzlement, police districts, 1972-78

Police district	No	1972	1973	1974	1975	1976	1977	1978
Oslo	1	.32	.40	.35	.24	.22	.19	.29
Halden	2	.09	.06	.29	.03	.09	.06	.03
Sarpsborg	3	.13	.15	.08	.05	.10	.05	.06
Fredrikstad	4	.03	.08	.09	.26	.11	.09	.11
Moss	5	.06	.04	.08	.04	.15	.09	.11
Follo	6	.06	.11	.09	.07	.01	.03	.04
Romerike	7	.09	.28	.86	.09	.06	.05	.06
Kongsvinger	8	.11		.06	.02	.04	.09	.11
Hamar	9	.09	.15	.26	.11	.10	.03	.14
Østerdal	10		.02		.04	.04	.06	.10
Gudbrandsd.	11	.06	.04	.16	.12		.03	.07
Vest-Oppl.	12	.13	.37	.19	.16	.14	.24	.05
Ringerike	13	.17	.05	.18	.06	.03	.04	.03
Asker & B.	14	.05	.19	.10	.10	.09	.10	.03
Drammen	15	.11	.25	.20	.15	.10	.10	.17
Kongsberg	16	.05	.13	.15	.10	.05	.10	
N.-Jarlsb.	17	.10	.04	.04		.06	.02	.04
Tønsberg	18	.05	.26	.11	.09	.07	.07	.10
Sandefjord	19	.17	.22	.51	.13	.24	.19	.16
Larvik	20	.03	.05	.14	.11	.11	.03	.03
Skien	21	.07	.18	.15	.13	.11	.09	.16
Telemark	22	.09	.15	.15	.06	.09	.02	.09
Notodden	23	.16	.08	.16			.04	.04
Rjukan	24		.13			.13		
Kragerø	25		.20	.07	.13	.13		
Arendal	26	.08	.13	.10	.13	.09	.10	.11
Kristians.	27	.20	.09	.13	.08	.14	.12	.09
Vest-Agder	28		.04	.08	.08	.06	.02	.06
Rogaland	29	.01	.07	.07	.05	.02	.02	.01
Stavanger	30	.06	.08	.04	.10	.10	.08	.09
Haugesund	31	.04	.04	.06	.05	.03		.01
Hardanger	32	.07	.11	.15	.04		.04	.04
Hordaland	33	.05		.03	.03	.04	.02	.02
Bergen	34	.22	.16	.13	.15	.15	.13	.14
Sogn	35	.02	.05	.03	.03			
Fjordane	36		.02			.02	.05	.06
Sunnmøre	37	.07	.18	.21	.09	.08	.09	.06
Romsdal	38	.02	.12	.04	.32	.04	.13	.15
Nordmøre	39	.10	.11	.06	.08	.02	.02	.03
Ut-Trønd.	40	.04	.05	.04	.03	.05	.04	.06
Trondheim	41	.24	.15	.12	.19	.07	.02	.10
Inn-Trønd.	42	.12	.37	.12	.03	.07	.08	.06
Namdal	43	.08	.06			.11	.11	
Helgeland	44	.13	.16	.04	.14	.04	.10	.03
Bodø	45	.23	.14	.23	.22	.09	.09	.16
Narvik	46	.17	.11	.25	.17	.06		.06
Lof. & Ves.	47	.08	.20	.20	.11	.15	.08	.10
Senja	48	.15	.06	.11	.06	.15	.02	.04
Troms	49	.19	.29	.25	.09	.11	.06	.06
Vest-Finnm.	50		.02	.05	.02	.14	.19	.07
Vardø	51	.10	.58	.38	.10	.10	.19	
Vadsø	52	.07	.13	.07	.07	.33	.07	
Sør-Var.	53	.09		.09	.18	.28	.09	.19

Table 26.1

Covariance matrix of logs of crime and clear-up rates of fraud and breach of trust

			CRIMES						CLEAR - UPS					
	1972	1973	1974	1975	1976	1977	1978	1972	1973	1974	1975	1976	1977	1978
C 1972	.6535													
R 1973	.3899	.6816												
I 1974	.3918	.4065	.6252											
M 1975	.4175	.4001	.3751	.5308										
E 1976	.3086	.3075	.3307	.3906	.5372									
S 1977	.3872	.2878	.3279	.3493	.3341	.6340								
1978	.3735	.2423	.2966	.3515	.3512	.4513	.5625							
C 1972	.6877	.3667	.3620	.4168	.2888	.3765	.3553	.7834						
L 1973	.3983	.5140	.3931	.4097	.2635	.2738	.2072	.3943	.5848					
E 1974	.3937	.4014	.6540	.4092	.3406	.3142	.2936	.3641	.4264	.8300				
A 1975	.4089	.3788	.3430	.5086	.3091	.2524	.3049	.4363	.4314	.4123	.6904			
R 1976	.3397	.2743	.3108	.4032	.5536	.3308	.3460	.3334	.2352	.3362	.3485	.6014		
U 1977	.3796	.2564	.2805	.3313	.3002	.5898	.4250	.3800	.2711	.2990	.2705	.3070	.6647	
P 1978	.4069	.2396	.3159	.3764	.3618	.4735	.5981	.3931	.2104	.3174	.3475	.3746	.4577	.6648

Table 26.2
Crime rates of fraud and breach of trust, police districts, 1972-78

Police district	No	1972	1973	1974	1975	1976	1977	1978
Oslo	1	2.68	3.12	2.46	3.03	3.21	3.02	2.99
Halden	2	.06	.29	.94	.29	.23	.40	.46
Sarpsborg	3	.51	.52	1.00	.55	.85	.87	.90
Fredrikstad	4	.69	.79	.62	.91	.62	.54	.59
Moss	5	.59	.84	.89	.58	.99	.82	.74
Follo	6	.75	.53	.51	.39	.20	.45	.48
Romerike	7	.46	.80	1.44	1.02	.71	.47	.49
Kongsvinger	8	1.11	.13	.39	.24	.55	.96	1.40
Hamar	9	.31	.19	.61	.65	.80	.87	.96
Østerdal	10	.45	.53	.35	.51	.52	.62	.26
Gudbrandsd.	11	.21	.25	.20	.26	.96	.29	.23
Vest-Oppl.	12	.32	.36	.62	1.03	1.04	.36	.28
Ringerike	13	1.00	1.07	.87	1.62	1.89	.88	.61
Asker & B.	14	.90	.90	.94	1.11	1.56	.81	.72
Drammen	15	.90	.80	1.83	.75	1.20	1.09	1.07
Kongsberg	16	.21	.28	.33	.60	.47	.39	.71
N.-Jarlsb.	17	.19	.27	.85	.46	.42	.63	.69
Tønsberg	18	.76	.32	.25	.65	.65	1.02	.71
Sandefjord	19	.39	1.42	.78	1.02	.83	.85	.74
Larvik	20	.16	.22	.30	.40	.83	.35	.61
Skien	21	.95	.93	1.22	1.26	1.48	1.47	.92
Telemark	22	.44	.80	.48	.78	.87	.71	1.15
Notodden	23	.35	.62	1.36	.19	.19	.62	.23
Rjukan	24	.25	.38	1.02	1.03	.39	.26	
Kragerø	25	.41	.20	.40	.33		.33	.26
Arendal	26	.50	.24	.41	.55	.50	1.08	.82
Kristians.	27	.98	.84	1.36	1.80	1.41	1.69	3.45
Vest-Agder	28	.28	.32	.18	.12	.21	.29	.19
Rogaland	29	.39	.56	.32	.51	.45	.32	.43
Stavanger	30	.92	.54	1.08	.58	1.30	.83	.57
Haugesund	31	.22	.12	.09	.26	.18	.48	.55
Hardanger	32	.59	.15	.59	.19	.19	.15	.11
Hordaland	33	.22	.04	.09	.11	.31	.16	.25
Bergen	34	1.35	1.26	1.61	1.20	1.26	.92	.96
Sogn	35	.02	.12	.13	.08	.20	.03	.05
Fjordane	36	.20	.18	.08	.16	.24	.16	.65
Sunnmøre	37	.28	.38	.34	.35	.72	.57	.41
Romsdal	38	.35	.37	.31	.72	.58	.30	.20
Nordmøre	39	.48	.42	.22	.43	.11	.70	.24
Ut-Trønd.	40	.12	.23	.25	.37	.37	.45	.22
Trondheim	41	1.11	.63	.71	1.01	.45	.08	.40
Inn-Trønd.	42	.35	.19	.49	.46	1.15	.64	1.11
Namdal	43	.33	.19	.22	.33	.17	.36	.33
Helgeland	44	.35	.51	.55	.60	.27	.41	.35
Bodø	45	1.78	.91	1.10	1.21	.56	.71	1.11
Narvik	46	.42	.34	.82	.26	.48	.55	.66
Lof. & Ves.	47	.55	.76	.66	.71	.53	.58	.52
Senja	48	.43	.36	.36	.31	.57	.48	.44
Troms	49	.43	.71	.64	.43	.73	.53	.69
Vest-Finnm.	50	.15	.33	.26	.42	.77	1.00	.56
Vardø	51	.48	.48	.67	.38	.68	.49	.39
Vadsø	52	.27	.07	.27	.59	.26	.13	.27
Sør-Var.	53	.28	.09	.28	.74	1.56	1.46	.19

Table 26.3
Clear-up rates of fraud and breach of trust, police districts, 1972-78

Oslo	1	1.59	1.94	1.13	1.23	1.30	1.44	1.70
Halden	2	.06	.20	.88	.29	.14	.23	.26
Sarpsborg	3	.31	.25	.65	.21	.60	.54	.71
Fredrikstad	4	.44	.69	.59	.73	.50	.33	.34
Moss	5	.49	.53	.70	.46	.84	.47	.48
Follo	6	.51	.25	.23	.27	.17	.34	.32
Romerike	7	.28	.49	1.17	.82	.51	.30	.34
Kongsvinger	8	.99	.11	.26	.13	.47	.83	1.10
Hamar	9	.19	.14	.40	.38	.61	.63	.64
Østerdal	10	.35	.47	.28	.40	.40	.56	.16
Gudbrandsd.	11	.10	.07	.12	.09	.83	.20	.16
Vest-Oppl.	12	.22	.31	.52	.88	.93	.26	.21
Ringerike	13	.93	.98	.78	.71	1.64	.73	.40
Asker & B.	14	.51	.48	.56	.79	.82	.54	.43
Drammen	15	.74	.52	1.31	.50	.90	.72	.73
Kongsberg	16	.10	.15	.28	.30	.35	.17	.39
N.-Jarlsb.	17	.19	.20	.77	.24	.22	.47	.59
Tønsberg	18	.67	.26	.21	.40	.51	.97	.47
Sandefjord	19	.30	1.26	.51	.73	.64	.61	.50
Larvik	20	.14	.05	.08	.27	.64	.13	.42
Skien	21	.64	.73	.89	.90	1.00	.73	.53
Telemark	22	.35	.50	.26	.50	.59	.51	.79
Notodden	23	.12	.55	1.17	.08	.08	.42	.11
Rjukan	24	.12	.25	.77	.77	.39	.13	
Kragerø	25	.41	.13	.27	.33		.20	
Arendal	26	.33	.17	.25	.39	.38	.90	.47
Kristians.	27	.85	.57	1.13	1.43	1.11	1.28	2.77
Vest-Agder	28	.24	.22	.04	.10	.12	.12	.09
Rogaland	29	.31	.49	.22	.45	.33	.20	.23
Stavanger	30	.56	.33	.93	.31	1.14	.59	.38
Haugesund	31	.21	.08	.09	.23	.13	.40	.30
Hardanger	32	.44	.11	.44	.11	.19	.07	.07
Hordaland	33	.02		.05	.07	.23	.09	.18
Bergen	34	.76	.64	1.01	.64	.67	.57	.59
Sogn	35	.02	.12	.10	.08	.10	.03	.03
Fjordane	36	.08	.13	.05	.14	.13	.14	.37
Sunnmøre	37	.22	.30	.26	.28	.62	.52	.32
Romsdal	38	.27	.25	.27	.51	.45	.26	.09
Nordmøre	39	.35	.34	.11	.41	.10	.68	.24
Ut-Trønd.	40	.10	.15	.15	.27	.21	.34	.16
Trondheim	41	.74	.44	.60	.71	.33	.05	.30
Inn-Trønd.	42	.14	.16	.40	.34	.98	.40	1.01
Namdal	43	.25	.17	.14	.19	.14	.22	.25
Helgeland	44	.23	.39	.39	.36	.17	.30	.25
Bodø	45	1.46	.70	.62	.96	.37	.53	.81
Narvik	46	.23	.08	.59	.14	.29	.37	.35
Lof. & Ves.	47	.37	.51	.36	.43	.31	.35	.30
Senja	48	.32	.28	.23	.27	.44	.40	.34
Troms	49	.20	.41	.43	.24	.45	.30	.46
Vest-Finnm.	50	.10	.17	.09	.02	.37	.44	.26
Vardø	51	.29	.39	.19		.39	.29	.29
Vadsø	52	.20		.20	.46	.13		.13
Sør-Var.	53	.19		.09	.64	1.29	1.46	.09

Table 28.1

Covariance matrix of logs of crime and clear-up rates of offence inflictin damage to property

	CRIMES							CLEAR-UPS						
	1972	1973	1974	1975	1976	1977	1978	1972	1973	1974	1975	1976	1977	1978
C 1972	.4288													
R 1973	.3891	.4904												
I 1974	.1973	.2246	.2694											
M 1975	.2065	.2422	.2299	.2955										
E 1976	.1796	.2134	.1937	.2596	.3123									
S 1977	.1055	.1718	.1351	.2009	.2155	.3430								
1978	.1934	.2096	.1452	.2000	.2174	.1873	.3193							
C 1972	.3449	.2648	.1461	.1378	.1190	.0602	.1648	.4670						
L 1973	.3099	.3834	.1905	.2220	.1944	.1545	.1758	.3030	.4855					
E 1974	.0994	.0956	.2075	.1601	.1548	.0778	.0525	.1519	.1786	.3326				
A 1975	.1739	.1803	.1599	.2020	.1742	.1298	.0980	.1380	.2364	.2090	.3061			
R 1976	.1423	.1414	.1201	.1889	.1559	.1559	.1048	.1327	.1839	.1681	.2011	.2849		
U 1977	.0503	.1052	.0777	.1346	.1579	.2305	.0996	.0689	.1783	.1216	.1510	.1953	.3776	
P 1978	.1269	.1684	.0946	.1522	.1778	.1691	.2262	.1273	.1930	.0899	.1316	.1383	.1852	.3190

Table 28.2
Crime rates of offence inflicting damage to property, police districts, 1972-78

Police district	No	1972	1973	1974	1975	1976	1977	1978
Oslo	1	.84	.70	.78	.77	.94	.78	.93
Halden	2	.46	.72	.60	.71	.54	.80	.63
Sarpsborg	3	2.10	2.14	2.01	2.02	1.46	1.80	1.71
Fredrikstad	4	2.36	2.81	1.85	2.93	3.53	2.47	2.66
Moss	5	1.14	.92	1.28	1.75	2.07	2.08	2.68
Follo	6	.94	1.33	1.07	1.16	.92	1.06	1.40
Romerike	7	.90	.79	1.08	1.02	1.27	1.47	1.68
Kongsvinger	8	.15	.33	.50	.40	.65	1.23	.79
Hamar	9	.53	.62	.87	1.01	1.12	1.17	1.19
Østerdal	10	.69	.57	.53	.69	.75	.96	.91
Gudbrandsd.	11	.73	.63	.82	.83	.77	.71	.98
Vest-Oppl.	12	.93	.81	.95	.94	1.28	1.01	1.52
Ringerike	13	1.22	1.66	2.15	2.01	1.77	1.94	2.66
Asker & B.	14	1.93	2.45	2.29	1.96	1.71	1.81	2.46
Drammen	15	1.14	1.48	1.19	1.88	1.85	2.33	2.37
Kongsberg	16	.82	1.15	.76	1.33	.77	.89	1.17
N.-Jarlsb.	17	1.00	.96	1.31	1.08	1.17	1.96	2.09
Tønsberg	18	1.59	.72	.51	1.05	1.05	.61	1.88
Sandefjord	19	2.73	2.84	3.21	3.29	2.31	2.29	3.86
Larvik	20	1.61	1.12	1.46	2.38	2.21	1.44	1.49
Skien	21	1.62	1.36	1.99	2.95	2.62	2.89	2.75
Telemark	22	1.07	1.29	1.74	3.47	2.62	2.91	3.70
Notodden	23	1.48	1.56	1.17	1.47	1.62	1.62	1.57
Rjukan	24	1.85	.38	.51	.77	.78	1.18	.65
Kragerø	25	1.15	.34	1.27	.67	.53	.20	.73
Arendal	26	.83	.98	.98	.75	.66	.46	1.28
Kristians.	27	2.56	2.15	1.75	2.35	2.24	2.49	3.77
Vest-Agder	28	.44	.54	.85	.68	1.02	.92	.63
Rogaland	29	.51	1.34	1.18	1.44	1.30	1.08	1.46
Stavanger	30	1.09	.52	.59	.58	.60	.53	.54
Haugesund	31	.67	.53	.81	1.19	1.59	2.15	2.65
Hardanger	32	1.32	.92	1.29	1.26	1.18	1.04	.97
Hordaland	33	.46	.40	.51	.63	.61	.61	.89
Bergen	34	2.79	2.61	2.89	2.72	2.73	2.74	3.68
Sogn	35	.10	.05	1.13	.76	.45	.61	.91
Fjordane	36	.83	.39	.35	.43	.50	.52	1.54
Sunnmøre	37	.92	.90	.77	.74	.73	.64	.74
Romsdal	38	.88	1.12	1.46	1.44	1.56	1.30	1.30
Nordmøre	39	1.01	1.53	1.20	1.36	.65	1.09	.64
Ut-Trønd.	40	.92	.74	.82	1.25	.95	1.35	1.40
Trondheim	41	2.32	1.56	1.93	.61	.26	.44	.53
Inn-Trønd.	42	1.04	.73	.74	.78	.98	1.15	.91
Namdal	43	.89	1.14	1.05	1.75	1.36	1.36	1.55
Helgeland	44	1.09	1.26	1.31	1.10	1.21	1.73	1.99
Bodø	45	2.01	1.55	1.75	1.42	1.50	1.56	1.39
Narvik	46	2.37	2.72	1.98	2.50	1.80	2.18	2.28
Lof. & Ves.	47	1.10	.97	.87	1.17	.96	1.44	1.69
Senja	48	1.07	1.00	.61	.63	1.05	.88	1.53
Troms	49	1.28	1.36	1.27	.95	1.43	1.22	2.97
Vest-Finnm.	50	.49	.98	1.44	1.67	2.14	2.60	1.77
Vardø	51	1.53	1.26	1.71	1.25	1.95	1.36	1.37
Vadsø	52	.47	.40	1.66	1.98	2.18	1.59	.40
Sør-Var.	53	2.26	1.78	3.89	2.95	3.31	.37	2.42

Table 28.3
Clear-up rates of offence inflicting damage to property, police districts, 1972-78

Oslo	1	.16	.16	.20	.20	.24	.25	.28
Halden	2	.17	.32	.14	.09	.20	.46	.20
Sarpsborg	3	.75	.64	.66	.43	.43	.39	.34
Fredrikstad	4	.42	.62	.37	.48	.57	.50	.61
Moss	5	.31	.25	.25	.27	.42	.22	.35
Follo	6	.06	.28	.15	.31	.20	.23	.18
Romerike	7	.16	.16	.34	.20	.26	.27	.32
Kongsvinger	8	.06	.06	.15	.07	.09	.27	.38
Hamar	9	.15	.14	.41	.31	.57	.41	.48
Østerdal	10	.22	.14	.12	.12	.40	.28	.20
Gudbrandsd.	11	.27	.21	.18	.19	.12	.17	.13
Vest-Oppl.	12	.27	.22	.32	.19	.38	.21	.26
Ringerike	13	.23	.52	.56	.47	.39	.45	.68
Asker & B.	14	.38	.33	.23	.31	.26	.29	.30
Drammen	15	.37	.30	.19	.25	.36	.29	.38
Kongsberg	16	.13	.18	.15	.28	.15	.10	.42
N.-Jarlsb.	17	.25	.16	.36	.20	.28	.24	.24
Tønsberg	18	.48	.09	.12	.23	.42	.10	.31
Sandefjord	19	1.16	1.12	.86	.86	.80	.75	1.00
Larvik	20	.19	.19	.30	.43	.40	.19	.27
Skien	21	.46	.42	.36	.47	.61	.53	.51
Telemark	22	.18	.39	.20	.19	.41	.33	.54
Notodden	23	.20	.23	.16	.31	.23	.27	.19
Rjukan	24	.49		.13	.39	.39	.52	.52
Kragerø	25	.27		.40	.13	.20	.07	.13
Arendal	26	.35	.70	.35	.26	.20	.09	.30
Kristians.	27	.84	.66	.47	.64	.75	.70	1.03
Vest-Agder	28	.16	.12	.33	.25	.35	.15	.15
Rogaland	29	.17	.50	.40	.61	.36	.31	.41
Stavanger	30	.87	.19	.25	.19	.33	.17	.07
Haugesund	31	.26	.23	.27	.23	.34	.63	.62
Hardanger	32	.48	.33	.55	.67	.30	.41	.34
Hordaland	33	.09	.13	.09	.16	.21	.17	.33
Bergen	34	.71	.47	.63	.44	.47	.51	.76
Sogn	35	.10	.02	.48	.15	.10	.13	.13
Fjordane	36	.31	.23	.24	.25	.16	.25	.42
Sunnmøre	37	.34	.39	.33	.23	.22	.18	.37
Romsdal	38	.45	.41	.38	.23	.43	.45	.37
Nordmøre	39	.34	.51	.43	.27	.21	.30	.13
Ut-Trønd.	40	.45	.32	.23	.42	.43	.61	.67
Trondheim	41	.33	.16	.24	.18	.12	.09	.13
Inn-Trønd.	42	.57	.56	.38	.41	.37	.25	.30
Namdal	43	.39	.47	.47	.53	.58	.64	.61
Helgeland	44	.51	.47	.42	.27	.42	.46	.60
Bodø	45	.49	.47	.57	.48	.33	.34	.46
Narvik	46	.68	.99	.45	.71	.37	.32	.38
Lof. & Ves.	47	.32	.28	.28	.48	.35	.56	.56
Senja	48	.23	.30	.19	.23	.38	.34	.34
Troms	49	.43	.28	.24	.18	.16	.23	.50
Vest-Finnm.	50	.15	.41	.47	.51	.56	.70	.44
Vardø	51	.48	.29	.57	.19	.39	.49	.49
Vadsø	52	.07	.20	1.33	1.06	1.38	.80	.20
Sør-Var.	53	.66	.47	1.20	.37	.46	.09	.37

Table 40.1

Covariance matrix of logs of crime and clear-up rates of aggravated larcenies

	C R I M E S							C L E A R - U P S						
	1972	1973	1974	1975	1976	1977	1978	1972	1973	1974	1975	1976	1977	1978
C 1972	.7134													
R 1973	.6631	.7242												
I 1974	.6529	.6508	.6997											
M 1975	.6802	.6877	.6550	.7331										
E 1976	.6638	.6470	.6601	.6909	.7426									
S 1977	.6695	.6516	.6666	.6885	.7395	.8008								
1978	.6077	.5914	.6224	.6222	.6433	.6733	.6709							
C 1972	.5606	.5023	.4794	.4891	.4472	.4509	.4233	.6829						
L 1973	.4660	.5734	.4463	.5047	.4269	.4355	.3786	.4489	.6282					
E 1974	.5024	.5027	.5247	.4971	.5158	.4992	.4233	.4337	.4242	.5582				
A 1975	.4921	.5103	.4736	.5435	.5036	.4852	.4331	.3958	.4607	.4171	.5554			
R 1976	.5712	.5620	.5537	.5956	.6280	.5967	.4996	.4730	.4435	.5182	.4804	.7037		
U 1977	.5106	.4976	.4919	.5022	.5914	.6733	.5052	.3620	.3976	.4355	.4216	.4988	.7664	
P 1978	.3841	.3640	.4033	.3558	.3657	.3833	.4137	.3644	.2765	.2919	.3004	.3576	.3435	.4322

Table 40.2
Crime rates of aggravted larcenies, police districts, 1972-78

Police district	No	1972	1973	1974	1975	1976	1977	1978
Oslo	1	21.11	23.87	26.31	28.00	27.31	28.01	35.15
Halden	2	6.87	7.05	6.02	7.62	6.25	5.43	5.91
Sarpsborg	3	4.35	5.26	6.29	7.64	7.01	5.78	8.09
Fredrikstad	4	8.78	10.69	6.02	13.14	13.59	10.09	9.46
Moss	5	4.22	5.28	5.62	7.02	8.32	9.51	9.24
Follo	6	5.18	5.55	6.63	6.91	5.82	6.01	6.85
Romerike	7	4.63	6.41	7.28	6.75	7.12	6.47	8.23
Kongsvinger	8	2.59	2.34	3.05	2.59	4.26	3.56	2.54
Hamar	9	2.75	5.24	2.90	3.94	4.05	4.22	4.47
Østerdal	10	1.47	1.69	2.09	1.45	2.62	2.64	2.67
Gudbrandsd.	11	2.49	2.25	1.55	2.46	2.90	2.88	3.08
Vest-Oppl.	12	4.00	4.27	5.92	5.95	5.85	3.53	4.57
Ringerike	13	7.03	9.26	11.24	8.18	9.04	8.02	7.91
Asker & B.	14	14.11	17.43	15.38	16.70	13.70	13.11	14.56
Drammen	15	9.40	10.99	9.79	12.67	10.21	12.31	15.61
Kongsberg	16	6.48	8.23	7.60	9.10	7.24	7.01	7.98
N.-Jarlsb.	17	6.02	5.86	5.83	4.44	4.78	5.69	6.99
Tønsberg	18	12.53	12.60	8.13	13.14	11.16	10.07	13.15
Sandefjord	19	8.67	7.37	8.70	8.84	10.68	6.61	9.38
Larvik	20	6.41	6.50	6.53	9.32	9.25	8.27	9.42
Skien	21	5.01	5.60	6.76	9.18	8.46	9.87	9.44
Telemark	22	4.35	7.97	7.85	11.16	11.31	9.40	12.38
Notodden	23	5.50	4.91	7.13	6.40	7.62	8.73	6.12
Rjukan	24	3.58	3.91	3.33	6.42	8.47	7.85	5.34
Kragerø	25	4.67	7.62	3.62	4.33	2.80	5.16	4.29
Arendal	26	5.31	4.36	4.60	6.88	6.05	4.36	6.87
Kristians.	27	8.14	10.56	10.44	11.69	11.63	9.38	12.08
Vest-Agder	28	.76	.94	1.30	1.44	1.33	2.13	2.12
Rogaland	29	4.07	5.19	3.75	4.39	4.53	3.71	4.62
Stavanger	30	6.28	6.56	5.73	7.55	6.78	5.77	8.28
Haugesund	31	5.32	4.83	4.75	6.43	6.61	7.19	10.25
Hardanger	32	5.46	2.66	2.92	4.94	2.00	1.34	3.58
Hordaland	33	2.78	2.76	3.16	3.51	2.71	3.13	3.72
Bergen	34	8.52	10.51	11.06	9.61	9.40	8.81	10.78
Sogn	35	.39	.47	.68	.68	.48	.25	.71
Fjordane	36	.28	.53	.53	.33	.32	.30	1.48
Sunnmøre	37	1.97	3.02	2.71	1.72	2.06	1.17	1.06
Romsdal	38	1.78	1.35	1.38	1.65	1.61	1.47	1.86
Nordmøre	39	2.81	2.60	1.68	2.10	2.26	2.20	1.96
Ut-Trønd.	40	1.66	1.83	1.98	2.18	2.54	3.02	3.27
Trondheim	41	12.98	12.10	11.81	10.48	12.79	11.35	12.80
Inn-Trønd.	42	1.63	1.64	2.09	1.83	2.56	3.22	3.58
Namdal	43	1.19	1.50	1.44	1.36	1.72	1.14	1.02
Helgeland	44	3.01	1.75	2.31	2.34	2.52	2.89	3.23
Bodø	45	3.82	3.36	3.54	3.73	3.03	2.83	3.04
Narvik	46	2.17	3.99	3.08	4.06	3.34	2.99	3.06
Lof. & Ves.	47	1.25	1.14	1.15	1.43	1.22	1.24	1.28
Senja	48	2.71	2.52	1.81	2.24	1.97	2.60	3.92
Troms	49	3.35	3.65	3.99	3.31	6.02	3.33	9.36
Vest-Finnm.	50	2.03	1.05	.92	2.56	4.69	3.46	2.75
Vardø	51	1.72	6.78	1.43	4.71	2.73	2.04	2.05
Vadsø	52	1.76	2.88	1.20	3.70	1.45	1.19	1.26
Sør-Var.	53	1.88	1.69	2.59	2.03	3.49	4.58	3.34

Table 40.3
Clear-up rates of aggravated larcenies, police districts, 1972-78

Police district	No	1972	1973	1974	1975	1976	1977	1978
Oslo	1	2.20	2.36	2.22	2.34	2.84	2.54	2.46
Halden	2	2.80	3.20	2.42	2.88	2.28	1.46	1.40
Sarpsborg	3	1.60	1.83	2.06	1.92	2.28	1.61	2.86
Fredrikstad	4	3.75	4.43	1.53	6.44	5.87	4.11	3.62
Moss	5	1.06	2.05	1.81	1.62	2.43	3.26	2.94
Follo	6	1.78	1.66	1.60	.95	2.16	1.61	1.27
Romerike	7	1.23	1.89	2.26	1.76	1.97	1.85	1.74
Kongsvinger	8	.81	.63	1.02	.75	1.98	1.57	1.10
Hamar	9	1.35	2.40	1.06	1.36	1.66	1.65	2.02
Østerdal	10	.51	.59	1.10	.28	1.07	.90	.79
Gudbrandsd.	11	.49	.44	.38	.66	.87	.98	.59
Vest-Oppl.	12	1.63	1.52	2.49	2.83	2.18	.81	1.09
Ringerike	13	1.65	2.76	3.79	2.21	3.32	1.31	1.99
Asker & B.	14	1.95	1.74	1.47	2.09	1.92	1.70	1.81
Drammen	15	2.49	2.65	1.52	2.23	2.40	2.53	2.56
Kongsberg	16	1.41	1.78	1.04	1.63	2.02	1.43	2.06
N.-Jarlsb.	17	3.08	2.10	1.84	1.12	1.33	1.56	2.05
Tønsberg	18	3.74	3.51	1.19	2.82	2.72	1.66	1.88
Sandefjord	19	4.17	2.62	3.59	2.48	4.37	2.69	3.43
Larvik	20	2.92	1.58	1.70	2.97	2.69	.99	1.49
Skien	21	1.57	2.02	2.15	2.20	2.57	2.02	1.62
Telemark	22	1.07	3.16	1.76	1.89	3.76	2.00	1.67
Notodden	23	2.38	1.09	2.85	1.75	.89	2.88	.96
Rjukan	24	.12	1.51	1.28	4.36	1.04	5.24	.52
Kragerø	25	1.42	4.05	1.41	.73	.47	2.78	1.06
Arendal	26	2.24	1.39	1.88	2.44	2.64	1.90	2.57
Kristians.	27	2.93	3.85	3.76	3.82	3.30	3.36	2.01
Vest-Agder	28	.46	.42	.20	.84	.21	.82	.78
Rogaland	29	2.99	3.25	1.90	2.69	1.97	1.34	1.69
Stavanger	30	2.76	2.26	1.86	2.36	2.23	1.80	2.14
Haugesund	31	3.17	3.15	1.77	1.59	1.50	1.56	1.19
Hardanger	32	2.67	1.03	.59	1.63	.81	.26	2.50
Hordaland	33	1.26	1.15	1.07	1.19	1.23	1.30	1.69
Bergen	34	2.76	2.49	2.50	1.71	1.74	1.18	1.71
Sogn	35	.10	.17	.25	.23	.18	.03	.28
Fjordane	36	.16	.29	.10	.19	.05	.14	.70
Sunnmøre	37	1.15	1.66	1.33	.74	1.22	.61	.70
Romsdal	38	1.05	.68	.59	.53	.45	.39	.72
Nordmøre	39	1.93	1.61	.72	.67	.97	1.22	.94
Ut-Trønd.	40	.52	.44	.75	.62	1.27	1.25	1.12
Trondheim	41	3.03	2.29	2.27	2.59	2.27	2.14	1.79
Inn-Trønd.	42	.88	.86	1.34	1.19	1.55	1.55	1.26
Namdal	43	.55	.75	.72	.64	.58	.64	.44
Helgeland	44	1.73	.61	.86	.94	1.30	.75	1.25
Bodø	45	2.48	1.86	2.17	2.11	.79	1.67	1.17
Narvik	46	.90	2.15	.74	1.45	.97	1.12	1.13
Lof. & Ves.	47	.90	.68	.61	.66	.56	.53	.55
Senja	48	1.41	1.42	.65	.84	.75	1.47	1.82
Troms	49	1.30	.93	1.23	1.12	1.45	1.06	1.70
Vest-Finnm.	50	.59	.17	.40	.30	.70	.93	.33
Vardø	51	.86	5.81	.95	2.02	1.37	.58	.68
Vadsø	52	1.02	2.28	.60	.99	.86	.27	.13
Sør-Var.	53	.75	.94	.46	.74	1.01	1.92	1.02

Table 41.1

Covariance matrix of crime and clear-up rates of simple larcenies

	|	CRIMES						|	CLEAR - UPS					
	1972	1973	1974	1975	1976	1977	1978	1972	1973	1974	1975	1976	1977	1978
C 1972	.4819													
R 1973	.4684	.5288												
I 1974	.4098	.4568	.4645											
M 1975	.3911	.4337	.4198	.4767										
E 1976	.3532	.3916	.3864	.4304	.4022									
S 1977	.3495	.3856	.3757	.3990	.3716	.3917								
1978	.3103	.3438	.3499	.3934	.3488	.3538	.4323							
C 1972	.3008	.2658	.2470	.1795	.1694	.1571	.1130	.4253						
L 1973	.3117	.3314	.2842	.2460	.2409	.2271	.1586	.3176	.4448					
E 1974	.2361	.2211	.2690	.1991	.1944	.1805	.1399	.2679	.2806	.3170				
A 1975	.1458	.1801	.1771	.2290	.1959	.1578	.1346	.1270	.1702	.1502	.2387			
R 1976	.1616	.1686	.1633	.1831	.1908	.1374	.0847	.1776	.2172	.1778	.1720	.3253		
U 1977	.1889	.1998	.1779	.1846	.1752	.1861	.1313	.2112	.2044	.1477	.1398	.1502	.3061	
P 1978	.1552	.1436	.1502	.1528	.1359	.1332	.1688	.1843	.1768	.1254	.1119	.1162	.1817	.2553

Table 41.2
Crime rates of simple larcenies, police districts, 1972-78

Police district	No	1972	1973	1974	1975	1976	1977	1978
Oslo	1	13.83	17.31	20.08	24.12	14.05	21.01	20.21
Halden	2	3.35	2.88	3.93	3.82	3.06	4.74	5.14
Sarpsborg	3	3.84	4.34	4.69	5.01	5.14	4.26	5.04
Fredrikstad	4	7.07	6.33	4.39	7.32	5.56	5.14	4.69
Moss	5	2.93	3.38	4.84	5.29	4.58	6.42	10.11
Follo	6	7.91	7.37	6.88	7.76	7.25	6.71	4.86
Romerike	7	5.12	6.32	6.73	7.34	7.32	8.17	7.89
Kongsvinger	8	2.25	1.45	3.01	2.15	2.67	3.26	2.71
Hamar	9	2.22	2.66	2.70	3.23	3.21	3.27	2.33
Østerdal	10	5.60	6.21	8.83	4.73	4.56	3.98	3.80
Gudbrandsd.	11	2.48	3.51	2.34	3.70	3.00	3.22	2.71
Vest-Oppl.	12	1.99	3.37	3.96	4.74	3.49	2.99	3.21
Ringerike	13	5.17	6.04	8.44	6.38	7.07	6.50	6.47
Asker & B.	14	14.57	16.36	7.29	7.48	6.01	6.61	6.16
Drammen	15	4.16	5.58	5.45	6.02	5.64	6.43	5.68
Kongsberg	16	3.88	3.93	3.93	3.48	3.43	3.74	3.57
N.-Jarlsb.	17	4.08	6.90	11.19	6.78	6.77	6.86	8.36
Tønsberg	18	8.72	11.56	10.92	15.01	13.45	11.80	17.32
Sandefjord	19	4.06	4.18	4.27	5.09	6.57	6.35	8.85
Larvik	20	2.07	3.02	6.43	13.31	11.32	7.52	9.29
Skien	21	8.74	6.50	12.66	4.82	4.98	5.95	6.51
Telemark	22	9.15	4.25	5.39	14.25	15.90	12.84	12.27
Notodden	23	3.28	3.47	4.52	4.35	5.10	5.58	3.79
Rjukan	24	4.81	4.54	3.58	5.26	3.78	6.41	5.47
Kragerø	25	3.52	6.54	5.36	3.87	3.99	5.03	5.88
Arendal	26	2.56	2.47	3.53	3.42	3.71	3.43	5.63
Kristians.	27	10.67	9.56	9.74	14.02	10.01	6.10	13.90
Vest-Agder	28	.68	1.00	1.93	2.36	2.59	1.88	1.99
Rogaland	29	2.59	3.14	2.49	2.31	2.97	2.99	2.74
Stavanger	30	5.00	5.49	5.92	5.09	5.15	4.15	5.22
Haugesund	31	2.10	1.59	1.82	2.51	3.17	3.53	3.39
Hardanger	32	3.52	1.81	3.21	3.56	3.33	1.89	1.49
Hordaland	33	1.65	1.20	1.97	1.74	1.51	1.56	2.30
Bergen	34	7.68	8.10	10.12	10.47	9.35	8.69	9.75
Sogn	35	.49	.50	.93	1.01	1.09	1.03	2.88
Fjordane	36	.80	.62	.50	.89	.76	.86	3.01
Sunnmøre	37	2.50	2.77	2.59	1.97	2.79	2.52	1.57
Romsdal	38	2.83	2.18	3.32	2.10	2.44	2.48	2.78
Nordmøre	39	3.04	2.14	1.88	1.45	1.37	1.92	1.21
Ut-Trønd.	40	1.57	1.36	1.67	1.82	1.91	2.46	1.97
Trondheim	41	6.43	5.80	5.84	4.52	4.83	4.71	7.80
Inn-Trønd.	42	1.65	2.21	1.92	2.53	2.96	1.70	1.66
Namdal	43	2.19	1.53	1.61	2.22	1.86	1.50	1.99
Helgeland	44	2.96	2.07	2.35	2.12	2.53	2.92	2.19
Bodø	45	4.55	3.89	4.99	4.03	3.20	3.14	4.18
Narvik	46	4.26	4.22	4.10	4.57	4.05	4.63	3.61
Lof. & Ves.	47	2.18	2.33	3.08	1.97	2.41	2.56	2.54
Senja	48	2.80	3.60	3.55	3.81	3.03	2.32	4.36
Troms	49	5.39	4.38	5.79	4.50	4.70	2.75	4.79
Vest-Finnm.	50	1.90	3.75	2.59	2.95	3.23	2.74	2.26
Vardø	51	6.23	6.20	5.43	6.05	7.90	4.08	4.39
Vadsø	52	1.83	2.14	2.72	1.65	2.18	2.12	1.53
Sør-Var.	53	4.98	6.48	8.99	7.37	8.81	6.32	7.62

Table 41.3
Clear-up rates of simple larcenies, police districts, 1972-78

Police district	No	1972	1973	1974	1975	1976	1977	1978
Oslo	1	2.87	3.12	3.43	3.54	1.80	1.87	1.69
Halden	2	1.01	1.35	1.20	.97	.77	1.63	1.37
Sarpsborg	3	1.01	.89	1.03	1.52	1.52	1.10	1.33
Fredrikstad	4	2.09	2.24	1.36	3.23	2.03	1.97	1.82
Moss	5	.75	.72	.95	.81	.93	1.20	1.22
Follo	6	.49	.68	.62	.64	.56	1.00	.55
Romerike	7	.54	.88	.83	.68	.88	.69	.55
Kongsvinger	8	1.29	.32	.92	.39	.56	.60	.67
Hamar	9	.77	1.04	1.05	1.34	1.48	1.25	.83
Østerdal	10	1.75	1.10	1.30	.83	.87	1.22	.83
Gudbrandsd.	11	.30	.37	.35	.74	.74	.59	.36
Vest-Oppl.	12	.53	.74	1.05	.85	.82	.53	.59
Ringerike	13	.93	1.06	1.72	1.56	.96	.96	.85
Asker & B.	14	.56	.67	.60	.88	.54	.56	.54
Drammen	15	.70	.97	.85	.89	.84	1.25	.96
Kongsberg	16	.54	.54	.96	.75	.90	.54	.49
N.-Jarlsb.	17	1.25	.63	1.11	.68	.90	.55	.77
Tønsberg	18	.95	.81	.88	1.40	1.15	1.25	1.09
Sandefjord	19	.77	1.45	1.13	.89	1.69	1.97	3.12
Larvik	20	.35	.65	1.24	3.11	1.49	.72	.61
Skien	21	1.58	2.44	3.97	.70	.78	1.12	.90
Telemark	22	.63	1.42	.81	1.02	1.22	.95	.99
Notodden	23	.78	.39	1.44	1.40	1.08	2.27	.65
Rjukan	24	.86	1.01	1.02	1.54	.13	3.01	
Kragerø	25	1.08	1.75	.94	.67	.27	.86	.99
Arendal	26	.60	.61	1.14	.86	1.29	1.13	1.42
Kristians.	27	1.80	1.07	1.13	.97	.95	1.30	1.01
Vest-Agder	28	.28	.24	.37	1.25	.44	.67	.59
Rogaland	29	1.32	1.42	.90	.98	1.47	1.13	1.00
Stavanger	30	1.30	1.39	1.32	1.13	1.33	1.07	1.12
Haugesund	31	.83	.82	.84	.72	.76	.67	.52
Hardanger	32	1.36	.70	1.99	1.45	1.81	.52	.75
Hordaland	33	.36	.31	.38	.47	.55	.60	1.02
Bergen	34	1.37	1.16	1.49	1.29	1.47	.96	1.12
Sogn	35	.10	.10	.38	.40	.25	.18	.23
Fjordane	36	.29	.19	.21	.32	.24	.30	.64
Sunnmøre	37	1.33	1.40	1.00	.67	1.12	.95	.55
Romsdal	38	1.54	.77	1.53	.70	.84	.99	.72
Nordmøre	39	1.93	1.03	.86	.56	.61	1.08	.53
Ut-Trønd.	40	.35	.24	.34	.51	.53	1.05	.80
Trondheim	41	1.36	.59	.76	.66	.69	.45	.85
Inn-Trønd.	42	.90	.88	.78	1.00	1.45	.93	.72
Namdal	43	.89	.69	.67	.83	.64	.42	.77
Helgeland	44	.93	.56	.67	.52	.76	.65	.79
Bodø	45	1.50	1.37	1.82	1.44	.95	1.13	1.57
Narvik	46	1.35	1.10	1.24	1.28	1.14	1.75	.92
Lof. & Ves.	47	.68	.76	.89	.74	.91	.83	.86
Senja	48	.90	.93	.88	1.28	.69	.80	1.36
Troms	49	1.63	.89	1.13	1.25	1.48	.64	.94
Vest-Finnm.	50	.49	.86	.31	.93	1.21	.79	.35
Vardø	51	2.30	2.32	2.47	1.06	2.54	1.46	.78
Vadsø	52	.27	1.47	1.20	.59	.92	.20	.27
Sør-Var.	53	1.32	2.35	1.39	1.29	1.84	1.46	3.07

Table 43.1

Covariance matrix of crime and clear-up rates of theft of motor vehicles

	C R I M E S							C L E A R - U P S						
	1972	1973	1974	1975	1976	1977	1978	1972	1973	1974	1975	1976	1977	1978
C 1972	.8289													
R 1973	.7845	.8251												
I 1974	.7554	.7660	.8242											
M 1975	.8161	.8083	.8527	.9706										
E 1976	.7641	.7480	.8227	.9296	.9437									
S 1977	.7467	.7186	.7410	.8708	.8338	.8173								
1978	.7497	.7319	.7371	.8466	.8007	.8023	.9779							
C 1972	.6029	.5173	.5133	.5549	.5552	.5172	.4982	.5689						
L 1973	.5901	.6188	.5708	.5658	.5299	.5146	.5210	.4310	.5730					
E 1974	.5091	.5230	.5886	.5595	.5535	.4845	.4835	.4143	.4521	.5146				
A 1975	.6069	.5992	.6514	.7576	.6815	.6271	.6146	.4466	.4699	.4771	.7301			
R 1976	.5445	.5109	.6017	.6708	.7177	.6098	.5706	.4488	.3825	.4477	.5186	.6272		
U 1977	.5372	.4972	.5048	.6272	.5903	.6136	.5778	.4121	.3766	.3605	.4932	.4705	.5513	
P 1978	.4937	.4726	.4830	.5163	.4881	.4903	.5505	.3627	.3746	.3648	.4190	.3748	.3872	.4463

Table 43.2
Rates of theft of motor vehicles, police districts, 1972-78

Police district	No	1972	1973	1974	1975	1976	1977	1978
Oslo	1	6.02	6.97	6.04	6.79	5.55	4.98	5.73
Halden	2	1.96	1.78	2.37	3.88	3.40	2.11	2.40
Sarpsborg	3	2.19	2.35	3.79	3.68	4.02	2.91	3.48
Fredrikstad	4	3.50	4.09	3.06	5.85	5.40	6.20	3.71
Moss	5	2.14	1.23	1.23	2.27	3.76	3.71	3.07
Follo	6	2.06	2.02	1.31	1.72	1.27	2.43	1.91
Romerike	7	1.52	1.59	2.17	1.98	2.11	2.77	2.66
Kongsvinger	8	.41	.35	.52	.42	.86	.85	.85
Hamar	9	.80	1.08	.86	1.56	1.17	1.42	1.06
Østerdal	10	.61	.67	.45	.48	.50	.54	.42
Gudbrandsd.	11	.31	.29	.32	.52	.54	.71	.43
Vest-Oppl.	12	.62	.75	.92	1.07	.99	.89	1.05
Ringerike	13	1.34	1.59	2.07	2.31	2.92	2.32	1.99
Asker & B.	14	4.54	8.06	6.56	10.91	5.01	4.74	5.78
Drammen	15	2.82	4.31	4.24	6.10	5.48	5.14	5.71
Kongsberg	16	1.41	.79	1.19	2.83	2.16	1.21	1.66
N.-Jarlsb.	17	2.06	1.59	2.54	1.68	2.77	2.69	3.31
Tønsberg	18	3.46	3.94	3.88	4.80	3.45	4.67	5.41
Sandefjord	19	2.82	3.11	3.94	6.20	4.67	4.69	5.26
Larvik	20	2.13	2.12	2.38	2.49	2.80	1.81	2.23
Skien	21	1.57	1.29	1.57	3.37	3.85	4.05	3.55
Telemark	22	1.79	1.79	2.59	4.00	5.33	3.78	4.26
Notodden	23	1.21	.82	1.17	1.44	1.66	1.62	1.15
Rjukan	24	.62	.76	.51	1.41	1.56	2.88	1.56
Kragerø	25	1.69	2.56	1.88	1.27	1.66	1.72	2.24
Arendal	26	1.77	1.22	1.83	2.06	1.93	2.41	3.29
Kristians.	27	2.95	4.01	3.14	5.11	3.69	3.47	4.36
Vest-Agder	28	.44	.44	1.04	.82	.83	.75	.80
Rogaland	29	1.15	2.44	2.32	1.44	2.08	1.60	2.08
Stavanger	30	2.95	2.50	2.95	3.12	2.96	2.96	2.96
Haugesund	31	1.77	1.52	1.20	2.11	2.74	3.81	5.03
Hardanger	32	1.39	.78	1.18	.71	.74	.74	.45
Hordaland	33	.56	.67	.73	.85	.84	.82	.77
Bergen	34	3.65	4.22	4.86	3.71	3.04	2.34	3.25
Sogn	35	.12	.20	.20	.20	.20	.18	.20
Fjordane	36	.16	.21	.10	.10	.05	.16	.54
Sunnmøre	37	.57	.91	.93	.46	.72	.52	.47
Romsdal	38	.80	.52	.61	.68	.47	.80	.69
Nordmøre	39	.71	.82	.53	.59	.53	.84	.41
Ut-Trønd.	40	.66	.56	.55	.75	.66	.88	1.06
Trondheim	41	5.31	4.74	5.72	5.88	4.31	5.59	5.46
Inn-Trønd.	42	.76	.72	.91	1.77	1.14	1.78	1.22
Namdal	43	.42	.47	.47	.44	.42	.31	.33
Helgeland	44	1.24	1.21	.95	1.01	1.23	.82	.75
Bodø	45	1.23	1.64	1.73	1.36	1.22	1.51	1.36
Narvik	46	.65	.59	.93	.82	.68	.86	.90
Lof. & Ves.	47	.50	.43	.46	.38	.51	.37	.56
Senja	48	1.05	1.02	.67	.80	.80	.88	1.30
Troms	49	1.57	1.25	.90	.64	1.19	.73	1.26
Vest-Finnm.	50	.20	.33	.26	.60	.65	.58	.49
Vardø	51	.77	.29	1.14	1.06	.39	.97	.10
Vadsø	52	.14	.27	.86	.53	.86	.40	.33
Sør-Var.	53	.75	1.22	1.95	2.39	2.57	2.56	3.44

Table 43.3
Clear-up rates of theft of motor vehicles, police districts, 1972-78

Police district	No	1972	1973	1974	1975	1976	1977	1978
Oslo	1	1.02	1.28	.88	1.20	.88	.82	2.81
Halden	2	.95	.83	1.40	1.68	1.34	1.00	.66
Sarpsborg	3	.71	.75	1.20	.76	1.31	.85	.97
Fredrikstad	4	1.55	1.84	1.16	2.89	1.89	2.62	.97
Moss	5	.71	.29	.41	.60	1.33	1.37	.87
Follo	6	.41	.88	.39	.62	.36	.82	.48
Romerike	7	.61	.65	.87	.52	.90	1.05	.87
Kongsvinger	8	.32	.26	.31	.13	.65	.34	.47
Hamar	9	.36	.27	.37	.48	.53	.54	.44
Østerdal	10	.35	.33	.16	.26	.30	.32	.28
Gudbrandsd.	11	.16	.07	.10	.07	.25	.27	.14
Vest-Oppl.	12	.37	.26	.46	.57	.47	.26	.35
Ringerike	13	.63	.89	1.10	1.27	1.61	.84	.77
Asker & B.	14	.61	1.93	1.10	2.59	.86	1.27	1.67
Drammen	15	1.00	1.26	.88	1.37	1.46	1.33	1.09
Kongsberg	16	.85	.31	.35	1.43	1.32	.52	.83
N.-Jarlsb.	17	1.17	.45	.89	.62	1.49	.99	1.18
Tønsberg	18	.95	1.18	1.00	1.14	1.08	1.37	1.45
Sandefjord	19	.77	.55	.89	1.59	1.85	2.45	.98
Larvik	20	.98	.68	.62	1.02	1.12	.56	.66
Skien	21	.69	.62	.47	.72	1.39	.78	.53
Telemark	22	.68	.65	.57	.98	2.27	1.29	.92
Notodden	23	.59	.35	.31	.62	.50	.85	.54
Rjukan	24	.12		.51	1.16	.65	1.96	.52
Kragerø	25	.47	1.42	.67	.40	.73	.46	.73
Arendal	26	1.11	.42	.99	.90	1.14	1.34	1.60
Kristians.	27	1.26	1.34	.98	1.61	1.04	.93	.90
Vest-Agder	28	.14	.22	.22	.55	.31	.33	.36
Rogaland	29	.64	1.23	.97	.64	.97	.63	.98
Stavanger	30	1.17	.70	.90	.68	.99	1.00	.79
Haugesund	31	1.00	.74	.41	.61	.67	.87	1.21
Hardanger	32	.95	.48	.55	.45	.44	.26	.37
Hordaland	33	.35	.42	.33	.35	.45	.57	.35
Bergen	34	1.07	1.06	1.45	1.10	.79	.55	.94
Sogn	35	.12	.10	.15	.10	.08	.08	.08
Fjordane	36	.05	.13	.06	.08	.03	.11	.36
Sunnmøre	37	.35	.62	.51	.23	.48	.31	.30
Romsdal	38	.53	.33	.29	.47	.34	.50	.37
Nordmøre	39	.55	.53	.37	.32	.33	.60	.37
Ut-Trønd.	40	.43	.29	.30	.34	.45	.55	.88
Trondheim	41	.64	.98	.83	1.45	1.30	1.20	.73
Inn-Trønd.	42	.53	.53	.66	1.28	.68	1.44	.65
Namdal	43	.30	.33	.39	.22	.25	.22	.28
Helgeland	44	.66	.55	.45	.47	.75	.41	.45
Bodø	45	.57	.90	1.04	.81	.54	.50	.72
Narvik	46	.42	.34	.40	.48	.43	.46	.55
Lof. & Ves.	47	.37	.30	.38	.30	.30	.33	.45
Senja	48	.55	.51	.42	.34	.61	.63	.80
Troms	49	.78	.50	.35	.35	.51	.37	.51
Vest-Finnm.	50	.10	.10	.07	.26	.33	.35	.16
Vardø	51	.57	.19	1.05	.10	.20	.68	
Vadsø	52	.07	.13	.47	.33	.59	.13	.27
Sør-Var.	53	.56	.56	1.02	1.47	1.10	1.46	1.86

Subject index